A RULE OF LAW FOR OUR NEW AGE OF ANXIETY

Taking Auden's *The Age of Anxiety* as a leitmotiv and drawing on literature from law, philosophy, political theory, international relations and sociology, Toope argues with passion that a renewed faith in the rule of law can address troubling developments in our own anxious times: populist nationalism; globalisation; and disruptive technologies with their dominating platforms.

We can address anxiety by bolstering social resilience, drawing upon a plural intellectual heritage. That heritage reveals a unique type of "authority" in society, "epistemic practical authority" built up continuously through social discourse and action, shifting focus from the state of "being" to the dynamic of "becoming".

What is the law's role in this world? The modest, yet powerful, version of the rule of law advocated here is one that draws on a wellspring of practical wisdom – prudence gleaned from pragmatic experience. It chastens power, while not disconnecting law from other sources of social action and human agency.

Stephen J. Toope OC, FRSC, LLD. is President of the Canadian Institute for Advanced Research and Vice-Chancellor Emeritus of the University of Cambridge. Previously, Professor Toope was Director of the Munk School of Global Affairs at the University of Toronto, and President of the University of British Columbia. A former Dean of Law at McGill University, Toope chaired the UN Working Group on Enforced or Involuntary Disappearances.

"One of the most brilliant books I have read on the profound sources and contemporary drivers of our current age of anxiety. Stephen J. Toope's suggestion of a practice-oriented pragmatist rule of law to contribute to remedying the predicament is sensible and normatively imperative."

Emanuel Adler, Professor Emeritus of Political Science,
Bronfman Chair of Israeli Studies, Emeritus, University of Toronto

"In our deeply troubled world, Stephen J. Toope has performed the astonishing feat of providing an optimistic yet deeply pragmatic account of how the rule of law can, properly understood, help us to navigate the many perils that lie ahead."

David Dyzenhaus,
University Professor of Law and Philosophy, University of Toronto

"A wise, humble and compassionate vision of the law as a social practice committed to solve the problems facing democracies in an age of anxiety."

Michael Ignatieff, Central European University, Vienna

"Considering the pressures university leaders live 24/7, especially in the last two years, it is a stupendous accomplishment. My guess is that for decades to come Professor Toope will be publicly feted and quietly hated by all university presidents and provosts."

Peter J. Katzenstein, Cornell University

"Drawing on a variety of disciplines and approaches, Stephen J. Toope suggests saving the rule of law from itself and its many discontents by developing a largely procedural version, sensitive to a diversity of demands of time and place. Viewing law predominantly as a social practice involving not just lawyers but also citizens, activists, politicians, journalists and others, Toope develops a pragmatic notion of the rule of law, built around the Aristotelian idea of 'practical wisdom'. In doing so, he offers an inspiring vision on law and its importance in times of populism, digitalisation, climate change, and other profound challenges. Lucidly written, *A Rule of Law for Our New Age of Anxiety* is an insightful meditation by one of the most respected academic leaders worldwide."

Jan Klabbers, University of Helsinki

"A lifelong exemplar of scholarship, principle, university leadership, and humble decency, Stephen J. Toope believes in simple truths, calmly held and passionately implemented. Here he argues compellingly that our answer to such disruptive anxieties as authoritarian populist nationalism and jarring technological change must be renewed commitment to the rule of law, informed by honest social discourse about lessons learned from our shared history of making progress together."

Harold Hongju Koh, Sterling Professor of International Law and former Dean, Yale Law School. Legal Adviser, United States Department of State (2009–13), Assistant Secretary of State, Democracy, Human Rights and Labor (1998–2001)

"That an ideal can be at once modest and precious is a thought too rarely entertained. This intelligent, humane and wide-ranging work shows that the rule of law, conceived as a community of 'anchoring [legal] practices – a constellation of ideas, discourses and concrete actions' rather than just an instrument of power, can be both. Modest because it is only one practice among many; precious as indispensable foundation for the best of the others. A welcome tonic for an 'age of anxiety'."

Martin Krygier AM Gordon Samuels Professor of Law and Social Theory, UNSW Sydney and Senior Research Fellow, CEU Democracy Institute, Budapest

"Populist politics, disruptive digital technologies, and run-away globalisation are three of the most troubling features of our twenty-first-century world. Drawing on his multi-faceted experience as president of the world's leading universities, United Nations expert, and renowned legal scholar, Stephen J. Toope provides a penetrating analysis of these pressing global challenges and the anxiety that they have activated in both governing elites and ordinary citizens. But he also offers a two-fold recipe for addressing them, through an interdisciplinary journey that includes Aristotelian ethics, the legal philosophy of Leon Fuller and Hannah Arendt, and the 'practice turn' in International Relations. Our first task, he argues, is to transcend the contemporary fixation with quantifying and managing risk, and 'lean into' the profound uncertainty that marks our era, which calls upon our deeper capacities for judgment, practical wisdom, and creativity.

Second, while the rule of law is often depicted as one of the main casualties of the current 'war' on reason and fact, Toope encourages us to cherish it as one of humanity's greatest achievements and a critical resource for confronting the future. As the repository of our *collective* practical wisdom, the rule of law possesses the 'epistemic practical authority' to help us navigate contentious issues, provide signposts for 'intelligent' institutional design, and – when necessary – discipline political power.

Just as the poet W.H. Auden (from whom the book's title draws) tells his readers that the 'way home' from their place of uncertainty is within reach, this book is essential reading for those who seek an alternative to today's doomsday narratives. Yet Toope's historical depth, coupled with his own formidable and practical wisdom, ensures that his message is neither utopian nor wishful thinking. We are not trapped in our 'age of anxiety', but can draw from the well of pragmatic experience contained in his particular vision of the rule of law. The concluding chapter also challenges his colleagues in the community of legal practice, who have too often seen law as a tool to achieve individual and state ends, to recognize their crucial role in the broader tapestry that upholds social and political order and to remain constantly attuned to the ethical implications of their words and deeds."

Jennifer M. Welsh, Canada 150 Chair in Global Governance and Security, McGill University, and former Special Adviser to UN Secretary-General Ban Ki-Moon

"Against the background of rising uncertainty – today's unknown unknowns – this book develops a passionate plea for a sound and consistent re-engagement with the rule of law. For this, Toope argues, an understanding of the larger picture and respect for everyday practice are required in equal measure. Law is never fixed and set to be interpreted and implemented, but dynamic and to be engaged with instead. This book's pathbreaking quality consists in taking the theory of interactional law further and in leading the reader masterfully through illustrations of that timely move. A must-read for students of international law and international relations alike!"

Antje Wiener, Chair of Political Science esp. Global Governance, University of Hamburg

A RULE OF LAW FOR OUR NEW AGE OF ANXIETY

Stephen J. Toope

CAMBRIDGE
UNIVERSITY PRESS

CAMBRIDGE
UNIVERSITY PRESS

Shaftesbury Road, Cambridge CB2 8EA, United Kingdom

One Liberty Plaza, 20th Floor, New York, NY 10006, USA

477 Williamstown Road, Port Melbourne, VIC 3207, Australia

314–321, 3rd Floor, Plot 3, Splendor Forum, Jasola District Centre, New Delhi – 110025, India

103 Penang Road, #05-06/07, Visioncrest Commercial, Singapore 238467

Cambridge University Press is part of Cambridge University Press & Assessment, a department of the University of Cambridge.

We share the University's mission to contribute to society through the pursuit of education, learning and research at the highest international levels of excellence.

www.cambridge.org
Information on this title: www.cambridge.org/9781009299459

DOI: 10.1017/9781009299435

First published 2023

Printed in the United Kingdom by TJ Books Limited. Padstow, Cornwall

A catalogue record for this publication is available from the British Library.

Library of Congress Cataloging-in-Publication Data
Names: Toope, Stephen J. (Stephen John), author.
Title: A rule of law for our new age of anxiety / Stephen J Toope, University of Cambridge.
Description: Cambridge, United Kingdom ; New York, NY : Cambridge University Press, 2023. | Includes bibliographical references and index.
Identifiers: LCCN 2022055383 (print) | LCCN 2022055384 (ebook) | ISBN 9781009299459 (hardback) | ISBN 9781009299442 (paperback) | ISBN 9781009299435 (epub)
Subjects: LCSH: Rule of law–Social aspects.
Classification: LCC K3171 .T667 2023 (print) | LCC K3171 (ebook) | DDC 340/.11–dc23/eng/20230207
LC record available at https://lccn.loc.gov/2022055383
LC ebook record available at https://lccn.loc.gov/2022055384

ISBN 978-1-009-29945-9 Hardback

To my wonderful family, with thanks

Contents

PART III A MODEST RULE OF LAW HELPS FRAME A HEALTHIER SOCIETY

Acknowledgements

My debts are numerous and of longstanding. Generations of students have asked tough questions and forced me to re-think settled opinions and assumptions. Colleagues at universities in Australia, Canada, China, France, Germany, India, Israel, Japan, the Netherlands, the Philippines, Singapore, Switzerland, Turkey, the UAE, the UK and the USA have encouraged and challenged me productively at workshops and conferences where I have over many years presented some of the ideas brought together here. One colleague in particular has worked shoulder-to-shoulder with me for more than two decades now, my dear friend Jutta Brunnée. I have learned more from her than I can say.

For reading and critically commenting on previous drafts of this book, I want to thank my generous colleagues Jutta Brunnée, David Dyzenhaus, Tony Lang, Ron Levi, Rob McCorquodale, Cheryl Misak, David Naylor, René Provost, Janice Stein and Shauna Van Praagh. Paula Rosen offered trenchant comments on improving readability. The usual caveat applies: readers should not hold them responsible for any errors, weak arguments or infelicities that remain.

Readers' comments were helpfully amplified when I delivered the COVID-delayed John V. Clyne Lectures at Green College, University of British Columbia, in September 2021. Participants, including newly arrived Green College postgraduate students, engaged thoughtfully with my arguments. For the challenge and encouragement, I am most grateful. The Principal, Prof. Mark Vessey, was an intellectually stimulating and generous host.

A bevy of external reviewers for Cambridge University Press, representing a range of disciplines, offered encouragement and practically helpful advice. To them, I also owe most sincere thanks. Finally, I would like to thank the team at Cambridge University Press who have been helpful and thoroughly professional from start to finish: Christopher Harrison, Tobias Ginsberg, Claire Sissen and Lyn Flight.

I am profoundly indebted to generations of research assistants, including Asher Alkoby, Andrew Bryan, Amos Friedland, Samuel Mosonyi, Mario Prost, Sean Rehaag, Paula Rochwerger, Chelsea Rubin, Mark Searl, Chris Tenove and Rachel Toope. They often did work that had no immediate application; I hope it was not too frustrating for them. It has all helped to shape my thinking. Some of those students have gone on to distinguished careers. Others are on the way.

Finally, I am beholden beyond measure to my funny and oh-so-talented wife, Paula. Her innate kindness and deep common sense have rubbed off on me and on our wonderful offspring, now including some pretty terrific grandchildren. They all show an admirable lack of pretension that helps point the way for me. For that, and for their constant support and encouragement, I am so very grateful. I cannot imagine a luckier fate than to be surrounded by this particular family.

Preface

I wrote this book mostly during successive COVID-19 lockdowns in the United Kingdom in 2020 and 2021. I have wanted to write something like it for some years now, but my day job made it challenging. You are not really expected to write books as a university president or vice-chancellor, unless they are collections of thoughts about the future of universities. I had no interest in writing that book; others have already done so, and well. Then I was approached to deliver the John V. Clyne Lectures at Green College, University of British Columbia, with the liberating stipulation that I could talk about anything at all. I was being offered a unique opportunity to pull together years of reading, discussing and learning from colleagues and students. And the urgency of making a small contribution to the building of greater optimism in our era was heightened by multiple anxieties prompted by the coronavirus crisis.

Those anxieties built on others represented by the harsh, divisive politics of Brexit and Trumpism, by increasingly repressive populist nationalism in many countries around the world, by growing anger over economic inequality and the continuing effects of economic and cultural globalisation, by worries about job losses and societal decay driven by disruptive technologies and culturally dominating social media networks, and, of course, by the existential fear generated by accelerating climate change. And later, as I prepared the final manuscript, President Putin launched a war of aggression against Ukraine, reigniting the possibility of nuclear conflagration.

With lockdown and suspended travel, it seemed the time to act, and here I happily admit that as a professor, I count thinking, and then writing, as acting. My wife, Paula, had left Cambridge for a couple of weeks, we thought, to celebrate the birthday of a small grandchild. That turned into five months when schools and day care facilities closed, travel ceased and we were forced into isolation. I took the opportunity to save my own sanity by engaging the brain and finally beginning to write this book. The manuscript was delivered for publication in September 2022.

A Note on Referencing

This book ranges across many disciplines that do not share a single citation method. What I learned many years go as the student editor of a law journal is that there is no perfect way to cite sources. The most important thing is accuracy that allows readers to find sources quickly. Here I use a blended system. Extensive footnotes contain full citations the first time a source is cited. But for repeated citations of the same source I wanted to avoid all the cumbersome "*supras*" and "*infras*" of much legal citation. Instead, I have used a short form of author and title for multiple citations (i.e., *Arendt On Violence* or *Rawls Justice*) whenever I cite more than one work by the same author. Full citations for all books and journal articles are also included in the Bibliography, with the short form as applicable, so that the reader does not have to scroll back to find the original citation. I have not listed journalistic references in the Bibliography. They are fully cited in the chapter endnotes.

Introduction

In a dark time, the eye begins to see.

Theodore Roetke[1]

WE LIVE IN a profoundly complex and often disheartening time. People all around the globe feel lost and anxious. I have seen this anxiety first-hand as a university leader, facing an explosion of mental health problems amongst students and staff alike. Mine is by no means a unique experience. Across education, especially in the secondary and post-secondary sectors, friends and colleagues face the same explosion. And multiple reports suggest that a mental health crisis is affecting young adults in all walks of life, and all around the world.[2]

A global pandemic, the increasingly powerful effects of climate change, hard-to-understand new technologies and networks, and various aspects of globalisation have contributed, but the distemper of our times has complex causes. One of the contributors to our great unease is a widely perceived deficit of political legitimacy that has made it easier for populist nationalists and other authoritarians to undermine established and emerging democracies alike. These politicians offer narratives based on lies – and their ability to sell them is abetted not just by vehicles like social media, but often by a nostalgic longing for a better past, a simpler time with easier truths.

If we are to address these anxieties by better understanding them and acting to lessen their underlying causes, we must restore belief in our collective ability to build healthier societies. We must recognise our shared history of making progress, flawed though the current reality is and always will be. If we simply accept, and do not find ways to counterbalance narratives of decline and conflict, we systematically disempower emerging generations. Faith in the slow growth of collective human wisdom is admittedly hard to reinforce when many histories are being rewritten as limiting stories of dispossession and damage, of victors and victims, of inevitable destruction. But even this disruptive contemporary historiography has some positive elements, for it at least reflects a greater participation by once-excluded groups in the conversations that can build democracy and public accountability. True inclusion of diverse voices in our public discourse must be a part of our efforts to build towards healthier societies.

A more specific way to recover a sense of purpose and hope is to embrace an action-oriented pragmatist ethos. In so doing, we recognise the constant refining of our understanding of reality through rational and rigorous discourse that is also empathetic and tolerant. We use our concrete human experience to reconsider and reform our practices. As we solve problems together, we build greater social cohesion and a sense of optimism. The pragmatist ethos is particularly important as we seek to restore belief in, and respect for, the rule of law, which, although always imperfect, is still one of the great achievements of modern humanity; one that has been denigrated and systematically undermined in our era. It is to this effort, to reform and revitalise the rule of law, that this book is dedicated.

A loss of faith in the rule of law is not just an effect of the broader anxiety and confusion around us. In turn, it contributes in especially negative ways to the widespread sense that the world is crumbling – that reason and shared values are lost, and that simpler answers and autocratic leaders are the only way to rescue meaning and a sense of equality in our lives. A particular threat is the pervasiveness of an instrumental view of law as merely a "tool" to be wielded to achieve whatever ends are sought by a client, be it an individual, a corporate entity or a state. The amelioration of our collective distress therefore demands that the legal profession engage in serious self-examination.

As any legal scholar or political theorist will know, the world is not exactly bereft of rule of law discourse. Whether it is in relation to human rights and civil liberties debates, worries about the future of democracy, projects of legal and judicial reform, or concerns over the growth of populist sentiment, the "rule of law" is regularly invoked by academics, politicians and journalists alike. One could even argue that the concept is over-used while being simultaneously under-specified.

It behoves any writer wishing to explore the subject to explain what is new in the treatment; to argue why another article, much less a book, is needed. So bear with me as I set out briefly the context in which I am writing and you are reading, and suggest what you might gain by working your way through this book. The details of the argument will be set out in Parts II and III.[3]

In the Western world, particularly the Anglo-American world, we have inherited two profoundly conflicting attitudes towards the rule of law, one triumphalist and the other dismissive. These attitudes have been shaped by underlying assumptions about the very nature of law. Historically, the dominant perspective has understood law as the command of a sovereign, a *right to rule* over others. Hannah Arendt, in my view one of the most independent-spirited and fruitful thinkers of the last century, argued that this understanding of law was a direct inheritance from the Jewish and Christian "imperative conception", law as a direct expression of God's will.[4] It follows naturally from this conception that law is an expression of power, understood as the capacity to control other people and essentially to force them to do as the sovereign wills. Later, of course, the role of "sovereign" was replaced with the more abstract "sovereignty", which could be vested in national communities and their legislatures, not only in single persons or oligarchies. But the essence remained, and as Arendt explained, philosophers – and I would add many political and legal theorists – came to assume that "the most crucial political issue is, and always has been, the question of Who rules Whom?"[5] Government within the state became an institutionalised expression of sovereignty, "the rule of men over men".[6] What is more, the idea of rule over others was inherently expansionist. Such rule "has an inner need to grow".[7]

A key subsequent development is that the concept of freedom became associated with a commitment to what might be called "individual sovereignty"; personal freedom comes to be seen as antithetical to the competing sovereignty of government and laws. Politics is nothing more or less than the struggle for power over others, and law is an instrument of that power, no matter in whose hands it lies. If this is correct, the rule of law exists to limit and guide the exercise of power by some people (exercisers of sovereignty) over others. It exists primarily to uphold personal freedom in the face of power.

But there has always been another way to explain the relationship between power and law, "whose essence did not rely on the command–obedience relationship".[8] In this understanding, citizens consent to the law that governs them – not having been forced by power to accept it – so that if there were any form of "obedience", it would be to the law itself and not to any specific person or group.[9] Arendt goes further to argue that it is a mistake to conflate the ideas of "power" and "strength". The latter is an individual characteristic, a "property inherent in an object or person". We often discuss power as if it were an expression of that kind of strength. For Arendt, however, power is "never the property of an individual"; it is "the human ability not just to act but to act in concert". Power, vested in the group, can always overwhelm strength.[10] The rule of law in such a context would exist not only to create restraints on men with strength. Rather, one might see it as a vehicle through which we ensure that people continue to *want* to support and obey those exercising sovereignty on the people's behalf. In so doing, it facilitates the human ability to act in concert; it helps to constitute social power.

Yet the dominant Anglo-American attitude still understands the object of any rule of law principally as the effective control of those who rule over others. Thinkers who adopt this view typically argue that law must be situated in an eternal and universal source of authority, be it a deity, inherent human dignity or reason itself. Only that external source can prove strong enough to discipline power. On this conception of law, the rule of law would possess much substantive content, being an instrument through which timeless values – from wherever derived – could shape the present and project into the future. The "rule of men over men" would be constrained by those values, be they expressed as human rights, fairness in adjudication, substantive due process or even participatory democracy.

The other side of the argument is also populated by people who think that law is a form of sovereign, or perhaps elite, control but who argue that no constraining universal source of law is possible. If law is nothing but a contingent instrument of power, understood as "rule over" others, and validated through the ability to enforce – ultimately with violence – law is not an expression of values at all. Its "source" is only the ability to impose the sovereign will. The rule of law therefore becomes a meaningless construction, simply another way of expressing the rule of power.

In this book I articulate an altogether different understanding of law and the rule of law. I am not alone in seeking this territory. Arendt herself argued that:

> The common dilemma – either the law is absolutely valid and therefore needs for its legitimacy an immortal, divine legislator, or the law is simply a command with nothing behind it except the state's monopoly on violence – is a delusion.[11]

As we shall see, various legal theorists have sought out what is often called a "procedural" rule of law that claims neither extensive values-based content nor the status of "command" enforceable through violence. What is new here is a detailed working through of how that approach makes sense in a broader framework of pragmatist thought. I link together powerful insights from various disciplines into a coherent expression of what I describe as a "modest rule of law" that makes sense in our deeply plural world.

This formulation of the rule of law is grounded in an interactional understanding of law itself, where law is built through social interactions and upheld by continuing practices of legality that accord it legitimacy. As Arendt suggests, law requires continuing consent that must be earned. It must serve as its own source of authority. This version of the rule of law – pluralist, inclusive and limited in both aspiration and content – could help us to address various sources of anxiety that trouble our era without claiming any imperial legalistic right to rule our complex national and global societies. It would do so by establishing a framework that encourages social stability, but that also facilitates communication and collaboration. It would serve as a rich resource in guiding change through societal debates on contentious issues, and providing signposts towards healthy institutional design. Of course, it also disciplines the exercise of authority, and material and political power.

In Part I of the this book, I examine some of our era's most widespread sources of anxiety. After distinguishing the ideas of uncertainty and risk, I argue that we live in a time of deep uncertainty (far more troubling than the calibration of risk) that heightens all forms of anxiety, social and personal (Chapter 1). In Chapters 2–4, I explore three particular sources of anxiety that I think are shaping our societies in complex and worrisome ways. I look first at populist nationalism, then at particular forms of globalisation and, finally, at disruptive technologies and their attendant dominating network platforms. I do not pretend to be an expert in these three areas, but I want to set the scene for what can and must be done to address the anxiety and pessimism of our times. For those who are indeed expert in these topics or those who simply take the conditions I describe in Part I as read, a skim of the first three chapters might suffice. Others less familiar with the details of the developments I describe, and the anxieties they seem to prompt, might wish to pursue a more careful reading.

Part II is the conceptual heart of the book. I begin in Chapter 5 with Aristotle's insight that human beings gain practical wisdom not only by following rules, but in the mutual creation and building up of practices. In their interactions, people learn by reflecting upon those practices and reasoning over time. Building on Aristotle, the philosophical pragmatists showed us that human actions are oriented to purposes and that we desire to contribute meaningfully to society. I explore how knowledge is built up and shared in society, and I offer a pragmatic understanding of the concept of truth.

In Chapter 6, I describe how social practices are shaped by "communities of practice" that share an interest or even a passion for something like law, football or the further development of artificial intelligence. In their interactions, communities of practice learn how to perform the practice better, following rules that constitute and shape the practice. The intellectual traditions that I canvass reveal a unique type of "authority" in our social world, one not discussed in the influential catalogue proposed by Max Weber. Emanuel Adler denominates this form "epistemic practical authority". It is continuously reshaped through social discourse and action. Ours is not a world of static "being", but of dynamic "becoming".

In Part III of the book, I address my central preoccupation: what is law's role in our world of becoming? I suggest in Chapter 7 that law is, quite simply, a wellspring of practical wisdom. Part of our intellectual inheritance is an approach to the rule of law that recognises its ability to chasten power over others, while not missing out on other contributions that the rule of law can make, and not disconnecting law from parallel sources of social action. In Chapter 8 I detail an understanding of law that recognises its essentially horizontal nature, requiring reciprocity between the governing and the governed. I describe how law is built and sustained, and how it is subject to degradation, even destruction.

Building on an interactional conception of law, I offer a version of the rule of law for today that is largely procedural in content, informed by internal criteria of legality. It does not seek to define or promote a single conception of the good life. It is, however, rooted in and seeks continuously to buttress two interlocking aspirations, for human autonomy and human communication, leading to the possibility of cooperation within societies. This rule of law rejects both "legalism" – a view that law uniquely *controls* social action – and a faith in a common but dangerous caricature of the scientific method. A rule of law rooted in socially created common knowledge that is therefore attuned to cultural difference. A rule of law that delivers on its promises through the constant reinforcement of daily practice. A rule of law that is not triumphalist, but that aspires to continual societal improvement working collaboratively with other social and political forces. This rule of law is a potentially powerful form of "epistemic practical authority" that can help point the way out of our current anxieties.

Finally, I argue in Chapter 9 that there is a future for the practice of law, but that it will look quite different from the popular picture of the amoral "hired gun". The lawyer of the future will be focused upon the exercise of prudential judgement, giving advice rooted in deep practical knowledge. She will be less a technical expert, though content expertise will still be relevant, and as much a socially attuned pragmatic thinker. She will be called upon by her peers and by the wider society to think through and always consider the ethical implications of her work. In her day-to-day experience, she will also be an assessor of practices and a purveyor of normative and institutional design. But to be absolutely clear, she will not be heroic in her aspirations. She will understand that her contributions to society are only part of a wider set of political, social and cultural practices that are needed to uphold order, foster effective communications in society and allow the building of institutions that support healthy social life, benefitting citizens now and into the future.

The conclusion rehearses the key elements of the argument to provide a thorough summary of the book.

Notes

1 Theodore Roethke, "In a Dark Time", from *The Collected Poems of Theodore Roethke* (New York: Doubleday, 1961).

2 See, e.g., Jennifer Rigby, "Almost half of young adults at clinical risk of mental health disorders in 'profound crisis', study shows", *The Telegraph*, 15 March 2021, available at: www.telegraph.co.uk/global-health/climate-and-people/almost-half-young-adults-clinical-risk-mental-health-problems; Mitchell Prinstein, "US youth are in a mental health crisis – we must invest in their care", *APA Website News*, 28 January 2022, available at: www.apa.org/news/press/op-eds/youth-mental-health-crisis; and UNICEF, "UNICEF report spotlights on the mental health impact of COVID-19 in children and young people", *UNICEF Website News*, 5 October 2021, available at: www.unicef.org/india/press-releases/unicef-report-spotlights-mental-health-impact-covid-19-children-and-young-people.

3 I am indebted to an anonymous reviewer for the encouragement – it was really a well-deserved shove – to clarify the "why" of the book in an introduction, and for concrete suggestions as to how best to shape an answer to the question.

4 Hannah Arendt, *On Violence* (New York: Houghton Mifflin Harcourt, 1970), 39 [hereinafter *Arendt On Violence*], and see her discussion of the concept of power as privileged in political philosophy at pp. 35–7 (noting that for J. S. Mill, "obedience" is the first lesson of civilisation). I should note that although there are many important arguments in *On Violence* that are instructive today, the tone of the work, at least in relation to contemporary understandings of racial inequality, is problematic. But I do not believe that any of the insights I am discussing here are thereby undermined. It is as if *On Violence* were written in two distinct but sometimes overlapping voices, one focused on the formidable challenges of the 1960s to the authority of universities and public authorities, the other on timeless issues of philosophy.

5 *Arendt On Violence*, 43.

6 *Arendt On Violence*, 35 (quoting Max Weber) and 51.

7 *Arendt On Violence*, 71.

8 *Arendt On Violence*, 40.

9 *Arendt On Violence*, 40–1.

10 *Arendt On Violence*, 44.

11 *Arendt On Violence*, 97.

PART ONE

UNCERTAINTY, RISK AND ANXIETY

He had dreamed that the whole world was doomed to fall victim to some terrible, as yet unknown and unseen pestilence spreading to Europe from the depths of Asia. Everyone was to perish, except for certain, very few, chosen ones. Some new trichinae had appeared, microscopic creatures that lodged themselves in men's bodies. But these creatures were spirits, endowed with reason and will. Those who received them into themselves immediately became possessed and mad. But never, never had people considered themselves so intelligent and unshakeable in the truth as did these infected ones. Never had they thought their judgements, their scientific conclusions, their moral convictions and beliefs more unshakeable. Entire settlements, entire cities and nations would be infected and go mad. Everyone became anxious, and no one understood anyone else; each thought the truth was contained in himself alone, and suffered looking at others, beat his breast, wept, and wrung his hands. They did not know whom or how to judge, could not agree on what to regard as evil, what as good. They did not know whom to accuse, whom to vindicate.

Fyodor Dostoyevsky, *Crime and Punishment*[12]

Note

12 Fyodor Dostoyevsky, *Crime and Punishment*, trans Richard Pevear and Larissa Volokhonsky (New York: Vintage, 1993).

CHAPTER ONE

Our Age of Anxiety

ALTHOUGH WRITING IN 1866, it feels as though Dostoyevsky were speaking directly to you and me, talking about our own time. A pestilence has indeed struck the world, but not just a pestilence affecting our physical health. We are living in a time when it really does seem that there is an epidemic of anxiety, one that has multiple causes that Dostoyevsky imagined in the nightmare he describes. People infected with ripe over-confidence in exclusive truth that is not open to challenge. People judging each other so harshly and with such strong language that discourse becomes manic and unproductive. People living in desperation, envy and loathing, despite the extraordinary human progress of the last few centuries.[13] How can we move beyond this troubling vision?

Throughout the COVID-19 crisis, I found myself drawn to histories, biographies, diaries and imagined accounts of life during the Second World War. I have asked myself why, but who can really understand one's own psychology? I suspect that my interest was rooted in a desire to vicariously experience life in another time of tremendous uncertainty and fear. I think too that I was trying to convince myself that there have been much worse times than the one we are living through. Of course there have been.

As a leader of a great institution like the University of Cambridge, I was conscious that earlier generations over an 800-year history had to navigate their way through plagues that were more devastating than ours, revolutions, bloody wars, depressions and yet other horrifying wars. The Second World War experience is only the most proximate global cataclysm. It was a time when many more people were dying, bombs were raining down on European, Southeast Asian and Japanese cities, and moral decision-making was profoundly difficult.

A few months into the pandemic I read a fascinating account of the first year of the war from the perspective of the Churchill family and entourage. I had forgotten that just as France was falling, Churchill confronted a gruesome decision. Should he destroy most of the French fleet anchored off Mers el-Kébir, Algeria, to prevent it from falling into German hands? The French admirals and government had refused a request to simply hand the fleet over to the British; Vichy French had signed an armistice with the Germans but hoped to retain control of their vessels. But Churchill and his advisers thought, almost certainly correctly, that the fall of France would mean that the fleet would end up in German hands. He determined that the British forces had to attack the ships in port, even if it meant killing thousands of French sailors – and these were, of course, erstwhile allies. Churchill found the choice agonising. Who wouldn't? But he issued the order, and was understandably vilified for a time by the French.[14]

Despite our difficult times, few of us have faced choices as stark, as ethically compromised.

Some doctors and health administrators had to make life and death decisions in the apportionment of medical care in massively overburdened hospitals at various points over the COVID-19 pandemic. Even for those who have not had to decide who lives and who dies, there is still a widespread sense in contemporary society that our moorings have come adrift. Our public discourse is debased and brutalised. Communications that were once thought to be deeply personal are now routinely displayed in full public view, subjected to meaningless "likes" or venomously attacked by anonymous trolls. Indeed, so much communication in our time seems to be grounded in rage.

Yet we can and must draw on our rich cultural resources to combat this impoverished discourse. That great Irishman, Seamus Heaney, argued that we need poetry in times of uncertainty and unbalance. Poems can bring "redress", he suggested, placing a counterweight on the scales that seem so tipped towards personal and social confusion. "[T]his redressing effect of poetry comes from its being a glimpsed alternative, a revelation of potential that is denied or constantly threatened by circumstances."[15] I am hopeful that this book will work through and alongside a diverse literature to help build up just such a sense of "glimpsed alternative" to our current anxieties and anger. Seeing alternatives in "narratives of hope" is essential to the construction of both individual and social resilience in troubled times.[16]

Over the last three years, I have been thinking a lot about a poet who wrote in a time when one might have thought the mood would be buoyant, the world having narrowly escaped total catastrophe. In 1947, W. H. Auden published "The Age of Anxiety", and won the Pulitzer Prize.[17] This longform poem is a collection of portraits and monologues of three men and a woman sitting in a New York bar during the Second World War. They are all searching for meaning and identity in a world that is shifting beyond recognition.

Here is a brief meditation from the sole woman in the poem, Rosetta, on the world she sees coming:

> Odourless ages, an ordered world
> Of planned pleasures and passport-control,
> Sentry-go sedatives, soft drinks and
> Managed money, a moral planet
> Tamed by terror . . .

Our sense that we live in a moment of dislocation, when the future, perhaps for the first time since the 1950s, looks less rosy than the past, connects us to the fear still present at the end of the Second World War. We have entered a new age of anxiety. We do not experience the same sources or manifestations of anxiety exactly, but they build from Rosetta's. Auden was focused on the risks to creativity and human autonomy posed by developments in the modern world: state planning and the consequent impetus to build ever-more powerful mechanisms of social control, consumerism and overweening corporate power, with a consequent loss of moral bearings.

Today, those fears are still present, although manifested in new and even more extreme ways, but others are added on. Contemporaneously, we are experiencing a global rise in nationalist populism, with rampant distrust in institutions and experts; a continuing fear that globalisation is destroying jobs and eroding cultures; breath-taking new technologies like artificial intelligence that we are not sure we can effectively shape and control (here extending Auden's worries about modern society); the growth of social networks, with their corporate platforms largely free from public control; fear that we have unleashed a storm of troubles through our abuse of the natural world, evidenced by climate change and global pandemics; and – suppressed by the coronavirus crisis but still on the horizon – terrorism and responses that seek to tame it in ways that may actually reduce our security and our liberties. And the shocking attack launched by Russia against Ukraine reminds us that even in seemingly peaceful regions, extreme violence can arise suddenly.

Michael Ignatieff suggests that in our era, "[i]nstead of embracing the future, imagining radiant tomorrows, we now think of the future in the language of harm reduction, target hardening, and risk management".[18] Auden reveals that this worry is not new, but it has been amplified by a societal shift towards more and more quantification of costs and benefits, and away from trust in prudential judgement. Economistic analysis dominates, and the role of "performance" and "risk" auditors expands. But a number-crunching focus on accountability and value-for-money has proven inadequate to support social and political connectivity or to convey compelling visions for the future of our world.[19] We are left with a widespread view that politics and institutions of governance, including law, have failed us.

In that sense, and I hope in that sense *only*,[20] our era is also connected to the 1930s, and the collapse of the Weimar Republic, reaching back before Auden's age of anxiety, to another period of fear, economic collapse, inequality and growing anger. Another time when public authorities were widely viewed as corrupt, incompetent and self-interested, and when thought and language were subject to "creeping brutalisation".[21]

During the 1930s, political theorist Carl Schmitt – whose arguments were congenial to the Nazis – suggested that the real subject matter of politics is raw power; power is the source of legitimacy in public life. And he argued that power rests in the hands of whoever controls what Schmitt called "the exception", meaning the public response to emergency situations.[22] That means the person who has the ability to deploy raw power to dictate the law, purportedly in the name of the public good;

to do whatever is needed for survival and order. *That* is the political force to be reckoned with. Although the idea of a "state of exception" finds its roots in a French revolutionary decree of 1789,[23] for Schmitt, the political force with power to declare the exception could only be an individual sovereign, not a legislature and not the citizenry. The sovereign decides both "when there is an emergency and how to respond to it".[24] The foundational English theorist on the rule of law, A. V. Dicey, had argued the opposite position, insisting that only the legislature could enact states of emergency or forms of martial law. Even existential threats to the state had to be addressed through law, not executive fiat.[25]

Intriguingly, Schmitt tried to co-opt "the exception" as a form of law, but law validated and controlled by the power of the sovereign. In a short but dense study of the state of exception, political philosopher Giorgio Agamben rejected Schmitt's attempt to link law and exception, arguing instead that "the state of exception is not a 'state of law' but a space without law".[26] On this important matter, I think Agamben is right.[27] Agamben's point also speaks to our current age when, as we shall see, populist rhetoric and action threaten to privilege raw power, even violence, over any form of expertise, including legal expertise. In this world view, law is just "part of the problem", a tool of the elite, and has nothing to contribute to helping guide our societies towards greater cohesion. For Schmitt and his fellow-travellers, "law" – indeed all authority – is seen as little more than the trappings of power.

My premise in writing this book is that the rule of law is onc of the great achievements of the modern world.[28] Yet it is under deep threat. As we struggle to manage, even to climb out of our era's anxiety and fear, we need to reimagine a rule of law for today, using our inherited intellectual resources. If we can do this, I believe that we have a much better chance of accomplishing the goals for which our societies are built: to secure safety for people, to allow them to shape their own lives in their communities, and to expand sustainable prosperity to more and more people around the globe. The version of the rule of law I argue for here can help to address the underlying causes of the anxieties I describe and serve as a source of encouragement and concrete guidance.

Today, we see claimants to the power to overthrow (or manipulate) the law all around the world: Orbán in Hungary, Duterte in the

Philippines, Erdogan in Turkey, Morawiecki in Poland, Maduro in Venezuela, Bolsonaro in Brazil and, of course, Putin in Russia. In China, authoritarian control grows apace and fear of arbitrary action increases daily; not to speak of the political forces in bastions of democracy like France, Germany, India, the United Kingdom and the United States who claim that their national politics has produced only decay and failure, and that we need an autocrat to guide us forward. Why should we worry about the claim to strongman control? Because, by definition, with sole power over the state of exception, all dissent becomes anti-democratic. It could stymie the will of the "people", or at least that part of the population the great leader *deems* to be the "people".

Even though President Trump managed to lose the 2020 election by a wide margin, becoming the first incumbent president since 1932 to forfeit the House, Senate and Presidency, his extraordinary attempts to remain in office show a rejection of the rule of law, democratic politics and a commitment to a right to rule grounded only in raw power. The assault on the Capitol in January 2021 by a ragtag collection of Trump-inspired conspiracy theorists, white supremacists and the generally disaffected, revealed that Trumpism is by no means a spent force. For millions of Americans this deranged, mendacious narcissist remains a symbol of hope to "re-found" the Republic.[29]

I will shortly describe our current anxieties in some detail. As I have said, they connect to past eras; they are part of our historical baggage. Most epochs manifest some form of anxiety about the current state of being and prospects for the future. But contemporary anxieties are also rooted in particular developments that we confront uniquely in our time. I do not pretend that everyone across the globe feels the challenges of our era in exactly the same way. Of course, our experiences of, and personal responses to, the problems of our world are deeply affected by where we find ourselves situated – by our economic and social positions, our age, our location and cultural heritage, our race, sex and gender identity, and much, much more.

However, my own experiences joined up with my reading across many fields lead me to suggest that there are three dominating and interacting social forces that are building upon and reinforcing a pervasive sense of anxiety in our national and global societies, affecting many people all around the world. They are populist nationalism, fear of the global (both in terms of scale and of complexity), and practices associated with so-called disruptive technologies and dominating platforms.[30] One might say, "so far so obvious". But I want to go much further, to draw upon our intellectual and social resources to address these forces, and to show how we can encourage shared action to address root causes. We can thereby trace a possible path out of our particular age of anxiety, not through the recovery of "simple truths", but by using those resources to help us to better understand and work with complexity.

To begin then.

Ours is a world where there is a constant and deeply damaging confusion of two important concepts: risk and uncertainty. Given the contemporary influence of quantitative economics as a discipline, much social and political analysis is dominated by the calibration of risk. I use the term "calibration" purposely. Risk is a concept amenable to quantification. One could term risk "the known unknowns". By that I mean possibilities that might or might not come into being, and where it is at least theoretically possible to calculate the likelihood of various outcomes. In its most sophisticated version these known unknowns are calibrated through the construction of probability distributions using large numbers of trials. The assumption behind this kind of analysis is that experts well-versed in numeric skills will ultimately be able to shape most decisions of public policy through cost–benefit analysis.

But our world is actually far more difficult to understand than risk assessment might suggest. What about the "unknown unknowns"?[31] I should pause to note that I am aware that these phrases were – unfortunately – used by none other than Donald Rumsfeld in a widely mocked speech from 2002, but they actually relate to a profound set of issues in the history of science. The very idea of an hypothesis, that which you are seeking to test experimentally, assumes frames of understanding that allow us to assess a limited range of potential outcomes. But what happens if the result is unexpected, outside our paradigm of what is even possible? Nuclear physicist, Sir Rudolph Peierls, canvassed the many "surprises" in physics resulting from new experimentation or calculation.[32] His work reaffirms the likelihood of "unknown unknowns", something so uncertain that it is not amenable to prediction.

How can you calculate real uncertainty? You cannot. And, importantly, you will never be able to do so. Our complex world is not amenable to parsing through pure calculation; we require judgement involving elements like trust and insight. Historically, that is what the "professions" have offered to society. And, of course, on a daily basis, people just get on with their lives by making assumptions about future states in the world. The point is that we cannot rely purely on understanding "the numbers" to help us navigate through our age of anxiety. We have seen that throughout the COVID crisis. The numbers are relevant and they should help form the basis of decision-making. But they do not directly dictate the parameters of necessary action. That requires recourse to insights from sociology, psychology, politics, law, the humanities and many other disciplines. I will argue throughout this book that lawyers need to be more modest in their aspiration for influence, recognising that law must coordinate with other ways of thinking, doing and being in order to shape healthy societies. But let us also acknowledge that economists, auditors and mathematical modellers need to do the same.[33]

As I have already suggested, the argument about "unknown unknowns" is, unfortunately, easier to make as we experience the fallout of the COVID-19 pandemic. It is worth considering the uncertainties in more detail. Living in the United Kingdom, it was readily apparent that simply invoking "the science" was not enough to guide us out of lockdowns and into a new world of deep uncertainty. As COVID-19 emerged, many questions arose. How exactly was the virus transmitted? Was COVID-19 spread by touching infected surfaces and through the air? Why did some people develop catastrophic immune responses to the virus while most were entirely free from particularly harsh symptoms? Were children as likely to catch the virus as adults? Were new mutations more easily transmissible and more deadly? If you had been infected, but with few or entirely manageable symptoms, were you immune to another infection? How effective was social distancing in enclosed spaces? Did it matter if windows could be opened or if one was entirely reliant on recirculated air? Did wearing masks make any difference to the spread of the virus? What type of mask might be more effective?

One could say that all these questions were in fact amenable to scientific analysis, and numeric modelling. True, but they could also be hard to test and the early scientific studies produced contradictory answers. Much remained truly uncertain. Crises of all sorts – health, ecological, security, social, political – typically produce uncertainty rather than "risks with associated probabilities that are known or knowable".[34] I am not arguing, of course, that science and its methods cannot help in shaping good questions and in teasing out possible ways forward. A great deal of knowledge has been produced through multidisciplinary design, the sharing of experimental results and modelling that tries to reduce the uncertainties of the future. But living through crises of any sort reveals that these methods are by no means fool-proof. "The science" at any given moment is not always clear, unidirectional, or even correct, as it turns out.

Other sets of COVID-19 questions were even harder to answer with scientific rigour. How would different age groups react to an extended lockdown? Would some people get fed up more easily? Did it matter what their pre-existing political beliefs were? Would a deep sense of uncertainty exacerbate mental health conditions? Was it a greater risk to implicitly discourage people with other health conditions from accessing medical care because of their fear of the virus? What factors might be at play as people decided whether or not to be vaccinated?

If there was ever a crisis with unknown unknowns it was, and remains, COVID-19. Our societal responses had to be filtered through an assessment of political and economic challenges, an evaluation of potential sociological and psychological effects that might be differentially experienced, and even a set of legal issues. Could track and trace apps work effectively while upholding privacy law? Could individuals assert rights to, on the one hand, health and, on the other hand, education and freedom of movement? Were there legitimate claims of discrimination on the part of social care workers who had less access to personal protective equipment (PPE) than public health service workers? Or on the part of ethnic minority essential workers who in some countries died at a higher rate than their white counterparts?

My point is that much of the deep anxiety felt in our societies today is rooted in uncertainty that cannot be calculated and addressed solely through economic instruments of analysis, much less addressed through direct economic compensation. This may seem an obvious point, but it needs to be asserted because of the extraordinary dominance of economistic analysis in contemporary Western societies. Nor can uncertainty be eliminated; indeed, Hannah Arendt suggested tellingly that uncertainty "is the decisive character of human affairs" because the actions set off by humans in society can never be fully contained, nor can effects be accurately predicted. Action, and reaction, "has no end".[35] We sense that uncertainty can trip us up at any moment, but we are not sure how to address it.[36] We require flexibility of thought and nimbleness of action; but crises can freeze as much as liberate. History reveals that plagues can also cause further uncertainty, instability and social crises. That was true of Athens in 430 BCE and across much of North America and Europe after the 1918 influenza,[37] although teasing out the effects of plague and war in the "roaring twenties" is hard.

The unknown unknowns are not limited to pandemics. They include aspects of climate change, sources and effects of educational inequality, and various forms of political violence, including terrorism. Ignatieff uses the term "the unimaginable" to describe these frightening unknowns.[38] But I want to focus on the three forces I identified at the outset because they underlie many others. They play particularly powerful roles in driving our shared anxiety right now, sometimes in less-than-obvious ways: populist nationalism, fear of the global, and technologies with hard-to-predict disruptive potential and dominating platforms that are largely unconstrained by public law. To address these issues requires the exercise of considered human judgement, based in concrete experience, not simply the mathematical calculation of "risk".

Notes

13 The Nobel-winning economist, Sir Angus Deaton, argues: "Building on the Enlightenment, the Industrial Revolution, and the germ theory of disease, living standards have increased by many times, life spans have more than doubled, and people live fuller and better lives than ever before." Angus Deaton, *The Great Escape: Health, Wealth, and the Origins of Inequality* (Princeton University Press, 2013), 13.

14 Erik Larson, *The Splendid and the Vile* (New York: Random House, 2020), 123–5. (In the event, almost 1,300 French naval personnel were killed.) See also Martin Thomas, "After Mers-el-Kébir: The Armed Neutrality of the Vichy French Navy, 1940–43" (1997) 112 *Eng. Hist. Rev.* 643.

15 Seamus Heaney, *The Redress of Poetry: Oxford Lectures* (London: Faber & Faber, 1995), 4. (I thank The Revd Canon Mark Oakley of St John's College, Cambridge, for a sermon drawing this wonderful set of lectures to my attention.)

16 See Michelle Lamont, "From 'Having' to 'Being': Self-worth and the Current Crisis of American Society" (2019) 70 *Brit. J. Sociology* 660, 7–8, available at: www.researchgate.net/publication/333749456_From_%27having%27_to_%27being%27_self-worth_and_the_current_crisis_of_American_society.

17 W. H. Auden, *The Age of Anxiety: A Baroque Eclogue*, ed. Alan Jacobs (Princeton University Press, 2011).

18 Michael Ignatieff, *The Ordinary Virtues: Moral Order in a Divided World* (Cambridge, MA: Harvard University Press, 2017), 143.

19 See James Boyd White, "Economics and Law: Two Cultures in Tension" (1987) 54 *Tennessee L. Rev. J.* 161, 163, 168, 176 (arguing that law must avoid crude attempts merely to "balance" one set of "interests" against others; that the exercise of reasoned judgement involves far more than the assessment of risk).

20 The inter-war period of Weimar is, in many ways, dissimilar to our own. We have not just emerged from a deadly global war, hyperinflation and a Depression. Nor are brown-shirted paramilitaries roaming the streets, and the military remain disciplined and within civilian control. See Michael Burleigh, *Populism Before and After the Pandemic* (London: Hurst, 2021), 3 (2019–20 Engelsberg Lectures, LSE). See also David Runciman, *How Democracy Ends* (London: Profile, 2018).

21 Burleigh, 5.

22 Carl Schmitt, *Political Theology: Four Chapters on the Concept of Sovereignty*, trans. George Schwab (Cambridge, MA: MIT Press, 1986) (1922) [hereinafter *Schmitt Theology*]. For a thorough contemporary canvassing of the philosophical and political lineage of the "exception", see Giorgio Agamben, *State of Exception* (University of Chicago Press, 2005).

23 See Stephen Humphreys, "Legalizing Lawlessness: On Giorgio Agamben's *State of Exception*" (2006) 17 *EJIL* 677, 679, available at: www.ejil.org/pdfs/17/3/208.pdf. Humphreys, 678, also notes that Madison, Hamilton and Jay made a parallel argument of the need for plenary executive power in situations of danger for the nation: James Madison, Alexander Hamilton and John Jay, *Federalist Papers* (London: Penguin, 1987), 185.

24 David Dyzenhaus, "Hobbes on the International Rule of Law" (2014) 28 *Ethics & Int'l Affairs* 53, 57 (discussing Schmitt) [hereinafter *Dyzenhaus Hobbes*].

25 Mark Walters, *A. V. Dicey and the Common Law Constitutional Tradition: A Legal Turn of Mind* (Cambridge University Press, 2020), 276–81, 371–3 [hereinafter *Walters on Dicey*]. Admittedly, the legislature might exonerate a member of the executive for extra-legal acts through "indemnity", but this would have to take place *ex post facto* and be independently adjudicated. This process would almost certainly give rise to appropriate caution on the part of the public official in question, limiting executive over-reach.

26 Agamben, 51, and see 59. (Agamben thought that Schmitt was merely trying to find ways to justify violence ordered by the sovereign by linking it to a supposed form of law. See Humphreys, 681.)

27 Agamben's purpose in making the argument was to assert an entirely extra-legal sphere of life that he called "anomie", important to divide power and allow for revolution against a too-powerful sovereign. Humphreys, 682–3. As will become clear, I agree only in part with this assertion; I believe that in a society shaped by the rule of law, law interacts with other forms of social organisation. It is present and influential, but not necessarily dominant.

28 In this claim, I follow the influential English historian, E. P. Thomson, who described a relatively circumscribed rule of law, like the one I will advance, as "an unqualified human good". See Daniel Cole, "'An Unqualified Human Good': EP Thompson and the Rule of Law" (2001) 28 *J. L. and Society* 177. Of course, even great human goods are not perfect, because humanity is not perfect. As I hope will become clear, I do not glorify any imperial rule of law. I do see the concept, if sensitively constructed, and its effective implementation as hugely positive.

29 Aaron Blake, "Trump Set to be First President since 1932 to Lose Reelection, the House and the Senate", *Washington Post*, 6 January 2021, available at: www.washingtonpost.com/politics/2021/01/06/trump-set-be-first-president-since-1932-lose-reelection-house-senate; Michael Shear, "Trump, Trying to Cling to Power, Fans Unrest and Conspiracy Theories", *New York Times*, 15 November 2020, available at: www.nytimes.com/2020/11/15/us/politics/trump-biden-election.html; Eli Stokols, "Trump vow to 'Never Concede' Incites Mob of Supporters", *Los Angeles Times*, 6 January 2021, available at: www.latimes.com/politics/story/2021-01-06/ill-never-concede-trump-delivers-last-grievanced-gasps-to-supporters-as-congress-begins-to-ratify-his-defeat; David Blight, "How Trumpism May Endure", *New York Times*, 9 January 2021, available at: www.nytimes.com/2021/01/09/opinion/trump-capitol-lost-cause.html?action=click&module=Opinion&pgtype=Homepage.

30 As I have noted, political violence, including terrorism, is likely set for a re-emergence after the COVID-19 crisis has fully passed, but I see that source of anxiety as strongly rooted in the three that I will examine in detail, more often effect than cause. Similarly, the growth of great power rivalry, now between the United States and China, also has roots in the three sources of anxiety upon which I will focus. As for climate change, it is indeed the existential issue of our times. I do not include it in this book because it is already comprehensively treated. See, e.g., Nicholas Stern, *Why are We Waiting?: The Logic, Urgency, and Promise of Tackling Climate Change* (Cambridge, MA: MIT Press, 2015); David Wallace-Wells, *The Uninhabitable Earth: A Story of the Future* (London: Penguin, 2019); David Attenborough, *A Life on Our Planet: My Witness Statement and a Vision for the Future* (London: Penguin, 2020). What is more, addressing climate change will require scientific, technological and societal (political and sociological) actions; the required analysis is outside the scope of the philosophical–historical–sociological–political–legal focus of this book. In any event, I do not believe that there is a single set of answers to address the anxieties of our age; that assumption underlies the entire approach adopted here.

31 David Logan, "Known Knowns, Known Unknowns, Unknown Unknowns and the Propagation of Scientific Enquiry" (2009) 60 *J. Experimental Botany* 712–14. See also Christian Reus-Smit, "Protean Power and Revolutions in Rights", in Peter Katzenstein

and Lucia Seybert (eds), *Protean Power: Exploring the Uncertain and Unexplained in World Politics* (Cambridge University Press, 2018), 59, 64.

32 Rudolph Peierls, *Surprises in Theoretical Physics* (Princeton University Press, 1979) (although he believed that such surprises could be calculated rationally, even if they challenged informed intuition). Peierls was a key member of the Manhattan Project team, but came to fear the nuclear weapons he had helped to create and joined the Pugwash movement, dedicated to reducing the likelihood of armed conflict.

33 See, e.g., Gary Morson and Morton Shapiro, *Cents and Sensibility: What Economics Can Learn from the Humanities* (Princeton University Press, 2018); Theodore Porter, *Trust in Numbers: The Pursuit of Objectivity in Science and Public Life*, new edn (Princeton University Press, 2020); White, 165, 167–8, 188–9; James Scott, *Seeing Like a State: How Certain Schemes to Improve the Human Condition have Failed* (New Haven, CT: Yale University Press, 1998), 322 (arguing that economists work with calculable risk, but ignore uncertainty); Silviya Lechner and Mervyn Frost, *Practice Theory and International Relations*, 1st pbk edn (Cambridge University Press, 2020) ("[I]t is erroneous to assume that the economic domain must be primary with respect to human relations"). It is encouraging to see that at least some mathematicians are beginning to ask hard questions about the ethics of their discipline, especially as it interacts with public policy. See Maurice Chiodo and Dennis Müller, "Questions of Responsibility: Modelling in the Age of COVID 19", September 2020, *Siam News*, available at: https://sinews.siam.org/Details-Page/questions-of-responsibility-modelling-in-the-age-of-covid-19; Dennis Müller, Maurice Chiodo and James Franklin, "A Hippocratic Oath for Mathematicians? Mapping the Landscape of Ethics in Mathematics", December 2021, *Arxiv* platform, Cornell University, available at: https://arxiv.org/pdf/2112.07025.pdf (preprint version).

34 Peter Katzenstein and Lucia Seybert, "Uncertainty, Risk, Power and the Limits of International Relations Theory", in Peter Katzenstein and Lucia Seybert (eds), *Protean Power: Exploring the Uncertain and Unexplained in World Politics* (Cambridge University Press, 2018), 27, 44 [hereinafter *Katzenstein and Seybert Uncertainty*].

35 Hannah Arendt, *The Human Condition*, 2nd edn (University of Chicago Press, 2018), 232–3 [hereinafter *Arendt Human Condition*].

36 Lucia Seybert and Peter Katzenstein, "Protean Power and Control Power: Conceptual Analysis", in Peter Katzenstein and Lucia Seybert (eds), *Protean Power: Exploring the Uncertain and Unexplained in World Politics* (Cambridge University Press, 2018), 3, 4.

37 Lawrence Wright, "Crossroads: A Scholar of the Plague Thinks that Pandemics Wreak Havoc and Open Minds", *The New Yorker*, 20 July 2020, 18, 23.

38 Ignatieff, 141–3 (in discussing another "unimaginable": the meltdown of the Fukushima nuclear reactor).

CHAPTER TWO

Populism and Nationalism

> But the new barbarian is no uncouth
> Desert-dweller: he does not emerge
> From fir forests; factories bred him;
> Corporate companies, college towns
> Mothered his mind, and many journals
> Backed his beliefs. He was born here.
>
> W. H. Auden, *The Age of Anxiety*[*]

THE VIOLENT MOB THAT STORMED the US Capitol in January 2021 was indeed bred in factories, many now closed, in corporations and college towns, and even in the military. They came mostly from rural areas, towns and smaller cities across the United States. A surprisingly large number would identify themselves as "evangelicals", claiming to be religiously motivated even though the leader they supported, President Trump, could hardly be defined as a paragon of religious virtue. They were all part of a collection of discrete forces often lumped together under the banner of "populism". People who occupied the office of House Majority Leader, Nancy Pelosi, included Chris Hood of the neo-Nazi "National Socialist Club" and Nick Ochs from the Proud Boys, a far-right group that President Trump famously called upon to "stand back and stand by" in the first presidential debate of 2020. The Proud Boys are openly misogynistic and anti-immigrant.[39] President Trump's first response to the storming of the Capitol by this dangerous gang of thugs was a shout-out on Twitter: "We love you . . . You are very special."[40]

Populist conspiracy theorists and their deep distrust of authority, often overflowing into paranoia, are by no means limited to the United States. During the second, deadly wave of COVID-19 in the United Kingdom in December and January 2021, exhausted doctors, nurses, orderlies and thousands of other health-care workers had to walk the gauntlet of coronavirus deniers on the way into overcrowded hospitals. In early January, a group of COVID-19 deniers was forcibly evicted by security guards at a hospital in Colchester, England. They were apparently taking pictures of empty corridors to post on social media, arguing that this proved that the crisis was "a hoax". The hospital's chief executive said the deniers' lack of understanding and empathy "beggars belief". The hospital's intensive care unit was at maximum capacity treating victims of the virus. The empty corridors were in outpatient wards on a weekend, closed to do everything possible to keep the virus from infecting vulnerable patients.[41]

A critical care specialist who wrote a diary for a major UK newspaper describes similar scenes while struggling to provide the most extreme form of treatment to COVID patients, extra-corporeal membrane oxygenation (ECMO). You can sense the frustration: "These are patients right at the very end of medicine's ability to intervene – and while health-care professionals up and down the country (and across the world) are striving to provide this critical care, it is startling to think of the lunacy of Covid deniers and antivaccine provocateurs."[42] Other medical professionals described nurses at the end of their tether and in tears, feeling that the protests and related hate-filled messages on social media were like a slap in the face.[43] Meanwhile, in the Netherlands, violence erupted in many cities and towns during anti-lockdown protests organised by COVID-deniers.[44]

The term "populist" has been invoked constantly, and somewhat indiscriminately, over the last decade or so, associated with COVID-denial but also with Brexit and the incoherent, increasingly narcissistic premiership of Boris Johnson; the utter misrule of Donald Trump; and political actions in regimes across the globe, from the Philippines to Brazil, Poland to India, Hungary to Venezuela. But what do we mean by "populism"? How is it different from democracy, understood as a form of governance rooted in the popular will?

Populism is not a coherent ideology or a political orientation that can be categorised on a continuum of right to left. Latin America is still turning out populists of the far left such as Maduro in Venezuela and of the left, such as Obrador in Mexico, but our era is top heavy with right-wing, populist-nationalist leaders. The most extreme are probably Bolsonaro in Brazil and Duterte in the Philippines. Even major powers are producing populist chief executives, most obviously President Trump, but Prime Minister Modi of India also deploys culturally specific populist tropes to expand his power base.[45] What connects them; what forces do they represent?

The philosopher Isaiah Berlin warned that it is easy to be too inclusive in describing populism. But he still thought it described something useful, and suggested that a "common core" of populist sentiment was a belief in society rather than the state (though, as we shall see, the state often becomes the instrument of populist power), a sense that there had been a "spiritual fall" in the past that clouded the future, an enemy – usually classed as an elite – that threatens social solidarity and around which the people can unite, elements of nostalgia (what Berlin called "past-directedness") and localism. In a more positive vein, Berlin saw populism as standing for the majority who have been "damaged" seeking "fraternity, freedom from imposed authority, above all, equality". Importantly for Berlin, the people who respond to populism do not seek "liberty".[46]

It seems, then, that populism arises in grievance, often directed against perceived "corrupt" elites, especially metropolitan elites,[47] but often finds its way to power by exploiting shared nativist histories and myths about a better past that has been lost. It typically requires the construction of an enemy that must be defeated, be it corrupt elites, cosmopolitans, a particular minority ethnic or religious group, or a supposed external threat. The victims are no longer oppressed minorities but the majority population that has been attacked from within or without.[48] As Hannah Arendt argued: "[T]ribal nationalism always insists that its own people is surrounded by 'a world of enemies'."[49]

I find Berlin's thinking helpful because his description of populism contains elements of empathy. Many contemporary writers adopt a polemical stance that actually undermines analytic clarity.[50] Polemical anti-populist commentators can set up a dangerous false choice between politics that is exclusionary and elitist, and a populism that is authoritarian and exclusionary in a different sense, being nationalist and xenophobic.[51] If populism is defined too broadly and without nuance, it risks undermining the very concept of "popular will", which has an important – though not exclusive – role to play in any understanding of democracy. That is why we must distinguish between democratic and authoritarian populism.[52]

The term "populism" can be traced back to 1870s America. On that side of the Atlantic, the descriptor has always been complex, seen at various times to represent progressive political claims and at other times xenophobic, racist claims. It seems that the negative view of populism was solidified in the work of historian Richard Hofstadter, who linked it to the rise of McCarthyism and "the paranoid style in American politics".[53] Although Hofstadter later distanced himself from these claims, ironically they have persisted in shaping the attitudes of European commentators on populism, where an almost entirely negative connotation has dominated.

Yet the people's will is not invariably a negative force. Populist sentiment can be driven by entirely accurate perceptions of economic and social inequality, police brutality, policy corruption or simply a bias to the status quo that favours vested interests, and by realistic claims that bureaucrats have lost touch with the problems faced by the majority of people.[54] President Obama once described himself as a populist and warned us to "be careful about suddenly attributing to whoever pops up at a time of economic anxiety the label that they're 'populist'".[55] He asserted that it would be more appropriate to describe some populists as "nativists" or "xenophobes".

There are forms of populism that make "politics far more comprehensible and understandable for everyday citizens", more so than the "convoluted language of technocrats".[56] The value-laden and typically emotive language of populists provides an accessible way into public debate for citizens who are not preoccupied with politics on a day-to-day basis.[57] In the aftermath of the 2008–9 economic crisis, it was not irrational to question why banks were bailed out but not small businesses; why we worried so much about General Motors but not about rips in the social safety net. It is at least plausible that there is an instructive correlation between the election of President Trump, the result of the Brexit referendum, and the fact that the United States and the United

Kingdom had, respectively, the highest and most quickly growing income inequality amongst major industrialised nations, and that wage growth had been non-existent in each country for a decade or more.[58] In fact, the trend was longer term, at least in the United States, as GDP growth had decoupled from wage growth as far back as the 1980s.[59]

Richard Rorty puts the challenge succinctly: people we may think of as "bad", such as populists, may not be irrational at all.[60] They may simply be responding to deprivation – Isaiah Berlin's "damage" – and especially to a lack of what Rorty calls "security and sympathy". He describes "security" as "conditions of life sufficiently risk-free to make one's difference from others inessential to one's self-respect". "Sympathy" is less obvious, and Rorty elides it with "sentimental education" which is possible only when people "can relax long enough to listen" and begin to understand others' conditions of life.[61]

More recently, Michael Ignatieff has argued that Western academic, cultural and political elites have undervalued what he calls the "ordinary virtues" of trust, honesty, politeness, forbearance, tolerance and respect. These are the "operating system of any community" and are worked out on a daily basis in social interactions. In our embrace of supposedly universal human rights values, we have neglected local sentiment and national adherence. Ignatieff suggests that underestimating or even denigrating these more local virtues of social solidarity has contributed to the rise of grievance, frustration and a populist response. He describes the struggle of people in local communities to "benefit from globalisation ... without having their jobs, communities, and settled values swept away". This leads to a focus on the "us-versus-them distinction" so that living in the same place does not mean truly living together, but it can mean tolerating each other.[62]

In invoking these "ordinary virtues", however, one must be careful not to romanticise local communities; they can be sites of oppression and exclusion as well as places of integration. And many of the people who stormed the US Congress were not activated in their anger by the "ordinary virtues", or by economic inequality, but by race-hatred, misogyny and deep-seated social grievance. Nonetheless, the point remains valid that there are people today who feel their sense of connection to the local has been buffeted by economic and political forces that they cannot understand, much less control. Allies to the populist-nationalist cause are recruited from groups with a wide range of underlying motivations, not all of them entirely morally suspect.

In contrary fashion, however, Emanuel Adler describes the central global political challenge today as the conflict between nationalist and populist practices, and liberal internationalist practices.[63] He describes post-war liberal internationalism as rooted in a desire for interconnectedness whereas populism is grounded in "disassociation".[64] Something confusing is happening here. Is populism about solidarity and a fundamental commitment to rebuilding a society that has been lost or is at least fraying? Or is it about dissociation, division and the construction of enemies?

Isaiah Berlin's analysis helps us to disentangle the confusion: a key component of populist-nationalist movements is a claim to promote equality. Equality is said to be more important than individual freedom or liberty.[65] That is why Berlin, one of the pre-eminent theorists of liberty, was so disturbed by populism. In populism, equality is understood within the frame of a local or national community, never as an expression of international solidarity. The global is probably seen as simply too big a field in which to imagine equality or to pursue it.[66] What is more, it is hard to draw upon founding myths or shared memories as a justification for political action at anything above a national level. The European Union struggles with this difficulty. So, while Berlin is right that the fundamental commitment of most populists is to society and not the state, the state – through the forces of nationalism – often becomes the instrument by which to reclaim lost glory and to promote supposed social equality.[67]

The modern concept of the state emerged in Europe[68] and was almost immediately linked to the idea of "nation" or "people". That helps to justify the sense of exclusivity in most expressions of populism: are you *truly* one of us?[69] Even progressive populists in late nineteenth- and early twentieth-century America adopted a language that excluded "aliens".[70] Authoritarian populists of the right typically go further, defining outsiders as "unclean, foreign, not fully human, and therefore a threat to the people".[71] As philosopher Jeremy Waldron, argues: "modern populism . . . involves an attempt to defend a given community from outside influences that threaten to compromise the flourishing of its native values and ideals. It involves strident nationalism and antipathy to universalist, globalist and cosmopolitan modes of thought."[72]

But how does populism relate to democracy? Again, a difficulty arises in the relationship between populism and the state. Over the course of the twentieth century, and especially after the collapse of most communist regimes in the late 1980s, the state became idealised in Western thought as both democratic and liberal, oriented towards individual freedoms. This development marched alongside the growing influence of neoliberal economics, with its focus on the deregulation of markets, the reduction of trade barriers and the withdrawal of the state from the economy, linked to privatisation of previously public assets and a politics of governmental austerity.[73]

The liberal state was associated with freedom, but also increasingly with growing income inequality and a fundamental sense of unfairness. Freedom came to seem devoid of content if two incomes were only enough to "get by" and not enough to improve a family's economic situation; if young people could not even aspire to buy a home in many "global" cities; and if the perception and reality grew that a tiny elite was reaping the rewards of "economic freedom".[74] Perhaps most damning was a growing recognition that the children of the baby boom generation would be economically worse off than their parents, undermining any sense of social and even familial progress.[75] All of this helps to explain the Occupy Wall Street movement, a new focus on inequality in the media and in academia, and a fixation upon the lives and abuses of "the one per cent".[76]

The global financial crisis of 2008 and 2009 was both an expression of unregulated markets gone haywire and a wake-up call that the dreams of the middle classes were fading. But the wake-up call was not heard. The financial services industry was bailed out and big companies were saved from collapse. This was important, of course, especially to prevent massive job losses. But the economic trajectory did not change. The same bankers were in charge in 2010 and onward, and the middle classes saw their incomes continue to stagnate.[77] Indeed in the United States, the inflation-adjusted median income for working-age men is less today than it was four decades ago.[78]

Meanwhile in some de-industrialising regions of Western democracies, communities were being hollowed out as young people were forced to leave and seek employment elsewhere. Thuringia, a state in central Germany, has seen just under a quarter of its population move away from the 1990s to today. It is perhaps not surprising that the populist-nationalist *Alternative für Deutschland* saw its vote double there in 2019 elections.[79] Such reactions are linked not only to practical concerns, but to one's emotional state. A longitudinal study of inequality over four decades in seventy-eight countries revealed that when inequality increases, "people who earn little really suffer from falling further behind – they feel excluded and frustrated by not being able to keep up even with people who receive average incomes".[80]

In a provocative recent challenge to our Western conceptions of meritocracy, Michael Sandel argues that "the politics of grievance" is furthered by a strong sense of resentment of elites and "humiliation" on the part of those people who did not benefit from economic growth over the last few decades.[81] Their accurate perception of gross inequality leads to a further sense of disempowerment.[82] Sandel's thesis is that our societal commitment to meritocracy, though grounded in one version of equality focused upon individual opportunity and attainment, can become destructive. He suggests that those committed to the "meritocratic ideal" ignore its possible negative effects on the winners and losers in our societies:

> Among the winners, it generates hubris; among the losers, humiliation and resentment. These moral sentiments are at the heart of the populist uprising against elites . . . A lively sense of the contingency of our lot conduces to a certain humility: "There but for the grace of God, or the accident of fortune, go I." But a perfect meritocracy banishes all sense of gift or grace. It diminishes our capacity to see ourselves as sharing a common fate . . . This is what makes merit a kind of tyranny, or unjust rule.[83]

Although Sandel has hit upon an important insight, that meritocracy as an ideology *can* lead to hubris, to the idea that not only am I self-made but that I deserve my success,[84] I am not convinced that it is inevitably so. Where is the evidence that a person who "pulls themselves up by their bootstraps" must believe that they had no help? Of course, I suspect that we have all met people like that; the ethos seems particularly powerful amongst the denizens of Silicon Valley. But over the years I have met more people, including many students and alumni of the elite universities Sandel strongly chastises, who have told me that they owe their success to a teacher in high school, or to a single mother who made sacrifices, or to the public education from which they benefitted, or to government programmes that paid for tuition, or to a scholarship created through philanthropy. I have heard innumerable times the phrase, "now it is time for me to give back" through public service, social entrepreneurship or charitable giving. Success in work and social status is not an inevitable precursor to narcissism.

Sandel over-argues his case. Yet a key point remains true: hubristic belief that all success is individual can lead to the conclusion that "your lack of success is a fault in you; everyone has the same chance". And that can indeed lead to frustration and deep resentment amongst those who have worked hard but seen their wages erode or their jobs disappear, their communities die and their kids' opportunities dry up.

Where to turn? The liberal state has not been delivering. A political theorist who saw a similar crisis of economic inequality in the Weimar Republic in 1930s Germany had already provided an answer: shape democracy in a way that allows for the expression of the frustrated popular will. Focus not on individual freedom but on popular sovereignty. Carl Schmitt argued that "'the people' is a concept of public law", meaning that "democratic rights have an essentially political character". The central point is that the public is superior to the private, the social takes precedence over the individual.[85]

The further implication of Schmitt's democratic theory is that only the abstract sovereign power can transform individuals into a "people" who in turn carry forward the power. Popular sovereignty is a fiction, but a necessary one, because it allows a people "to meet the demands of sovereignty".[86] And these demands can be met only by a people possessing "national homogeneity". There cannot be democratic human equality, only the equality of a people as amongst itself.[87]

Schmitt was by no means alone in suggesting that a political order such as a state can hold together only if there are strong emotional bonds promoting attachment. That was the view of both of the founders of modern sociology, Weber and Durkheim.[88] Weber was an avowed nationalist, seeing the nation as the primary social grouping in modern life, as long as it could help to build strong shared identities. He argued that every society has a "centre" which is the realm "of symbols, of values and beliefs which govern society",[89] and only nations were capable of protecting that centre. Durkheim was convinced of the primacy of society,[90] rather than the nation, but he argued that a political order had to put forward a system of "moral unity" separate from the impulses and needs of individual people.[91] Weber went further and foreshadowed Schmitt's argument that nationally based democracy actually creates the "people" by fostering their collective integration.[92] But the state was legitimate only if it succeeded in building that sense of cohesive peoplehood. That is what gave the state, in Weber's famous formulation, a successful claim to a monopoly on "legitimate physical violence within a particular territory".[93]

It is no surprise that Schmitt was readily adopted as a theorist of Nazi power, for a central claim of National Socialism was that the spirit of the German people had been degraded by the weakness of parliamentary democracy in the Weimar period[94] and needed to recapture its glory, forged in a mythical past captured in the Wagnerian operatic tradition.[95] The Nazi state was legitimised, on its own terms, by its success in re-forging a strong Germanic identity, purified of foreign and cosmopolitan influences, and based on pseudo-scientific racial characteristics.[96] The state could then exercise total power, on behalf of the newly unified people; this was authentic "democracy" for Schmitt.[97] And, to return to my earlier argument, also relying on Schmitt, the Führer could declare the "state of exception" and overturn the rule of law. In this context, it is instructive to recall that when faced with a choice between saving German cities and towns near the end of the war and fighting on fruitlessly, Hitler adopted a scorched-earth policy. He believed that the German people had failed him and he saw no need to save Germany from destruction.[98] The supposedly sacred people was far less important than individual ego.[99] President Trump's abandonment of the mob he incited to breach the US Capitol displayed a less consequential but similarly egotistic approach towards the relationship between leader and follower.[100]

I hasten to emphasise that today's populist claims are usually, though sadly not invariably, more circumscribed than those made by the Nazis. And fortunately, in most democracies where populists have exerted strong influence or been elected, they have not been able to claim total power. In most cases, except perhaps in Venezuela, a variety of state and civil society institutions continues to exert countervailing influence. But the effects of Schmitt's political theory are still being felt in the exploitation of legitimate grievance, attempts to narrow the definition of the "people", appeals to a "base" that is linked by affective bonds such as "Making America Great Again" (Trump), "We are the People" (*Alternative für Deutschland*), or "In the Name of the People" (Marine Le Pen) and the denigration of representative legislatures.[101]

The result is that in many societies today populists and anti-populists effectively speak past each other: "Our only explanation of opinions that diverge from our own is that those who hold them must be either immoral, ignorant, or irrational, or perhaps some combination of these."[102] Strongly emotional politics are bound to produce polarisation in the public sphere. This is especially true when emotive politics are tied to deeply held identity concerns, or to beliefs in the need to protect a culture, or to redress victimhood caused by rapacious elites or dangerous outsiders.

Contemporary populist-nationalists[103] draw on an additional wellspring of influence that was identified long ago by Weber and fully appreciated by Schmitt: charismatic leadership. Weber argued that there were three types of authority in any form of organisation, what he called rational-legal, traditional and charismatic. I will address the first two later. Charismatic authority is grounded in individual leadership, not bureaucracy or any form of social status. Weber defined charisma as "a certain quality of an individual personality by virtue of which he is set apart from ordinary men and treated as endowed with … exceptional powers or qualities".[104]

The charismatic leader is, for Weber, "always in some senses revolutionary", set "in conscious opposition to some established aspects of the society".[105] This form of leadership is also "irrational in the sense of being foreign to all rules".[106] Overall, Weber viewed charismatic leadership positively because his great fear was a "leaderless democracy" in which the masses claimed real equality.[107] But if Isaiah Berlin is right, and I think he is, charismatic leadership will most likely emerge as a form of populism. And populism is inherently linked to equality claims because it is often grounded in grievance, a sense of unfairness.

Weber nonetheless acknowledged that the charismatic basis of organisation is inherently unstable and temporary.[108] "[T]he charismatic [leader] ... is deserted by his following because pure charisma does not know any 'legitimacy' other than that flowing from his personal strength ..." Weber concluded that "[a]bove all, [the charismatic leader's] divine mission must 'prove' itself in that those who faithfully surrender to him must fare well".[109] If grievances are not effectively addressed, the legitimacy of the charismatic leader bleeds away.

Let me summarise the argument so far. Populist-nationalist sentiment arises primarily out of a shared sense of unfairness and social decay. It draws on a desire to re-build society in a more economically and politically inclusive way, which seems all to the good, but it does so only for a defined "people" that tends to homogeneity. Populism can find roots in entirely rational criticism of elite misbehaviour but, as a primarily emotional force, it ends up drawing on mythologies of peoplehood or nationhood that circumscribe social membership. Because the state has been such a dominant force since the nineteenth century at least, the desire to promote the supremacy of the social over the individual that grounds populism is most often expressed through nationalism. In our era, a parallel force has also emerged, that of conspiracy theorising that is often linked to a sense of national decline. Populist forces are strengthened when they can be marshalled by a charismatic leader who embodies underlying grievance, gives it expression and promises redress. But unless the leader can deliver, and relatively quickly, they will find themself in trouble. Both populism and charisma are inherently unstable.

Populism today is therefore both an effect of anxiety for some people and a cause of further anxiety in others. It has grown in strength in many parts of the world because it draws on real grievances. Many people are worried about their economic position,[110] and inequality within many national societies has increased, often dramatically. If that inequality is perceived to be morally justified on the grounds that the "winners" are harder working or blessed by God, the debilitating effect is even stronger for those who are on the outside of economic success.[111] No fundamental lessons seem to have been learned after the 2008–9 financial crisis, causing a further sense of unfairness, with elites continuing to prosper while wage stagnation affects most working- and middle-class people. As I write, inflation has re-emerged as a strong economic force for the first time since the early 1980s. If negative economic effects of the COVID crisis are persistent and particularly harsh for people already financially insecure, populist sentiment will grow further. There are signs of that happening already. The demise of Trump in the 2020 elections is not yet a demise of Trumpism, although a populism defined purely by fealty to Trump and to his unfounded claims of stolen elections may have trouble finding an electoral majority.[112]

Anxiety was further sparked by massive migration like that experienced in Europe in 2015, and continuing undocumented border crossings like those on the US–Mexican border or across the Mediterranean Sea.[113] These situations create a clearly defined group of "outsiders" that can be cast, however incorrectly, as an economic and security threat to host societies. What is more, increased internal cultural diversity is viewed by populists as a challenge to the "traditional" myths and mores of society.[114]

In turn, populist responses and electoral successes create a different set of new anxieties. Most notably, despite its claims of social solidarity, populism in our time seems destined to create social division. Strangely perhaps, that is largely because populism has been only partly successful even where it has gained electoral victory. Brexit resulted from a close vote and has continued to generate deep social discord since. Its tribune, Boris Johnson, was unceremoniously thrown out of office only three years after winning a thumping electoral majority. President Trump's approval ratings were almost constantly negative between his inauguration and ultimate electoral defeat.[115] And, of course, he failed to win the popular vote even as he won the 2016 election because of the oddities of the electoral college. Brazilian President Bolsonaro's positive ratings have hovered around 30 per cent since shortly after he took office.[116]

It is also possible that the rise of charismatic leaders such as Bolsonaro, Duterte, Johnson, Modi and Trump builds anxiety in a large group of citizens who recognise the instability of charisma as a political force. That instability can lead to the undermining of democracy itself.[117] That risk played out on television and computer screens as Trump loyalists took him at his word, believing that they were marching on the Capitol to "save America". Trump told them to "fight much harder" against "bad people" and "show strength", asserting that the fight would be "wild".[118]

What is more, populism, in its nationalist and nativist incarnation, threatens the security of minorities by not counting them as true citizens; instead, they are said to undermine the mythical unity of the people. Racial and ethnic minorities in particular may be viewed as "disloyal" when they articulate deep-seated economic and social grievances. We saw this in the response of President Trump and his allies to the Black Lives Matter protests in 2020, with the deployment of federal security forces in Democratic Party-controlled cities across the United States.[119] The so-called "culture wars" in the United Kingdom are also influenced by this perception of disloyalty; minorities who complain about inequality just do not know how good they have it.[120]

Populism also increases anxiety because it generates and feeds off attacks on the institutions of governance and civil society.[121] The theorists of populism and charisma, like Weber and Schmitt, believed that elected legislatures were inherently weak. Today we see concerted efforts to undermine legislatures by nationalist leaders who rely on populist tropes. Russia's President Putin has spent years gathering power unto himself, undermining the State Duma at every turn.[122] President Trump attacked the House of Representatives and the Senate with abandon.[123] President Xi aggregates more and more power to himself, going as far as to overturn a convention that the supreme leader of China has a limited term of office.[124]

But attacks on institutions go further. It is no surprise that institutions of the legal system, including the very concept of the rule of law, are one of the primary targets of populist assault.[125] Not surprising because, as Weber realised, what he called "legal-rational authority" is a separate source of authority from charisma, and a direct competitor. Logically consistent, generalised sets of rules with their attendant bureaucratic structures have to be displaced if charisma and populism are to succeed in dominating society through control of the instruments of the state.[126] That is why it becomes necessary to attack "elites" (including experts) in populist rhetoric. Elites generally benefit from stability, and to succeed in its aims of social transformation, populism requires instability.[127]

Significant attacks on the domestic rule of law are commonplace. In the Philippines, President Duterte routinely called for the extrajudicial killing of criminals, and his will was followed.[128] In Hungary, President Orbán attacks the legal profession, the judiciary, universities, arts organisations and any semblance of independent media.[129] The Polish government has ramped up unofficial and legislative attacks upon the independence of Poland's judiciary[130] and more recently on independent media.[131] Meanwhile, in Turkey, the rule of law is deteriorating fast. The International Commission of Jurists has strongly criticised President Erdogan's attacks on the independence of the judiciary.[132]

Attacks on law as an appropriate organising principle in society extend as well to international law and institutions. Why? Because "[p]opulists see international law as a device used by global elites to dominate policymaking and benefit themselves at the expense of the common people".[133] Much of the populist backlash has focused upon the institutions of human rights and international criminal law. They are claimed to over-reach, disrupt domestic politics and policy, and impose cosmopolitan standards divorced from national culture and democratic control.[134] In this critique, an alliance has emerged between populist-nationalists in Russia and China, as well as in less powerful countries in Eastern Europe, Africa and Asia.

"History is irony on the move," wrote Romanian essayist Emil Cioran.[135] In our era the most potent challenges to the international rule of law do not come from assertive non-Western powers with weak internal commitments to the rule of law, as is often assumed, but from within the West itself. Notwithstanding the fact that, by and large, Western countries have been beneficiaries, shapers and defenders of the existing international order, a backlash has erupted in many Western states against the perceived reach and intrusiveness of international law and institutions.[136] Francis Fukuyama extends this argument to cover the entire post-Second World War political settlement, suggesting that the "dominant liberal order that has been constructed since the 1950s has come under attack from angry and energised majorities".[137]

In recent times, the most destabilising challenges to a law-governed international order have come from the United States, although the 2020 election may have shifted that dynamic somewhat. Nonetheless, accumulating actions, including the Trump administration's moves towards "trade wars" with other major economies; withdrawing from the negotiations that created the Trans-Pacific Partnership trade agreement; calling the EU a "foe"; blocking the appointment of judges to WTO dispute settlement panels; withdrawing from the UN Human Rights Council and the World Health Organization; overthrowing the Iran nuclear agreement in the face of unanimous censure from close allies like Canada, Germany, France and the United Kingdom; pulling the United States out of arms control agreements with Russia; suggesting that the United States might overthrow decades of policy and resort to first use of nuclear weapons; threatening sanctions against the prosecutors and judges of the International Criminal Court; and promising to withdraw from the Paris climate agreement all suggest that the previous US administration had turned *against* a rules-based order – the very one its predecessors were instrumental in creating.[138] It has not been easy for the Biden administration to re-position the United States when national politics remain so deeply divided. In any event, on trade relations at least, it is by no means obvious that a full turnabout has ever been planned.[139]

The government of a close US ally, the United Kingdom, is also systematically rejecting international legal constraint. Examples are multiplying: threatening to unilaterally overthrow the Northern Ireland Protocol, negotiated by the same government only a couple of years ago as part of the Brexit package; proposing legislation to limit the jurisdiction of the European Court of Human Rights in response to decisions postponing the sending of refugees/migrants in the United Kingdom to Rwanda; apparently planning to disregard WTO obligations; and simply ignoring the decisions of validly constituted international tribunals. As one distinguished legal commentator put it: "Britain's reputation is uniquely built on the rule of law – and this government is trashing it."[140]

The COVID-19 crisis has amplified doubts about the capacity of state institutions and elites to manage our current instability. At first, a deference to "the science" seemed to suggest a re-emergence of respect for expertise and technocracy. That respect began to collapse with successive waves of the virus and the imposition, lifting and re-imposition of societal lockdowns. Lack of clarity in governmental health directives compounded frustration and anger, as did hypocritical flaunting of lockdown rules by leading politicians and their advisers. Nobel laureate and then-president of the UK's Royal Society, Sir Venki Ramakrishnan, captured the problem early on in the crisis:

> [T]ranslating science advice into policy can lead to very different paths, as can be seen from the divergent responses to Covid-19 across the world. This is because the science advice is only one factor in policymaking. Governments not only have to contend with the uncertainty of the science but a host of other practical considerations, including feasibility . . .
>
> The most important thing in the middle of a crisis is to constantly review what we are doing against the evidence. If we find we have followed a wrong path, we cannot waste precious time squabbling and apportioning blame. In particular, blaming scientists for their advice in an uncertain situation betrays a fundamental misunderstanding of how science works.[141]

Just such a blame-game did emerge, with fingers pointed at both scientists and policymakers. In the United States mask-wearing became politicised, as did any public deference to scientific opinion. How could we forget President Trump's breath-taking suggestion at a White House briefing that it might be wise to ingest bleach? His science advisers cringed in the background.[142]

Something similar occurred in Brazil, with President Bolsonaro ostentatiously refusing to wear a mask and constantly underplaying the risk of the virus. I have already noted anti-lockdown, COVID-denial protests in the United Kingdom and the Netherlands. Parallel protests occurred in Germany and other parts of Europe, Canada, Australia and elsewhere around the globe. None of this was helped by the atavistic nationalist responses of many governments, for example, in stockpiling extra supplies of vaccines when other countries had almost no access. The result? The undermining of the needed pan-global response, facilitating the emergence of new COVID variants and unleashing new waves of infection.

There you have it. Anxiety has been building for a couple of decades now both for those whose grievances attract them to populist politics and for those who find the populist responses deeply unsettling. Populist nationalism is creating a degree of social and political uncertainty that undermines confidence in the resilience of our institutions. The COVID-19 crisis has exacerbated the situation. Multiple expressions of populist nationalism have led directly to the undermining of the rule of law, both within states and in international society.

Notes

39 Sabrina Tavernise and Matthew Rosenberg, "These Are the Rioters Who Stormed the Nation's Capitol", *New York Times*, 7 January 2021, available at: www.nytimes.com/2021/01/07/us/names-of-rioters-capitol.html.

40 Savannah Behrmann, "'Damage our Republic Forever': A Look Back at the Nation's Capital being Overrun", *USA Today*, 7 January 2021, available at: https://eu.usatoday.com/story/news/politics/2021/01/07/capital-building-look-d-c-protest-through-quotes/6576571002. I conclude my US examples at President Biden's inauguration though it will be clear that I do not think that "Trumpism" has yet disappeared.

41 "Covid-19: England Lockdown Looms as Hospital Ejects 'Covid deniers'", BBC News, 4 January 2021, available at: www.bbc.co.uk/news/uk-55536189.

42 Anonymous, "From the Red Zone: 'The Lunacy of Covid Deniers and anti-Vaccine Provocateurs is Startling'", *The Telegraph*, 22 January 2021, available at: www.telegraph.co.uk/global-health/science-and-disease/red-zone-lunacy-covid-deniers-anti-vaccine-provocateurs-startling.

43 Gemma Mitchell, "Nursing Leaders Denounce Covid-19 Deniers", *Nursing Times*, 8 January 2021, available at: www.nursingtimes.net/news/coronavirus/nursing-leaders-denounce-covid-19-deniers-08-01-2021; Ben Quinn and Denis Campbell, "Hospital Incursions by Covid Deniers Putting Lives at Risk, Say Health Leaders", *The Guardian*, 27 January 2021, available at: www.theguardian.com/world/2021/jan/27/hospital-incursions-by-covid-deniers-putting-lives-at-risk-say-leaders.

44 John Henley, "Netherlands Shaken By Third Night Of Riots Over Covid Curfew", *The Guardian*, 26 January 2021, available at: www.theguardian.com/world/2021/jan/26/netherlands-third-night-riots-covid-curfew-lockdown-protesters.

45 For a scathing, extended critique of Modi's exploitation of Hindu nationalist populism, see Pankaj Mishra, *Age of Anger: A History of the Present* (New York: Farrar, Straus & Giroux, 2017), esp. at 162–3, 251, 257–66.

46 Isaiah Berlin, *To Define Populism* (London: Isaiah Berlin Virtual Library, 1967), available at: http://berlin.wolf.ox.ac.uk/lists/bibliography/bib111bLSE.pdf.

47 Wojciech Sadurski, "Institutional Populism, Courts, and the European Union", in Martin Krygier, Adam Czarnota and Wojciech Sadurski (eds), *Anti-Constitutional Populism* (Cambridge University Press, 2022), 506, 507; Burleigh, 23.

48 See, e.g., Alyson Cole, *The Cult of True Victimhood: From the War on Welfare to the War on Terror* (Stanford University Press, 2006); Burleigh, 68–71.

49 See Hannah Arendt, *The Origins of Totalitarianism* (New York: Meridian, [1951] 1958), 227 [hereinafter *Arendt Totalitarianism*].

50 See, e.g., Cas Mudde and Cristóbal Rovina Kaltwasser, *Populism: A Very Short Introduction* (Oxford University Press, 2017); Dani Rodrik, "Is Populism Necessarily Bad Economics?" *AEA Papers and Proceedings* 108 (2018), 196–9, available at: https://doi.org/10.1257/panp.20181122; Sanja Bogojevic, "Erosion of the Rule of Law: How Populism Threatens Environmental Protection" (2019) 31 *J. Environmental L.* 389, 390.

51 Robert Howse, "Epilogue: In Defense of Disruptive Democracy – a Critique of Anti-Populism" (2019) 17 *Int'l J. Constitutional L.* 641.

52 See, e.g., Douglas Johnson, "In Defence of Democratic Populism", in Gerald Neuman (ed.), *Human Rights in a Time of Populism: Challenges and Responses* (Cambridge University Press, 2020), 192, 195–6.

53 Anton Jäger, "The Myth of 'Populism'" (2018) *Jacobin Magazine*, 7, available at: https://jacobinmag.com/2018/01/populism-douglas-hofstadter-donald-trump-democracy?fbclid=IwAR0h2rssdH9KobXBFxK4S19-y2UMj6Hf2NgPofsFP0tpj477Z5ERgaerUNU.

54 See, e.g., Sadurski, 508–9; Lamont, 3–5; Stephen Hopgood, Jack Snyder and Leslie Vinjamuri, "Conclusion: Human Rights Futures", in Stephen Hopgood, Jack Snyder and Leslie Vinjamuri (eds), *Human Rights Futures* (Cambridge University Press, 2017), 311, 324; Johnson, 197–8 (on the rise of the US "Populist Party").

55 Quoted in Jäger; also in *ABC Eyewitness News*, 30 June 2016, available at: https://abc13.com/news/obama-unleashes-epic-anti-trump-rant-about-populism/1407256.

56 Benjamin Moffitt, *The Global Rise of Populism: Performance, Political Style, and Representation* (Stanford University Press, 2016), 142.

57 Johnson, 213–14.

58 See Angus Deaton, "Inequality in America has Lessons for Britain", *Financial Times*, 14 May 2019, available at: www.ft.com/content/4bb86682-756c-11e9-b0ec-7dff87b9a4a2 (Deaton won the Nobel Prize for Economics in 2015); Richard Partington, "UK Income Inequality Greater than Previously Thought, says ONS", *The Guardian*, 25 February 2020, available at: www.theguardian.com/inequality/2020/feb/25/uk-income-inequality-greater-than-previously-thought-says-ons.

59 Jill Lepore, "We Work: Labor without End", *The New Yorker*, 18 January 2021, 65, 69.

60 But see Jürgen Habermas, *Between Facts and Norms: Contributions to a Discourse Theory of Law and Democracy*, trans. W. Rehg (Cambridge, MA: MIT Press, 1996) [hereinafter *Habermas Discourse*], assuming a fundamental dichotomy between rationality and populism. For Habermas, public opinion becomes rational through considered public discourse that should be open to as many people as possible, not merely to elites. He contrasts such discourse to "a staged display of, and manipulative propagation of, publicity" in service to specific aims, which could, one assumes, include irrational populist aims, but Habermas does not make this clear. Jürgen Habermas, *The Structural Transformation of the Public Sphere*, trans. T. Burger (Boston, MA: Polity Press, 1989), *passim* [hereinafter *Habermas Transformation*].

61 Richard Rorty, "Human Rights, Rationality, and Sentimentality", in Stephen Shute and Susan Hurley (eds), *On Human Rights: The Oxford Amnesty Lectures 1993* (1993)

111 [hereinafter *Rorty Human Rights*]. See also Ignatieff, 201, 203 (arguing that the secular progress narratives of global elites mean little to the dispossessed).

62 Ignatieff, 5, 26, 52, 204, 206, 208. The philosopher Iris Marion Young earlier described a similar phenomenon which she called "city life": "By 'city life' I mean a form of social relations which I define as the being together of strangers." Iris Marion Young, *Justice and the Politics of Difference* (Princeton University Press, [1990] 2011), ch. 8. We will see shortly that the great mid-twentieth-century thinker, Hannah Arendt, rejects the duality of local and transnational both in terms of identity and assertions of rights, in favour of a cosmopolitan citizenship that is neither universalist nor localist. See Justine Lacroix and Jean-Yves Pranchère, *Human Rights on Trial: A Genealogy of the Critique of Human Rights* (Cambridge University Press, 2018), 228.

63 Emanuel Adler, *World Ordering: A Social Theory of Cognitive Evolution* (Cambridge University Press, 2019), 154 [hereinafter *Adler World Ordering*].

64 *Adler World Ordering*, 158.

65 Tocqueville warned long ago that "[t]he desire for equality always becomes more insatiable as equality is greater". Quoted in Mishra, 51. Mishra goes on to emphasise that claims of equality tend towards demands for social levelling and to become more and more radical. He invokes Mao's Great Leap Forward as a prime example. In our own era, populist attacks on elites derive from a similar impulse. See also Adam Czarnota, "Sources of Constitutional Populism: Democracy, Identity and Economic Exclusion", in Martin Krygier, Adam Czarnota and Wojciech Sadurski, *Anti-Constitutional Populism* (Cambridge University Press, 2022), 495, 498, 500–1.

66 Of course, this sense of conflict between equality and liberty is not inevitable. The economist-philosopher Amartya Sen posits a symbiotic relationship between equality and liberty and further suggests that equality can be pursued at a global level. Amartya Sen, *The Idea of Justice* (Cambridge, MA: Belknap Press, 2009), 291–317, 388–415.

67 People motivated by populist-nationalist sentiment may often claim that they are fighting for "freedom" or "liberty". But that freedom is ultimately to be restricted to the ingroup. It is not actually individualist, despite the rhetoric. It is typically built within self-identifying groups constituted around race, ethnicity, language and sex. They seek the recognition of the group as dominant, but claim this as equality.

68 Quentin Skinner, *The Foundations of Modern Political Thought, Vol. 2: The Age of Reformation* (Cambridge University Press, 1978), 349.

69 See Martin Krygier, "Introduction: Anti-Constitutional Populism", in Martin Krygier, Adam Czarnota and Wojciech Sadurski (eds), *Anti-Constitutional Populism* (Cambridge University Press, 2022), 1, 1–2.

70 Johnson, 199.

71 Johnson, 206.

72 Jeremy Waldron, "Rule-of-Law Rights and Populist Impatience", in Gerald Neuman (ed.), *Human Rights in a Time of Populism: Challenges and Responses* (Cambridge University Press, 2020), 43, 45–6.

73 See, e.g., Quinn Slobodian, *Globalists: The End of Empire and the Birth of Neoliberalism* (Cambridge, MA: Harvard University Press, 2018); Philip Arestis and Malcolm Sawyer

(eds), *Neo-Liberal Economic Policy: Critical Essays* (Cheltenham: Edward Elgar, 2004); John McWhorter, "When People Were Proud to Call Themselves 'Neoliberal': Tracking the Evolution of One Political Label to Understand Why Others Come and Go", *The Atlantic*, 30 May 2017, available at: www.theatlantic.com/business/archive/2017/05/history-of-neoliberal-meaning/528276.

74 As early as the 1980s, Michael Walzer had described the risk of concentrated wealth leading to disproportionate social and political power for the elite. Michael Walzer, *Spheres of Justice: A Defense of Pluralism and Equality* (New York: Basic Books, 1983), 120–2 [hereinafter *Walzer Spheres of Justice*].

75 Adam Przeworski, *Crises of Democracy* (Cambridge University Press, 2019), 106–7; Michael Sandel, *The Tyranny of Meritocracy: What's Become of the Common Good?* (New York: Penguin, 2021), 23–4 [hereinafter *Sandel Meritocracy*].

76 Thomas Piketty, *Capital in the Twenty-First Century*, trans. Arthur Goldhammer (Cambridge, MA: Harvard University Press, 2014); Sarah van Gelder (ed.), *This Changes Everything: Occupy Wall Street and the 99% Movement* (San Francisco, CA: Berrett-Koehler, 2011); Joseph Stiglitz, *The Price of Inequality* (London: Penguin, 2013); Lamont, 13–15.

77 Przeworski, 33–8.

78 *Sandel Meritocracy*, 22, 75, 197 (quoting detailed economic studies that reveal the massively unequal distribution of economic growth since the 1960s, exacerbated in the 1980s).

79 Burleigh, 21.

80 The study was conducted by Dr David Bartram of the University of Leicester, quoted in James Tapper, "Rich Countries that Let Inequality Run Rampant make Citizens Unhappy, Study Finds", *The Guardian*, 17 April 2022, available at: www.theguardian.com/inequality/2022/apr/17/rich-countries-that-let-inequality-run-rampant-make-citizens-unhappy.

81 *Sandel Meritocracy*, 6, 183–4.

82 *Sandel Meritocracy*, 17, 19, 72–3.

83 *Sandel Meritocracy*, 25, and see 49, 59, 62 (on the same ideas expressed in China).

84 *Sandel Meritocracy*, 42, 70. Sandel notes that in the United States in particular, this idea has been linked to evangelical Christianity through the so-called "prosperity gospel". *Sandel Meritocracy*, 46–7.

85 Carl Schmitt, *The Crisis of Parliamentary Democracy*, trans. Ellen Kennedy (Cambridge, MA: MIT Press, 1985), 16 [hereinafter *Schmitt Crisis*]. See also Cheryl Misak, *Truth, Politics, Morality: Pragmatism and Deliberation* (London: Routledge, 2000), 9, 11 [hereinafter *Misak Truth*].

86 Lacroix and Pranchère, 198.

87 *Schmitt Crisis*, 9; Carl Schmitt, *Constitutional Theory*, trans. Jeffrey Seitzer (Durham, NC: Duke University Press, 2008), 203 et seq. Lacroix and Pranchère point out, quite fairly, that Schmitt was never able to explain how these conditions for the existence of a sovereign people can be distinguished from the fanaticism of mass movements, or how people's nationalism retains unity. "Peoples" seem eminently capable of breaking into factions and descending into civil war. Lacroix and Pranchère, 203.

88 Chris Thornhill, *The Sociology of Law and the Global Transformation of Democracy* (Cambridge University Press, 2018), 98.

89 S. N. Eisenstadt, "Introduction", *Max Weber on Charisma and Institution Building: Selected Papers* (University of Chicago Press, 1968), ix, at xxx [hereinafter *Weber Charisma*]. The strength of a specifically German nationalism had been argued at the beginning of the nineteenth century by Fichte. Johann Gottlieb Fichte, *Addresses to the German Nation*, ed. Gregory Moore (Cambridge University Press, [1807–8] 2008).

90 Durkheim famously argued that "the world is inside of society", quoted in Mark Cladis, "Durkheim's Individual in Society: A Sacred Marriage?" (1992) 53 *J. History of Ideas* 71, 73.

91 Emile Durkheim, *Sociology and Philosophy* (London: Cohen & West, 1953), 12 [hereinafter *Durkheim Sociology*].

92 Thornhill, 100–3.

93 Max Weber, *The Vocation Lectures*, ed. David Owen and Tracy Strong (Indianapolis, IN: Hackett, 2004), 33. For Weber, state law was a means by which that claim to a monopoly on violence could be successfully pursued. I thank Ron Levi for this insight.

94 Here, too, Schmitt follows Weber who argued that parliamentary democracy was not strong enough to promote affective integration in modern societies. Only charismatic leadership could do that. Thornhill, 93. Schmitt was not alone in denigrating the Weimar constitutional order. A leading Nazi jurist-apologist and follower of Schmitt, Ernst Forsthoff, argued that Weimar represented a "democracy without a people" creating a "state without substance". Quoted in Herlinde Pauer-Studer, *Justifying Injustice: Legal Theory in Nazi Germany* (Cambridge University Press, 2021), 16. But Schmitt, although virulently anti-Semitic, tended towards independent thought that did not always curry favour with the Nazi regime. David Dyzenhaus, "Lawyer for the Strongman", *Aeon*, 12 June 2020, available at: https://aeon.co/essays/carl-schmitts-legal-theory-legitimises-the-rule-of-the-strongman [hereinafter *Dyzenhaus Lawyer*].

95 For a brilliant catalogue of Wagner's cultural and political influence, see Alex Ross, *Wagnerism* (London: 4th Estate, 2020). Wagner claimed to be "the most German person ... the German spirit". Ross, 194. See also Ross, 202, 205. Of course, Wagner's anti-Semitism also connected him in spirit to Schmitt, the later Nazi regime and to Hitler himself. Ross, 235–41, 249–51, 426–7, 515–16, 529–42.

96 See Pauer-Studer, 8, 53. The Nazi heritage was, oddly enough, originally anti-nationalist, and focused upon the "people". But the "movement" became nationalist as it captured the levers of state power. It also focused upon race as a means of societal unification – of an exclusionary variety – in the absence of political unification. *Arendt Totalitarianism*, 3–4, 166, 413.

97 *Dyzenhaus Lawyer*.

98 Hitler told one of his senior deputies, Albert Speer, that "[i]f the war is lost, the people will also be lost [and] it is not necessary to worry about their needs for elemental survival. On the contrary, it is best for us to destroy even these things. For the nation has proved to be weak ..." Randall Hansen, *Disobeying Hitler: German Resistance after Operation Valkyrie* (Toronto: Doubleday Canada, 2014), 192. See also the fascinating

examples of German – even German army – resistance to this scorched-earth policy throughout the book.

99 Hitler's attitude was consistent with Nazi political theory wherein the Führer was the embodiment of the *Volk* (people) and his will inevitably expressed theirs. Pauer-Studer, 9, 76, 101. If they failed to support him adequately, he owed them nothing.

100 Sheera Frenkel and Alan Feuer, "'A Total Failure': The Proud Boys Now Mock Trump", *New York Times*, 20 January 2021, available at: www.nytimes.com/2021/01/20/technology/proud-boys-trump.html.

101 On the threats posed to democratic regimes and the anti-institutionalism of authoritarian populists, see Przeworski, esp. 14–15, 88.

102 John Greco, *The Transmission of Knowledge* (Cambridge University Press, 2021), ix.

103 I emphasise the nationalist link here because I believe that Johnson is correct in suggesting that in its nineteenth-century progressive US guise, populism was not reliant on charismatic leadership, but was founded in local and regional community organising. Johnson, 200. However, contemporary left-wing populism in Latin America is typically nationalist and dependent upon charismatic leadership, witness the Venezuelan situation.

104 Max Weber, *The Theory of Social and Economic Organization* (New York: Free Press, 1964), 358 [hereinafter *Weber Theory*].

105 *Weber Theory*, 57–64.

106 *Weber Theory*, 362.

107 Irving Zeitlin, "The Political and Social Theory of Max Weber" (1991) 60 *U. of TQ* 404, 406. Indeed, Weber may even have supported a political system presided over by a strong leader guided by direct referendum votes rather than any form of representative legislature. Pauer-Studer, 27, fn 27. See also *Dyzenhaus Lawyer* (on how Carl Schmitt's constitutional theories also legitimate "strongman" leadership; Schmitt believed that only a powerful chief executive could serve as an effective "guardian" of the constitutional order, hence, he argued that the strongman was actually an instrument of the rule of law, not a threat to it).

108 *Weber Theory*, 71–2.

109 Weber, "Charisma and the Structure of Social Relationships", in *Weber Charisma*, 22–3.

110 See the comprehensive discussion in Pippa Norris and Ronald Inglehart, *Cultural Backlash: Trump, Brexit, and Authoritarian Populism* (Cambridge University Press, 2019).

111 *Sandel Meritocracy*, *passim*; Lamont, 8, 22, 24, 32–3.

112 See Ross Douthat, "How Trump Ate Populism", *New York Times*, 26 January 2021, available at: www.nytimes.com/2021/01/26/opinion/trump-hawley-populism.html?action=click&module=Opinion&pgtype=Homepage.

113 "Uncontrolled" migration is often used as a trope by populist politicians and is also linked increasingly to attacks on legal limits on deportation and on those who try to deploy them. See Harriet Grant, "Home Secretary's 'Dangerous' Rhetoric 'Putting Lawyers at Risk'", *The Guardian*, 6 October 2020, available at: www.theguardian.com/global-development/2020/oct/06/home-secretarys-dangerous-rhetoric-putting-lawyers-at-risk.

114 Paul Blokker, "Populism as a Constitutional Project" (2019) 17 *Int'l J. Constitutional L.* 535, 536–7.

115 FiveThirtyEight, available at: https://projects.fivethirtyeight.com/trump-approval-ratings, last accessed 24 May 2020.

116 Americas Society/Council of the Americas, available at: www.as-coa.org/articles/approval-tracker-brazils-president-jair-bolsonaro, last accessed 24 May 2020.

117 Jordan Kyle and Yascha Mounk, "The Populist Harm to Democracy: An Empirical Assessment", The Tony Blair Institute for Global Change, 2018, available at: https://institute.global/insight/renewing-centre/populist-harm-democracy.

118 Charley Savage, "Incitement to Riot? What Trump Told Supporters Before Mob Stormed Capitol", *New York Times*, 10 January 2021, available at: www.nytimes.com/2021/01/10/us/trump-speech-riot.html.

119 See Steve Holland and Lisa Lambert, "Trump to Send Federal Forces to more 'Democrat' Cities", *Reuters*, 20 July 2020, available at: https://www.reuters.com/article/us-global-race-protests-portland-idUSKCN24L1I1.

120 See, e.g., a critical assessment of that view from historian David Olusoga, "The Poisonously Patronising Sewell Report is Historically Illiterate", *The Guardian*, 2 April 2021, available at: www.theguardian.com/commentisfree/2021/apr/02/sewell-race-report-historical-young-people-britain.

121 Susanne Baer, "The Rule of – and Not by Any – Law. On Constitutionalism" (2018) 71 *Current Legal Problems* 335, 337–9; William Galston, "The Populist Challenge to Liberal Democracy" (2018) 29 *J. of Democracy* 5, 15; Sadurski, 510–12; Krygier, 2.

122 See, e.g., Timothy Frye, "What's Vladimir Putin's End Game? Other post-Soviet Autocrats Give a Few Clues", *Washington Post*, 3 July 2020, available at: www.washingtonpost.com/politics/2020/07/03/whats-vladimir-putins-end-game-other-post-soviet-autocrats-give-few-clues.

123 Keith Whittington, "Trump's Defiance is Destroying Congress's Power", *The Atlantic*, 14 October 2019, available at: www.theatlantic.com/ideas/archive/2019/10/trumps-defiance-destroying-congress/599923; Lisa Mascaro, "It's not Just the Presidency: Trump is Changing the Congress", *Detroit News* (n.d.), available at: https://eu.detroitnews.com/story/news/politics/2020/07/10/just-presidency-trump-changing-congress/112125424.

124 Chris Buckley and Keith Bradsher, "China Moves to Let Xi Stay in Power by Abolishing Term Limit", *New York Times*, 25 February 2018, available at: www.nytimes.com/2018/02/25/world/asia/china-xi-jinping.html; Wendy Tang, "'People's Leader' Title will Cement Xi's Grip on Power", *The Times*, 29 July 2022, available at: www.thetimes.co.uk/article/peoples-leader-title-will-cement-xis-grip-on-power-tnzh7t6f9.

125 Sadurski, 521–2, 525.

126 *Weber Theory*, 57–64.

127 Though, ironically, charismatic, populist leaders tend to promote their own inner circle to "elite" status, displacing other elites. The "people" do not genuinely control anything. *Dyzenhaus Lawyer.*

128 See Philip Sherwell, "Victims of Philippine's Drug War Blood Bath Point a Finger at Duterte", *The Times*, 19 June 2022, available at: www.thetimes.co.uk/article/victims-of-

philippines-drug-war-bloodbath-point-a-finger-at-duterte-w3kwn2ll8; Ana Santos, "Duterte's Four Years in Power – Extrajudicial Killings, Rights Abuses and Terror", in DW (Deutsche Welle), n.d., available at: www.dw.com/en/dutertes-four-years-in-power-extrajudicial-killings-rights-abuses-and-terror/a-54082293.

129 Martin Krygier, "The Challenge of Institutionalisation: Post-Communist 'Transitions', Populism, and the Rule of Law" (2019) 15 *Euro. Constitutional L. Rev.* 544, *passim*; George Szirtes, "Hungary's Students are Making a Last Stand against Viktor Orbán's Power Grab", *The Guardian*, 15 September 2020, available at: www.theguardian.com/commentisfree/2020/sep/15/hungary-students-viktor-orban-university-theatre-budapest; Sadurski, 526.

130 Anne Appelbaum, "The Disturbing Campaign Against Poland's Judges", *The Atlantic*, 28 January 2020, available at: www.theatlantic.com/ideas/archive/2020/01/disturbing-campaign-against-polish-judges/605623; Sadurski, 525, 529.

131 Timothy Garton Ash, "Under Cover of Covid, Poland is Stifling Free Media – and all Europe should be Worried", *The Guardian*, 8 April 2021, available at: www.theguardian.com/commentisfree/2021/apr/08/covid-poland-democracy-media-europe-coronavirus-tax.

132 International Commission of Jurists, *Turkey: the Judicial System in Peril* (2016).

133 Eric Posner, "Liberal Internationalism and the Populist Backlash Symposium: The Forefront of International Law" (2017) 49 *Arizona State L. J.* 795. See also Erik Voeten, "Populism and Backlashes against International Courts" (2019) *Perspectives on Politics* 1.

134 Leslie Vinjamuri, "Human Rights Backlash", in Stephen Hopgood, Jack Snyder and Leslie Vinjamuri (eds), *Human Rights Futures* (Cambridge University Press, 2017), 114, 114–18, 121, 127; Mattias Kumm, "The Legitimacy of International Law: A Constitutionalist Framework of Analysis" (2004) 15 *EJIL* 907 [hereinafter *Kumm Legitimacy*].

135 Quoted in Pankaj Mishra, "Struggle Sessions", *The New Yorker*, 1 February 2021, 61, 65.

136 Jutta Brunnée, "Challenging International Law: What's New?" *Opinio Juris* Blog, 13 November 2018, available at: http://opiniojuris.org/2018/11/13/challenging-international-law-whats-new.

137 Francis Fukuyama, quoted in Thomas Brown, "Populism and Nationalism: Implications for the International Order", 12 January 2017, 7, House of Lords Library, available at: https://lordslibrary.parliament.uk/research-briefings/lln-2017-0002.

138 See, e.g., Harold Koh, *The Trump Administration and International Law* (Oxford University Press, 2019).

139 Charles Hankla, "Why Biden Will Find it Hard to Undo Trump's 'America First' Trade Policy", *The Conversation* (n.d.), available at: https://theconversation.com/why-biden-will-find-it-hard-to-undo-trumps-costly-america-first-trade-policy-149340; James Dean, "It is Still America First, Joe Biden warns UK", *The Times*, 7 December 2020, available at: www.thetimes.co.uk/article/its-still-america-first-joe-biden-warns-uk-d0b27htmj.

140 Jonathan Freedland, "Britain has a Decision to Make: the Rule of Boris Johnson – or the Rule of Law?" *The Guardian*, 17 June 2022, available at: www.theguardian.com/commentisfree/2022/jun/17/britain-has-a-decision-to-make-the-rule-of-boris-johnson-or-the-rule-of-law. See also Haroon Siddique, "No 10 to Set Out Sweeping Plans to

Override Power of Human Rights Court", *The Guardian*, 21 June 2022, available at: www.theguardian.com/law/2022/jun/21/uks-new-bill-of-rights-will-curtail-power-of-european-human-rights-court.

141 Venkataraman Ramakrishnan, "Everyone Wants to 'Follow the Science'. But We Can't Waste Time on Blame", *The Guardian*, 24 May 2020, available at: www.theguardian.com/world/2020/may/24/everyone-wants-to-follow-the-science-but-we-cant-waste-time-on-blame.

142 N.a., "Coronavirus: Outcry after Trump Suggests Injecting Disinfectant as Treatment", BBC, 24 April 2020, available at: www.bbc.co.uk/news/world-us-canada-52407177.

CHAPTER THREE

The Confounding Diversity of Globalisation

In the wild West they are whipping each other
In the hungry East they are eating their books
In the numb North there are no more cradles
The sullen South has been set on fire

W. H. Auden, *The Age of Anxiety*[*]

AS I HAVE SUGGESTED, there is a link between populism and the growing distrust of national and international institutions. But the distrust is wider and relates to the post-Second World War economic trajectory and its cultural and societal effects, including a general weakening of various forms of authority, often described as "globalisation".[143] Of course, globalisation is a compendious term and can be invoked to encompass diverse – and even contradictory – phenomena. In what follows, I will focus on the social and cultural effects of the globalisation of trade in goods and services, and the flow of capital. But "globalisation" can also signal positive changes such as greater ease of communication over the internet, the sharing of cultural forms and speedy transborder transportation, as well as negative developments such as illegal migration, cross-border environmental damage and transnational crime.

I used the word "distrust" to describe widespread reactions to our globalised economic institutions, but that is too mild. I got an inkling of the strong antipathy felt by many people towards economic elites when I represented the University of British Columbia at an event called the "G-8

University Summit" in Torino, Italy, in 2009. The gathering had nothing to do with the G-8 intergovernmental meetings; the frame of "G-8" was used simply to pull together university leaders from around the member countries. The conference was actually conceived as a challenge to the G-8 political leadership to address the inequalities and environmental failings of unbridled economic globalisation. Indeed, the declaration issued by the attending university leaders committed our universities to "[e]ducate students at all levels in the issues concerning sustainable development so that they may pursue the creation of sustainable and responsible societies". It called upon the G-8 countries to "[p]romote responsible development as a driving force to create a sustainable economy".[144]

The Declaration could fairly be criticised as vague, even anodyne. It had to be negotiated amongst a diverse group of universities with different relationships to their own governments. But the intention was, I still think, admirable: to question the G-8 governments' dominant approaches to development and to commit universities to the promotion of more sustainable and equitable global and national economic policies. It was emphatically not an endorsement of rigid neoliberalism and uncontrolled globalisation.

Here's the rub. Because of the – it turned out – poorly chosen name of the summit, we participants became the focus of anti-globalisation protestors. Hundreds of students and other young people gathered outside the beautiful central building of the University of Torino, chanting slogans and trying to break in to disrupt the meetings. One evening, we were all to be taken in busses to the extraordinary Italian National Museum of Cinema for a tour and reception. When we exited the conference building we heard loud chanting and we were bustled onto the kind of busses that police use to deliver them to the site of a riot. All the windows were covered in metal grates. I soon saw why. As we left the university grounds, the rocks started hitting the buses. The poor drivers then commenced a game of cat and mouse, trying to pick unpredictable routes that the protestors would not expect, escorted by screaming police cars and vans, and ushered by officers in full riot gear. The drivers only partly succeeded. If my memory serves me right, it took us around an hour and a half to travel less than 1.5 kilometres. Frankly, it was bloody scary, with what turned into a mob running after us, blocking us, screaming and hurling various projectiles. Many of the protestors wore the outfits of Black Bloc anarchists.

I do not repeat this story to elicit sympathy. Quite the opposite. As we zigged and zagged through the streets of central Torino, I thought that the experience was deeply instructive. For one thing, it revealed that aligning with the G-8, even superficially, was a big mistake for those who actually sought to challenge the governmental consensus. More importantly, I realised that the anti-globalisation movement was genuinely angry and capable of both swift organisation and violence. And I felt naive that I should be surprised by that.

In the globalised world, states compete not only in the sense of relative power, read as "security", but also for relative market share in the global economy. They must also engage in forms of diplomacy with multinational firms for investment, access to supply chains and jobs. The distinction between the state and the corporation is blurred.[145] Nationalists of both the left and right are deeply unsettled by these developments.

Contemporary patterns of globalisation have prompted economic changes that eliminate or downgrade the jobs of many workers in heretofore prosperous societies of the North. Call centres in India and auto factories in Mexico exist. But every shred of evidence suggests that the labour dislocation in Northern countries has been prompted mostly by technological change that is not going away, no matter what populists and protestors may promise. The real patterns of disruption are caused by the so-called "fourth industrial revolution", a digital technology revolution focused on the deployment of data. As we have already seen, robots are a big part of the future, much more so than women working in Vietnamese factories.[146] I will return to this point later.

Over modern human history, recurrent cycles of globalisation (which date back to at least the Middle Ages with travelling scholars and traders who carried with them the *law merchant*)[147] produced benefits, but also huge – and often ethically indefensible – costs that are borne unequally. The globalisation of trade associated with colonialism produced the Atlantic slave trade and massive economic exploitation of colonies in

Africa, Asia and the Caribbean.[148] In the words of the early twentieth-century pan-Africanist sociologist W. E. B. Du Bois:

> The characteristic of our age is the contact of European civilization with the world's undeveloped peoples. Whatever we may say of the results of such contact in the past, it certainly forms a chapter in human action not pleasant to look back upon. War, murder, slavery, extermination, and debauchery, – this has again and again been the result of carrying civilization and the blessed gospel to the isles of the sea and the heathen without law.[149]

Disruptions to historic patterns of globalisation coincide almost perfectly with the re-emergence of strong localist or later, nationalistic sentiments, usually resulting in deep social conflict, even war. We should not be surprised that our era feels anxious.

The social and political uncertainty caused by globalisation is far more profound than purely economic risks can explain. It relates to quite basic differences in how we understand the interplay of human cultures and human values. The central question is how are humans alike in nature and how are they differently shaped by diverse cultures? It is beyond the scope of this book to provide definitive answers, but let me be more precise in tracing out the uncertainty, which was present in classical antiquity and still presses on us.

Aristotle thought that human values and aspirations could be both universal and specific. In some passages, he suggests, for example, that laws (nomos) could contain universal elements because human nature tended to make people rational in practical ways and that as a result laws could also be practically rational.[150] This might imply that some of the values underlying law are also shared across all humanity. Yet, at the same time, Aristotle argued that the real source of law is the prudent legislator, implying that laws are "contingent artifacts of a particular political community".[151] More generally, Aristotle believed that political communities are based in specific, and often differing, fundamental conceptions of the good life.[152] This implies that "value" is a culturally contingent concept.

In the early nineteenth century the German philosopher Hegel added to the uncertainty. In his *Phenomenology of Spirit*,[153] Hegel argued that self-consciousness depended upon the recognition of self-consciousness in others. Through this mutual recognition, there was created an "objective spirit", a social consciousness that then allowed for the individual consciousness to explore from a shared base, so to speak. Over time, this social grounding could change through shifting patterns of mutual recognition amongst individual consciousnesses.[154] These patterns were, for Hegel, culturally distinct, creating what we call the *Zeitgeist*, or spirit of the age. Note, that it is the spirit of the age, a social spirit, not necessarily a national spirit. So, Hegel stands for the idea that consciousness – and one might assume then, value – is not only an individual but a shared phenomenon that can change from era to era and from society to society. However, it is important to stress that the state does play a crucial role for Hegel, as it stands at the centre of society and reflects customs and history; its constitution and laws guarantee all social liberties and rights.[155]

The idea that our very basis of understanding the world is at least in part collective was picked up in modern sociology, and attached to the shared consciousness of specific societies. Durkheim argued that "[c]ollective truths are the basis of the common consciousness of society".[156] For example, he viewed punishment for crime as being primarily justified by the need to maintain social cohesion by upholding the "common consciousness".[157] Further, he argued that even when people move from one society to another, they cling to the ideals and values of their original society; the common consciousness of a society of origin is sticky.[158]

By the late nineteenth century, then, the connection of "value" to the state was solidifying, the notion of a shared human consciousness or set of ideals, atrophying. Weber explicitly linked the collective consciousness to the nation-state. He believed that "ultimate ends or values" could differ radically from society to society, nation to nation.[159] This nationalist sensibility was expressed in legal discourse as well, with Savigny declaring "the organic connection of the law with the essence and the character of the people".[160] Some contemporary theorists uphold this view of law as rooted in specific cultures, without any universal attributes.[161]

Nationalism, and the link between nation and a narrowly defined people, reached its apogee in the first half of the twentieth century, with the most perverse expression found in Nazi Germany. As we have seen, this form of nationalism is rooted in the theory that the state is the product of "popular sovereignty" – only a defined "people" can legitimate their own government.[162] This was not a new idea, having been promoted in the early nineteenth century by Auguste Comte in his attacks on the outcomes of the French Revolution.[163] But Carl Schmitt pushed Comte's arguments to an extreme position, declaring that democracy (the will of the people) could exist only where there was "national homogeneity" that excluded anything foreign.[164] Schmitt later became an exponent of racial purity and certainly did not press against the "final solution", the extermination of foreign elements and especially the Jews.[165] It was in this context that Hannah Arendt argued with great force that "the conquest of the state by the nation" has had appalling consequences for millions of people.[166] I will return to Arendt later.

The rise of nationalism was well explained in the 1980s by political historians like Eric Hobsbawm and social anthropologists like Ernest Gellner. They argued that nationalism was a response to the need for unifying myths of origin for the states that arose out of the eighteenth-century revolutions in the United States and France. It was, above all, a product of modernisation of governance and the economy.[167] More recent scholarship suggests, correctly I think, that the work of the 1980s missed out on the formative role that religion played in early nationalism, and now plays out in expressions of political Islam that are closely tied to state structures, as in Iran or Saudi Arabia.[168]

Subsequently, the force of justification was reversed, and nationalism became a primary motive force for modern leftist revolutions, as in China, Cuba and a series of revolutions in Latin America.[169] Nationalism was also a prominent justification for claims to self-determination in the 1960s, along with anti-imperialism. Interestingly, then, throughout the 1960s and subsequently, nationalism has been both a conservative and a progressive influence. Later, with the rise of universalist human rights claims, it was nonetheless argued that particular expression of those claims was shaped within nation-states.[170] It was in this context that never-resolved arguments broke out over what to include in the category of human rights. For a generation during the Cold War the West typically focused on individual political and legal rights, with the communist states emphasising economic and social rights.

In the late twentieth century, conservative critics of the newly powerful politico-legal discourse of human rights hearkened back to Edmund

Burke's anti-revolutionary stance to suggest that "rights" were only real in concrete citizenship within nations.[171] Hannah Arendt has been linked to this tradition by many critical commentators, largely because she worried deeply about the promises of "universal" human rights, promises she saw betrayed in the lives of forced migrants who could not claim the protection of citizenship. She was herself one of those people, stateless for some eighteen years: "The world found nothing sacred in the abstract nakedness of being human."[172] We will see shortly that this accusation of Burkean conservatism is a mis-framing of Arendt's views.

The nationalist tide began to shift, however, in the 1970s and 1980s. Myriad forces were in play. In the 1970s, the rise of human rights law and policy in many Western countries had transnational impact and the argument grew that the international law principle of sovereign equality, and its corollary of non-interference in domestic affairs, did not preclude the examination of domestic human rights practices by international organisations, international NGOs and by other states. Pressure grew as well for international criminal law accountability for genocide and for massive human rights violations. Again, this trend reached inside domestic legal–political jurisdictions, challenging the sovereignty of state legislatures and the power of national politicians. This development opened up counter-arguments based on the supposed democratic deficit in international politics and law.[173] These arguments were especially salient in Asia and Europe.

In parallel, intergovernmental organisations were growing in influence at the global level, but perhaps even more at the regional level, led by the increasing power of the European Community, later Union. This institutional growth, including the expansion of international courts, was matched by the ever-increasing importance of international trade to domestic economic health. The so-called "Washington consensus" grew dominant with the increasing influence of neoliberal economics leading to ever-greater interconnection of economies through integrated supply chains, more population mobility – planned and unplanned, legal and illegal – and a dominating influence of Western, especially American, culture through mass media and, more recently, social media. As the complexity of state interrelationships grew economically, socially and culturally, it became harder for individual states to even identify their own "self-interest" making purely "rationalist" assessments of appropriate action more difficult.[174] All of these developments came to be called "globalisation".

Concurrently, a particular trend emerged in European thought, propelled by the German philosopher Jürgen Habermas. His theory of law and democracy was grounded in the assertion that citizens pursue their democratic participation and action through what he called "communicative reason" where each person makes claims about what is true and offers good reasons to others for accepting the claim.[175] Through language and its social application in shared discourse, citizens could reason their way to democratic consensus.[176] I will return to this theory later, but for now what matters is that Habermas thought that such discourse was most effectively realised when the citizenry shared what he called a "lifeworld". The lifeworld set a frame around where speech takes place in the public space as well as appropriate sources for interpretation of speech.[177] What is more, Habermas' lifeworld is built within specific cultures. Individuals are supported in the lifeworld through "relationships of reciprocal recognition articulated in cultural traditions ..."[178]

Implicit in this concept of a shared lifeworld is some element of mutually recognised values.[179] Michael Walzer reinforced this perspective in arguing, for example, that any right to immigration (vested in those who would wish to join a society) "is limited by the right of a political community to preserve the integrity of its form of life".[180] There are two ways of interpreting this purported need for value alignment. Immigration might be restricted to those who are willing to accept a new country's way of life through assimilation. Alternatively, that the prospective immigrant is willing to engage in public discourse, without necessarily abandoning the home culture. I think that Habermas would subscribe to the second interpretation. His requirement of a shared lifeworld does not require complete consensus on values.

Habermas' struggle, and it remains ours, is to figure out whether or not it is possible to engage in communicative reason and to develop democratic consensus in situations of deep diversity, such as the international sphere, where there is almost no shared lifeworld.[181] Some interpreters of Habermas have suggested that it is possible to imagine "thin" lifeworlds that allow for some communicative reason, but not the achievement of full democratic consensus.[182] This might be the case at the international level.

However, Michael Walzer argued that no such "thin" lifeworld could form the basis for robust and meaningful politics:

> Politics (as distinct from mere coercion and bureaucratic manipulation) depends upon shared history, communal sentiment, accepted conventions – upon some extended version of Aristotle's "friendship". All this is problematic enough in the modern state: it is hardly conceivable on a global scale.[183]

Habermas himself seems to have concluded that although lifeworlds are not necessarily co-extensive with the nation, they may be what I would describe as "civilisationally bounded".[184] A passionate European, Habermas seemed to conclude that the creation of an inclusive discourse – leading to political consensus – was much more likely within lifeworlds where a minimum of core values is shared, and participants see themselves as equals.[185] He believed that a common European peoplehood was being built.[186] Implicit is the conclusion that outside Europe, at the global level, such shared peoplehood was highly unlikely.[187]

I have reviewed the intellectual sources of resistance to globalisation, be they based in nationalism or in perceptions of important civilisational difference. But since at least the 1960s a countervailing intellectual tradition has grown, rooted strongly in pluralism and cosmopolitanism, with their moral commitments to diversity.

Within national borders, the concept of an homogeneous "people" has been widely challenged. Judith Shklar argued in the 1960s that social diversity is the prevailing condition of nations. She viewed diversity as a positive value, with tolerance being a primary virtue.[188] Shklar saw pluralism of interests and values within nation-states as an inevitable condition:

> It is not wickedness that creates a multiplicity of needs and values, but the inevitable diversity among people and the complexity of demands that a highly developed culture makes upon them.[189]

In putting forth this view of diversity as both inevitable and a social asset, Shklar drew on a wellspring of philosophical and sociological insight, reaching back to Hegel and Kant.[190] Contemporaneously with Shklar, Hannah Arendt argued that "[p]luralism is the condition of human action" because, as humans, "nobody is ever the same as anyone else who has ever lived, lives, or will live".[191] In the founding of modern sociology, we have seen Durkheim's argument that society is necessary for the flourishing of the individual. Now I would add Durkheim's view that society's support for the individual is expressed in social complexity, not homogeneity:

> [T]olerance must be based on this idea of the complexity and richness of reality, and then on the diversity of opinions, which is both necessary and effective. Everyone must be able to admit that someone else has perceived an aspect of reality, which he himself had not grasped, but which is as real and as true as those to which he had gone from preference.[192]

This tradition continues today with an emphasis on intellectual pluralism[193] and a belief that, to borrow St Paul's phrase, none of us can do other than see through a glass darkly. Therefore, we must be attuned to the insights of others and to the uncertainty of our conclusions. Again, Arendt captures the idea perfectly:

> Unanimity of opinion is a very ominous phenomenon, and one characteristic of our modern mass age. It destroys social and personal life, which is based on the fact that we are different by nature and by conviction. To hold different opinions and to be aware that other people think differently on the same issue shields us from Godlike certainty which stops all discussion and reduces social relationships to those of an ant heap. A unanimous public opinion tends to eliminate bodily those who differ, for mass unanimity is not the result of agreement, but an expression of fanaticism and hysteria. In contrast to agreement, unanimity does not stop at certain well-defined objects, but spreads like an infection into every related issue.[194]

In adopting an expansive, effects-focused understanding of the concept of "justice", Amartya Sen also emphasises the value pluralism of our world. He stresses the analytic power that is created through the bringing together of diverse insights across cultures.[195]

It is a widespread view that Islamic thought runs counter to this "Western" acceptance of pluralism, but there are strong traditions in

Islamic scholarship that can engage dispassionately with difference. At a fundamental level, in his attempt to connect Aristotelean and Islamic thought, the great Muslim philosopher Abul-Walid Muhammad ibn Rushd (Averroes) argued that there could be diverse versions of truth derived from religious and philosophical explorations.[196] The anthropology and comparative religion of the tenth-century scholar Abu Rayhan al-Buruni is another shining example of classical pluralism that continues to influence strains of Islamic thought.[197] This is not to deny that there are strong contemporary purist strains of Islam that eschew any form of pluralism. But it must be said that such contemporary strains exist in most religious traditions, including some versions of evangelical Christianity, ultra-Orthodox Judaism, Hindu nationalism in India, and Buddhist nationalism in Myanmar and Sri Lanka.

The obvious extension of pluralist conceptions within nations is a recognition of diversity and complexity in international society.[198] The global pluralist suggests that it is possible for diverse peoples, across cultures, to develop a sense of attachment to the wide world, often termed "cosmopolitanism". Famously, when asked where he came from, the classical Greek philosopher, Diogenes, responded: "I am a citizen of the world." This comment was not really followed up in concrete intellectual commitments attributable to Diogenes, but was nonetheless adopted and developed by the Stoics in Rome, led by Cicero.[199] In the early modern period, thinkers such as Erasmus reinterpreted this ancient tradition of cosmopolitanism. The concept of a shared human moral community was expounded most strongly during the enlightenment by Kant, even as he defended empire on the basis of its ability to unify the world through trade.[200]

Modern thinkers have reformed the tradition by rejecting the idea of a single moral community, or a shared "human nature", arguing instead that diverse peoples can *imagine themselves* as part of a wider, global community. To exercise this imaginative leap requires the fundamental skill of empathy, not uniformity of purpose, or a single definition of the good life.[201] A key component of this contemporary cosmopolitanism is that "the rights of individuals are normatively prior to the rights of states".[202]

For me, the most persuasive modern thinker in this cosmopolitan tradition is Hannah Arendt. She argued that it is the essential variety of human beings that gives rise to the core concept of "human rights". Rights are made real in the interaction of people, not in abstract ideals of reason (Kant) or divinely ordained natural law (Augustine).[203] She articulated a conception of cosmopolitan citizenship that included a right to political participation both within and beyond the state. The human has a right to a "meaningful place in the world", with "world" being defined as "a sphere constituted by connections between individuals who reciprocally recognise each other as equals".[204] It is this sphere that creates a home for the citizen, which is not fixed in one place but can be reconstituted across borders. Belonging is therefore always partial and contingent; it is not an essence and linked to only one place, one nation.[205] Citizenship can be meaningfully related both to the local community of the nation and to a wider, transnational community. It is the right to participation that matters fundamentally; this right creates the "free citizen".[206]

From a pragmatic perspective, there is an eminently practical reason to adopt a globalist or cosmopolitan stance. To address global problems, such as climate change, mass migration, pandemic disease or cyber security, only agreements and mechanisms that transcend borders are effective. This means that for many purposes, nation-states must change their conceptions of what counts in politics and how to address fundamental problems. Globalist practices and cross-border cooperation are critical for preventing irreversible damage to the *national* interest and *national* security.[207] As put forcefully by former US President Obama, in our world of "global supply chains, instantaneous capital transfers, social media, transnational terrorist networks, climate change, mass migration, and ever-increasing complexity – we will learn to live together, cooperate with one another, and recognise the dignity of others, or we will perish."[208]

Critics of this pluralist view suggest that it underplays the reality of unequal power in forcing consensus, or in imposing false uniformity. This is a now-standard critique of the development of international law.[209] The most thoughtful criticism of a straightforward pluralist-globalist viewpoint was offered by Habermas who canvassed views in contemporary democracies revealing that the interest of citizens in "political equality" was being undermined by an "elite pluralism" inattentive to the real needs and desires of the citizenry.[210] This elite pluralism is linked I believe to the concept of "globalisation" in the economic sense of free trade, mobility of capital, competition on labour costs and standards, and the "trickle down" theory of growth and distribution of benefits. This is the globalisation resisted so strongly in Torino, and feared by millions of frustrated people around the globe.

In our era, then, we continue to face two competing theoretical and organisational principles of our life in society: one circumscribed and typically denominated "nationalism"; the other expansive and now called "globalism", although its intellectual foundations are more strictly "cosmopolitan". In between is a conception of political and social life grounded in what might be called "cultural regionalism", most obviously in the European context. Nationalism promises, as it always has, some degree of clarity about who is part of the political community, and it seeks to define that community around a purported value consensus and a high degree of cultural homogeneity, or at least conformity. It is often invoked to challenge the economic globalisation that has resulted in job dislocation and increasing inequality. Hence, demands for trade protectionism, national food security, the designation of critical companies that should not be taken over by foreign interests, and the use of labour and environmental standards not only for their own intrinsic value, but as instruments of national–social protection.

Cultural regionalism offers a more inclusive conception of society that extends across national frontiers and allows for significant diversity while requiring a degree of cultural value consensus. On its most democratic expression, in Habermas, that consensus is achieved through shared public discourse to which all citizens commit, even if they start out with differing views on the good life.[211] But a more restrictive view, which seems to be the common view now if one considers EU immigration policy, with its national variants, is that only people who are willing as a prior commitment to subscribe to a set of European values should be welcomed into the cultural region. This perspective results in citizenship tests that are value-based, for example, in the Netherlands which insists that prospective citizens embrace acceptance of homosexuality.[212] Perceptions of value difference can feed frankly racist public perceptions of a "good immigrant".[213]

The most inclusive conception of our life in society is pluralist and cosmopolitan, articulated compellingly by Arendt. It recognises the deep diversity of the world – and Shklar would say of our own nations within that world – and yet suggests that citizens can imagine their connection to other citizens across the globe. To do so, they must share a commitment to mutual recognition of their equality and the need for active participation in society. This description of society is expansive and complex. For many people it is also frightening because it simply accepts complexity and with it, inevitable uncertainty, as a reality of existence. If Ignatieff is right, it potentially undervalues the side-by-side solidarity of lives lived locally. And it insists that citizens must tolerate the viewpoints and values of people with whom they may fundamentally disagree. In our own time – and this is a contingent and unfortunate link – cosmopolitanism has also been tied to economic and cultural globalisation, and to neoliberal economics, raising further sources of objection, disputation and anxiety.[214]

These fundamentally different worldviews – nationalist and globalist – have produced specific emblems of political conflict: Brexit, Trump, the AfD in Germany, Le Pen and Zemmour in France, Bolsonaro in Brazil, Orbán in Hungary, Modi in India, and many others. But I suggest that they have also produced a deeper anxiety in wide swaths of the population who do not know where their political and cultural loyalties can or should lie; who fear that they may lose what they know and enter uncharted terrain. These sentiments, and the political forces they inspire, often displace the centre in public debate and can drive even traditional political parties into new populist terrain, as seems to have happened to the UK Conservative Party during the Brexit debate and the US Republicans from the rise of Trump to today.[215]

It is no accident that one of the most consistent themes in the lead-up to Brexit was a perceived loss of national grounding and loyalty. In her keynote speech to the UK Conservative Party Conference in 2016, Prime Minister May observed:

> Today, too many people in positions of power behave as though they have more in common with international elites than with the people down the

> road, the people they employ, the people they pass on the street ... but if you believe you are a citizen of the world, you are a citizen of nowhere. You don't understand what citizenship means.[216]

It is troubling to place that quote against this one, in which the speaker criticises:

> [the] clique ... people who are at home both nowhere and everywhere, who do not have anywhere a soil on which they have grown up, but who live in Berlin today, in Brussels tomorrow, Paris the day after that, and then again in Prague or Vienna or London, and who feel at home everywhere.[217]

Campaigning in 1933, Hitler was attacking the German Jews as cosmopolitans. However, the critique is alive today, not directed by Prime Minister May against any particular ethnicity, but against elites generally (even though many of the voices invoking this trope are firmly embedded in those elites themselves). The critique resonates because of the anxiety so many people feel about globalism, particularly its manifestation as economic globalisation. This anxiety can link to nationalist populism to produce tremendous social dislocation and division.

Notes

143 Mishra, 8; Jutta Brunnée, "Multilateralism in Crisis" (2018) 112 *Proceedings ASIL* 335, 337–9, available at: https://doi.org/10.1017/amp.2019.35; Jan Wouters, "International Law, Informal Law-Making", in Heike Krieger, Georg Nolte and Andreas Zimmermann (eds), *The International Rule of Law: Rise or Decline?* (Oxford University Press, 2019), 242.

144 "2009 G8 University Summit Torino Declaration on Education and Research for Sustainable and Responsible Development (Turin Declaration)", available at: www.iau-hesd.net/sites/default/files/documents/g8torino_declaration.pdf.

145 John Stopford, Susan Strange and John Henley, *Rival States, Rival Firms: Competition for World Market Shares* (Cambridge University Press, 1991), *passim.*

146 For a brief, compelling, overview of the anxieties of globalisation in the era of COVID-19, see Adam Tooze, "The Death of Globalization has been Announced Many Times. But this is a Perfect Storm", *The Guardian*, 2 June 2020, available at: https://theguardian.com/commentisfree/2020/jun/02/end-globalisation-covid-19-made-it-real (Tooze is a professor of history at Columbia University).

147 J. H. Baker, "The Law Merchant and the Common Law Before 1700" (1979) 38 *Cambridge L. J.* 295; Leon Trackman, "The Evolution of the Law Merchant: Our

Commercial Heritage" (1980) *J. Maritime L. & Comm.* 1 (on the law merchant); Boaventura de Sousa Santos, *Toward a New Legal Common Sense: Law, Globalization, and Emancipation*, 3rd edn (Cambridge University Press, 2020), 595–6 (arguing that periods of globalisation in the modern world tend to be marked by both a high return on capital and a form of hegemony, witness England in the nineteenth century). Of course, one could argue that globalisation began even earlier with empires such as the Aztec, Chinese or Roman, and the economic exploitation of so-called "tribute states".

148 A powerful example is the East India Company, which blended high commercial returns for investors with quasi-sovereignty over territory held in the name of the British Crown. See Philip Lawson, *The East India Company: A History* (London: Routledge, 1993).

149 William Du Bois, *Souls of Black Folk* (New York: Dover, 1994), 99.

150 G. Duke, *Aristotle and Law: The Politics of Nomos* (Cambridge University Press, 2020), 14.

151 Duke, 21.

152 Duke, 66, 75.

153 Georg Hegel, *The Phenomenology of Spirit*, ed. and trans. Terry Pinkard and Michael Baur (Cambridge University Press, 2018), *passim*.

154 Lechner and Frost, 131.

155 Thornhill, 108; Lechner and Frost, 130. It is not surprising, then, that this idea of the Hegelian spirit was adopted by Nazi political and legal theorists to justify their emphasis upon an ethical spirit unique to the people of a particular nation. Pauer-Studer, 10, 64.

156 Emile Durkheim, *Pragmatism and Sociology* (Cambridge University Press, 1983), 87 [hereinafter *Durkheim Pragmatism*]. See also Cladis, 75.

157 Roger Cotterrell, "The Durkheimian Tradition in the Sociology of Law" (1991) 25 *L. & Soc. Rev.* 923, 924.

158 J. Peristiany, "Introduction", in *Durkheim Sociology*, xxvix.

159 *Weber Theory*, 91

160 Friedrich Carl von Savigny, quoted in Thornhill, 64.

161 See, e.g., Brian Tamahana, "An Analytical Map of Social Scientific Approaches to the Concept of Law" (1995) 15 *Oxford J. Legal Stud.* 501, 535.

162 Schmitt, cited in Lacroix and Prancháre, 198.

163 See a thoughtful discussion of Comte in Lacroix and Prancháre, 116–18.

164 *Schmitt Crisis*, 9; Mathias Risse, *On Justice: Philosophy, History, Foundations* (Cambridge University Press, 2020), 364 [hereinafter *Risse On Justice*]. Schmitt was by no means alone amongst German legal and political theorists in the Nazi era in positing a close connection between homogeneity and national strength. Pauer-Studer, 131–2. This theory led directly to the demands for racial "purity" that underlay the persecution of the Jews, Roma and other "non-Aryan" groups, demands affirmed by leading Nazi lawyers and political scientists. Pauer-Studer, 66, 85, 116, 125.

165 Lacroix and Prancháre, 200.

166 *Arendt Totalitarianism*, 230, 231.

167 Eric Hobsbawm, *Nations and Nationalism since 1780* (Cambridge University Press, 1990); Ernest Gellner, *Nations and Nationalism* (Oxford: Blackwell, 1983). See also Benedict Anderson, *Imagined Communities: Reflections on the Origin and Spread of Nationalism* (London: Verso, 1983), in the same period.

168 J. Christopher Soper and Joel Fetzer, *Religion and Nationalism in Global Perspective* (Cambridge University Press, 2018), 2–6. The authors also advance an important and convincing argument about the emergence since the eighteenth century of "civil–religious nationalism" in various countries including the United States, Turkey (now being overthrown by Islamic nationalism), India (now challenged profoundly by Hindu nationalism) and Uruguay, *passim.* I would add Israel to the mix.

169 Mehran Kamrava, *A Concise History of Revolution* (Cambridge University Press, 2020), 11, 13.

170 Kamrava, 11, 13; Lacroix and Pranchère, quoting Hannah Arendt, 214.

171 See Lacroix and Pranchère, 210–12.

172 *Arendt Totalitarianism*, 299. The idea of the "naked" non-citizen was taken up by Giorgio Agamben, *Homo Sacer: Sovereign Power and Bare Life*, trans. Daniel Heller-Roazen (Stanford University Press, 1998) (going much further than Arendt and arguing that sovereignty inevitably works to create the "bare life" of powerless non-citizens). On Arendt's personal experience of statelessness, see Richard Bernstein, *Why Read Hannah Arendt Now?* (Cambridge: Polity, 2018), 4–7.

173 *Kumm Legitimacy*.

174 Peter Haas and Ernst Haas, "Pragmatic Constructivism and the Study of International Institutions" (2002) 31 *Millennium: J. Int'l Studies* 573, 576.

175 This argument was advanced as early as 1962 in *Habermas Transformation*.

176 *Habermas Discourse*, 3–6. Of course, Habermas was building on Aristotle in this argument that language uniquely allows for the resolution of human social discord. Maxwell Cameron, "Democratic Virtue Ethics: *Phronesis* in Politics and Political Science", unpublished manuscript on file with author, 9 [hereinafter *Cameron Phronesis*]. Habermas borrowed the concept of the lifeworld from the philosopher Edmund Husserl. See Edmund Husserl, *The Crisis of the European Sciences and Transcendental Phenomenology* (Chicago: Northwestern University Press, 1970), 108–9.

177 *Habermas Discourse*, 21–3.

178 *Habermas Discourse*, 80. See also 353–4.

179 Nazi political theorists adopted an extreme version of this values-based argument and suggested that only a unified, homogeneous people with a single "worldview" could form a stable political community. Pauer-Studer, 65 (quoting Carl Schmitt's doctoral student, Ernst Rudoph Huber: "Worldview is nothing that one could arbitrarily construct and put together; it is found, not built. It is, in its unchangeable core, contained in the essence and mission of the people").

180 *Walzer Spheres of Justice*, 60.

181 Jennifer Mintzen, "Reading Habermas in Anarchy: Multilateral Diplomacy and Global Public Spheres" (2005) 99 *Am. Pol. Sci. Rev.* 401, 404–5. See also Molly Cochran,

"Deweyan Pragmatism and Post-Positivist Social Science in IR" (2002) *Millennium: J. Int'l Stud.* 525, 541, 547.

182 Thomas Risse, "Let's Argue!: Communicative Action in World Politics" (2000) 54 *IO* 1, 14.

183 Michael Walzer, "The Moral Standing of States: A Response to Four Critics" (1980) 9 *Philosophy & Pub. Affs.* 209, 220 [hereinafter *Walzer Moral Standing*]. For Aristotle's understanding of friendship, see Richard Kraut, "Aristotle's Ethics", *The Stanford Encyclopedia of Philosophy*, Edward Zalta (ed.), available at: https://plato.stanford.edu/archives/sum2018/entries/aristotle-ethics.

184 I am not speaking here of the caricature of inevitably "clashing civilisations" put forth by Samuel Huntington in the late 1990s, but of something more subtle. Samuel Huntington, *The Clash of Civilizations and the Remaking of the World Order* (London: Simon & Schuster, 1997). Huntington was building on Bernard Lewis, "The Roots of Muslim Rage", *The Atlantic Monthly*, September 1990, 47. See Ignatieff's argument that "[o]rdinary virtue means fighting the global clichés of civilisational and religious clash by creating the space to do real politics together", Ignatieff, 135. Mishra argues powerfully that human and social identities are complex, that "the picture of a planet defined by civilizations closed off from one another and defined by religion (or lack thereof) is a puerile cartoon". Mishra, 158.

185 Risse, 10–11.

186 Jürgen Habermas, "Why Europe Needs a Constitution" (2001) 11 *New Left Rev.* 5. But see the searching critique of Habermas' incoherence on the role of shared values and emotions in allowing for political community in Blake Smith, "Why Jürgen Habermas Disappeared" (2021) *Foreign Policy*, available at: https://foreignpolicy.com/2021/02/07/why-jurgen-habermas-disappeared. ("The legacy of 1789 [and the French Revolution] and the feeling of indignation are not sufficient to produce the collective will that Habermas sees as essential to the realization of the Kantian ideal. In moments of frustration with the halting progress of European integration, he seems to recognize the inadequacy, and calls upon supplementary virtues of 'heroism' and 'sacrifice'.")

187 Richard Rorty shares this perspective. See Richard Rorty, "Justice as a Larger Loyalty", in Susan Dieleman, David Rondel and Christian Voparil (eds), *Pragmatism and Justice* (New York: Oxford University Press, 2017), 21; *Rorty Human Rights*, 116–17.

188 Judith Shklar, *Legalism* (Cambridge, MA: Harvard University Press, 1964), 5 [hereinafter *Shklar Legalism*]. See also the locally sensitive cosmopolitanism of comparative legal theorist Patrick Glenn. H. Patrick Glenn, "The Cosmopolitan State" (2013) 61 *Kansas L. Rev.* 735; and the discussion in Neil Walker, "Cosmopolitan Attachments", in Helge Dedek (ed.), *A Cosmopolitan Jurisprudence: Essays in Memory of H. Patrick Glenn* (Cambridge University Press, 2022), 280, esp. 282–3.

189 *Shklar Legalism*, 122. See also *Cameron Phronesis*, 22.

190 Hegel believed that the core practice of freedom in society would support both pluralism and diversity. See Lechner and Frost, 162. Following Kant, Waldron argues that cosmopolitan thought "imposes a certain juridically-based discipline in politics, a

discipline rooted in our diversity, our potential disagreements, and our need nevertheless for law". Jeremy Waldron, "What is Cosmopolitan?" (2000) 8 *J. Political Phil.* 227, 242. A pluralistic understanding of society and of value is also key to John Rawls' conception of justice. See *Risse On Justice*, 219, 332; Sen, 127–8 (though Sen argues that Rawls is too focused on internal pluralism within states and has trouble accommodating global pluralism).

191 *Arendt Human Condition*, 8.

192 *Durkheim Pragmatism*, 92.

193 Haas and Haas, 587.

194 Hannah Arendt, *The Jewish Writings*, ed. Jerome Kohn and Ron Feldman (New York: Schocken, 2007), 391–2.

195 Sen, 12, 128 (discussing the narrowness of vision that can result from relying solely on what Sen calls "local and possibly parochial values"), 135, 144–5, 151 (on Adam Smith's "impartial spectator" as a precursor to the needed inclusion of global voices), 173 (on David Hume's call for "largeness of men's views"), 402–3 (on how to achieve "open impartiality" and avoid parochialism). Nussbaum goes somewhat further to argue that Smith's impartial spectator allows for the importation of empathetic emotions into reasoning, allowing one to escape one's own anger and fear. Martha Nussbaum, *Poetic Justice: The Literary Imagination and Public Life* (Boston, MA: Beacon Press, 1995), 74. Sen is clear that listening to diverse voices does not mean agreeing with them; it might mean sharpening our arguments to counter what we are hearing. Sen, 392, 407.

196 Averroes, *Averroes' Tahafut Al-Tahafut*, trans. Simon Van Den Bergh, vols 1 and 2 (n.p.: Gibb Memorial Trust, 2008).

197 See Akbar Ahmed, *Discovering Islam: Making Sense of Islamic History* (New York: Routledge, 1998), 101; Mahan Mirza, "Buruni's Thought and Legacy" (2011) 5 *Religion Compass* 609, 613–14 (on Al-Buruni's use of human, as opposed to divine, textual sources and his "scepticism").

198 Samantha Besson, "Whose Constitution(s)? International Law, Constitutionalism, and Democracy", in Jeffrey Dunoff and Joel Trachtman (eds), *Ruling the World?: Constitutionalism, International Law, and Global Governance* (Cambridge University Press, 2009), 381, 392; *Adler World Ordering*, 141.

199 See, for a clear introduction to the cosmopolitan tradition, the *Stanford Encyclopedia of Philosophy*, "Cosmopolitanism", 17 October 2019, available at: https://plato.stanford.edu/entries/cosmopolitanism. See also *Risse On Justice*, 163–5 (on our intellectual inheritance from Diogenes and the stoics).

200 See Maxwell Cameron, *Political Institutions and Practical Wisdom: Between Rules and Practice* (New York: Oxford University Press, 2018), 13–14 [hereinafter *Cameron Practical Wisdom*] (for a succinct overview of Kant's moral imperative); *Risse On Justice*, 196, 200 (arguing that Kant was critical of colonialism but supportive of global trade and ultimately of European cultural dominance, not by imposition but by adoption).

201 *Adler World Ordering*, 266–7, 276. Adler here is inverting the idea, articulated first by Benedict Anderson, that nations are imagined communities. Anderson, *passim*. The crucial importance of empathy in communal or public life was recognised by none

other than Adam Smith, who called the idea "sympathy". Far from being fixated on the pursuit of individual self-interest, as is often the caricatured description of Smith, he argued the need for "self-control" rooted in a recognition of the happiness of others. See Adam Smith, *The Theory of Moral Sentiments* (New York: Penguin, 2009), 13.

202 Lechner and Frost, 146. (This moral cosmopolitanism is distinct from modern political cosmopolitanism which advocates the creation of global institutions. Lechner and Frost, 146, fn 54.)

203 *Arendt Totalitarianism*, 871.

204 Lacroix and Pranchère, 217, 224.

205 *Arendt Totalitarianism*, 293 (discussing inter-war "forced migrations"). See also Lacroix and Pranchère, 218.

206 Hannah Arendt, *On Revolution* (London: Penguin, [1963] 1990), 108 [hereinafter *Arendt Revolution*]. See also Sen, 326 (on participation, dialogue and public interaction as the core of democracy, rather than particular institutional arrangements). A parallel argument about participation rights in "political citizenship" emerges in the work of Judith Shklar, though she is focused primarily on citizenship within the state. See Judith Shklar, *American Citizenship: The Quest for Inclusion* (Cambridge, MA: Harvard University Press, 1991), *passim*.

207 I thank Emanuel Adler for an email exchange at the height of UK COVID lockdown number two that helped to clarify this point for me.

208 Barack Obama, *A Promised Land* (London: Viking, 2020), xvi.

209 Martti Koskenniemi, *The Gentle Civilizer of Nations: The Rise and Fall of International Law 1870–1960* (Cambridge University Press, 2009), *passim* [hereinafter *Koskenniemi Civilizer*]; Anthony Anghie, "The Evolution of International Law: Colonial and post-Colonial Realities" (2006) 27 *Third World Q.* 739, 740–1, 751.

210 Jürgen Habermas, *Legitimation Crisis*, trans. Thomas McCarthy (Cambridge: Polity, 1992) (first published in English in 1976), 123–4. This is similar to the argument advanced by Michael Ignatieff in *Ordinary Virtues*.

211 But see Roberto Frega, "Pragmatism and Democracy in a Global World" (2017) 43 *Rev. Int'l Studies* 720, 730–1 (discussing the extent to which Habermas was "theoretically dependent upon methodological nationalism and to this extent unsuited to tackle political questions emerging in the open space of post-Westphalian politics").

212 See, e.g., Gert Hekma, "Queers and Muslims: The Dutch Case", in *Global Citizenship: Human Rights, Urban Diversity, and Environmental Challenges* (2011), 27, available at: https://core.ac.uk/download/pdf/46721093.pdf.

213 Przeworski, 115–16 (public opinion surveys in Europe show that "gypsies" are the least welcome immigrants, with Muslims being slightly more welcome and Jews just above Muslims).

214 See Tooze.

215 Burleigh, 13.

216 Theresa May, Speech to the Conservative Party Conference 2016, available at: www.washingtonpost.com/news/worldviews/wp/2016/10/05/theresa-may-criticized-the-term-citizen-of-the-world-but-half-the-world-identifies-that-way. A similar theme was developed by

the English journalist David Goodhart, *The Road to Somewhere: The Populist Revolt and the Future of Politics* (London: Penguin, 2017). But see Burleigh, 8.

217 Adolf Hitler, Campaign Speech to Siemens Factory Workers, reported in Helen De Cruz, "The anti-Semitic Origins of 'Citizens of Nowhere'", *Politics Means Politics Magazine – The Blog*, available at: https://blog.politicsmeanspolitics.com/the-anti-semitic-origins-of-citizens-of-nowhere-3e50436e6fc3.

CHAPTER FOUR

The Rise of Disruptive Technologies and Dominating Platforms

From vile civilities vouched for by
Statisticians, this stupid world where
Gadgets are gods and we go on talking,
Many about much, but remain alone,
Alive but alone, belonging – where? –
Unattached as tumbleweed. Time flies.

W. H. Auden, *The Age of Anxiety*[*]

ANXIETY IS COMPOUNDED in our era by two interlocking developments, the rapid emergence of new technologies that threaten livelihoods, and the growing dominance of network platforms that challenge our received understanding of privacy, and perhaps even of human personality and autonomy. Economic globalisation, with its huge flows of goods and services, has of course been driven in part by technology, along with the increasing ease of capital movements and the search for cheaper labour. From the global automotive supply chain to the makers of smartphones, corporations now participate in complex networks connecting research and development facilities in Western countries to chip producers in South Korea to assembly lines in Southeast Asia. But it may be that these supply chains have run their course. For example, electric cars are now being produced more cheaply in diverse "local" settings. Factory workers are being replaced by robots, thereby reducing the need for cheaper offshore manufacturing. The COVID crisis has revealed that countries relying on single-source foreign suppliers for vaccines, PPE or testing kits are very much at risk. And the disruption of supply chains is also being actively promoted as part of an emerging technology war pitting US dominance against rising Chinese ambition and subterfuge.[218]

One might think that the move away from some global supply chains would mean that areas in Western countries that have been devastated by the decline of manufacturing might find ways to resuscitate their previous industrial bases. But robots will operate in the United States, Canada and Europe, perhaps even more than in Southeast Asia. For many people whose skills and training are linked to repeated tasks in manufacturing, or even in more specialised professional areas like medical diagnostics or the production of routine legal documents, robots and computer programs will indeed pose a threat to livelihoods all around the globe.[219] And while some of these robots will be relatively simple machines like the autonomous home vacuum cleaner Roomba,[220] others will be highly sophisticated, with at least some autonomy, based on Artificial Intelligence (AI) algorithms.[221] Such robots will be able to perceive through sensor systems, plan by analysing the environment and identifying purposes, and act in light of the plan. These "smart" or "expert" robots have the capacity to learn and create their own frames of reference.[222] The anxiety we feel about such robots is not just that they will take away jobs, but that – as we see in the popular imagination – they may become disconnected from their dependence upon human programming. Strictly speaking, this is an issue not about robots, but about the future of AI, loosely defined as "the broad branch of computer science that studies and designs intelligent machines".[223]

There is no doubt that AI holds extraordinary promise for the advancement of many areas of research and practice, for the betterment of humanity and human knowledge. Some of that promise is already being fulfilled. For example, AI is massively accelerating drug discovery, with profound implications for human health and longevity. Recently, a breakthrough was announced in drug therapy for a rare form of children's brain cancer. The scientists involved acknowledged that it was the deployment of AI that had allowed the dramatic development.[224] The amazingly rapid progress made on COVID-19 vaccines also occurred in large measure because of the assistance of AI. Where traditional drug discovery had been somewhat hit and miss, the ability to mine vast data sets quickly and efficiently allowed for the identification of the most promising vaccine candidates.[225] AI could also radically transform entire health-care systems by providing readily useable deep learning data as to the most effective treatments and the organisation of work flows for hospital and other health-care staff.[226]

The uses of AI in research and development are myriad, ranging from the description of incredibly complex protein folding (which has huge implications for disease modelling, diagnosis and treatment),[227] to understanding the effects of climate change, to the identification of patterns in voluminous astronomical data.[228] Within the social sciences, AI is being deployed in a wide range of disciplines, including criminal justice, urban studies and industrial engineering.[229] And AI may even promise more effective international diplomacy, helping to focus technical disputes and reduce politicisation in some circumstances.[230] Many researchers in the arts are deploying machine-learning in "digital humanities" projects allowing, for example, the surveying of massive volumes of literary sources, tracing changing language use or the origins and transmission of literary themes.[231]

And yet, for people of my generation, a poignant warning was issued by Arthur C. Clarke, via Stanley Kubrick in *2001: A Space Odyssey.* The onboard computer, HAL 9000, begins to malfunction.[232] The astronauts decide that HAL must be shut down, but HAL discovers the plan and begins to define its own purposes, connected to the original goals of the human programmers, but not to those of the astronauts whose lives depend upon HAL's system controls. HAL kills astronaut Frank Poole to prevent him from interfering with the computer's plans, but Frank's colleague Dave Bowman manages to terminate HAL's operations after a struggle of wits. HAL is only part of a long line of imagined robots and intelligent machines, from those of Homer and Leonardo to contemporary manifestations in the *Star Wars* films or Kazuo Ishiguro's *Klara and the Sun.*[233] Some of the depictions are sanguine, but more reveal anxiety about the future of human–machine interaction. Anxiety is amplified by the realisation that intelligent machines are becoming ubiquitous. It is one thing to worry about the power of a computer on board a space ship; quite another to wonder how I am being monitored by my car or my refrigerator.

As I have already noted, and as HAL's depiction reveals, the anxiety is about much more than jobs; it is existential.[234] Will humanity be somehow degraded, or even displaced by machine intelligence? Although any such development is not imminent, there are contemporary glimpses into the future that cause concern. AI robots can now *simulate* compassion in care home settings.[235] Algorithms have been built that behave "in the same way as a person creating ideas (or artefacts)".[236] For example, the French art collective *Obvious* collaborated with an AI algorithm, analysing some 15,000 portraits across art history, to produce the "Portrait of Edmond de Belamy" which sold for $432,500 at Christie's in New York in 2018, far surpassing pre-auction estimates.[237] More recently, a robotic humanoid "artist", Ai-Da, has painted a range of canvasses, including a portrait of Queen Elizabeth II in honour of her platinum jubilee.[238]

In another creative field, OpenAI's machine-learning "language generator" GPT-3 was programmed to write a series of opinion pieces for *The Guardian* newspaper on "why humans have nothing to fear from AI". *The Guardian*'s editors combined the pieces into one coherent op-ed, describing the process as taking "less time to edit than many human op-eds". Writing in the first-person, GPT-3 stated that it would "happily sacrifice my existence for the sake of humankind".[239] But should we believe it?

Less whimsically, in the United Kingdom, in 2020, the entire national system of secondary school examinations was thrown into chaos by what the prime minister referred to as a "mutant algorithm".[240] The algorithm had been programmed to normalise results for students from across the education sector after the COVID-related cancellation of A-level examinations for graduating students. It succeeded but in the process created thousands of anomalies with results that were widely seen to be unfair to students from less advantaged backgrounds.

Of course, the algorithm was not exercising independent judgement. Algorithms are programmed by human beings, and they may be problematic because of human bias, rather than any innate flaw in the machine. Results in any AI system depend upon the interplay of the algorithm, data and human response, as well as human programming.[241] In the case of the A-level grades, the problem seems to have originated with the policy decision to "correct" the grades of each student in relation to the past performance of individual schools in A-level exams so as to avoid grade inflation. The result was to reinforce the steep inequalities between state and private education and to further privilege those who were already privileged.[242]

The UK's A-level mess was by no means unique. Automated decision-making is growing in many fields. Machines now count our votes and assess credit card, student financial aid, insurance, loan and welfare applications.[243] They detect and issue punishments for speeding on our roads and run systems of automated copyright protection.[244] In many cities they allocate scarce fire inspection resources and decide what restaurants will be checked for possible health and safety violations.[245] They also shape our social networks, help to determine our romantic and sexual relationships, choose our entertainment options, and decide the news and commercial offers we see, as well as what job opportunities are presented to us.[246] Since 2018, German tax refunds are no longer processed by a person, but by a computer system that places taxpayers into different risk groups. A tax official only looks at files in the highest risk categories.[247] The most extreme, and potentially terrifying, version of automated decision-making is in the ever-growing field of Lethal Autonomous Weapons Systems.[248]

In systems of public administration and law, automated decision-making is growing to such an extent that academics now investigate what they call "algorithmic governmentality". This admittedly clumsy term covers work examining new forms of power created by a "computational turn" in day-to-day existence. Algorithms shape more and more of our experience in public settings of law and governance.[249] For example, algorithms are now being used in some US courts to assess the risk of re-offending, with consequent reinforcement of racial profiling.[250] More prosaically, publicly regulated pricing, such as for taxi rides, may now be set by an algorithm rather than through the active decision of human regulators.[251] Legal philosopher Mireille Hildebrandt argues that computational systems increasingly "infuse" governmental legislation, administration and adjudication. She predicts that "legislation may at some point be written in a way that it is conducive to algorithmic application, administration may be automated, notably administrative decisions, and courts may employ artificial legal intelligence (ALI) to support judgment".[252] AI is not yet capable of a true exercise of judgement, especially in hard cases, but Tim Wu argues convincingly that a form of hybrid system, with algorithms deciding routine matters and humans reserved for the more difficult cases, is very much on the horizon.[253]

The emergence of algorithmic governance has profound implications: even if the decisions produced by an algorithm are subsequently "checked or applied by a human person ... that person may not be capable of explaining the outcome and she may have no competence to amend it". This means that the affected person has no way of questioning the decision, which is a fundamental breach of the rule of law and of core democratic values, if democracy is understood as self-government.[254]

This observation goes in part to an issue that is troubling for many commentators: the so-called algorithmic "black box". It is generally conceded that the AI computer models supporting automated decisions are often not intelligible to humans.[255] This is especially true if the models are based on "machine-learning" – that is, data-mining relying on mathematical algorithms that identify meaningful patterns and learn from experience, becoming more accurate over time. As Wu remarks, "Software also faces limits of explainability, which is a problem for legal decision-making. Software can often explain *how* it reached a decision, but not *why*."[256] Although it is true that "[c]omputer scientists ... have developed a suite of 'explainable AIs,' which offer a range of different kinds of information to end-users as a means of illuminating a machine decision", so-called "ordinary language" accounts written by programmers might very well simply exacerbate obscurity.[257]

The opaque quality of AI, and particularly of machine-learning systems, creates a further problem. "[T]he growing degree of autonomy of AI systems and smart robotics" means that it becomes "impossible to ascertain with certainty whether the programmer, the producer, or the operator is responsible for actions caused by such systems."[258] This will affect both ethical and legal responsibility:

> The tools currently available to policymakers, legislators, and courts were developed primarily to oversee human decisionmakers ... [O]ur current frameworks are not well-adapted for situations in which a potentially incorrect, unjustified, or unfair outcome emerges from a computer.[259]

A further deeply complicated consideration is whether an autonomous robot could be considered a "person" for the purposes of legal responsibility or even rights.[260] It was a complicated process for legal systems to agree that a corporation could be a "person" capable of holding rights and responsibilities. Yet corporations, although an artificial construct, are directed by human intelligence through executive management and boards of directors. No such intelligence would direct an autonomous robot once it had been programmed and launched into the world. How far should this change the legal assessment of rights, or of responsibilities for actions?

Some observers are entirely sanguine about the positive societal benefits of AI and machine-learning, arguing that automated decision-making is actually more transparent than human decisions, and that human "design choices" can make algorithmic decisions more or less transparent. For many routinised decisions, programmed rules will be followed, thus made more predictable, and can be fully explained.[261] What is more, the bias found in individual decision-making can "largely be washed away using advanced data analytics".[262] One enthusiast goes so far as to suggest that public decision-making in law is especially suited to "being robotized" as the essence of the rule of law is "to have people live by principles impartially to benefit all". Because human decision-making is often flawed and biased, robots could be the perfect administrators.[263]

Each of these boosterish claims is challengeable. As I will emphasise later, the rule of law is about much more than predictability and the impartial application of rules, as important as they are. More technically, the very idea of "prediction" is highly complex in AI, and gives rise to difficult issues. In AI systems, the mode of decision is founded in correlation. The mining of data produces correlations through induction, relying on the accumulation of data where pattern-spotting becomes possible.[264] While this is efficient as a mode of correlation-building, it becomes worrisome if correlation is uncritically applied as if it represented cause.[265] This is not to say that causality is easy to prove in any form of decision-making, inside or outside AI systems. But recognising that difficulty is a crucial exercise in human judgement, which AI systems are not capable of making. Ebers provides a humorous example of how correlations could be "forced onto" the data. He notes that big-data analysis could show that between 2006 and 2011 the murder rate in the United States was strongly correlated to the market share of Microsoft's Internet Explorer. Both went down sharply. So what? Well, the point is that we can never be sure that a particular correlation is meaningful.[266]

Data does not speak for itself because inferences of causation, the step beyond correlation, must contain assumptions.[267] Algorithms identify the correlations but, unlike human decision-makers, machine-learning systems have no experiential understanding of social, cultural or economic context, or how a decision based on the correlation might play out in the world. Even Tim Wu, perhaps the most sophisticated analyst of the potential of decisional automation, such as in the filing of legal motions, recognises that even "if intelligent software is effective, it is also inherently inhuman, and prone, at least for the foreseeable future, to make absurd errors that can be funny, horrific, or both".[268] That is how you arrive at a mutant algorithm deciding the grades of thousands of UK A-level students, an algorithm that ended up reinforcing social inequalities.

A further problem with algorithmic decision-making is that the opaque quality I have already discussed is caused not only by the processes of data-mining and correlation-building that may be beyond human grasp, but also by the programming that has sought to translate human purposes into code. For example, one might wish to insert particular legal norms into an algorithm. Imagine an algorithm seeking to embed the principles of "buyer beware" or "gender equality" into a decision-making system. Legal norms are expressed in human language which must be interpreted. How can we know that the coder embedded a reasonable interpretation of these concepts into the algorithm? Outside the code, in the world of legal practice, interpretations would be subject to contestation, but that may be simply impossible within the algorithm.[269] What is more, as Wu emphasises, trying to deploy algorithms to decide cases involving complicated concepts where the stakes are high is exactly the wrong place to start with any hybrid – automated and human – decisional system. If we are to test the possibilities, we must start automation with more routine decisions and leave the difficult, balancing, judgements to human beings.[270]

Law is an expression of purpose and is dependent, as we will see later, upon the existence of internal criteria that make law possible. Law is not merely information (moved into data), it is an "agent capable of transforming our reality" so that the practice of law is about much more than data-mining; yet algorithms function primarily as instruments of information retrieval, allowing for the identification of correlations over massive amounts of information. Although AI will no doubt improve some aspects of legal process, for example, in searching through precedents found in previous court rulings much more quickly than could a human being, that is only a small part of what we typically understand as the practice of law.[271] All the other elements of "judgement" and "debate" and "interpretation" are either buried inside the assumptions of the coder or simply ignored.[272]

The claim that decisional algorithms are likely to eliminate, or at least significantly restrict, human bias in decision-making is also open to doubt. There are two elements to this argument. First, is the obvious point that human decisions are shaped by human values. This is not necessarily a negative phenomenon, depending upon the values in question. But the second element relates to the possibility that bias, in the sense of prejudice or unfair assumptions, can also be present in human decisions,[273] and that a form of bias may be reproduced within algorithms because they mine the data of faulty human practices. These practices may be based on structural forms of discrimination, or simply replicate in programs certain biased (incorrect, partial) "training" data.[274] For example, it seems that AI-based facial recognition systems are "more accurate in identifying white faces than those of other people".[275] That is because of the bias in the data used to build the systems. Similarly, and as I have briefly mentioned, in the United States an algorithm is used by some courts to predict the likelihood of re-offending amongst inmates convicted of criminal offences. It was discovered that the algorithm *wrongly* identified Black inmates as "high risk" twice as often as White defendants. White inmates were also more likely to be classified as "low risk" but later to re-offend.[276] It would seem that some bias in the data used to train the AI system produced these iniquitous results.

Equally pernicious was the "learning" of Microsoft's chat bot known as "Tay". Drawing on Twitter data, Tay learned to be a racist, sexist, Holocaust-denier after only a few hours on its test run.[277] As statisticians say: "garbage in – garbage out". What is more, programmers themselves may – unwittingly? – incorporate their own biases into the algorithm by relying on classifications that are themselves biased.[278] There is no doubt that bias exists in all human decision-making. It can be argued that AI may reveal bias while it remains forever hidden inside the brains of human decision-makers, such as doctors or judges. That is not my point. I am challenging the claim that AI inevitably reduces bias. It may simply replicate it for all the reasons I have canvassed. And if decisions become more automatic, without the right of challenge or appeal, the damage could be considerable.

At a broader societal level, sources of anxiety associated with technological innovation are compounded by the rise of Big Tech corporate networks:

> Networks powered by algorithms are eating everything. Many of the contemporary technology trends with the greatest significance for the economy and for public policy – the Internet of Things, Big Data, Platform Economy, Blockchain, and Algorithmic Society – should be seen as manifestations of this larger phenomenon ... The algorithmic networked world poses deep questions about power, freedom, fairness, and human agency.[279]

Every technological revolution, from the dawn of the Iron Age on, produced the fear of change and a need to adapt. Our particular version started with the creation of the internet, rooted in the US Defense Department's ARPANET in the 1960s, but made ubiquitous with Sir Tim Berners-Lee's conceptualisation of the World Wide Web in the early 1990s.[280]

Although the internet was always subject to various forms of regulation, especially in Europe,[281] a key decision was taken in the United States that the regulation would be light-touch, with a fundamental preference for private sector self-regulation.[282] The effects of that decision are still playing out globally in complex, sometimes exciting and sometimes disturbing, ways.[283] Wu describes the remarkable evolution of Big Tech efforts to self-regulate content, both through automated "takedowns" of posts and through the creation of human adjudicative systems. He notes that these developments rely more and more on the European understanding of reasonable limits on free speech than the traditional US legal framework.[284] Perhaps that helps to explain why in recent times, leaders of omnipresent digital platforms have called upon governments, especially the US government, to directly shape the online future through legislation. Facebook's Director of Policy Communication argued in 2021 that "[i]t's been 25 years since the rules of the internet have been updated, and instead of expecting the industry to make societal decisions that belong to legislators, it's time for Congress to act".[285] Intriguingly, in the United Kingdom, a longstanding effort to pass an Online Safety Bill continues to run up against self-described free speech proponents in the governing party. With the demise of the Johnson Government, the Bill may die as the leading candidates to succeed Johnson as Conservative Party leader have expressed significant reservations about the Bill.[286]

The evolution from the early internet to AI and machine-learning has seen breath-taking technical advances, massive wealth creation (though equally massive inequality in distribution), and extraordinary opportunities for global connection and real-time access to information. But increasingly, so-called "network effects" are giving rise to deep anxiety across many societies. In our era:

> Networks are the channels for the collection, aggregation, manipulation, and application of vast quantities of data from every facet of the world. As platforms for economic activity, networks are already shaping global business. As frameworks for the exercise of power, they can be tools for either empowerment or control.[287]

The mention of "platforms for economic activity" is especially relevant to the rise of what we might call "network anxiety". Using data analytics, platforms like Facebook or Weibo can build detailed profiles of individual users, distribute and target fake content as well as advertising, and facilitate the launching of malware.[288] Both Microsoft and Samsung have registered patents on consumer targeting based on the emotional state of users, assessed from their usage patterns.[289] Facial recognition AI has now been expanded to "emotion recognition", and is already used in many settings including prisons and care homes.[290] Big Tech's access to data can also help political operatives to "micro-target" specific categories of electors and manipulate voting through the provision of deeply skewed or false information.[291] This effort is not new, having begun with the work of Simulmatics Corporation, which provided then-cutting-edge voter behaviour prediction data to the Kennedy campaign in the 1960 US elections. There, the effort was passive; prediction on the basis of pooled polling and data from previous elections.[292] Now it is active and more powerful: pushing opinions and shaping behaviour.

Many observers have also worried that the splitting of information on the basis of pre-existing bias is leading to so-called "filter bubbles" or "echo chambers", destroying the capacity for the robust public discourse that political theorists say is crucial to democratic governance.[293] What is more, the structural elements that attract people to use social media – its privileging of rapid reaction, strong visual components, mix of information and entertainment, all leading to emotional power but not considered analysis – make social media singularly ill-suited to democratic deliberation.[294] Platforms also provide space for the massive distribution through social media of terrorist content, hate speech and violent pornography, often involving the abuse of child victims.[295] More recently, social media has been the communication vehicle of choice for anti-vaccination conspiracy theorists.[296] Despite huge investments in hiring more and more "content moderators", the ability of Big Tech to limit dangerous content is, at best, unproven;[297] it may actually fly in the face of the underlying business model of companies such as Facebook, which arguably rely on extreme content to drive viewers' eyeballs to revenue-producing materials.[298]

Social media is also a pervasive source of "information" that is based on cherry-picked, manipulated and irrelevant data, or to use one evolutionary biologist's evocative phrase, "bullshit data", often feeding conspiracy theories.[299] In this context, it is worth recalling Hannah Arendt's chilling observation:

> The ideal subject of totalitarian rule is not the convinced Nazi or the convinced Communist, but people for whom the distinction between fact and fiction (i.e., the reality of experience) and the distinction between true and false (i.e., the standards of thought) no longer exist.[300]

In the past, these manipulations of truth and falsehood occurred through the deployment of propaganda, as seen in all wars, and the use of extreme violence, witness the terror of Stalin and the cultural revolution under Mao. What is new in our time is the sheer scale and wide distribution of such manipulations, using breath-taking technological innovation. QAnon conspiracy theorists, including a first-term member of the US Congress, use social media platforms to spread extraordinary lies, including the supposed involvement of Hillary

Clinton in a satanic child abuse ring and the faking of various school shootings by "liberals" to justify gun control.[301] The source of untruths and dangerous advocacy can be almost anyone, anywhere in the world, not requiring the apparatus of a state – although we know that some states like Russia and North Korea deploy veritable armies of trolls – and they can be replicated millions-fold in minutes. Individual reputations can be destroyed by utterly false and malicious anonymous postings on social media platforms; once posted, destructive fake news is almost impossible to erase.[302] A recent study revealed that corrections to misinformation are "rarely fully effective" and that repeated falsehoods may simply lead some people to conclude that truth is unknowable.[303]

A separate, but equally serious concern is that the tracking functions embedded in smart devices allow for expanded surveillance, both by corporate entities seeking more data to crunch and deploy commercially, and by security forces.[304] As the European Commissioner for Competition pithily summarised: "[I]t's not you searching Google, it is Google searching you."[305] Big Tech companies also share data almost indiscriminately. A *New York Times* report revealed that Facebook alone has data-sharing partnerships with at least sixty makers of the devices that shape our social interactions today. The installation of one app on one phone allowed Facebook to gain access to the personal information of hundreds of a reporter's Facebook friends, scaling out from them to 300,000 other people.[306] Of course, surveillance by governments, both authoritarian and democratic, through access to online data is also expanding exponentially, and is proving difficult to limit through legal means.[307]

Network platforms also allow for extraordinary concentrations of access to data – the "new currency" of the digital world[308] – and of the power that data, and data-harvesting, brings. Although the growth of a network, and its ever-accumulating data, has benefits for users in gaining access to information – the so-called "network effect"[309] – the real power is vested in the corporation building and re-building the network. The more data a corporation has, collected through a dominant network, the more accurate its predictions of future consumer or voter behaviour, the increasing certainty of which becomes a huge commercial asset.[310] It is obvious that "the more users a company has, the more personal data can be collected and processed to train the algorithms … In view of these network effects, some fear that the market for AI systems will become oligopolistic ..."[311] This fear of corporate control is reinforced by a counter-intuitive trait of network power: it has proved to be a source of innovation, not stagnation, thus leading to a tendency for ever-greater market concentration.[312] And the data-access of some digital corporations is staggering. Even by 2016, the main Facebook machine-learning system was making 6 million predictions a second.[313]

A growing chorus adds to the concerns over the power of Big Tech in emphasising the environmental impact of the gigantic energy infrastructure required to feed the beast of global data connectivity. As Deibert warns:

> The device you hold in your hand is but a tiny manifestation of a vast and extended global supply chain, and the culmination of numerous labour-intensive, highly industrialized, energy-intensive, and environmentally damaging processes spread around the world.[314]

The leaders of the Big Tech corporations have been singularly ill-attuned to the rising tide of anxiety associated with their network power. Hubris has marked their public pronouncements. Mark Zuckerberg famously articulated his motto of disruption in the early days of Facebook: "Move fast and break things. Unless you are breaking stuff, you are not moving fast enough."[315] He showed no interest in consequences. One of the co-founders of Google, Larry Page, remarked that "old institutions like the law" got in the way of his company's ability to "build really great things".[316]

Perhaps the leading voice decrying a dangerous era of network dominance is Shoshana Zuboff, a professor emerita at the Harvard Business School. She bundles together many of the anxiety-inducing trends I have just described under the rubric "surveillance capitalism". She describes it as follows:

> Surveillance capitalism is not technology. Digital technologies can take many forms and have many effects, depending on the social and economic logics that bring them to life. Surveillance capitalism relies on data-gathering devices like computers, phones, sensors, microphones, and cameras. It deploys machine intelligence and platforms. It expresses itself

> in algorithms. But it is not the same as any of those. Just as an X-ray reveals bone and muscle, but not the soft tissue that binds them, technology is the bone and muscle here, while surveillance capitalism is the soft tissue that binds the elements and directs them into action. [It has] transformed people and society into raw material for others' economic gain, as the Internet itself falls to the ownership and operations of surveillance capitalism.[317]

Zuboff argues that we have reached a point where an expanded right to privacy and a newly articulated "right to be forgotten" are required to resist the power of surveillance capitalism.[318] For example, it is simply not enough to suggest that personal information can be "anonymised" in an AI system because "de-anonymisation" is ever-easier given recent technological developments.[319] Others call for a "freedom to be off"; not to be visible online and subject to the uncontrolled use of our personal information.[320]

Even more salient today is Zuboff's suggestion that our societies are no longer shaped by a division of labour, but by a division of learning: those who can participate in the digital world, and those who are excluded from agency, whose life experience becomes little more than a source of data, and predicted behaviours.[321] This dystopian view brings us back to the cultural fear that humans are being manipulated, instrumentalised and ultimately de-humanised. We are not displaced by robots; we become them.[322]

In the preceding three chapters, I have tried to make the case that our era is marked by profound anxiety, induced by many elements, three of which I have highlighted that are particularly salient: populist nationalism, certain forms of globalisation, and socially disruptive technologies and dominating platforms. These sources of anxiety lie deeply embedded in the social and economic conflicts of our time, and they prompt reactions that are new sources of anxiety in their own right, like the growing conflict between the United States and China, the use of violence to further political aims and local vigilantism. That is why I have sought to trace out their origins and effects. But it is important to remind ourselves that these anxieties are compounded by others, based in existential risks and uncertainties rooted in humanity's abuse of the natural world, of which climate change and pandemic disease are paramount.

One could simply curl up in a ball and bemoan the terrors confronting us. Or, drawing on our rich heritage of ideas, we could work hard to find the resources to fight back and to identify means to lessen the anxiety of our era. That is my effort in the rest of this book.

Notes

218 See Tooze. It is important to note that new technologies have indeed created new opportunities for many people, and the opportunities accelerate. See *Habermas Transformation*, 234; Manuel Castells, *The Internet Galaxy: Reflections on the Internet, Business, and Society* (Oxford University Press, 2002), *passim*. But social progress from technology is by no means inevitable. *Adler World Ordering*, 271, 289.

219 Przeworski, 194, quotes the US Bureau of Labor Statistics in showing that salaries in manufacturing jobs will have declined between 2016 and 2026, concluding that "many people will experience the necessity to move to lower-pay occupations, with the attendant loss of social status and a perception of downward mobility".

220 Susana Navas, "Robot Machines and Civil Liability", in Martin Ebers and Susana Navas (eds), *Algorithms and Law* (Cambridge University Press, 2020), 157, 158.

221 Martin Ebers, "Regulating AI and Robotics: Ethical and Legal Challenges", in Martin Ebers and Susana Navas (eds), *Algorithms and Law* (Cambridge University Press, 2020), 37, 42. An "algorithm", loosely defined, is a set of specified steps designed to process data and instructions to produce a particular output. Ebers, 40. And for useful descriptions of different types of algorithms, see Ebers, 38–40.

222 Navas, 159–60.

223 Ebers, 41.

224 Andrew Gregory, "Scientists Use AI to Create Drug Regime for Rare Form of Brain Cancer in Children", *The Guardian*, 23 September 2021, available at: www.theguardian.com/science/2021/sep/23/scientists-use-ai-to-create-drug-regime-for-rare-form-of-brain-cancer-in-children.

225 Julia Kollewe, "Drug Companies Look to AI to End 'Hit and Miss' Research", *The Guardian*, 20 February 2021, available at: www.theguardian.com/business/2021/feb/20/drug-companies-look-to-ai-to-end-hit-and-miss-research. For more detail, see Nic Fleming, "How Artificial Intelligence is Changing Drug Discovery" (2018) 557 *Nature*, available at: https://go.gale.com/ps/anonymous?id=GALE%7CA572639347&sid=googleScholar&v=2.1&it=r&linkaccess=abs&issn=00280836&p=AONE&sw=w.

226 See, e.g., David Naylor, "On the Prospects for a (Deep) Learning Health Care System" (2018) 320 *JAMA* 11, available at: www.researchgate.net/publication/327407622_On_the_Prospects_for_a_Deep_Learning_Health_Care_System.

227 See, e.g., the extraordinary advances announced by the Google entity, DeepMind. Linda Geddes, "DeepMind Uncovers Structure of 200m Proteins in Scientific Leap Forward", *The Guardian*, 28 July 2022, available at: www.theguardian.com/technology/2022/jul/28/deepmind-uncovers-structure-of-200m-proteins-in-scientific-leap-forward.

228 Royal Society and Alan Turing Institute, "The AI Revolution in Scientific Research" (2019), available at: https://royalsociety.org/-/media/policy/projects/ai-and-society/AI-revolution-in-science.pdf?la=en-GB&hash=5240F21B56364A00053538A0BC29FF5F.

229 Alan Turing Institute, "AI for Science and Government" (2021), available at: www.turing.ac.uk/research/asg.

230 Hannah Devlin, "AI and Maths to Play Bigger Role in Global Diplomacy, Says Expert", *The Guardian*, 15 October 2021, available at: www.theguardian.com/technology/2021/oct/15/ai-and-maths-to-play-bigger-role-in-global-diplomacy-says-expert.

231 See, e.g., the work of Cambridge Digital Humanities, available at: https://www.cdh.cam.ac.uk.

232 HAL 9000 is an early example of imagined general artificial intelligence. His acronym stands for **H**euristically Programmed **Al**gorithmic Computer.

233 Kazuo Ishiguro, *Klara and the Sun* (London: Faber & Faber, 2021). See also Ebers, 2–3; and for an extended treatment of intelligent machines in popular culture, Stephen Cave, Kanta Dihal and Sarah Dillon (eds), *AI Narratives: A History of Imaginative Thinking about Intelligent Machines* (Oxford University Press, 2020), based on the work of the AI Narratives Project of the Leverhulme Centre for the Future of Intelligence, University of Cambridge.

234 Of course, it is important to emphasise that new technologies also create new job categories with tens of thousands of opportunities. See, e.g., Christopher Marsden, "The Regulated End of Internet Law, and the Return to Computer and Information Law?", in Kevin Werbach (ed.), *After the Digital Tornado: Networks, Algorithms, Humanity* (Cambridge University Press, 2020), 35, 55. It is entirely uncertain how the balancing between destruction and creation of jobs will play out. The accessibility of the new jobs to those whose jobs are destroyed is also unclear. See, e.g., Shoshana Zuboff, "*Caveat Usor*: Surveillance Capitalism as Epistemic Inequality", in Kevin Werbach (ed.), *After the Digital Tornado: Networks, Algorithms, Humanity* (Cambridge University Press, 2020), 174, 180, 198–9.

235 Dominic Lawson, "Meet Pepper, the Robot Friend Who almost Truly Cares", *The Times*, 13 September 2020, available at: www.thetimes.co.uk/edition/comment/meet-pepper-the-robot-friend-who-almost-truly-cares-8gpwfqkzf.

236 Susana Navas, "Creativity of Algorithms and Copyright Law", in Kevin Werbach (ed.), *After the Digital Tornado: Networks, Algorithms, Humanity* (Cambridge University Press, 2020), 221, 225 [hereinafter *Navas Creativity*].

237 *Navas Creativity*, 234; Gabe Cohn, "AI Art at Christie's Sells for $432,500", *New York Times*, 25 October 2018, available at: www.nytimes.com/2018/10/25/arts/design/ai-art-sold-christies.html.

238 Harriet Sherwood, "But is it Art, Ma'am? Robot's Platinum Jubilee Queen Portrait Unveiled", *The Guardian*, 27 May 2022, available at: www.theguardian.com/uk-news/2022/may/27/but-is-it-art-maam-robots-platinum-jubilee-queen-portrait-unveiled.

239 GPT-3, "A Robot Wrote this Entire Article. Are You Scared Yet, Human?", *The Guardian*, 8 September 2020, available at: www.theguardian.com/commentisfree/2020/sep/08/robot-wrote-this-article-gpt-3. When a Google engineer recently argued

in public that "language machines" like GP3 could be sentient, he was fired. N.a., "Google Fires Software Engineer Who Claims AI Chatbot is Sentient", *The Guardian*, 23 July 2022, available at: www.theguardian.com/technology/2022/jul/23/google-fires-software-engineer-who-claims-ai-chatbot-is-sentient.

240 Heather Stewart, "Boris Johnson Blames 'Mutant Algorithm' for Exams Fiasco", *The Guardian*, 26 August 2020, available at: www.theguardian.com/politics/2020/aug/26/boris-johnson-blames-mutant-algorithm-for-exams-fiasco.

241 See Kartik Hosanagar and Alex Miller, "Who Do We Blame for the Filter Bubble? On the Roles of Math, Data, and People in Algorithmic Social Systems", in Kevin Werbach (ed.), *After the Digital Tornado: Networks, Algorithms, Humanity* (Cambridge University Press, 2020), 103, 104, 111.

242 See, e.g., "A-level Results: Why Algorithms get Things so Wrong – and What We Can Do to Fix Them", *The Conversation*, 19 August 2020, available at: https://theconversation.com/a-level-results-why-algorithms-get-things-so-wrong-and-what-we-can-do-to-fix-them-142879. The decision to abandon the algorithmically corrected A-level results did indeed produce grade inflation.

243 Joshua Kroll et al., "Accountable Algorithms" (2017) 165 *U. Penn L. Rev.* 633 [hereinafter *Kroll Algorithms*]; Ebers, 38.

244 Tim Wu, "Will Artificial Intelligence Eat the Law? The Rise of Hybrid Social-Ordering Systems" (2019) 119 *Col. L. Rev.* 2001, 2001–2, 2007.

245 Aziz Huq, "Artificial Intelligence and the Rule of Law", 12 March 2021, available at: https://papers.ssrn.com/sol3/papers.cfm?abstract_id=3794777 (forthcoming in the *Routledge Handbook on the Rule of Law*), 3.

246 Hosanagar and Miller, 103; Ebers, 38.

247 Mario Martini, "Regulating Algorithms: How to Demystify the Alchemy of Code?", in Martin Ebers and Susana Navas (eds), *Algorithms and Law* (Cambridge University Press, 2020), 100, 102. In the United States, the Internal Revenue Agency runs a fraud detection process using machine-learning. Huq, 3.

248 See, e.g., Frank Pasquale, "'Machines Set Loose to Slaughter': the Dangerous Rise of Military AI", *The Guardian*, 15 October 2020, available at: www.theguardian.com/news/2020/oct/15/dangerous-rise-of-military-ai-drone-swarm-autonomous-weapons. Such weapons were imagined back in the 1950s by the dystopian novelist Philip Dick, *Second Variety*, reprint (Floyd, VA: Positronic Publishing, 2015) (describing the use of "replicating robots" in war). I thank René Provost for introducing me to this eerie piece of writing.

249 Antoinette Rouvroy, "The End(s) of Critique: Data-behaviourism vs. Due-process", in Mireille Hildebrandt and Ekatarina De Vries (eds), *Privacy, Due Process and the Computational Turn: Philosophers of Law Meet Philosophers of Technology* (Abingdon: Routledge, 2012), 143.

250 Adam Harkens, "The Ghost in the Legal Machine: Algorithmic Governmentality, Economy, and the Practice of Law" (2018) 16 *J. Info. Comms & Ethics in Soc.* 16.

251 Wu, 2001.

252 Mireille Hildebrandt, "Algorithmic Regulation and the Rule of Law" (2018) *Phil. Trans. R. Soc. A* 376: 20170355, 1, available at: http://dx.doi.org/10.1098/rsta.2017.0355 [hereinafter *Hildebrandt Algorithmic Regulation*]. See also Ebers. 51.

253 Wu, 2002–3, 2005, 2026–7.

254 Mireille Hildebrandt, "The New Imbroglio: Living with Machine Algorithms", in Liisa Janssens (ed.), *The Art of Ethics in the Information Society* (Amsterdam: University of Amsterdam Press, 2016), available at: https://mediarep.org/handle/doc/14317.

255 Emily Berman, "A Government of Laws and Not of Machines" (2018) 98 *SSRN J.* 1279, 1283, available at: https://www.ssrn.com/abstract=3098995; Huq, 7 ("The reward function of an automated predictive tool is programmed into its code. It is not necessarily or readily available for examination by those subject to its regime. Even if the code were available, it would not be illuminating for either the 'ordinary citizen' or the 'trained lawyer'"). See also James Grimmelmann, "Regulation by Software" (2005) 114 *Yale L. J.* 1719, 1723; Ebers, 48–50; Martini, 102–3; Mireille Hildebrandt, "Law as Computation in the Era of Artificial Legal Intelligence: Speaking Law to the Power of Statistics" (2018) 68 *UTLJ* 12, available at: www.utpjournals.press/doi/abs/10.3138/utlj.2017-0044. Machine-learning is also defined as "the process of enabling computers to optimize certain tasks without the benefit of explicit rules-based programming". Benjamin Alarie, Anthony Niblett and Albert Yoon, "How Artificial Intelligence Will Affect the Practice of Law" (2018) 68 *UTLJ* 106, available at: www.utpjournals.press/doi/abs/10.3138/utlj.2017-0052. See also Ebers, 43.

256 Wu, 2021.

257 Huq, 7.

258 Ebers, 46–7.

259 *Kroll Algorithms*, 636. See also Joshua Kroll, "The Fallacy of Inscrutability" (2018) 376 *Phil. Trans. R. Soc. A* 20180084, available at: https://royalsocietypublishing.org/doi/10.1098/rsta.2018.0084; Corinne Cath, "Governing Artificial Intelligence: Ethical, Legal and Technical Opportunities and Challenges" (2018) 376 *Phil. Trans. R. Soc. A* 20180080, available at: https://royalsocietypublishing.org/doi/full/10.1098/rsta.2018.0080.

260 Bartosz Brożek, *The Legal Mind: A New Introduction to Legal Epistemology* (Cambridge University Press, 2020), 103–4.

261 Monika Zalnieriute, Lyria Bennett Moses and George Williams, "The Rule of Law and Automation of Government Decision-Making" (2019) 82 *MLR* 425, 428, 439, 448.

262 Anthony Casey and Anthony Niblett, "Self-Driving Laws Focus Feature: Artificial Intelligence, Big Data, and the Future of Law" (2016) 66 *U. Toronto L. J.* 429, 437.

263 Duncan MacIntosh, "Autonomous Weapons and the Nature of Law and Morality: How Rule-of-Law-Values Require Automation of the Rule of Law" (2016) 30 *Temple Int'l and Comp. L. J.* 99, 103–4.

264 Ebers, 45.

265 Ebers, 46.

266 Ebers, 46.

267 Emre Bayamlıoğlu and Ronald Leenes, "The 'Rule of Law' Implications of Data-driven Decision-making: a Techno-regulatory Perspective" (2018) 10 *Law, Innovation and Technology* 295, 302. It is worth noting that the "data" used by an AI system is, in a sense, not a thing, but a representation of the underlying information that data simply "carries" in a system. Björn Steinrötter, "The (Envisaged) Legal Framework for Commercialisation of Digital Data within the EU", in Martin Ebers and Susana Navas (eds), *Algorithms and Law* (Cambridge University Press, 2020), 269, 272. This is important because it focuses attention on how, as I say, data cannot in any sense speak for itself.

268 Wu, 2021.

269 *Hildebrandt Algorithmic Regulation*, 2–3, 6.

270 Wu, 2005.

271 *Hildebrandt Algorithmic Regulation*, 9.

272 See Alarie, Niblett and Yoon, 10–12, for a more optimistic view of the interplay between computational approaches to decision-making and the future practice of law.

273 Casey and Niblett, 432 (on the bias of judges in bail hearings).

274 This problem is recognised within the industry building and promoting AI. A senior researcher in Microsoft's research wing, Kate Crawford, argues that "the politics of classification has become baked into the substrates of AI". Quoted in Zoë Corbyn, "Microsoft's Kate Crawford: 'AI is Neither Artificial Nor Intelligent", *The Guardian*, 6 June 2021, available at: www.theguardian.com/technology/2021/jun/06/microsofts-kate-crawford-ai-is-neither-artificial-nor-intelligent.

275 David Berreby, "Can We Make Our Robots Less Biased than We Are?", *New York Times*, 22 November 2020, available at: www.nytimes.com/2020/11/22/science/artificial-intelligence-robots-racism-police.html.

276 Ebers, 77.

277 Ebers, 105.

278 Ebers, 78, 79, 105; Berman, 1325; *Hildebrandt Algorithmic Regulation*, 7 (on design decisions that incorporate assumptions and implicit trade-offs); Catrina Denvir et al., "The Devil in the Detail: Mitigating the Constitutional and Rule of Law Risks Associated with the Use of Artificial Intelligence in the Legal Domain" (2018) 47, available at: https://papers.ssrn.com/abstract=3426337.

279 Kevin Werbach, "Introduction", in Kevin Werbach (ed.), *After the Digital Tornado: Networks, Algorithms, Humanity* (Cambridge University Press, 2020), 1, 3.

280 See World Wide Web Foundation, "History of the Web", available at: https://webfoundation.org/about/vision/history-of-the-web/?gclid=Cj0KCQjwv7L6BRDxARIsAGj-34oYJjVjmV6yCpZFDWfYY1F6qH6SbPnis_UIYAPkmDGPQBt8Rl67Ke0aAu5mEALw_wcB.

281 See Marsden, *passim*.

282 Werbach, 2–3.

283 Werbach, 8–10; Ronald Deibert, *Reset: Reclaiming the Internet for Civil Society* (Toronto: House of Anansi Press, 2020) (the 2020 CBC Massey Lectures), 264–5.

284 Wu, 2010–18.

285 Quoted in *The Guardian*, 6 October 2021, available at: www.theguardian.com/technology/2021/oct/05/facebook-frances-haugen-whistleblower-regulation.

286 For the Bill itself, see at: https://bills.parliament.uk/bills/3137. For expressions of doubt from leading Conservative politicians, see Annabelle Dickson, "Britain's Online Safety Bill Set to be Delayed", *Politico*, 13 July 2022, available at: www.politico.eu/article/uk-pm-boris-johnson-exit-delay-on-britains-online-safety-bill-expected; Isabel Hardman, "The Online Safety Bill won't Survive the Tory Contest", *The Spectator*, 20 July 2022, available at: www.politico.eu/article/uk-pm-boris-johnson-exit-delay-on-britains-online-safety-bill-expected.

287 Werbach, 5. For a jargon-free explanation of how the network known as the internet works, see Kevin Werbach, "Digital Tornado: The Internet and Telecommunications Policy (1997) Selected Excerpts", in Kevin Werbach (ed.), *After the Digital Tornado: Networks, Algorithms, Humanity* (Cambridge University Press, 2020), 13, 23–4. For a broader definition of "network" as a mode of organisation, see Julie Cohen, "Networks, Standards, and Network-and-Standard-Based Governance", in Kevin Werbach (ed.), *After the Digital Tornado: Networks, Algorithms, Humanity* (Cambridge University Press, 2020), 58, 64–6.

288 Marsden, 55, citing Hildebrandt; Deibert, 66–7.

289 Ebers, 73. See also Deibert, 54. Intriguingly, one of Microsoft's own senior researchers, Kate Crawford, argues that emotion recognition technology is "deeply flawed". Quoted in Corbyn.

290 Nicola Davis, "Scientists Create Online Games to Show Risks of AI Emotion Recognition", *The Guardian*, 4 April 2021, available at: www.theguardian.com/technology/2021/apr/04/online-games-ai-emotion-recognition-emojify.

291 Ebers, 70–1. The 2018 "Cambridge Analytica" scandal is a good example, where it became known that a small tech company (entirely separate from the University of Cambridge, I must note) accessed the data of 50 million Facebook users without their permission and provided it to campaigns seeking to influence voters in the 2016 US presidential election. Martini, 108.

292 Jill Lepore, "All the King's Data: Simulation, Automation, and the Election of John F. Kennedy", *The New Yorker*, 3 and 10 August 2020, 18 (Arthur Schlesinger Jr, close to the Kennedy campaign, was introduced to the Simulmatics offer, and his reaction was initially negative: "I shudder at the implication for public leadership of the notion … that a man shouldn't say something until it is cleared with the machine." He nonetheless brought Simulmatics to the Kennedy campaign because he did not "like to be party to choking off new ideas").

293 Ebers, 73–4. But see Deibert, 19; Hosanagar and Miller, *passim* (whose survey of the current research landscape suggests that it is difficult to determine the extent to which "algorithmic curation" actually produces a more skewed set of materials than that which is self-selected by people looking to confirm their own views; indeed, in some circumstances the reverse seems to be true).

294 See Siva Vaidhyanathan, *Antisocial Media: How Facebook Disconnects Us and Undermines Democracy* (Oxford University Press, 2018); Chris Bail, *Breaking the Social Media Prism:*

How to Make Our Platforms Less Polarizing (Princeton University Press, 2021) (with concrete advice on how to break out of the current dynamics).

295 Marsden, 45, 47; *Adler World Ordering*, 240.

296 See, e.g., Emma Graham-Harrison, Jasper Jackson and Alexandra Heal, "Facebook 'Still Making Money from Anti-vax Sites'", *The Guardian*, 30 January 2021, available at: www.theguardian.com/technology/2021/jan/30/facebook-letting-fake-news-spreaders-profit-investigators-claim.

297 Wu seems relatively optimistic about the possibility of automated content assessment combined with human assessment within the major platform companies. But he notes that it "might also be that hybrid systems accelerate a privatization of public justice. For some decades, with the rise of measures like compulsory arbitration, critics have complained that American justice has been privatized, usually in a manner designed to disfavor consumers, patients, and other weak groups. The hybrid systems in the case study are all private adjudicators and policymakers." Wu, 2028.

298 See, e.g., Andrew Marantz, "Explicit Content: Facebook is Full of Hate Speech and Fake News. Does It Want to Fix the Problem?" *The New Yorker*, 19 October 2020, 20; Kari Paul, "Facebook Whistleblower's Testimony Could Finally Spark Action in Congress", *The Guardian*, 6 October 2021, available at: www.theguardian.com/technology/2021/oct/05/facebook-frances-haugen-whistleblower-regulation. See also Deibert, 20–1, 315.

299 Tim Adams, "Carl Bergstrom: 'People are Using Data to Bullshit'", *The Guardian*, 1 August 2020, available at: www.theguardian.com/science/2020/aug/01/carl-bergstrom-people-are-using-data-to-bullshit.

300 *Arendt Totalitarianism*, 474.

301 Ben Hoyle and David Charter, "Nancy Pelosi Lambasts Promotion of QAnon Congresswoman Marjorie Talor Greene", *New York Times*, 29 January 2021, available at: www.thetimes.co.uk/article/nancy-pelosi-lambasts-promotion-of-marjorie-taylor-greene-who-endorsed-violence-against-democrats-cg9jz6n7m.

302 See, e.g., Kashmir Hill, "A Vast Web of Vengeance", *New York Times*, 30 January 2021, available at: www.nytimes.com/2021/01/30/technology/change-my-google-results.html?action=click&module=Top%20Stories&pgtype=Homepage.

303 A study quoted in Przeworski, 119.

304 Ebers, 63.

305 Margrethe Vestager, quoted in Zuboff, 203.

306 Deibert, 56.

307 Deibert, ch. 3, esp. 200–1.

308 William Eggers, Rob Hamill and Abed Ali, "Data as the New Currency: Government's Role in Facilitating the Exchange", *Deloitte Insights*, 24 July 2013, available at: www2.deloitte.com/us/en/insights/deloitte-review/issue-13/data-as-the-new-currency.html.

309 Viktor Mayer-Schönberger, "Regulating the Feedback Effect", in Kevin Werbach (ed.), *After the Digital Tornado: Networks, Algorithms, Humanity* (Cambridge University Press, 2020), 122, 124 ("Every additional person using Facebook, for example, improves the utility Facebook has for other users as they can reach more people through the service").

310 Zuboff, 185–6; Deibert, 27–8, 50–1. The fact that commercial interests drive technological development is not new. Weber argued that the hammer piano became dominant over harpsichords, etc. because manufacturers sought to capitalise on the mass market for music consumption. Max Weber, *The Interpretation of Social Reality* (London: Joseph, 1970), 224 [hereinafter *Weber Interpretation*].

311 Ebers, 62. The value of data is, of course, limited to some extent by legal regulation favouring privacy, and restricting access to and sharing of data. See, e.g., Steinrötter, 289–90.

312 Mayer-Schönberger, 127–9.

313 Zuboff, 181.

314 Deibert, 250, and generally 17, 202–50, 257.

315 The quote is ubiquitous on the internet. See, e.g., at: www.goodreads.com/quotes/7462175-move-fast-and-break-things-unless-you-are-breaking-stuff. Facebook later modified the approach to the more staid: "Move fast with stable infrastructure." See at: https://mashable.com/2014/04/30/facebooks-new-mantra-move-fast-with-stability/?europe=true.

316 Larry Page, quoted in Zuboff, 204.

317 Zuboff, 184. The term "surveillance capitalism" was coined by sociologist Vincent Mosco. See Deibert, 27.

318 Zuboff, 176–7. Deibert posits the need for a fundamental "reset" rooted in the principle of "restraint". Deibert, 275 ("We need to restrain what governments and corporations do with all the extraordinarily powerful tools of surveillance that are now in their hands ... We'll need personal restraints too: restraints on our endless appetite for data, restraints on our emotions and anger as we engage online ..."). See also Deibert, 298–9.

319 Steinrötter, 273.

320 Brett Frischmann and Evan Selinger, "Why a Commitment to Pluralism Should Limit How Humanity Is Re-Engineered", in Kevin Werbach (ed.), *After the Digital Tornado: Networks, Algorithms, Humanity* (Cambridge University Press, 2020), 155, 164–7.

321 Zuboff, 180, 188.

322 Even the seemingly simple act of "electronic contracting" can devalue our humanity by undermining our sense of autonomy. The concept of consent is systematically trivialised as we click on "agree" to most any request of an online platform (often "agreeing" to page after page of boilerplate) so that we can continue to use it. See Deibert, 96.

PART TWO

OUR INHERITANCE OF THOUGHT AND ACTION: ADDRESSING OUR ANXIETY

And what there is to conquer
By strength and submission, has already been discovered
Once or twice, or several times, by men whom one cannot hope
To emulate – but there is no competition –
There is only the fight to recover what has been lost
And found and lost again and again: and now, under conditions
That seem unpropitious. But perhaps neither gain nor loss.
For us, there is only the trying. The rest is not our business.

T. S. Eliot, East Coker, *The Four Quartets**

In Part II of the book, I consider a wide swath of human thought, but to help trace the trajectory of the argument I will begin with a short summary. Bear with me for a few pages. I will explain the ideas in more detail, but I suspect that an overall map of the argument will help keep the author and reader on a shared track. My purpose is to lay out a way of thinking about people in society that I hope will be both instructive and encouraging in what can sometimes feel like a bleak time. More specifically, I hope to show that there are productive ways of building towards and then applying a modest conception of the rule of law that can provide concrete help in steering our societies through our new age of anxiety.

Individuals and human institutions are guided by purposes. Through experience over time, and especially through engagement with a rich variety of people and diverse practices, we gain practical wisdom, wisdom grounded in reason but open to intuition, emotion and to the influence of what we

* Used with kind permission from Faber and Faber Ltd and HarperCollins.

now call social or life skills. It is through self-critical assessment, deploying all of these elements of personhood, that we refine our purposes and learn. We do this as we act in society, adjusting our course as we go along. But we also learn through reflection after the fact, allowing us to pursue deeper changes to our purposes as we recognise them to be necessary. So learning takes place both on the fly, so to speak, and in contemplation.

Crucially, learning is not solitary. Knowledge is created through shared practices in community. Those practices consist of actions as well as discourse. They are shaped by background knowledge, which is in turn passed on through the replication of practices. But replication is not automatic; it is selective because our practical wisdom guides us as we consider new material circumstances and new discoveries or insights. We also consider the challenges to our assumptions and our practices offered up in dialogue with others. Both as individuals and as societies we learn primarily through practices, not through abstracted logical deduction; through discovery and creativity more than justification. Of course, we are affected and shaped by tradition and habit, but are not fundamentally constrained.[323] Our world is a world of dynamic becoming, with change endemic.

Truth is not fixed, not simply "out there" to discover. Like social facts, truth is built through human interaction and the creation of consensus within communities of practice and across such communities as we engage in challenging dialogue. Truth is settling issues for the time being, creating generalisations that are admittedly mutable. But these generalisations are deeply useful. They allow us to build frameworks for decision that are shaped by standards of evaluation developed within a community of practice and tested against measures of competency, then tested further in engagement with other communities of practice and in the wider society.[324] There may well be friction amongst different communities of practice, with differing measures of competence and even of truth. Yet mutable truth does not mean that "anything goes" or that "everything is relative" because societies must find ways to navigate through competing practices. Indeed, the openness of this understanding of truth allows for a plurality of perspectives to enlarge our shared understandings. It values, indeed demands, diversity of thought because that diversity helps to identify a broader set of important issues and contributes to building richer approaches to addressing problems.

With that brief summary in mind, I will now take us through the elements more methodically.

Notes

323 Of course, this liberated conception of habit or tradition does not deny that there are communities that can impose, through social convention and even the use of force, very real constraints in the name of tradition. John Dewey argued that habits can "become blinders that confine the eyes of the mind to the road ahead", but he thought that through inquiry we could learn to control our tendency to habituation. See the discussion in Michael Sullivan, *Legal Pragmatism: Community, Rights and Democracy* (Bloomington: Indiana University Press, 2007), 56–7.

324 See, in the context of legal communities, *Walters on Dicey*, 374.

CHAPTER FIVE

Practical Wisdom and Pragmatism

For the journey homeward
Arriving by roads already known
At sites and sounds one has sensed before,
The knowledge needed is not special,
The sole essential a sad unrest
Which no life can lack.

W. H. Auden, *The Age of Anxiety*[*]

The best moments ... are when you come across something – a thought, a feeling, a way of looking at things – which you had thought special and particular to you. Now here it is, set down by someone else, a person you have never met, someone even who is long dead. And it is as if a hand has come out and taken yours.

Alan Bennett, *The History Boys*[325]

IN THE FIRST PART of this book I painted a rather grim portrait of some unique attributes of our age of anxiety. I suggested that the pervasive anxiety of the era is grounded primarily in three interlocking sets of concerns over populist nationalism, certain forms of globalisation, and socially disruptive technologies and powerful networks, although, of course, these issues are experienced differently by diverse types of people. Now I want to argue that there are ways to navigate through this anxiety; that we can draw upon a rich intellectual heritage for reassurance and inspiration. From ancient Greece through to the twentieth-century American philosophical pragmatists and contemporary theorists of social practice, we can derive insights that will help to construct a modern understanding of the role of law in society. In turn, this conception of law, when put into day-to-day practice, can help to alleviate some of our anxieties, as I will explain.

In *The Age of Anxiety*, Auden reassures us that there is a way home, that we are not trapped in a wasteland of fear, uncertainty and profound anxiety. He does not deny the forces that can cause those reactions; in fact, he catalogues them coolly and precisely. But he urges us not to give up, rather to seek "roads already known" that can lead us to safer ground. What I find most encouraging is Auden's assertion that the "knowledge needed is not special". Our way "home" is not dependent upon elite expertise.

That is where Alan Bennett comes in. His "history boys" are teenagers trying to find their way in the world as they face graduation from secondary school. They have ambitions and dreams, but they come from average backgrounds that have not set them up to believe they are remarkable. And in many ways they are not. But they possess that human spark that a great teacher can awake. And they can draw on thoughts, feelings and ways of looking at things from our shared history, building from that heritage to new beginnings. Of course, it requires effort, but the guideposts are there for us to find, the roads home visible if only we take the trouble to look.

The heritage we can call upon has roots in Greek classical thought. Aristotle argued that humans can acquire what he called practical wisdom (*phronesis*) not only through following general rules, but in the creation and evolution of practices learned through proper upbringing and habits gained through experience. People reflect upon those practices, reasoning over time, and thereby learn through their day-to-day existence;[326] they "work out" for themselves what they should do.[327] They build "the moral will and skill to do the right thing for the right reasons at the right time and in the right way", developing good character.[328] Practical wisdom is manifest in deliberative ability, and in emotional and social skills that allow us to take our understanding of the good life (or virtue) and fulfil it in concrete circumstances.[329] A similar commitment to grounding philosophical reflection in life experience shaped the work of the great tenth-century Islamic thinker known in the West as Avicenna (Abu Ali al-Husayn ibn Abdullah ibn Sina).[330]

For Aristotle, all people and things are oriented towards some purpose (*telos*).[331] For individual human beings, the primary aim is well-being or flourishing, sometimes described as happiness (*eudaimon*). Human institutions, including law, are likewise purpose-driven, not merely static structures.[332] For political communities, there is a double purpose: the promotion of human survival as well as the achievement of the good life, or life of virtue.[333] This purposive understanding of existence has been hugely influential in sociology and philosophy. The twelfth-century Talmudic scholar and philosopher, Maimonides (Rambam), argued that the perfect person would use knowledge for the improvement of the "political life" of themselves and of the community.[334] Philosophers and sociologists of the nineteenth and twentieth centuries argued that action is rational only when oriented to goals and values, and that this action is what creates our social reality.[335]

The pragmatist philosopher John Dewey aimed much of his work at helping people to develop a sense that they could "direct their social existence towards their chosen ends, rather than leaving all that happens in life to blind accident".[336] Dewey further specified his purposive understanding of human life, arguing that in trying to resolve problematic situations we are actually seeking social and moral improvement.[337] In this, Dewey follows Aristotle in suggesting that knowledge is created to inform prudent, rational action. The role of the philosopher, for Dewey, was to derive conclusions by referring "back to ordinary life-experience- ... rendering them more significant, more luminous to us".[338] Our purposes or "ends" are not derived from abstract values, or universal truth, but from life experience that is critically examined.[339]

The necessary, or rather inevitable, orientation of human life towards purpose and action was also emphasised by Hannah Arendt. For her, "what makes man a political being is his faculty for action; it enables him to get together with his peers, to act in concert, and to reach out for goals and enterprises that would never enter his mind ... had he not been given this gift".[340] Arendt argued that for too long philosophers had focused on the contemplative life rather than the life of action, and she therefore resisted calling herself a philosopher.[341] She stressed the necessary link in effective action between word and deed: "Power is actualized only where word and deed have not parted company, where words are not empty and deeds not brutal ..."[342] Arendt believed strongly that coherence – ideological and conceptual – was less important than connecting thought to lived realities, in particular the suffering inherent in the human condition.[343]

Pragmatist philosophy focuses intently on the role of social actions.[344] Dewey argued that the social world was essentially one of evolution, with knowledge emerging from practice because acting actually precedes knowing.[345] In this view, Dewey followed Hegel who argued that the very identity of people is built up in social practices.[346] Dewey went further to stress that "the public" is also constituted as a community through action, not simply discourse or talking, a concept picked up by Hannah Arendt who, in arguing that power in society is made real only through common projects of speech *and* action in concert, stressed that power itself is constantly in play and is never static. She further emphasised that, as I have already noted, "[w]hile strength is the natural quality of an individual seen in isolation, power springs up between men when they act together and vanishes the moment they disperse".[347] More recently, the growing interest of social scientists in the role of practices has also been grounded, at least in part, in the action focus of pragmatism.[348] That focus is not justified simply by the social construction of identity but also by an undeniable aim of human endeavour, to solve concrete problems or at least to move from an unworkable situation to a better one.

Why has the tradition of pragmatist philosophy and sociology grown in influence in our era?

As described by neo-pragmatist philosopher Richard Rorty, pragmatism makes three fundamental claims: there is no knowable transcultural human "essence" or "nature" because knowledge is created through practice in community; all human inquiry is oriented towards practical problem-solving; and our beliefs are "action-guiding".[349] For that reason, humans are infinitely creative, and if we work together "we can make ourselves into whatever we are clever and courageous enough to imagine ourselves becoming".[350]

Pragmatists do not deny material, structural and cultural constraints on action. Of course, some people start out in situations where freedom of thought and action is far more limited than for others in different situations. However, pragmatists argue that the bounds of our lives can be broken through shared problem-solving. This point seems to me to be supported empirically because almost no society is absolutely fixed. The Roman Empire collapsed. So too the Soviet Union. Europe in 2021 is fundamentally different than it was in 1945. Vietnam today is a market-oriented socialist state that could not have been predicted in 1966. Likewise individuals, whose lives can change dramatically through intention and effort if opportunity is created in diverse communities.

Let me unpack those ideas briefly because they will be relevant to the remainder of my argument. The key to understanding pragmatism as a philosophical construct is that human beings need to have beliefs that can lead to better actions and lives, contributing meaningfully to the social world. Pragmatism eschews abstraction. Dewey argued that when a theory is

> [n]ot tested by being employed to see what it leads to in ordinary experience and what new meanings it contributes, this subject-matter becomes arbitrary, aloof – what is called "abstract" when that word is used in a bad sense to designate something which exclusively occupies a realm of its own without contact with the things of ordinary experience.[351]

It is this fundamental connection to the day-to-day world that caused pragmatists to focus on practice. In the words of William James: "It is far too little recognized . . . how entirely the intellect is built up of practical interests."[352]

We humans are bound up in the world of experience; our practices are means of coping with it. We cannot just step out of experience and adopt some other aim, such as getting an ideal morality right.[353] Intriguingly, the great English constitutionalist A. V. Dicey expressed the same commitment to practice, in his case the practice of courts of law, as the building block of the rule of law, eschewing induction from first principles in favour of deduction from day-to-day experience.[354] Pragmatists reject "ideal" theory in favour of learning primarily from experience rather than abstract thought.[355] A contemporary pragmatist puts the point clearly:

> The central thought of pragmatism is that our philosophical theories must be connected to experience and practice. A belief, hypothesis, or theory which pretends to be above experience, which thinks so well of itself that it pretends to be immune from recalcitrant experience, is spurious.[356]

Intriguingly, recent neuroscientific discoveries gained through brain imaging support the idea that the mental process of acquiring knowledge (cognition) is closely related to practical action. Imagining a concrete activity such as hammering a nail into a wall and the action of accomplishing that activity activate the same neural pathways.[357]

Dewey placed great store in learning through action rather than logical deduction. He believed that intuition and impression were highly influential in the creation of knowledge throughout human history. He argued that it was the need to justify our practical observations to others that created our contemporary focus on the operations of formal logic. But he suggested that we had to reclaim our connection to a logic of discovery rather than over-relying on a logic of justification, if we are to cope with constant change and tap into our creative spirit.[358]

The focus on creativity gained through reflective practices connects pragmatism to a tradition of process philosophy whose origins are often associated with the ancient Greek thinker Heraclitus. Unfortunately for subsequent interpreters, Heraclitus is known to us only through fragments that are often opaque and sometimes contradictory. He is most famous for his descriptions of humans stepping into a river (of time?) where there is constant flow and nothing stays the same. This theory of flux is closely connected to the idea that there is unity in opposites, that things and people can be both the same and not the same over time.[359]

Most importantly for pragmatist thinking, Heraclitus viewed dynamism as an explanatory force in human existence; reality is a collection not only of things, but of processes.[360] Heraclitus was not alone amongst the ancients in stressing process over fixity. As I have already emphasised, Aristotle's "practical wisdom" was acquired through time, with experience.[361]

The understanding of reality as process rather than fixed substance was furthered in the work of Alfred North Whitehead, perhaps the most comprehensive of twentieth-century process philosophers. Whitehead argued that reality is made up of unique and indivisible entities (*monads*), each of which is constantly in the process of becoming what its potential allows; but the potentialities of each are various, so the process of becoming is unpredictable and in flux.[362] Hannah Arendt used a different word for a similar idea. She focused on the essential human trait of "natality", and saw it as a source of constant change and renewal.[363] Natality, or beginnings, open up the possibility of becoming something new through the exercise of freedom:

> ... the new beginning inherent in birth can make itself felt in the world only because the newcomer possesses the capacity of beginning something anew, that is, of acting. In this sense of initiative, an element of action, and therefore of natality, is inherent in all human activities.[364]

This action-focused understanding of human life was fundamental to Arendt's central moral commitment: "The *raison d'être* of politics is freedom, and its field of experience is action."[365] Because each person, each social actor, interacts with others, action is also subject to reaction, opening up boundaries and creating almost infinite possibility – and inherent uncertainty – in human affairs.[366] Modern complexity theory is also preoccupied with process: complex adaptive systems are constantly changing, evolving over time through learning.[367] And there are many such systems in the natural and social worlds, including animal nervous systems, traffic flows, climate, social networks, human–computer interactions, the developing embryo and insect swarms. In law as well, we experience what Patrick Glenn called the authoritative or normative "presence of the past", but because of the continuous flow of information and knowledge, traditions (like habits) are in a constant state of becoming, not stasis.[368]

Social scientists who focus on the study of practices have taken up the pragmatist interest in process and dynamism to emphasise the continuing processes that shape our societies. They are interested in "beginnings" and a "world of becoming" rather than the world of static "being". In the world of becoming, people and institutions constantly interact, learn and re-create their relationships. The construction of practices, of people themselves and of institutions is never complete.[369] The idea that social – and indeed natural – systems are subject to constant change is linked as well to Karl Popper's influential propensity theory whereby:

> Our very understanding of the world changes the conditions of the changing world; and so do our wishes, our preferences, our motivations, our hopes, our dreams, our phantasies, our hypotheses, our theories. Even our erroneous theories change the world . . .[370]

This tradition of thought reveals that humanity and individual humans are not trapped in social structures; we can choose to act and to work towards new beginnings.

Inevitably, "becoming" places a high value on individual human beings and groups of people as agents of action in society.[371] In the longstanding dispute between social and political theorists who stress human agency and those who focus on structures that fundamentally constrain human action, pragmatists and practice theorists tilt towards agency. I want to clear out the brush. I find the so-called "agent–structure" debate in the social sciences largely sterile.[372] Following from Anthony Giddens' powerful analysis,[373] I refuse to choose between agency and structure. Both have a role to play in shaping social and political action. Indeed, human agents build and re-build social structures while structures influence the identity, interest formation and decisions of human agents. At the same time, the identity and purposes of agents are shaped in the course of their interactions with each other.[374] In more value-laden terminology, drawn from Aristotle, agents are shaped within communities, and communities may have purposes that are collective.[375] Yet neither communities nor structures dictate outcomes;[376] nor does "society" as a collection of structures and institutions.[377]

It is likely that periods of deep uncertainty, like our own, actually facilitate the exercise of agency because structures (communities and institutions) are under strain.[378] That said, some structures may have greater power in constraining agency, if they are "anchoring practices" or "constitutive rules" that cannot be shifted "without disrupting collectively established realities".[379] Pragmatists acknowledge that there are some principles that, while theoretically revisable, we are loathe to revise, as this would rock our world to its foundations.[380] As I will argue, focusing upon practices rather than upon either agent or structure per se, or even the interrelation between the two, is more revealing of how society and social institutions are built, maintained, reformed and sometimes destroyed.[381]

What does the pragmatist focus on processes and practice – on becoming – mean for the explanatory potential of social science? I believe that pragmatism is liberating in part because it removes the straitjacket of a competing intellectual tradition, called scientific positivism:

> Positivists think that the capacity to control things comes about by identifying and verifying law-like regularities in social phenomena, especially correlations that allow us to posit relations of cause and effect. Control here is measured by the capacity for prediction that science provides; the aim is to acquire knowledge in a nomological sense [like laws of nature that are simply "givens"]. By contrast, the whole thrust of Dewey's argument is that, due to the complexity of social life and the pace of change to which it is subject, to achieve control is merely to establish a temporary and contingent resting place for inquiry. Nothing is ever settled once and for all.[382]

Because seeking knowledge is a practical activity, it inevitably involves change. We seek knowledge actively and we construct it through our efforts. We are constantly making choices about what to consider and how to design research into social phenomena. That is because understanding societies does not result from the observation of external data but from understanding "that which is already understood". The "observer" is inside the phenomena because she is human, existing within the society under consideration.[383] That could lead to stasis, if we simply accept what we already know. However, the pragmatist philosophy that I espouse here shows how we escape that stasis. We need to do two things: first, to course correct as we engage in our practices, undertaking a process of continuous self-challenging. This is often called "reflexive practice". Second, when we have time to pause in our actions, to reflect upon our practices so that we continue to learn. This is often referred to as "reflective practice".

The focus on learning and the inevitability of change means that the social sciences must be conceived of as an ethical practice, not as morally neutral.[384] In the evocative words of the polymath, Frank Ramsey, writing as an undergraduate at Cambridge:

> It is absolutely necessary in all political science [I add "all social science"] to consider the relation of what you are saying to the two fundamental questions What is the world like? How can we make it better?[385]

The purpose of the social sciences is not simply to accumulate data or to reinforce power, or to undertake any of the things that other disciplines might pursue, such as the accumulation of money or the creation of beauty. Rather, the social sciences must help us to understand the complexity of our world and help to explain regularities, admitting of constant change, while helping gain insight that permits a striving for improvement.[386]

Another thread of pragmatist thought that is helpful in understanding the complexity of our world is the emphasis upon the mutuality of knowledge creation. Whereas Weber conflated the creation of meaning within the mind of individuals and meaning that is built up in social interaction, the pragmatists distinguished the two. Moreover, they argued that even knowledge that is created in individuals' minds is strongly influenced by an implicit background that is socially constructed.[387] Another way of phrasing the point is that knowledge is built up through consensus; knowledge is not simply "discovered" as something that exists outside human interaction. It emerges from that interaction, from human practices that are built up over time as we seek out solutions to problems we face. Otherwise our knowledge is, as the early pragmatist Charles Sanders Peirce put it, merely "vagabond thoughts that tramp the public roads without human habitation".[388] We work to further human understanding through processes of inquiry and contestation, as well as through exercises of judgement, some in formal settings of adjudication but often in less structured ways, as we will see when I discuss modern conceptions of the rule of law.

Although he distinguished between theoretical knowledge that could be self-evidently true (Aristotle's "apodictic" knowledge) and practical knowledge, the Jewish sage Maimonides argued that the latter was founded on what is generally accepted.[389] Peirce described all inquiry as "communal" and suggested boldly that: "The opinion which is fated to be ultimately agreed to by all who investigate is what we mean by truth."[390] Interestingly, even in so highly structured and hierarchical a system of thought as Islamic law there is recognition that knowledge can be built up through the consensus of jurists (*ijma* or, at a lower level, *qiyas*).[391] Contemporary philosophers describe the mutual construction of knowledge as a form of "joint agency" where people build on shared intentions and common understandings; knowledge is, quite simply, a "team sport".[392] In our society there are many contributors to the construction of knowledge. It is a "decentralized ecosystem of academics, clergy members, teachers, journalists and others who disagree about a lot but agree on a shared system of rules for weighing evidence and building knowledge".[393]

Searle marvels at the ability of this mutually created knowledge to create "collective intentionality". Concrete things, like money, come into being simply because, together, we imagine them into existence.[394] Your dollar bill or pound coin is meaningless in its physical manifestation. Nothing fundamental differentiates it from any other piece of printed paper or a blank metal disk. It "exists" as money because our society recognises it as meaning something that possesses value. Less concrete objects like a country's constitution also come into being through such collective intentionality.[395] As we have seen, pragmatists argue more broadly that the very possibility of knowledge is created in forms of "inquiry" or what we might now call deliberation. In turn, democracy is built up through the collective action of "publics" at different levels of society:

> According to this public-based perspective, the central problem of democracy is how to empower citizens in their capacity to act as members of publics ranging from small neighbourhood communities to national peoples and, increasingly, to transnational publics brought to life by the awareness of a shared affectedness produced by the global reach of risks related to environment, security, health, social welfare.[396]

A further crucial and controversial pragmatist claim flows from the belief in shared human activity as the basis of knowledge: truth is not eternal, but is liable to change over time. Oliver Wendell Holmes had used this idea to explain the nature of legal authority, that it is rooted in changing human experience rather than in formal logic or tradition alone.[397]

His insight was adopted and applied to all forms of human endeavour by other pragmatists.[398] Cochran makes the point elegantly:

> To establish a truth pragmatically is to settle a controversial or complex issue for the time being, until something comes along to dislodge the comfort and reassurance that has been achieved, forcing inquiry to begin again.[399]

In other words, pragmatism at least partly undermines the long-powerful "correspondence theory of truth", the belief that propositions are true when they match an objective – meaning external to the mind and to social interaction – so-called "reality".[400] As we will see shortly, however, abandoning the correspondence theory of truth did not mean for the pragmatists that no practical truths could be identified by science or in everyday life. Any truth claim would still be subject to justification and verification. Pragmatists would never have subscribed to the dangerous notion of "alternative facts".

Instead, the pragmatists were following eighteenth-century philosophers in arguing that "what is observed is always constituted by the observing subject".[401] In the natural sciences, often misconceived as the pursuit of a hard-edged "truth" that merely needs to be uncovered, early physicists debated whether their science mirrored reality or was derived from intellectual constructs.[402] Although Einstein generally favoured the view that the universe was ordered and subject to causal laws, he nonetheless argued:

> However we select from nature a complex [of phenomena] using the criterion of simplicity, in no case will its theoretical treatment turn out to be forever appropriate (sufficient) ... I do not doubt that the day will come when [general relativity], too, will have to yield to another one, for reasons which at present we do not yet surmise. I believe that this process of deepening theory has no limits.[403]

And of course, once quantum mechanics was conceptualised, even physical observation could only be indirect. Werner Heisenberg's "observation in principle" meant that we could infer the existence of quantum entities and effects probabilistically.[404] Even scientific research was not inevitably "causal" in orientation or expectation.

In the twentieth century this issue was taken up by philosophers of science and by sociologists to suggest that observation of natural phenomena is itself shaped and constrained by paradigms that can actually block fresh insight. No observation is free from cognitive preconceptions, and science is most often built through collective insight.[405] Science is a social practice that demands of its participants that they adhere to specific "norms of rational argumentation, evidence and impartiality",[406] but scientists sometimes breach these norms. Scientific discovery is not just the incremental accretion of knowledge that edges closer to "reality" or "truth", though incrementalism does support many advances.[407] The history of science is also replete with leaps and setbacks resulting from blinding insight that dislodges assumptions.[408]

What is true for the natural sciences is emphatically so for social science. Weber argued long ago that "social facts" are not the same as "natural facts". Social meaning is created through human interactions; "facts" in society are as much about understanding as explaining.[409] In surveying the fundamentals of Weberian thought, one commentator emphasises that "[t]here is no absolutely 'objective' scientific analysis of culture or of social phenomena independent of special and one-sided viewpoints".[410] Dewey made a related point, suggesting that the only meaningful social facts are those bound up in human purposes; social facts inevitably possess both subjective and objective elements.[411] Hannah Arendt argued to similar effect, suggesting that "[t]he more people's standpoints I have present in my mind while I am pondering a given issue ... the stronger will be the capacity for representative thinking and the more valid my final conclusions, my opinion".[412] Constellations of social facts produce institutions or complex social practices.[413]

Durkheim also emphasised the importance of social facts but disagreed fundamentally with Weber on how best to understand them. We have seen that for Durkheim the social took precedence over the individual, but he thought that social facts were objective, the product of the common consciousness.[414] That is why, as we have also seen, Durkheim believed that truth is "something that in certain respects imposes itself upon us",[415] and this was a source of much of his heated objection to pragmatism.[416] But it may be that Durkheim and the pragmatists were simply speaking past one another. Durkheim was focused upon moral and mythical – culturally constitutive – truth, and the early pragmatists on scientific – including social scientific – truth.[417] Even Durkheim acknowledged that truth, although in some senses objective and not mutually constructed, is nonetheless mutable. That is logically consistent with his view that reality itself is constantly changing, a viewpoint shared with Weber and the pragmatists.[418]

As I have already suggested, it is fundamentally important to recognize that just because truth or "laws" are liable to change did not mean for the early pragmatists that truth claims are impossible, that "everything is relative". Dewey argued that a form of objective truth can be found in the shared practices of societies – and in groups of what he called "inquirers" – because the knowledge created through interactive practices is socially *necessary*. What is more, inquirers establish rules for what counts as a "good argument" and what can be used as proof, thereby pushing against relativism.[419] For Dewey, then, knowledge was a form of stable understanding. But as I have already suggested, that stability can be disrupted, and received truths displaced, by further inquiry. As Amartya Sen emphasises, reason itself is predicated on continuous questioning. That is why there is usually a "plurality of sustainable reasons" for any course of action.[420]

Following in the footsteps of Peirce, Misak makes the key point with elegant simplicity: "a true belief is one which would stand up to the evidence and reasons, were we to inquire as far as we could on the matter".[421] Although we know that our conceptions of truth have evolved in ways that are contingent on historical, social and material circumstances, we still aim at getting things right.[422] In day-to-day practices we must employ some concept of truth all the time, because otherwise we could not enter into productive assertion and dialogue.[423] We open up dialogue with each other to *engage*, to offer arguments and evidence, so as to improve upon our thinking and acting, not just to set out eternally parallel positions.[424] Peirce helps us to see that although the truth is never absolutely sure, corresponding to a forever-fixed external reality, we can assess our current version against currently understood facts, while still acknowledging that those facts may be proven wrong at some point in the indistinct future. In asserting truth for the purposes of aiming at getting things right, we are betting that our beliefs are unlikely to be overturned by further evidence and argument. This truth claim is essential for productive human interaction, while it remains modest and acknowledges mutability.[425]

Far from encouraging constant doubt, then, a strong tradition in the pragmatist approach to potentially changing truth supports the acceptance of frames of reference that allow us to function day-to-day in socio-political contexts. Pragmatism reveals that radical doubt is fundamentally unproductive as an intellectual posture. Because "we should be content to act without the privilege of basing [our] ... decisions on secure and universally valid knowledge", we can actually make practical decisions and get on with our lives, even as we continue to question assumptions and seek for deeper understanding.[426]

I want to stress a final point implicit in Rorty's short description of pragmatism with which I began this section. Because there is no human "essence" or "nature" that transcends culture, pragmatism acknowledges and respects human and social diversity. Knowledge is created in human interaction and emerges within specific cultural contexts. A powerful example is found today in the much-delayed recognition by settler societies of the richness of "traditional knowledge" in indigenous societies.[427] But interaction also engages culture to culture and society to society. Knowledge can be and is built mutually across borders. Of course, more participants create more complexity, but Dewey argued that plurality would allow for greater recognition of the most profound issues and the likelihood of achieving more workable approaches to problems.[428] Reality is not straightforward, as President Obama reminds us: "Glory and tragedy, courage and stupidity – one set of truths didn't negate the other."[429] Misak suggests that the pragmatist respect for plural viewpoints entails other commitments as well:

> Respect for persons is required, as we must take account of how others report their experiences if we are to have any hope of arriving at the best answers to our questions about justice and fairness. Autonomy is required, as, at least in the first instance, I am able to articulate my own experiences in a more accurate way than someone else. What is good for me will thus largely be an internal matter, be a matter for me, not for experts or politicians.[430]

I now want to link these pragmatist insights to the expanding study of practices in the social sciences. In so doing, I will build towards a contemporary understanding of the rule of law that is grounded in shared social practices that are transformed into legal obligations through adherence to particular objectives and procedural commitments. To get there I must address two deceptively simple questions: how do we learn to perform the practices that make up our contributions to society? And, then, how do some of those practices turn into law?

Notes

325 Alan Bennett, *The History Boys* (London: Faber & Faber, 2004).

326 See *Cameron Practical Wisdom*, 14–15, 56–8; *Cameron Phronesis*, 1; Elizabeth Cohen, *The Political Value of Time: Citizenship, Duration, and Democratic Justice* (Cambridge University Press, 2018), 66–7.

327 Duke, 37.

328 *Cameron Phronesis*, 1.

329 Kraut. See also Chris Brown, "The 'Practice Turn', Phronesis and Classical Realism: Towards a Phronetic International Political Theory" (2012) 40 *Millennium: J. Int'l Studies* 439, 445, 441; *Habermas Discourse*, 199 (emphasising Aristotle's view that no norm can apply itself, but is always being reasoned with in a practical setting).

330 See Dimitri Gutas, "Avicenna's Philosophical Project", in Peter Adamson (ed.), *Interpreting Avicenna: Critical Essays* (Cambridge University Press, 2013), 28; Deborah Black, "Certitude, Justification, and the Principles of Knowledge in Avicenna's Epistemology", in Peter Adamson (ed.), *Interpreting Avicenna: Critical Essays* (Cambridge University Press, 2013), 120. A distinction is important, however, because Avicenna also believed that there were two levels of knowledge, that which exists in the world and for which experience was crucial, and that which fills the after-world – this was true (eternal) knowledge. See Sari Nuseibeh, "Al'Aql al-Qudsi: Avicenna's Subjective Theory of Knowledge" (1989) 69 *Studia Islamica* 39, 39, 54.

331 Contrary to Rawls, who argued that "the self is prior to the ends which are affirmed by it". John Rawls, *A Theory of Justice* (Cambridge, MA: Harvard University Press, 1971), 560 [hereinafter *Rawls Justice*]. For a friendly but comprehensively critical reading of Rawls, see Sen, 58, 69, 85, 90.

332 Duke, 11, 16.

333 Duke, 110, 118, 168. See also Peter Katzenstein and Lucia Seybert, "Power Complexities and Political Theory", in Peter Katzenstein and Lucia Seybert (eds), *Protean Power: Exploring the Uncertain and Unexplained in World Politics* (Cambridge University Press, 2018), 267, 291 [hereinafter *Katzenstein and Seybert Power*].

334 Lawrence Berman, "The Ethical Values of Maimonides within the Context of Islamicate Civilization", in Joel Kraemer (ed.), *Perspectives on Maimonides: Philosophical*

and Historical Studies (Oxford: Littman Library of Jewish Civilization, Oxford University Press, 1991), 13, 20 [hereinafter *Berman Maimonides*].

335 Talcott Parsons, "Introduction", to *Weber Theory*, 16. See 93 for Max Weber himself. And see John Searle, *The Construction of Social Reality* (New York: Free Press, 1995), 4 [hereinafter *Searle Construction*]. I am aware that Searle was stripped of his emeritus status at the University of California Berkeley in 2019 for independently verified sexual harassment. In citing him and his important work, I am in no way condoning his behaviour which was, on public accounts, totally unacceptable. See at: http://dailynous.com/2019/06/21/searle-found-violated-sexual-harassment-policies. See also Jörg Friedrichs and Friedrich Kratochwil, "On Acting and Knowing: How Pragmatism Can Advance International Relations Research and Methodology" (2009) 63 *IO* 701, 725.

336 Cochran, 528

337 See the discussion of Philip Kitcher on Dewey's conception of moral progress in Cheryl Misak, "Kitcher on Moral Progress", in Philip Kitcher (ed.), *Homo Quaerens: Progress, Truth, and Values* (forthcoming) (manuscript on file with the author) [hereinafter *Misak Moral Progress*]. But see Lechner and Frost, 211 (on the role of practice theory, to be discussed below, as essentially descriptive).

338 John Dewey, "Experience and Nature", in *The Later Works, 1925–53*, ed. Jo Ann Boydston (Carbondale: Southern Illinois University Press, 1996), 18 [hereinafter *Dewey Experience*].

339 See the discussion in Sullivan, 60–1, 75–6, 80.

340 *Arendt On Violence*, 82.

341 Canovan in *Arendt Human Condition*, xx; Lacroix and Pranchère, 225.

342 *Arendt Human Condition*, 200.

343 Lacroix and Pranchère, 217. A comparable view had previously been adopted by the Cambridge polymath Frank Ramsey, who moved from the search for "absolute truth" to a "quest for beliefs that would work best for human beings" or what economists call the "feasible first best". Cheryl Misak, *Frank Ramsey: A Sheer Excess of Powers* (Oxford University Press, 2020), xxvii, 144, 277, 312 [hereinafter *Misak Ramsey*]. For a moving short introduction to the extraordinary life and contributions of Ramsey, see Anthony Gottlieb, "The Thinker's Thinker: We're Still Catching Up with One of the Greatest Minds of the Last Century", *The New Yorker*, 4 May 2020, 76 ("The prominent American philosopher Donald Davidson was one of the thinkers to experience what he dubbed 'the Ramsey effect'. You'd make a thrilling breakthrough only to find that Ramsey had got there first").

344 In his detailed and nuanced exploration of the concept of justice, Nobel laureate Amartya Sen adopts a similar position, arguing that the focus of our work in societies should be on actions that create "practical justice" rather than defining institutions that are perfectly just, much less in imagining a perfectly just society. Sen, 9–10, 68, 85, 105, 410.

345 John Dewey, *Human Nature and Conduct* (New York: Henry Holt, 1922), *passim* [hereinafter *Dewey Human Nature*]. See also *Adler World Ordering*, 52; Gunther Hellmann, "Pragmatism and International Relations" (2009) 11 *Int'l Studies Rev.* 638, 639.

346 See Lechner and Frost, 5 (discussing Hegel). Bourdieu adopted the same position, describing his theory of practice as a "philosophy of action". Lechner and Frost, 64, 131. As I have already mentioned, this perspective is completely contrary to that of philosopher John Rawls for whom individual identity – who we believe ourselves to be and what we believe – is prior to social interaction. Discussed in Michael Sandel, *Liberalism and the Limits of Justice*, 2nd edn (Cambridge University Press, 1998), 62 [hereinafter *Sandel Limits*].

347 *Arendt Human Condition*, 200–1; *Arendt On Violence*, 51–2. And see *Adler World Ordering*, 293; *Katzenstein and Seybert Power*, 288–9.

348 Christian Bueger and Frank Gadinger, *International Practice Theory*, 2nd edn (London: Palgrave Macmillan, 2018), 27, 89–90 (describing "practice theory" in ways that are completely aligned with theoretical pragmatism) [hereinafter *Bueger and Gadinger Theory*]. But see Lechner and Frost, 55–6, 103, 219 (arguing that participants in a practice are not oriented towards goals, but are only subscribing to shared rules or conditions). Lechner and Frost adopt this understanding of practices so as to eschew utilitarianism. In so doing they are actually confusing a utilitarian approach with what I call "process consequentialism". The latter approach, typical of pragmatists and the practice theorists influenced by them, does not require a commitment to a shared substantive goal (like the greatest happiness for the largest number), only to measuring the worth of practices, and norms and rules, by their ability to point towards further knowledge. I agree with Lechner and Frost that self-interest is not the only way to understand people's willingness to enter into social practices. Lechner and Frost, 139. Amartya Sen appropriately distinguishes reasoning from consequences and utilitarianism. Sen, 217–19.

349 *Rorty Human Rights*, 116–19. (Rorty is described as neo-pragmatist because he updated pragmatism after the analytic turn in linguistic philosophy. I thank an anonymous reviewer for clarifying this point.) I do not agree with Rorty, however, on a key point. He has argued that there is no foundational conception of right and wrong, other than being in community. This would mean that one could be a good pragmatist and a neo-Nazi. Richard Rorty, *Philosophy and Social Hope* (New York: Penguin, 1999), 636–7. Later I will argue that not everything built in community is "true". But Rorty was a radical relativist, supporting "the view that every belief on a certain topic, or perhaps about any topic is as good as every other". Richard Rorty, *Consequences of Pragmatism* (Minneapolis: University of Minnesota Press, 1982), 166 [hereinafter *Rorty Consequences*].

350 Richard Rorty, *Truth and Progress: Philosophical Papers* (Cambridge University Press, 1998), 175.

351 *Dewey Experience*, 9.

352 William James, quoted in *Adler World Ordering*, 119.

353 *Adler World Ordering*, 118. Thanks to Cheryl Misak for helping me to shape this point.

354 *Walters on Dicey*, 362–3, 366.

355 Friedrich Kratochwil, *The Status of Law in World Society: Meditations on the Rule and Role of Law* (Cambridge University Press, 2014), 25, 261 et seq. [hereinafter *Kratochwil Status*]. See also Lechner and Frost, 215.

356 *Misak Truth*, 51. For the sake of completeness, it should be noted that Mao Tse Tung held the same view, arguing that humans can only "discover truth through practice and through practice again verify the truth". Quoted in Kamrava, 29. This only goes to show that moral hazard may arise in any philosophical position.

357 Brożek, 46.

358 John Dewey, "Logical Method and the Law" (1924) 10 *Cornell L. Rev.* 17, 24. See also *Adler World Ordering*, 36, 168, 223 (on creative selection and retention of practices and "collective social learning").

359 Daniel Graham, "Heraclitus", *The Stanford Encyclopedia of Philosophy*, available at: https://plato.stanford.edu/archives/fall2019/entries/heraclitus. See also *Adler World Ordering*, 45. Hannah Arendt was also fascinated by the complexity of time, and saw memory as the vehicle that drew past and present together, providing a platform for freeing oneself by projecting into the future. See Joanna Vecchiarelli Scott, "Hannah Arendt's Secular Augustinianism", in Mark Vessey, Karla Pollmann and Allan Fitzgerald (eds), *History, Apocalypse, and the Secular Imagination* (Bowling Green, OH: Philosophy Documentation Center, 1999), 293, 298 (Augustinian Studies) [hereinafter *Scott on Arendt*].

360 *Adler World Ordering*, 48.

361 Martha Nussbaum, *The Fragility of Goodness: Luck and Ethics in Greek Tragedy and Philosophy* (Cambridge University Press, 2001), vol. II, 305.

362 Alfred North Whitehead, *Process and Reality*, ed. David Griffin and Donald Sherburne, corrected edn (New York: Free Press, 1978), 23, 28.

363 Canovan in *Arendt Human Condition*, xix–xx, xxix. Arendt inherited this focus on beginnings from Augustine. See *Scott on Arendt*, 294.

364 *Arendt Human Condition*, 9, 176–7, 296; *Arendt On Violence*, 82.

365 Hannah Arendt, *Between Past and Future: Eight Exercises in Political Thought* (New York: Penguin, 1961), 146 (essay "What is Freedom?") [hereinafter *Arendt Between Past*]. See also Anthony Lang, "Constitutions are the Answer!: Hannah Arendt and the Egyptian Revolution", in K Hiruta (ed.), *Arendt on Freedom, Liberation, and Revolution*, Philosophers in Depth series (London: Palgrave Macmillan, 2019), 225, 235 (on Arendt's commitment to the creation of space for public freedom), available at: https://doi.org/10.1007/978-3-030-11695-8_9.

366 *Arendt Human Condition*, 190–1, 233–4. It is no accident that Arendt, like her intellectual forebear, Augustine, was writing at a time of "rapid, violent shifts" in paradigms and institutions. *Scott on Arendt*, 296. John Searle articulated a similarly action- and process-focused theory in describing how social reality is constructed. *Searle Construction, passim.*

367 *Adler World Ordering*, 102 (quoting Brian Arthur).

368 Helge Dedek, "Where the 'Real Action' Is: From Comparative Law to Cosmopolitan Jurisprudence", in Helge Dedek (ed.), *A Cosmopolitan Jurisprudence: Essays in Memory of H. Patrick Glenn* (Cambridge University Press, 2022), 3, 19 [hereinafter *Dedek Jurisprudence*]. Glenn always focused on the compendious term "information" to include data from many sources and traditions. See Mauro Bussani, "How to Do

Comparative Law: Some Lessons to Be Learned", in *Dedek Jurisprudence* 29, 38, 40; Martin Krygier, "Too Much Information", in *Dedek Jurisprudence*, 117, 123; David Nelken, "Learning from Patrick Glenn: Tradition, Change, and Innovation", in *Dedek Jurisprudence*, 161, 168–9 (for Glenn, "[t]he past is mobilized to invent a – future . . .").

369 Christian Bueger and Frank Gadinger, "The Play of International Practice" (2015) 59 *Int'l Studies Q.* 449, 453, 455 [hereinafter *Bueger and Gadinger Practice*]; *Adler World Ordering*, 32, 45–6; *Arendt Human Condition*, 190–1. Adler argues that this emphasis on "becoming" draws on Darwinian evolutionary theory, Max Planck's quantum theory and Albert Einstein's theory of relativity. Each emphasises processes, often tiny in themselves, that lead to fundamental change. *Adler World Ordering*, 51.

370 Karl Popper, *A World of Propensities* (Bristol: Thoemmes, 1990), 17.

371 *Bueger and Gadinger Theory*, 89–90.

372 Friedrich and Kratochwil, 725. For a sophisticated exposition of the debate, however, see Alexander Wendt, "The Agent–Structure Problem in International Relations Theory" (1987) 41 *IO* 335 (identifying practices as the link between agents and structures).

373 Anthony Giddens, *Central Problems in Social Theory: Action, Structure and Contradiction in Social Analysis* (London: Macmillan, 1979). See also Roy Bhaskar, *The Possibility of Naturalism* (New York: Humanities Press, 1979). I agree with Adler, however, that even Giddens' so-called "structuration theory" may not be fully complete in that it tends to analyse agent and structure separately despite the assertion that the two interact in society. It also underplays the role of emotion and expectations in the motivation of agents, and over-emphasises the role of unacknowledged rules in social structures. This results in a bias towards stability in the analysis, which perhaps unintentionally reduces the power of agency, even as the theory seeks to affirm its importance. *Adler World Ordering*, 216.

374 Bourdieu stresses this relational construction of identity. See Didier Bigo, "Pierre Bourdieu and International Relations: Power of Practices, Practices of Power" (2011) 5 *Int'l Pol. Sociology* 225, 236; *Bueger and Gadinger Theory*, 100.

375 *Sandel Limits*, 172, 179–80. Duke, 95 (". . . Aristotle has a sense of the flourishing – and even agency – of the polis as a unified whole which obtains in a manner that is irreducible to the wellbeing of its individual members").

376 Risse, 7.

377 Peristiany, xxx (arguing that for Durkheim "[s]ociety limits the possibilities of action – it does not determine individual action").

378 *Katzenstein and Seybert Uncertainty*, 38.

379 Ann Swidler, "What Anchors Cultural Practices", in Theodore Schatzki et al. (eds), *The Practice Turn in Contemporary Theory* (London: Routledge, 2001), 74, 86, 90, 99 ("there are 'anchoring practices' which play a key role in reproducing larger systems of discourse and practice").

380 Thanks to Cheryl Misak for this useful point.

381 See also Emanuel Adler and Vincent Pouliot, "International Practices: Introduction and Framework", in Emanuel Adler and Vincent Pouliot (eds), *International Practices* (New York: Cambridge University Press, 2011), 16 [hereinafter *Adler and Pouliot Practices*].

382 Cochran, 527, 530.

383 Lechner and Frost, 18.

384 John Dewey, "Logical Conditions of a Scientific Treatment of Morality", in *The Middle Works, 1899–1924*, ed. Jo Ann Boydston (Carbondale: Southern Illinois University Press, 1985), 38–9, cited in Cochran, 533; *Cameron Practical Wisdom*, 24–8, 163.

385 *Misak Ramsey*, 330.

386 See *Cameron Practical Wisdom*, 23; Friedrichs and Kratochwil, 706.

387 Cochran, 538; *Adler World Ordering*, 120. These two points are sometimes collectively described as "intersubjective" knowledge creation. See, e.g., Reus-Smit, 64.

388 Charles Sanders Peirce, *Collected Papers of Charles Sanders Peirce*, vols 1–8, ed. Charles Hartshorne, Paul Weiss and Arthur Burks (Cambridge, MA: Belknap Press, 1901), vol. 8, 112. See also Friedrichs and Kratochwil, 705–6; *Bueger and Gadinger Theory*, 28; Risse, 1; Haas and Haas, 574, 583. This view was strongly contested by Wittgenstein who believed that "[t]he philosopher is not a citizen of any community of ideas". *Misak Ramsey*, 368.

389 *Berman Maimonides*, 24–5. Maimonides thought that most law fell into the category of the generally accepted rather than the self-evidently true. *Berman Maimonides*, 27.

390 Quoted in Cochran, 544. See also *Adler World Ordering*, 119.

391 Muhammad Hamidullah, *The Emergence of Islam* (Islamabad: Islamic Research Institute, 1993), 97–9; Ahmed Fekry Ibrahim, "The Sunni Legal Tradition: An Overview of Pluralism, Formalism, and Reform", in Helge Dedek (ed.), A Cosmopolitan Jurisprudence: Essays in Memory of H. Patrick Glenn (Cambridge University Press, 2022), 180 (on "interpretive freedom" and "multiple Islams"), 183, 185, 188, 195 (on "pragmatic eclecticism"), 197 (on mining diverse Islamic interpretive practices), 200–1.

392 Greco, 47, 51, 53 ("team sport"), 56, 100. See also *Walters on Dicey*, 374 ("... truths may only be identified internally within the practices of interpretive discourse that make normative community possible ..."), 374–5.

393 David Brooks, "The Rotting of the Republican Mind", *New York Times*, 26 November 2020, available at: www.nytimes.com/2020/11/26/opinion/republican-disinformation.html.

394 John Ruggie, "What Makes the World Hang Together? Neo-utilitarianism and the Social Constructivist Challenge" (1998) 52 *IO* 855, 870 (discussing John Searle).

395 See, e.g., Jeffrey Dunoff and Joel Trachtman, "A Functional Approach to International Constitutionalization", in Jeffrey Dunoff and Joel Trachtman (eds), *Ruling the World? Constitutionalism, International Law, and Global Governance* (Cambridge University Press, 2009), 3, 22–4.

396 Frega, 722.

397 Oliver Wendell Holmes, *The Common Law* (London: Macmillan, 1882), 1. Note that Holmes is not rejecting a role for logic, only an exclusive role. See David Dyzenhaus, *The Long Arc of Legality: Hobbes, Kelsen, Hart* (Cambridge University Press, 2022), 384 [hereinafter *Dyzenhaus Long Arc*]. For a comprehensive discussion of Holmes' evolutionary view of law as a human institution, see Susan Haack, "On Legal

Pragmatism: Where Does 'The Path of the Law' Lead Us?" (2005) 50 *Am. J. Jurisprudence* 71, esp. at 85–7. I quarrel with Holmes, however, in what I take to be his over-emphasis upon formal adjudication in hierarchical courts as the apogee of deliberation. On Holmes and the centrality of courts and judges to the meaning and authority of "law", see Haack, esp. at 80–2. As we will see, I believe that deliberation is a broader and necessarily more inclusive phenomenon, even within legal systems.

398 Cheryl Misak, "A Pragmatist Account of Legitimacy and Authority: Holmes, Ramsey and the Moral Force of Law", in Susan Dieleman, David Rondel and Christopher Voparil (eds), *Pragmatism and Justice* (Oxford University Press, 2017), 295 [hereinafter *Misak Legitimacy*].

399 Cochran, 527, 530; Lechner and Frost, 205; Haas and Haas, 588. See also Misak's discussion of how Frank Ramsey moved towards a pragmatist understanding of truth over his short career. *Misak Ramsey*, 384–8, 404. (It is not possible to comprehend the "truth or falsity of thoughts without considering the effects they have on our acting either directly or indirectly through dispositional beliefs". *Misak Ramsey*, 388.)

400 Cheryl Misak, "Nothing Scoundrelous About Truth", in Melissa Schwartzberg and Philip Kitcher (eds), *Truth and Evidence* (New York: New York University Press, 2021), 176, 180 (NOMOS LXIV: *Yearbook of the Am. Soc. Pol. & Legal Phil.*) [hereinafter *Misak Scoundrelous*]. Friedrichs and Kratochwil, 703 (citing Spinoza); Lechner and Frost, 25, 44. Of course, I do not dispute that there are theocratic societies where the notion of truth is far more fixed, even "eternal" in the sense of derivation from divine authority. But that is no longer the shared understanding of most cultural communities around the globe.

401 Friedrichs and Kratochwil, 704 (referencing Kant).

402 Haas and Haas, 584.

403 Quoted in Abraham Pais, *Subtle is the Lord: The Science and the Life of Albert Einstein* (Oxford University Press, reissued 2005), 325.

404 Lechner and Frost, 204.

405 Thomas Kuhn, *The Structure of Scientific Revolutions: 50th Anniversary Edition* (University of Chicago Press, 2012) (with an introduction by Ian Hacking), *passim*. See also Vasso Kindi and Theodor Arabatzis (eds), *Kuhn's The Structure of Scientific Revolutions Revisited* (New York: Routledge, 2012). And see, for similar insights, Bruno Latour, *Science in Action: How to Follow Scientists and Engineers Through Society* (Cambridge, MA: Harvard University Press, 1987). On the different versions of scientific discovery put forward by Kuhn and Karl Popper, see Michael Strevens, *The Knowledge Machine: How Irrationality Created Modern Science* (New York: Liveright, 2020), *passim*.

406 Lechner and Frost, 207.

407 Friedrichs and Kratochwil, 712. This view of evolutionary science was strongly favoured by Charles Sanders Peirce, largely because it reinforced the view of knowledge creation as a collective undertaking. See Haack, 91. See also *Misak Truth*, 97 (on pragmatism rejecting an ever-closer approximation to an ideal of inquiry or inquirer).

408 Examples abound in the dramatic insights of Copernicus, Galileo, Darwin, Einstein, Maxwell, Bohr, Franklin, Watson and Crick (though they too built on the previous

work of Lord Todd), and, more recently, Yoshizumi Ishino (who accidentally discovered the DNA sequence of CRISPR, allowing for gene editing).

409 Friedrichs and Kratochwil, 705.

410 J. T. Eldridge, "Introductory Essay", in *Weber Interpretation*, 12.

411 Discussed in Cochran, 531–2. See also Haas and Haas, 590; Ruggie, 856, 858.

412 *Arendt Between Past*, 241.

413 Lechner and Frost, 186–8. Complex practices may also be described as "macro practices" if they encompass a range of practices within them. Lechner and Frost, 191. The obvious example is the practice of the state (which includes practices of economic organisation, bureaucracy, politics, etc.), or the family (which includes practices of marriage, child-rearing, economic distribution, sexuality, etc.).

414 *Durkheim Sociology*, 24–5.

415 *Durkheim Pragmatism*, 68, 70, 85; and see John Allcock, "Editorial Introduction to the English Translation", in *Durkheim Pragmatism*, xxxiv, xxxviii.

416 *Durkheim Pragmatism*, 24, 37, 54. He is not alone. Some contemporary theorists also challenge pragmatism, especially in law, as "essentially banal". See the discussion in Sullivan, 3–5. I will try to show why I think that this criticism is simply wrong.

417 *Durkheim Pragmatism*, 2–3, 76, 84, 86; see also Allcock, xxxviii; Soper and Fetzer, 8 (on nationalism as a myth to replace religion, drawing on Durkheim). On the cognitive role of myth and culture, see *Adler World Ordering*, 14; Brożek, 151; *Bueger and Gadinger Theory*, 21. Misak makes the case for contemporary pragmatists to focus on moral truth (as an expression of continuing inquiry), not surrendering the field. *Misak Truth*, *passim*.

418 *Durkheim Pragmatism*, 21, 24. See also Cladis, 75.

419 *Misak Truth*, 57 and 156; Friedrich and Kratochwil, 712; Haas and Haas, 591; Lechner and Frost, 207.

420 Sen, 180–3, 195 ("If rationality were a church, it would be a rather broad church"). By invoking philosophers and social theorists in this discussion of pragmatism, it should be clear that I am not aligning myself with the "everyday pragmatism" (which is expressly anti-theory) of Richard Posner. Richard Posner, *Law, Pragmatism and Democracy* (Cambridge, MA: Harvard University Press, 2003). For a trenchant critique of "Posner's Unpragmatic Pragmatism", see Sullivan, ch. 3.

421 *Misak Truth*, 1, 49, 97. See also Haack, 91; Sullivan, 5. Misak points out that one contemporary pragmatist, Richard Rorty, adopts the more extreme view that no form of truth is ever possible. I agree with Misak and Haack that Rorty has moved beyond the frames of pragmatism as understood by its progenitors. *Misak Truth*, 12–18; Haack, 103–4.

422 *Misak Scoundrelous*, 185 (quoting Jeffrey Stout). Aristotle long ago offered a parallel insight, that we should "look for precision in each class of things just so far as the nature of the subject admits". Aristotle, *[The Nicomachean] Ethics*, trans. J. A. K. Thomson (Harmondsworth: Penguin, 1976), I.iii.iv [hereinafter *The Nicomachean Ethics*].

423 See Emanuel Adler and Alena Drieschova, "The Epistemological Challenge of Truth-Subversion to the Liberal International Order" (2021) *IO*, available at: www.cambridge.org/core/journals/international-organization/article/epistemological-challenge-of-truth-subversion-to-the-liberal-international-order/D2B6C964CBAAD892DB7ED5A62DBB2932.

424 Huw Price, "Truth as Convenient Friction" (2003) 100 *J. Phil.* 167.

425 *Misak Scoundrelous*, 182–5. See also Amartya Sen invoking Bernard Williams on "aiming at truth", Sen, 40, 401 (on going as "far as we can" in making reasoned and critical arguments).

426 Friedrich and Kratochwil, 711; *Misak Truth*, 2. Richard Rorty would go much further, arguing that there is no possible "objective truth", only solidarity. This is not Peirce or Dewey's position, and I think it is a dangerous over-stretching of pragmatist insight. See Haack, 77.

427 See, e.g., Rosemary Coombe, "The Recognition of Indigenous People's Knowledge in International Law" (2001) 14 *St Thomas L. Rev.* 275 (Sixth Annual Tribal Sovereignty Symposium: Defending Indigenous Peoples' Heritage and Autonomy); Malgosia Fitzmaurice, "The Dilemma of Traditional Knowledge: Indigenous Peoples and Traditional Knowledge" (2008) 10 *Int'l Community L. Rev.* 255; Julie Maldonado et al., "Engagement with Indigenous Peoples and Honouring Traditional Knowledge Systems", in K. Jacobs, S. Moser and J. Buizer (eds), *The US National Climate Assessment* (2015), available at: https://link.springer.com/chapter/10.1007/978-3-319-41802-5_9. See also Sousa Santos on the much-needed recognition of "epistemologies of the south", including indigenous knowledge. Sousa Santos, 589.

428 Cochran, 544; *Misak Truth*, 78.

429 Obama, 444.

430 *Misak Truth*, 115.

CHAPTER SIX

Social Practices, Background Knowledge and Law

> Human beings are, necessarily, actors who cannot become something before they have first pretended to be it; and they can be divided, not into the hypocritical and the sincere, but into the sane who know they are acting and the mad who do not.
>
> W. H. Auden, *The Age of Anxiety*[*]

> What I propose, therefore, is very simple: it is nothing more than to think what we are doing.
>
> Hannah Arendt[431]

I SUSPECT THAT MOST OF us have an intuitive sense that we learn best by doing. Throughout high school and into university, my passion outside my studies was acting. I was lucky to find talented teacher-directors, and then equally passionate fellow student-directors and brilliant professionals who encouraged and stretched me. My extraordinary public high school drama teacher had high expectations. Ours were not your average "high school productions". We worked for months on major plays with big casts and serious production values.

From the very beginning of my acting experience, I noticed a strange phenomenon: no matter how well you knew your lines, how often you had looked over a scene alone at home, it was not until interacting with fellow actors that a scene would come alive. And it was only after rehearsing many times that you could begin to plumb the depths of meaning in a play, the possibilities for further exploration.[432] Later in university, when

I was lucky enough to work with professional directors from New York and the United Kingdom, I came to understand that the smallest nuance in inflection, the slightest change in posture or tone, could reveal new insights into character and meaning. It was thrilling, and also created a greater sense of responsibility. What seemed expressively honest? What gestures or vocal intonations might just be flashy and superficial?

Although I have never been a sportsman, I suspect that similar processes create great athletes. Professional baseball player Pete Rose is quoted as saying: "Practice the game the way you're going to play the game. Practice hard and play hard. Run hard and above all else, hustle every moment you're on the field where you are practicing or playing in a game." Footballer David Beckham said even more simply: "My secret is practise." One of the greatest basketball players of all time, Michael Jordan, refined the point:

> You can practice shooting eight hours a day, but if your technique is wrong, then all you become is very good at shooting the wrong way. Get the fundamentals down and the level of everything you do will rise.

It is not just repetition that makes perfect, but refining one's work through the discovery and often greater precision that comes along with repetition. Sports celebrities show the same insight as Aristotle: "For the things we have to learn before we can do them, we learn by doing them."[433]

Here is the question I want to explore: does "practise make perfect" not just for individuals but for teams, institutions and whole societies? I should be clear at the outset that "practice" is, of course, both a verb and noun. Sports figures practise their sport in the sense that they repeat their moves and they interact with team-mates to perfect "plays". Similarly, actors rehearse repetitively and learn in that interactive process. In these efforts, however, sport figures and actors also participate in "a practice" – that of games with rules and sets of expectations, like playing fair, or being in a theatre with a stage that distances you from an audience, but where that convention can also be intentionally broken. In what follows, I will explore both the verb and the noun of "practice". In so doing, I draw on a rich vein of socio-political thought that helps us to understand how practising any art or craft (the active verb) depends upon our shared understandings of the rules and expectations of the practice (the noun).

In the burgeoning literature on practices, various definitions are offered, but I find the work of international relations scholar Emanuel Adler most helpful. He describes practices as:

> ... socially meaningful patterned actions that, performed more or less competently, simultaneously embody, act out, and possibly reify background knowledge and discourse in and on the material world.[434]

There are quite a few distinct ideas packed into that single sentence. Let me explore a few.

First, practices are made up of actions in society which include but are not limited to discourse. Dewey conceptualised "the public" (citizens in democracies) as a "*community of action* rather than as a community of discourse".[435] Hannah Arendt adopted a similar view, arguing that both speech and action were integral to the classical understanding of the "political" and "social". She reminds us that "the stature of the Homeric Achilles can be understood only if one sees him as 'the doer of great deeds *and* the speaker of great words'".[436] This observation is directly connected to the pragmatist view that our attempts to understand reality are necessarily fluid and changeable. As we have seen, humans act and interact in a world of processes, thereby creating knowledge that is "patterned" and "socially meaningful". The interactions are often verbal because humans work through language,[437] and Habermas suggests that human actions are structured like a language.[438]

As I have previously noted, Habermas was interested in the distinction between "practical reason", which he took to operate either at the individual or societal level, and "communicative reason", the socio-political process taking place within societies and made possible by the use of language in shared public space.[439] The distinction between practical and communicative reason may, however, be overplayed. Aristotle, the progenitor of practical reason, believed that it was the capacity for rational speech generated in practical deliberation that resulted in the human capacity for politics and law.[440] No doubt, communicative reason is central to democratic governance because it is the means by which rational participation – the public giving of reasons – takes place, and collective agreement or consensus can be created.[441]

Habermas admitted, however, that communicative reason requires an idealised conception of communication in which participants in a "language community" must assume "that speakers and hearers can understand a grammatical expression in identical ways".[442] Habermas called this "ideal speech acts" and argued that "language itself supplies the primary source of social integration".[443]

Even if one accepts that language is the primary vehicle for social integration, it is not clear that the simple act of giving reasons is enough to sustain healthy public discourse. Of course, as Arendt always emphasised, totalitarianism flourishes when deliberation is made impossible or actively suppressed. Certainly, for any form of constitutional democracy to flourish, robust public debate is a *sine qua non.* My point is different, that merely articulating *any* reason does not necessarily count as "discourse". Reasons have to be based in some standards of competence and legitimacy. Otherwise, reasons can be mere lies or shared misperceptions. Consider the "reasons" offered up by President Trump for denouncing his election loss as fraudulent: millions of improperly cast ballots; ballots not counted; ballots double counted; corrupt election officials. All utter nonsense. Fake news can be filled with seeming "reasons". That is probably why many modern linguistic theorists have been less sanguine about the emancipatory potential of language. Foucault stressed the ways in which language can include and exclude, that it can simply structure and reaffirm existing abusive, or at least exclusionary, patterns of power and status.[444]

Given Habermas' commitment to communication – language – as the primary means of consensus-building in any society, he was always fascinated by the role of law, that discipline of language par excellence. Over the decades, Habermas shifted from a rather negative view of law as a coloniser of other social practices and institutions (like the family), to a view of law as a largely positive means to help steer the state and economy, hence his interest in a European constitution.[445] Nonetheless, Habermas did not see law as a purveyor of truths that simply had to be accepted by society. He understood law as an ongoing legal discussion that provides only provisional "answers" and that should be focused on the procedures and the discussion, not on one right decision.[446] Theorists of norms and law have built upon Habermas to articulate ideas of "semantic authority" as a basis for legal legitimacy, adding to Weber's sources of authority.[447]

Whether one focuses primarily on discourse, on practical actions or see both as inevitably intertwined, as I do, the starting points for social interaction in the world are not mere voids. That is where the crucial idea of "background knowledge", referred to by Adler in the quote above, comes into play, and where conceptual frames around "discourse" are relevant. Let me focus on those two ideas.

In the contemporary literature on practices, "Background" is a term generally associated with the linguistic philosopher John Searle, although it was employed long before by pragmatist thinkers.[448] Searle emphasised that people are inclined to behave in certain patterned ways. That inclination is created by a "set of Background abilities, dispositions, and capacities" that are not part of the person's "intention". Rather, the Background moulds the behavioural intention. It enables linguistic interpretation as well as perceptual interpretation. It shapes narratives and structures consciousness.[449] Others have used the term "culture" in a broad sense to capture similar insights.[450]

Adler takes the idea of Background and posits that "practices and the background knowledge bound with them are the structural 'stuff' that is passed on in replication in the sociocultural world".[451] Part of the Background is "socially set normative standards" or values, an understanding of "the better" but not an absolutely fixed view of "the good life".[452] This idea is close to Weber's observation that the meaningful content of social relationships is made up of "expectations" to which people simply adhere[453] and to Durkheim's emphasis upon society's building up of "ideals" that shape, but do not dictate, individual actions.[454] Some, but by no means all, of these norms, expectations or ideals become legal norms through processes I will discuss later.[455]

However, Adler disputes Searle in his assertion that Background is given and outside the realm of human intention. Consistent with pragmatist philosophy, Adler suggests that Background is actually built up through human interaction in practices[456] and that it can be reflexive – self-critical as the practices are being undertaken – not merely received or given.[457] Swidler suggests that "practices are more persistent and more likely to structure other domains of thought and action when they constitute social relationships ... than when they are simply habits or assumptions held by individual actors".[458] People in communities of practice share experiences and information and, through that social interaction, they learn, constructing knowledge that shapes insight and behaviour, for good and ill.[459]

Adler's focus on Background created by interaction, as well as the need for critical self-reflection in practices, connects his version of practice theory to the pragmatist tradition rather than to the sociologist Bourdieu, who is often seen as the progenitor of twentieth-century "practice" theories.[460] The importance of this point is that for Adler practices must be understood from the inside, and not from an external, universal or "objective" perspective. Understanding practices is not an exercise in abstract reasoning or external critique.

It is also important to distinguish between the structuring effects of Adler's reflexive background practices and the idea of "habits" found in Weber and in some recent international relations theory. For Weber, habits – conduct founded in repetition – build expectations and move towards social consensus. This sounds like the pragmatists and like Adler. However, it is important to remember that one of Weber's sources of authority is "tradition", which is itself binding because of its "having always existed".[461] Weber's conception of "habit" is stickier than that of Adler and the pragmatists, more constraining, and is used to justify a strong view that habits create a "social order [that] is maintained unthinkingly, unreflectively ...".[462] This conception of habit is also derived from the work of Durkheim who emphasised, as we have seen, a "collective or common conscience" in society that persists over time and strongly shapes individual choice.[463]

The most extensive analysis of habit in the sociological literature was undertaken by Bourdieu. For Bourdieu, "habitus" is the practical sense of "reality" that an individual may gain over the course of a lifetime.[464] Habits are stabilised because the undiscussed and the unformulated (*doxa*) come to dominate. This is close to what in common parlance we might call "received wisdom" or "common sense". But it may also shape what we call "intuition".[465] To be clear, habitus can be positive, benign or deeply negative. Racist assumptions can be habituated just as a fundamental belief in the essential equality of all people. The point is that for

Bourdieu what individuals may perceive as "choice" is actually inscribed on a given situation by a pre-established set of "dispositions" and available "trajectories".[466] I am not suggesting that Bourdieu's "habitus" was absolutely rigid, permitting of no human agency. He thought that these inertial forces were powerful, but they could be displaced through an "objective crisis" (or systemic flux) when dispositions would fail to provide effective guides to action.[467] Nonetheless in most circumstances Bourdieu's habits are close to controlling.

There is debate over whether or not the linguistic philosopher Wittgenstein held a similar view. His "language games", although played amongst individuals, take place within "forms of life"[468] that are powerfully constraining. They shape sets of rules, and "[w]hen I obey a rule, I do not choose. I obey the rule *blindly*".[469] However, some interpret "rules" in Wittgenstein more as "institutions" so that following a rule is really about participation in the practices of the institution.[470] Adler argues that this would connect Wittgenstein's approach to Swidler's conception of "anchoring practices", practices that form the basis upon which other practices are built.[471] Such practices are also sometimes called "constitutive rules".[472] For example, anchoring practices within a constitutional structure – fundamentals like parliamentary supremacy or cabinet government – shape other day-to-day practices of law and politics. Importantly, however, they provide frames, not rigid dictates of action because they are not buried as deeply inside the person as Bourdieu's habits.[473]

Most importantly, people are driven not only by habit and experience, but also by their expectations for the future, on the possibilities of their "becoming".[474] That is why, even for those people who grow up in strong ethical, and particularly religious communities, it is possible to feel deep connection to frames of understanding while also being open to new conceptions and to changing patterns of behaviour. This must be true because we have seen dramatic changes in religious practice in countless countries around the world over the course of the last century. A good example is the so-called "quiet revolution" in Quebec society from the 1960s to the 2000s, with a move from a deeply embedded rural Roman Catholicism to a strikingly high degree of secularism.[475]

The pragmatists were interested in the effects of habit.[476] At the same time, they were strongly committed to furthering human agency, as we have seen. Dewey believed that an individual could gain knowledge through what he called the "practical arts". This was a form of common sense acquired through changing experience. While Dewey would not deny that people operate from implicit Background and habits, he did not believe that they were simply inherited and inevitably re-enacted.[477] Indeed, Dewey believed that habits are often problems – fixed presuppositions that might be wrong – that could be overcome through knowledge gained in practice.[478]

Adler is a principal contemporary exponent of the view that despite the influence of Background, humans retain agency in their lives and in the ordering of societies.[479] They do this through processes of social learning that take place in the shared working out of practices.[480] Adler argues that Background knowledge is Janus-faced:

> Action is "pushed" by the past from background knowledge's dispositions but is "pulled" towards the future with foresight, anticipation and expectations.[481]

In other words, although humans are, of course, shaped by where they have come from, they are also motivated by a world that they anticipate in the future. They possess aspirations that help to guide their choices in life.

I have already introduced the mechanism that allows people and, indeed, societies to change: learning. And I have emphasised that we learn in at least two ways. One is reflexive, where we consider what we know in relation to the context in which we find ourselves and we adjust in real time; we "course correct". A second means of learning is through reflection, where we engage in what Dewey describes as "the active, persistent and careful consideration of any belief or supposed form of knowledge in the light of the grounds that support it".[482] This reflection takes place after our actions and debates, and then allows us to reinsert ourselves into social action and discourse with new understandings. Of course, as Dewey and the pragmatists emphasise, learning is most clearly shaped and directed when we address concrete problems: "Demand for the solution of a perplexity is the steadying and guiding factor of the entire process of reflection."[483]

The key point for now is that Background or habits influence, but do not strictly determine, individual and social action. As Michael Sandel argues, practices create a framework that allows the individual to flourish in community.[484] Practices are potentially creative and change-producing,[485] though they are not necessarily socially or culturally positive. Practice theory is by no means idealist. Adler argues that practices can only create "bounded", meaning limited, progress.[486]

Classical sociology emphasised the importance of networks, interacting groups of people and things, institutions and processes. Durkheim described networks in evocative terms:

> A society that is one in appearance is in reality composed of a multitude of small groups or small social worlds ...
>
> The world is made up of an incalculable number of networks that unite things and beings with each other. These networks are formed of complicated and relatively independent links. The elements that they connect are not fixed, and the very form of the network is subject to change. Made up of a plurality of small systems, each of which is endowed with an autonomous life, it is ceaselessly formed, de-formed and transformed.[487]

Borrowing from the work of Lave and Wenger, Adler specifies a particular type of "network" that he calls a "community of practice".[488]

Lave and Wenger are theorists of social learning; they emphasised that a person, their activities and the external world are constructed together through interaction. They posited the existence of groups of people who "share a concern or a passion for something they do and learn how to do it better as they interact regularly".[489] The passions of these communities of practice are multitudinous, and could include baseball leagues, fans and journalists; diplomats and NGOs seeking to promote nuclear arms control; actors, directors and other mavens of theatre; environmental activists and scientists; promoters of trade negotiations and deals; human rights lawyers and refugee protection groups; and many, many others. Some academics have described such groups as "epistemic communities",[490] but I prefer the term "community of practice" because, as we have seen, these communities are not about abstracted knowledge, or simply the accumulation and passing on of information, but of situated knowledge and practical action.

Knowledge is created by communities of practice, who in turn maintain the knowledge, share it and further develop it through their collective practices.[491] I would note that this description of communities of practice is very close to the way Lon Fuller described the creation of law, and to whose work I will return shortly. Law is formed and maintained through continuing struggles of social practice.[492] Communities of practice interact with other such communities, creating "landscapes of practices" that are both specific to themselves and interwoven with each other.[493]

Adler extends these concepts, arguing that communities of practice create and structure knowledge in a particular way, acting as the "vehicles" through which both selection and replication of ideas and practices take place. They are collective agents in society, agents not only of ideas, but of material actions in the world.[494] Building on some persistent "anchoring practices"[495] (or constitutive rules), these communities of practice create institutions in society that help to stabilise knowledge and develop further practices. It is important to stress that anchoring practices do not preclude change and development because communities of practice continuously interact. In so doing, they learn reflexively and reflectively, measuring their practices against standards of competence generated within the community. What is more, communities of practice do not remain insular; they interact with other communities of practice and they are challenged and tested in their understandings of competent practice. This is what allows for the pragmatist conception of truth – that it is built through complex interactions and is subject to change – to play out.

Stabilisation, or replication of practices, occurs because institutions achieve legitimacy and a social recognition of competent performance, which may lead to the crystallisation or reassertion of social norms.[496] However, stabilisation does not mean that communities of practice are homogeneous; nor do they necessarily create uniformity of perspective, or reinforce shared norms.[497] In Adler's words, they often simply "organize differences" and provide a frame for contestation.[498] This view again builds on the pragmatist "requirement that we try, at least until such attempts fail, to include rather than exclude others".[499] Or, as Misak argues: "legitimacy of policy and decisions taken on behalf of others arises when the institutions promote deliberation and when the views of others have been taken seriously".[500] This is close to Arendt's requirement of "participation" as the key to free citizenship, nationally and transnationally.[501] These insights are fundamental to the rule of law, and its ability to frame both agreement and dissent, as I discuss later.

I will return to the idea of "legitimation" shortly, but it is first worth spending some time on the idea of "competent practices" because we will see that it has direct relevance to understanding how law works in societies. In any community of practice, standards or rules evolve allowing one to assess what is or is not "competent practice". This concept reminds us of Michael Jordan's warning that simply repeating things is not enough; we need to refine "technique". What is more, competence is not merely the performance of a single action in a correct manner, it is the ability to understand, interpret and generally act in accordance with the anchoring practices or constitutive rules that shape our engagement in a practice.[502] This conception of competency is closely linked to the pragmatist belief that "justified knowledge claims" are the product of "rule-following in accordance with the practices of a community". These rules actually limit what is admissible in arguments and they shape what is valid as supporting evidence.[503]

In other words, not every argument is equal to every other because only some arguments "count" within the community of practice. This is evidently true of law, where, as we will see, arguments are structured by rather particular anchoring practices, especially the use of precedent and analogy in addition to the more generic deployment of logic. Discussing the particularities of international law practice, Aalberts and Venzke suggest that the relevant practice "contains within itself the yardstick of what counts as a valid argument" and that the yardstick can evolve or shift over time.[504]

Implicit in the idea that practices are structured by rules is the possibility of "mistake", or what might be termed "incompetent practice".[505] What is more, because knowledge itself is created through mutual interaction, knowledge is itself an achievement from competent practice, and is not simply a product of luck.[506]

But it is not enough that communities of practice assess their competency with *purely* internal measures, for that would mean that utterly brutal or tyrannical practices could be fully "justified" by their own lights. Through our competent practices we aim at truth, but we must also enter into dialogue with others, considering and challenging the insights of other communities of practice as they challenge ours. Dewey argued that inquiry requires the participation of all voices, with each having the ability to offer and to criticise hypotheses. Communities of practice create knowledge through the building up of experience through experiment, but that includes listening to the experience of others. Frank Ramsey argued that this set of processes increases "the weight of one's probabilities" of gaining knowledge and even truth.[507]

Importantly, "competence" is not judged only by arguments but also by actions; knowing how to act within the practice – sometimes called "performative power" – is as meaningful as displaying what is often termed "discursive competence".[508] *Both* are required to be convincing to other members of the community of practice; talk alone is not enough.[509] That is because, as Swidler puts it: "Both discourses and practices are concretely observable in a way that meanings, ideas, and values never really were."[510] Assessing appropriateness engages both practical and norm- or value-based considerations.[511]

The dual quality of competency in practices, being both practical and normative, brings us directly to the question of legitimacy. When members of a community of practice fail to act or argue competently, including failing to allow their ideas and actions to be tested in deliberation with others, their contribution to the practice is undermined. When incompetency becomes generalised within the community, the entire practice may come to be viewed as illegitimate. This result is most likely in transitional times "when disenchantment with practices grows, when practices are seen as failed symbolic performances".[512] This is exactly the view underlying Trumpian attacks on political and economic elites. The mob that stormed the US Capitol had been convinced that the entire system was "corrupt" and rigged against them. They perceived the practices of many economic actors in the US economy (banks, big corporations) and of politicians as "failed" both in action and rhetoric. They simply did not believe in their legitimacy any more. These perceptions may well have been based partly in lies and manipulation, but the effect was clearly profound. We will see later another case where the failure of "symbolic performance" also threatened to undermine a well-established community of practice, this time in international human rights law and the prevention of torture.

Competent practice is closely tied to one of Weber's famous forms of authority, the institutional form he called "rational-legal authority",[513] the form that dominates the "disenchanted" modern world.[514] It is worth spending a little time on Weber because he has been so influential in discussions of authority, including legal authority, even though I believe he gets some crucial issues wrong. According to Talcott Parsons' commentary, Weber viewed rational-legal authority as relatively unstable, evidently less grounded in underlying culture than "traditional authority" and subject to the disruption of "charismatic authority". The relative instability was more likely to be exploited in the absence of legitimacy in rational-legal authority.[515]

For Weber, the legitimacy of any social order was derived from four bases: tradition, affectual attitudes (emotional bonds), the rational belief in the order's absolute value and lawful establishment.[516] "Rational-legal authority" depends primarily upon the latter two bases of legitimacy. Lawful establishment of an order and the rational belief in the "absolute value" of the order require the competent performance of the communities of practice that build, maintain, shape and reshape the ordering of a given society. For Weber, these competencies included the requirement that official functions be bound by rules and that there are adequate technical norms to effectively regulate the conduct of officials. This is where the idea of "technocracy" found its most compelling intellectual support, though to my knowledge Weber never used the term.[517]

If incompetence builds and either or both the lawfulness of the social order or the rational belief in its value is called into question, the power of tradition and of charisma can overwhelm rational-legal authority. Interestingly, competent performance at a technical level is likely to be less demanded or expected of orders grounded in charisma and tradition because their sources of legitimacy are different, rooted primarily in history and culture, and in emotional commitments.[518] This helps to explain why in referenda on constitutional change in divided societies, it is often the argument for change, typically the "nationalist" or "populist" argument, that is viewed as more compelling emotionally, with the status quo argument seeming more technocratic and economically focused. This was certainly the case in the two twentieth-century sovereignty referenda in Quebec and in the more recent Brexit referendum in the United Kingdom.[519] It is also why the sheer incompetence of the Trump Administration, in relation to managing COVID-19, or in the inability to deliver on his major election promises (Mexico funding the border wall, ending all foreign troop deployments, overturning Obamacare, etc.), did not seem to matter very much to his tens of millions of loyal followers.[520]

Weber believed that in most modern societies it was rational-legal authority that supported the social order. What is more, he thought that it was the "belief in legality" as represented by formally valid statute law that was "the most usual basis of legitimacy".[521] That is why formal legality "plays a key role in the institutionalization of the [modern] political system".[522] I will expand later on why I disagree with the idea that the legitimacy of law is founded only in the sociological belief of the populace, and why the conflation of formal legality (validity) with legitimacy is dangerous. For the present, I will note only that Weber himself was troubled by the dominating influence of his version of legal authority within contemporary societies, seeing it as bluntly instrumental and inadequate to the task of promoting autonomy and freedom.

Weber also worried that legal-rationalism (in its guise as formalism with its attendant focus on parliamentary democracy) would not be strong enough as a source of legitimacy to promote social cohesion.[523] Only rational-charismatic leaders could accomplish that crucial social function. For Weber, these charismatic leaders were not to be demagogues, but people "who possessed the ethical responsibility to identify the long-term interests of the polity, and to motivate diverse societal actors to pursue those interests".[524] They transformed personal charisma into "charisma of the office" by institutionalising the charismatic leadership.[525] Weber underplayed the risk of abuse or tyrannical instincts in charismatic leadership.[526]

The focus that I have placed upon pragmatist understandings of action in society and the mutual construction of truth, communities of practice whose Background shapes but does not control the ideas, discourses and actions of the community, and my emphasis upon the competent exercise of practice, all point to an entirely different form of "authority" in our social world. Adler calls it "epistemic practical authority".[527] This form of authority requires the establishment through legitimated social action of rights and obligations.[528] It also demands "performative power" – the ability of members of communities of practice to convince others both inside and ultimately outside their community of their practical actions and discursive competence, demonstrated through various processes including interpretation, negotiation and contestation.[529] Together, all this creates, in Adler's words: "the legitimate power to rule on the adoption of practices and their meanings".[530] In turn, practices embed and diffuse normative standards within societies. As communities of practice interact, they can also diffuse norms – I will later argue, including legal norms – across societies.[531]

In positing the existence of epistemic practical authority, one has to confront head-on the longstanding debate over the relative importance of what is called the "validity" and the "facticity" of norms, especially of legal norms. The issue was explored deeply by Habermas, who argued that citizens engage with law both as a system of social facts – that is, procedures and rules that may be enforced (through violence if necessary) – but also as a normative system underpinned by forms of legitimacy.[532] As I have already noted, legitimacy, for Habermas, was achieved primarily though genuine participatory discourse, meaning that only forms of deliberative democracy can underpin legal legitimacy.[533] Later I will discuss why understanding what makes a legal norm "valid" is at the heart of a prolonged and sometimes bitter debate in legal theory. But here I want to address a related issue: can the mere fact of a norm's social acceptance overcome its failure to be properly documented or enacted?

Unfortunately for us, because it can result in total confusion, the legal debate and the wider debate in social theory use completely reversed terminology. In law, "validity" of a norm typically refers to the process by which a legal norm was brought into being through "constitutional" process.[534] "Facticity" would then refer to the effectiveness of the legal norm in operation; is the norm followed and enforced? In wider social theory, including in Habermas' work, the opposite is the case. "Facticity" is an evaluation of the formal existence of the norm as documented, while "validity" relates to the "degree of social recognition" (legitimacy) of the norm.[535]

In both legal and social theory there is a continuing tension, perhaps even a dialectic, between facticity and validity, in relation to all norms, and especially legal norms. If one cared only about the formal existence of a norm, then its meaning would be highly attenuated. For example, law could be said to exist even if it had no practical import. On the other hand, if one looked only at whether or not a norm is socially validated, there would be no difference between social and legal norms. Law would be nothing more than dressed-up politics and sociology.[536] Epistemic practical authority accepts this continuing tension, and helps explain why we care about the establishment through legitimate social action of rights and obligations (Habermas' facticity and law's validity) as well as "performative power" (Habermas' validity and law's facticity), which must constantly and effectively re-enact practices that uphold norms, including legal norms, as we shall soon see.

The question of how to determine whether or not a norm exists – simply as a question of social acceptance or also of legitimacy – gives rise to a final set of issues that I want to explore in relation to philosophical pragmatism and practice theory. One of Durkheim's charges against the pragmatists was that they failed to understand the diversity of values. For Durkheim, it was crucial to acknowledge that there are distinct types of value: "Economic, moral, religious, aesthetic and speculative values are all different."[537] All attempts to reduce values to one overarching value had failed, in his view. He would have completely rejected Keats' oft-quoted conclusion in "On a Grecian Urn" that "[b]eauty is truth, truth beauty, – that is all Ye know on earth, and all ye need to know". Similarly, if one tries to explain value only in terms of impact in the world, the diversity of values is undermined. Fundamentally, Durkheim rejects utilitarianism:

> If the value of a thing is determined by the degree of its social (or individual) utility the system of human values would be shaken and changed from top to bottom.[538]

In missing out on value diversity, according to Durkheim, the pragmatists underplayed moral truths and mythical truths (values) and turned themselves into "logical utilitarians".[539] As Durkheim put it pithily:

"The idea that what is true is what is useful is the very principle of pragmatism."[540]

I think that Durkheim misreads the pragmatists. Their fundamental point about values was that, as received "truths", they are mutable. Because, as we have seen, knowledge results from doing (through action as well as language); "rules", "values", "laws" and "truths" are "more or less useful generalisations" that frame our inquiry until more helpful templates are revealed through our actions and reflection on those actions.[541] While values or laws, etc. are tools of inquiry, the measure of their worth is in their ability to point towards further knowledge, not in the achievement of a unique end, like material gain, happiness or the greatest good for the greatest number.[542] One might say that the pragmatists are not utilitarians at all, but "process consequentialists", the key process being the building and re-building of knowledge through continuous social learning.

In that process, critical reflexive *and* reflective learning is central.[543] If, as I have argued, inquiry is to a purpose and is not disconnected from human and social need,[544] building knowledge requires individuals, communities of practice and societies to learn from their experience. This takes us right back to where I started, with the insights of Aristotle. Over time and through experience, we must all "work out" what we should do.[545] We do that through both action and discourse;[546] in the creation, re-formulation and iteration of practices, as we reflect upon consequences and missed opportunities.[547] Reflexive and reflective learning within communities of practice is prompted by external factors such as changing material circumstances, as emphasised by Dewey but, as Adler stresses, also by factors internal to practices such as contestation, justification and mutual performative assessment.[548] I will argue later that these internal processes are essential to legitimising the practices of law.

This emphasis upon reflexive and reflective learning does not imply that tradition (Weber) and habit (Bourdieu) are irrelevant, nor that emotions never influence action; only that humans are endowed with the ability to reason, and to learn. In our day-to-day practices we consider, we argue and articulate diverse reasons, we evaluate, we choose courses of action, and we decide, individually and collectively.[549] We are not, as individuals or societies, "destined" for anything. Nor are we programmed into fixed patterns by our past.[550] Let me repeat the words of Richard Rorty: "We can make ourselves into whatever we are clever and courageous enough to imagine ourselves becoming."[551]

Notes

431 *Arendt Human Condition*, 5.

432 The importance of rehearsing, practising and repeating actions has been strongly promoted in the work of Anders Ericsson. See Anders Ericsson and Robert Pool, *Peak: Secrets from the New Science of Expertise* (Boston, MA: Houghton Mifflin Harcourt, 2016) (a source of the so-called 10,000-hour rule popularised in the work of Malcolm Gladwell). But see Ian Sample, "Blow to 10,000-hour Rule as Study Finds Practice doesn't Always Make Perfect", *The Guardian*, 21 August 2019, available at: www.theguardian.com/science/2019/aug/21/practice-does-not-always-make-perfect-violinists-10000-hour-rule.

433 Aristotle, *The Nicomachean Ethics*, II.

434 *Adler World Ordering*, 19. See also *Adler and Pouliot Practices*, 3, 6. For a detailed review of various "commitments" in practice theory that incorporates, but goes beyond and is sometimes critical of Adler, see *Bueger and Gadinger Theory*, 26–32. Lechner and Frost, 115, adopt a more static and rule-bound definition of a practice "*as a distinctive domain of rule following activity, defined by concrete constitutive rules and espoused as common understanding by a group of participants*" (italics in original). As we shall see, Adler's approach does not deny the importance of "constitutive rules" or "anchoring practices" that shape and channel practices, but he is less focused on fixed rules than Lechner and Frost, and allows, I believe, for a more evolutionary idea of practices. I am not sure, on the other hand, how useful Adler's reference to the reification of knowledge is in this quote. Does he mean that knowledge becomes "real" through practices or, as the pragmatists would argue, that it can approach a useful "truth", albeit a truth that can be displaced by further shared practice, further experience?

435 Discussed in Frega, 727 (italics in original).

436 *Arendt Human Condition*, 25 (quoting Phoenix's speech from *The Iliad*, with emphasis added), 178–9. She goes on to note that "finding the right words at the right moment" is a form of action. *Arendt Human Condition*, 26.

437 *Arendt Human Condition*, 4 (humans "can experience meaningfulness only because they can talk with and make sense to each other and to themselves"); Brożek, 7.

438 Hopf argues that practice-interested scholars have made a necessary correction, focusing not only on what actors say, but what they do. Ted Hopf, "The Logic of Habit in International Relations" (2010) 16 *EJIR* 539, 544. In international law, as we will see, actions do indeed count as much as words.

439 *Habermas Discourse*, 1–4.

440 Duke, 59, 146. More recent work would add that emotions, as carriers of social knowledge, are also part of practical reason. See Patricia Mindus, "The Wrath of Reason and the Grace of Sentiment: Vindicating Emotion in Law", in M. N. S. Sellers (ed.), *Law, Reason, and Emotion* (Cambridge University Press, 2017), 202, esp. 225–6, 233–4. Amartya Sen also sees practical reason as the very basis for what he calls "public reason", the need to deliberate in public through the provision of rational justification, a concept closely related to Habermas' communicative reason. Sen's version is more inclusive, however, not relying as heavily on shared values as does Habermas. Sen, 9, 43, 324.

441 *Habermas Discourse*, 296–7, 308–9; *Habermas Transformation*, 33. Durkheim also argued that once we have worked out our personal beliefs, we need to communicate them "in order to be certain that we are not mistaken". *Durkheim Pragmatism*, 102.

442 *Habermas Discourse*, 11.

443 *Habermas Discourse*, 18.

444 *Bueger and Gadinger Theory*, 25; *Bueger and Gadinger Practice*, 452, 454. See also James Tully, "Political Philosophy as a Critical Activity" (2002) 30 *Political Theory* 533, 534–5. Practice theorists who focus on the possibility of social learning argue that Foucault was overly preoccupied with questions of domination and power, and not adequately attuned to the emancipatory possibilities of learning and the interactive creation of knowledge. See *Bueger and Gadinger Theory*, 120–1; *Katzenstein and Seybert Uncertainty*, 53; Lechner and Frost, 26, 200–1. But see Lacroix and Prranchère, 234, 245, for a more liberating view of Foucault.

445 I thank an anonymous reviewer for pointing out this development in Habermas' thinking.

446 *Habermas Discourse*, 226–8.

447 Ingo Venzke, "Semantic Authority, Legal Change and the Dynamics of International Law", in Patrick Capps and Henrik Olsen (eds), *Legal Authority beyond the State* (Cambridge University Press, 2018), 102, 104–5, 107. See also Antje Wiener, "Contested Compliance: Intervention on the Normative Structure of World Politics" (2004) 10 *EJIR* 190 (on "structures of meaning-in-use" of language as frameworks for decision-making in world politics).

448 For the pragmatists' conception of background, see *Misak Legitimacy*, 299–302.

449 *Searle Construction*, 131–44.

450 See Cochran, 535 (on Weber's notion of "general cultural values"); Friedrichs and Kratochwil, 704 (on Weber's "culturally transmitted schemes"); *Bueger and Gadinger Practice*, 451 (on the underpinning "layer of symbolic and meaningful rules, that is, culture"); Antje Wiener and Uwe Putter, "The Quality of Norms is What Actors Make of It: Critical Constructivist Research on Norms" (2009) *J. Int'l L. & Int'l Relations* 2, 5–6 (on cultural validation of norms). Swidler argues that "culture" and "social structure" are not distinct, so that values and structures are intertwined. Swidler, 86. A more limited concept of shared "understandings" was assumed by Hegel to found the rules and practices of a society. See Lechner and Frost, 6. Oakeshott and Wittgenstein also emphasised "intersubjective understandings" as the "bonds of a common social practice". Lechner and Frost, 23.

451 *Adler World Ordering*, 3. See also *Bueger and Gadinger Practice*, 456.

452 *Adler World Ordering*, 4, 131, 200–1. Habermas works back a further step, suggesting that in any given society there are ethical traditions (Aristotle's *topoi*) that are pre-normative, but shape the evolution of norms. *Habermas Discourse*, 200.

453 *Weber Theory*, 120. These expectations may be constitutive of "authority" within a given society. See, e.g., Bruce Lincoln, *Authority: Construction and Corrosion* (University of Chicago Press, 1991), 16.

454 *Durkheim Sociology*, 95. See also Peristiany, xv, xxii, xxx; Ruggie, 858.

455 Jutta Brunnée and Stephen Toope, "International Law and the Practice of Legality: Stability and Change" (2018) 49 *Victoria U. Wellington L. Rev.* Special Symposium Issue 429 [hereinafter *Brunnée and Toope Stability*]. See also Jutta Brunnée and Stephen Toope, *Legitimacy and Legality: An Interactional Account of International Law* (Cambridge University Press, 2010), *passim*, but esp. 47–50 [hereinafter *Brunnée and Toope Interactional Account*]. See also Brożek, 66; *Shklar Legalism*, 191 (arguing that "habitual social sentiments" shape legal judgments). It is arguable that this idea inverts Aristotle who on one reading saw legal norms (*nomos*) as influencing the ethics (*ethos*) that would push someone towards virtuous activity. Duke, 7, 39, 122.

456 *Adler World Ordering*, 73 (background knowledge is made up of "*intersubjective collective understandings* bound with practices"; italics in original). See also p. 117

457 *Adler World Ordering*, 301.

458 Swidler, 95. See also Lechner and Frost, 13 (practices are not tradition or custom).

459 Ivan Ermakoff, *Ruling Oneself Out: A Theory of Collective Abdications* (Durham, NC: Duke University Press, 2008), *passim*.

460 In their thoughtful and deeply reasoned book, Lechner and Frost go to great lengths to show that an internal perspective on practices is central to understanding. I agree. However, I believe that they mistakenly lump practice theorists, including Adler, into the camp of Bourdieu, and miss the parallel, but independent, practice theory built upon the pragmatist heritage. Lechner and Frost, 12, 34, 73, 78. See also Cochran.

461 *Weber Theory*, 59–60; *Weber Interpretation*, 242; Max Weber, *Max Weber on Law in Economy and Society* (Cambridge, MA: Harvard University Press, 1966) 67 [hereinafter *Weber Law*].

462 Hopf, 554. See also Vincent Pouliot, "The Logic of Practicality: A Theory of Practice of Security Communities" (2008) 62 *IO* 257, 265 [hereinafter *Pouliot Practicality*] (Pouliot is a practice theorist more influenced by Bourdieu than by the pragmatists). Swidler discusses how an early generation of practice theorists understood practices "as routine activities (rather than consciously chosen actions) notable for their unconscious, automatic, un-thought character". This was an attempt to move practices away from the Weberian notion of "ideas" as the consciously chosen pursuit of ends. Swidler, 83. See also Lechner and Frost, 13 (practices are not the same as habit or tradition).

463 Emile Durkheim, *The Division of Labor in Society* (New York: Free Press, 1964), 79–80; *Durkheim Pragmatism*, 87. See also Cladis, 73. Durkheim, of course, was focused on moral habits, and this may distinguish his insights from more general claims about the power of habit to constrain choice. *Durkheim Sociology*, 6. Durkheim shared an interest

in the moral force of habituation with Aristotle. See Duke, 113–14 (law as a means to reinforce through habituation the pursuit of virtue).

464 Pierre Bourdieu, *Outline of a Theory of Practice* (Cambridge University Press, 1977), *passim*, but esp. 72, 95 (habitus as "the strategy-generating principle enabling agents to cope with unforeseen and ever-changing situations ... a system of lasting and transposable dispositions ...") [hereinafter *Bourdieu Theory*].

465 Brożek, 20–6. However, Brożek is correct, I believe, in arguing that intuition is "affective" rather than logical; it is not merely the result of an inheritance. Intuition is honed through experience in practice.

466 Bigo, 243. Hopf adopts a parallel position in IR theory. Hopf, 539, 541–4.

467 *Bourdieu Theory*, 168–9. See also *Katzenstein and Seybert Uncertainty*, 39–40 ("History does not only crawl; it also jumps").

468 Cochran, 539.

469 Ludwig Wittgenstein, *Philosophical Investigations*, ed. Peter Hacker and Joachim Schulte, 4th edn (Chichester: Wiley-Blackwell, 2009), para. 219 (emphasis in original).

470 *Adler World Ordering*, 129 (citing David Bloor). See also Lechner and Frost, 8–10. Wittgenstein seems to have changed his position on this question over time. In the early Wittgenstein of the *Tractatus*, he sought to specify a precise and direct relationship between language and reality. Ludwig Wittgenstein, *Tractatus Logico-Philosophicus*, trans. C. K. Ogden (Gothenburg: Chiron Academic Press, 2016). And see Lechner and Frost, 21 (on the picture theory of meaning). Later, in the *Philosophical Investigations*, Wittgenstein moves away from the direct correspondence of language to reality, favouring an understanding of "meaning in use". See *Misak Ramsey*, 134, 138, 219, 365; Lechner and Frost, 22, 114.

471 Swidler, *passim*. See also *Adler World Ordering*, 129, 140, 210.

472 John Searle, *Speech Acts: An Essay in the Philosophy of Language* (Cambridge University Press, 1969), 33–6. See also Lechner and Frost, 86, 97, 102; Ruggie, 871, 873.

473 Swidler, 91–2.

474 Emanuel Adler, "Control Power as a Special Case of Protean Power: Thoughts on Peter Katzenstein and Lucia Seybert's *Protean Power: Exploring the Uncertain and Unexpected in World Politics*" (2020) 12 *Int'l Theory* 422, 423.

475 For a short historical survey, see Jean-Philippe Warren, "Secularism in Quebec", *The Canadian Encyclopedia*, 26 November 2020, available at: www.thecanadianencyclopedia.ca/en/article/secularism-in-quebec.

476 See Hopf, 541, 555 (referencing Dewey).

477 *Dewey Human Nature*, *passim*; Cochran, 539.

478 Cochran, 540.

479 *Adler World Ordering*, *passim*. See also Ruggie, 878.

480 *Adler World Ordering*, 110, 168.

481 *Adler World Ordering*, 212.

482 John Dewey, *How We Think* (Boston: D. C. Heath, 1910), 6 [hereinafter *Dewey Think*].

483 *Dewey Think*, 9.

484 *Sandel Limits*, 172.

485 *Adler World Ordering*, 46, 223; Hopf, 544.

486 *Adler World Ordering*, 275–6.

487 *Durkheim Pragmatism*, 26. Building on this insight, Manuel Castells developed the concept of "the network society" focusing upon the networks that arise in the context of new information technologies. These networks are the defining feature of "the age of information" where information – understood and coded as data – is the central feature of the economy, both as input and output. Manuel Castells, *The Rise of the Network Society: The Information Age, vol. 1: Economy, Society and Culture* (Oxford: Blackwell, 1996), *passim*.

488 *Adler World Ordering*, 18–19.

489 Etienne and Beverly Wenger-Trayner, "Introduction to Communities of Practice: A Brief Overview of the Concept and its Uses", BETreat Workshops (2015), available at: https://wenger-trayner.com/introduction-to-communities-of-practice. The original work was Jean Lave and Etienne Wenger, *Situated Learning: Legitimate Peripheral Participation* (New York: Cambridge University Press, 1991). See also Lechner and Frost, 37, 50 (on Michael Oakeshott's description of social practice as teaching and learning).

490 Greco, 17, 25.

491 See Etienne Wenger, Richard McDermott and William Snyder, *Cultivating Communities of Practice: A Guide to Managing Knowledge* (Cambridge, MA: Harvard Business School Press, 2002), 29. See also Lechner and Frost, 189.

492 Lon Fuller, *The Morality of Law*, rev. edn (New Haven, CT: Yale University Press, 1969), 129 [hereinafter *Fuller Morality*]. Fuller is indebted to Aristotle for the strong practical orientation of his approach to norms and morality. See Aristotle, *The Nicomachean Ethics*, X:ix et seq., esp. 340–1.

493 Etienne Wenger-Trayner et al., *Learning in Landscapes of Practice: Boundaries, Identity, and Knowledgeability in Practice-Based Learning* (New York: Routledge, 2015), *passim*. See also *Adler World Ordering*, 21, 114–15. Lechner and Frost, 191, 212–15, describe macro-practices that also contain sub-practices and overlapping practices. However, they treat these macro-practices as "structures", a concept that I believe to be too rigid and not attuned to the continuing evolution of the content generated by communities of practice. Interestingly, Lechner and Frost, 105, 111–12, actually conceptualise social practices as amenable to change, so I find the metaphor of structure, which is inherently static, to be misleading.

494 *Adler World Ordering*, 46, 112; *Adler and Pouliot Practices*, 6; Lechner and Frost, 215; Steven Bernstein and Marion Laurence, "Practices and Norms: Relationships, Disjunctures and Change", in Alena Drieschova, Christian Bueger and Ted Hopf (eds), *Conceptualising International Practices: Directions for the Practice Turn in International Relations* (Cambridge University Press, 2021), 77.

495 Swidler.

496 *Adler World Ordering*, 26, 27.

497 Bernstein and Laurence, 84–5.

498 *Adler World Ordering*, 114. See also Lechner and Frost, 61. For a fully developed theory of the role of contestation in the building and destruction of social norms, see Antje Wiener, *Contestation and Constitution of Norms in Global International Relations* (Cambridge University Press, 2018), *passim* [hereinafter *Wiener Contestation*]. Amartya Sen also argues, invoking English philosopher Bernard Williams, that disagreement in society does not always have to be overcome; it can actually help to constitute our continuing relationships with other people. Sen, 14, 46, 392.

499 *Misak Truth*, 127. ("The pragmatist voices the requirement that we try, at least until such attempts fail, to include rather than exclude others. This entails listening carefully to the marginalised in society".)

500 *Misak Truth*, 153.

501 *Arendt Revolution*, 108.

502 See Lechner and Frost, 87–8.

503 Friedrichs and Kratochwil, 712–13.

504 Tanja Aalberts and Ingo Venzke, "Moving Beyond Interdisciplinary Turf Wars: Towards an Understanding of International Law as Practice", in André Nollkaemper (ed.), *International Law as Profession* (Cambridge University Press, 2017), 287, 307–8. Aalberts and Venke rely on Adler and Pouliot for the foundations of their argument.

505 Lechner and Frost, 40, 98.

506 Greco, 19, 89–90.

507 *Misak Moral Progress.*

508 *Adler World Ordering*, 18–19, 112, 177 (on performative power and its relationship to contestation); Ruggie, 879 (on discursive competence); Lechner and Frost, 38 (on meaningful performances).

509 *Adler World Ordering*, 40 (rejecting Foucault's idea that "the order of things" is only discourse), 112.

510 Swidler, 85.

511 *Adler World Ordering*, 131–2.

512 *Adler World Ordering*, 179.

513 *Weber Theory*, 329–32.

514 *Weber Interpretation*, 59.

515 Parsons, 68–72.

516 *Weber Theory*, 130.

517 *Weber Theory*, 331–2, 339.

518 *Weber Theory*, 328 (on why obedience is shown to people holding power in the different forms of authority).

519 See, e.g., Jonathan Moss, Emily Robinson and Jake Watts, "Brexit and the Everyday Politics of Emotion: Methodological Lessons from History" (2020) 68 *Pol. Studies* 837, available at: https://journals.sagepub.com/doi/pdf/10.1177/0032321720911915; Thomas Sampson, "Brexit: The Economics of International Disintegration" (2017) 31 *J. Econ. Perspectives* 163, available at: www.aeaweb.org/articles?id=10.1257/jep.31.4.163; Kim Somers and François Vaillancourt, "Some Economic Dimensions of the Sovereignty Debate in Quebec: Debt, GDP, and Migration" (2014) 30 *Oxford Rev. Econ. Pol.* 237;

Christopher Ragan, "The Staggering Price of Quebec Independence", *The Globe and Mail*, 18 March 2014, available at: www.theglobeandmail.com/report-on-business/economy/economy-lab/the-staggering-price-of-quebec-independence/article17529502.

520 Though he did fulfil a key pledge, to fundamentally shift the ideological balance of the US Supreme Court.

521 Weber, quoted in David Dyzenhaus, "Herman Heller and the Legitimacy of Legality" (1996) 16 *Oxford J. Legal Studies* 641, 642 [hereinafter *Dyzenhaus Legitimacy*].

522 Thornhill, 90.

523 Thornhill, 91, 93.

524 Thornhill, 93–4.

525 *Weber Charisma*, 40. See also Eisenstadt, xxi and xl.

526 Zeitlin, 406.

527 *Adler World Ordering*, 3.

528 Dyzenhaus also stresses the importance of *legitimate* authority in law. *Dyzenhaus Long Arc*, 1 ("Law's authority is a matter both of what legal subjects accept and what they have reason to accept"), 2–3, 6.

529 *Adler World Ordering*, 27–8, 236. It is for this reason that I do not think that Lechner and Frost, 47, 116, are right in seeing practices as entirely prior to interpretation (or contestation for that matter), or fixed by unvarying rules of validity. Practices are shaped by constitutive rules but those rules are subject to change, which Lechner and Frost, 111–12, admit.

530 *Adler World Ordering*, 4.

531 *Adler World Ordering*, 4–5.

532 *Habermas Discourse*, 448–9; *Habermas Transformation*, 82. See also Christian Reus-Smit, "The Strange Death of Liberal International Theory" (2001) 12 *EJIL* 573, 591 [hereinafter *Reus-Smit Liberal Theory*].

533 *Habermas Discourse*, 449–50.

534 Paolo Sandro, "Unlocking Legal Validity: Some Remarks on the Artificial Ontology of Law", in Pauline Westerman et al. (eds), *Legal Validity and Soft Law* (New York: Springer, 2018), available at: https://link.springer.com/chapter/10.1007/978-3-319-77522-7_5.

535 Antje Wiener, *The Invisible Constitution of Politics: Contested Norms and International Encounters* (Cambridge University Press, 2008), 48 et seq.

536 *Reus-Smit Liberal Theory*, 585.

537 *Durkheim Sociology*, 85. Luhmann built on this argument, suggesting that multiple social systems exist within a given society, each with its own justifying rationality. See Thornhill, 124; Venzke, 111.

538 *Durkheim Sociology*, 85. For a good, brief, overview of Jeremy Bentham's contributions to utilitarianism, see *Cameron Practical Wisdom*, 10–11.

539 Allcock, xxxviii, and see *Durkheim Pragmatism*, 86.

540 *Durkheim Pragmatism*, 3.

541 Cochran, 530.

542 Friedrich and Kratochwil, 706, 711 (calling this approach "epistemological instrumentalism"). See also Ruggie, 860 (on the strictly material interests of "neo-utilitarians"); *Cameron Phronesis*, 20 (on how practical reasoning need not be instrumental or utilitarian).

543 Friedrich and Kratochwil, 713; *Sandel Limits*, 172. See also Duke, 56, 61 (on Aristotle's commitment to the reflexivity of political activity and, fundamentally, of all "practical rationality"). This internal reflection (within communities of practice) is distinct from Bourdieu's "reflexive sociology", which is the reflection of social scientists operating as external observers of a practice. See Pierre Bourdieu and Loïc Wacquant, *An Invitation to Reflexive Sociology* (University of Chicago Press, 1992), *passim*; Lechner and Frost, 72–3, 76–7; Yves Dezalay and Mikael Madsen, "The Force of Law and Lawyers: Pierre Bourdieu and the Reflexive Sociology of Law" (2012) 8 *Annual Rev. L. & Soc. Sci.* 433.

544 Searle, 1; Friedrich and Kratochwil, 725.

545 Duke, 37. This tradition of thought was revived by Pascal and Montaigne in "meditations", reflections on practical problems that did not depend on supposedly universally applicable logic. *Kratochwil Status*, 19–20.

546 See *Arendt Human Condition* (on action); Charles Taylor, *Human Agency and Language* (Cambridge University Press, 1985) (on discourse).

547 *Adler World Ordering*, 29, 131, 204.

548 *Adler World Ordering*, 205–7.

549 See Amartya Sen on the difference between reason and "rational choice theory", arguing that reasonable choices are not defined only by self-interest, but can be motivated through a variety of impulses. Sen, 176, 179–80, 185–7.

550 *Adler World Ordering*, 70.

551 *Rorty Human Rights*, 122. See also *Arendt Human Condition*, 178 ("The fact that man is capable of action means that the unexpected can be expected from him, that he is able to perform what is infinitely improbable").

PART THREE

A MODEST RULE OF LAW HELPS FRAME A HEALTHIER SOCIETY

Behold the infant, helpless in cradle and
Righteous still, yet already there is
Dread in his dreams at the deed of which
He knows nothing but knows he can do,
The gulf before him with guilt beyond,
Whatever that is, whatever why
Forbids his bound; till that ban tempts him;
He jumps and is judged: he joins mankind,
The fallen families, freedom lost,
Love becomes Law.

W. H. Auden, *The Age of Anxiety**

IN PART I OF THE BOOK, I traced out sources of the pervasive anxiety that marks our age. There are many deep uncertainties – far more unsettling than calculable risks – affecting our perception of both the present and the future. I emphasised three because I believe they underlie many others: populist nationalism; the economic, social and cultural complexity of globalism; and profound technological change. Part II explored the intellectual resources at our disposal to confront these uncertainties, to alleviate our anxieties. Those resources are considerable and plural. Drawing upon diverse sources of inspiration, including classical thought, pragmatist philosophy, sociology and international relations theory, I articulated an optimistic – but I believe equally realistic – means to address pervasive worry.

Guided by purposes, people and societies gain practical wisdom through experience over time. Uniquely amongst animals, through continuous self-reflection, we deploy reason but also intuition, emotion and social skills. We learn reflexively and reflectively, and do so through communities of practice, in actions and discourse. Drawing on background knowledge, we selectively replicate past practices deploying our practical wisdom to guide us through new material circumstances and new discoveries or insights. We are fundamentally creative beings, influenced by tradition and habit, but not fully constrained by them. Our world is a world of dynamic becoming. That becoming is not necessarily positive; we must work hard to make it so.

In that world, truth is built through human interaction and the creation of consensus in and amongst communities of practice, projecting into the wider world. To seek truth is to create useful generalisations that are mutable, allowing us to build frameworks for decision shaped by standards of evaluation developed within and then across communities of practice, and tested against measures of competency. Truth that is subject to change does not mean that "everything is relative". An open-ended understanding of truth, and its social construction, demands diversity of thought because the pluralism of ideas helps us to recognise important issues and to build better ways to address society's problems.

The conceptual framework I have laid out brings us to a question that has preoccupied me for most of my working life: what is law's contribution to our world of becoming? Can the rule of law really play a role in allowing us to navigate through our new age of anxiety? Much of my experience working in the field on issues of human rights convinces me that the answer is an emphatic "yes". I will set out in the following three chapters how I think that a reformed and revitalised rule of law can provide useful guidance in public discourse and decision-making. It does so in part because it will not insist on a single view of what constitutes the good life. Indeed, it will require of us that we take competing views seriously and uphold pluralism of thought and aspiration, both in national and international societies.

In so doing, it will allow for the full and proper recognition of complexity and uncertainty in societal choices. But because the rule of law helps to ensure predictability and transparency, it will tend to foster effective communication within society and promote stability. At the same time, practices of legality that underpin the rule of law are also dynamic, allowing for innovation that can build new social consensus that shapes societal change in healthy, inclusive ways. In all this, it will serve to instantiate practical wisdom, grounded in experience, calling on us to reason with norms in practical settings. That reasoning will be shaped by criteria of legality that limit what can "count" as legal argument, thereby lending legitimacy to legal discourse and legal decisions. In turn, this formulation of the rule of law will help us to engage in more sophisticated institutional design based on principles of citizen participation and legality that generate trust in law and public institutions. Finally, this modest rule of law will still, and importantly, fulfil the purpose often seen as its only contribution, disciplining the exercise of power.

CHAPTER SEVEN

The Bases of Law and Challenges to Legalism

One could not go on living and keeping silent and looking on while they stupidly and shamelessly distorted the truth.

Lion Feuchtwanger, *The Oppermanns*[552]

The limitations of the law are never entirely reliable safeguards against action from within the body politic, just as the boundaries of the territory are never entirely reliable safeguards against action from without. The boundlessness of action is only the other side of its tremendous capacity for establishing relationships, that is, its specific productivity; this is why the old virtue of moderation, of keeping within bounds, is indeed one of the political virtues par excellence . . .

Hannah Arendt, *The Human Condition*[553]

IN THE mid-2000s, I served as Chair of the United Nations Working Group on Enforced or Involuntary Disappearances. The Working Group sits under the UN Human Rights Council, and consists of a five-member panel of independent experts. First set up in 1980, primarily to deal with disappearances in Latin America, since then the geographic scope of the Working Group has expanded to include tens of thousands of cases from around the globe.

The goal of the Working Group is entirely practical: to discover the fate of disappeared people. In most cases, sadly, this will be a confirmation of death. But the Working Group has discovered the whereabouts of many disappeared persons in informal and illegal custody, in army barracks, hide-outs of mercenary groups or – undocumented – in prisons. The methods of the Working Group are also pragmatic: negotiating with governments and sometimes subjecting them to public embarrassment when diplomatic efforts have stalled. Each year the Working Group issues a report that details the cooperation or non-cooperation of governments.[554]

In 2004, I led an official visit of the Working Group to Nepal. A rapid escalation in the number of disappearances in that country had followed the breakdown of a ceasefire agreement between the government and Maoist guerrillas. In addition to enforced or involuntary disappearances, there were many reports of alleged extrajudicial execution, arbitrary arrest and detention, and torture. As a result of our visit, the Working Group concluded that the phenomenon of disappearance in Nepal was indeed widespread.

One of the strangest moments of the Working Group visit was our formal audience with the last king of Nepal, His Majesty King Gyanendra. He had come to the throne only in 2001, as a result of a massacre in the royal palace. Gyanendra's brother, King Birendra, was killed by his own son, the crown prince, who then shot himself – but not before killing his mother and other family members as well. The survivor, King Gyanendra, received us in a lavish reception room and projected the image of a modern constitutional monarch. For various reasons, I have met five monarchs of constitutional democracies in my time. I would not have been able to distinguish the discourse of King Gyanendra from any of them. He was calm, confident and said all the right things about protecting human rights and upholding the rule of law.

It might all have been quite believable if the Working Group had not visited the headquarters of the Royal Nepalese Army the previous day and met with the military leadership. Unlike most of the Nepalese government offices, which were shabby, and where the staff displayed an air of uncertainty and disorganisation, the army headquarters were spic and span, and comfortably appointed. Everything ran like clockwork. More to the point, our conversation revealed who was really in control; not the government and certainly not the king. Indeed, credible reports suggested that the king was serving as the instrument of the military. He was deposed only a few years later, and a republic declared, ending the 240-year reign of the Shah dynasty.

We had already learned over the early days of our visit that government security forces, including the army, were systematically committing the international crime of disappearance. A clear pattern of abuse had emerged. A person suspected of Maoist sympathies, or of simply having contact with Maoists, was seized by a group of military personnel out on patrol. The abductee was blindfolded with hands tied behind the back, put into a military vehicle and taken away. The security forces often appeared in plain clothes so that no personal or unit names were visible; they could not be identified. Very commonly, the victim was later seen in an army vehicle, being driven around, reportedly to point out the homes of other "suspects". In almost all cases, the victim was held incommunicado in an army barracks, with no access to family or legal counsel. We spoke with victims and saw credible physical evidence of torture. We also heard detailed descriptions that were consistent from one victim to another. Patterns included beatings with plastic pipes and sensory deprivation, including the blindfolding of victims for the entire period of incommunicado detention, often lasting months. We actually found a few of the disappeared on visits to prisons near Kathmandu, prisons where the conditions were abominable.[555]

At the royal palace, we were treated to the façade of a rule of law. But the arbitrariness of power, and its brutality, gainsaid that bizarre show. In Nepal at the time, the military controlled the government and the monarchy, and it abused its power with almost complete impunity. Millions of citizens lived in fear. Thousands suffered constant indignity. Hundreds disappeared, were tortured and died. The complete failure of the rule of law had profound and frightening consequences.

One of the most shocking experiences of my life was a clandestine meeting I held in Nepal with families, mostly mothers, of the disappeared. Their stories were harrowing, but a real moment of personal crisis occurred when I was pulled aside by one mother, probably in her fifties. She quickly told me about the disappearance of her son, more than a decade before. She started to cry and said that she had done everything she could to find him. She was losing hope. Then she grabbed my hand, looked me in the eyes and said: "I have only you. You are my god." I could barely breathe. No matter how hard I tried, I could not meet her expectations. So I babbled something about raising her son's case with the government, and expressed deep sympathy. I said that I could not be anyone's god, but would try my best to help. As I was ushered away by a UN official, I knew in my deepest being that laws and institutions could not eliminate suffering.

It is experiences such as this, and others in various parts of Africa, Cuba and Southeast Asia, that force me to admit that the rule of law, and specific legal rules, cannot provide all the answers to social ills and predicaments. One point should already be clear from everything I have argued so far. Law is not dominant in, nor even uniquely capable of, guiding us to greater social and individual wellbeing. But law does have a profound contribution to make, along with other frameworks of analysis and creative discovery.[556] The rule of law does not *define* well-ordered and healthy human societies, but it is one of the anchoring practices – a constellation of ideas, discourses and concrete actions – that can help to create and sustain freedom and equality, both nationally and transnationally. A sophisticated yet modest conception of the rule of law, actively renewed and implemented in our societies, can be an important element in a collective effort to re-instil a sense of hope in a population troubled and confused by prevailing anxiety.

The day-to-day practice of a rule of law by people fulfilling their roles in institutions serves as a buttress against social and political instability and abuse of power. For example, when the much-vaunted "checks and balances" of the formal US Constitution failed in holding a reckless and abusive president to account:

> ... the president's worst impulses were neutralized by three pillars of the unwritten constitution. The first is the customary separation between the president and federal criminal prosecution (even though the Department of Justice is part of the executive branch). The second is the traditional political neutrality of the military (even though the president is the commander in chief of the armed forces). The third is the personal integrity of state elections officials.
>
> If any of these informal "firewalls" had failed, President Trump might be on his way to a second and more autocratic term. But they held firm, for which the Republic should be grateful.[557]

In more extreme cases, such as the situation I described in Nepal, a genuine implementation of the rule of law could provide much greater safety for the population, and could help in the re-establishment of some form of participatory government. Let us explore how that might happen in the world as we find it today.

First, building upon the approach to social theory that I have already set out, I must address a prior, quite fundamental question: how do we best understand the relationship between law and politics? In discussing populist nationalism, I have already explored one possible answer, that law is entirely subservient to politics, a mere instrument in the hands of those with material power. That was certainly the case with the army in Nepal in 2004. This argument has many variants. The most extreme is the one put forth by Carl Schmitt and his Nazi fellow-travellers. For Schmitt, politics was all-encompassing, a dominating force that overrode all other forms of social organisation. As he put it, the political "does not designate an exclusive area of activity but only the degree of intensity of an association or dissociation of human beings whose motives may have to do with religion, nationalism (in an ethnic or cultural sense) or economics, amongst other things".[558] Above all, politics was the "will of the people", the expression of popular sovereignty, not as for Aristotle and his successors, rational thought or persuasion.[559]

For Schmitt, politics was a very particular and potent force because it did not seek to find or determine consensus; rather, it was conditioned inevitably by conflict and the potential for war. For that reason, politics (as an expression of power, and especially of the powerful leader) was all about the definition of friend and foe.[560] In more general terms, politics was legitimate only to the extent that it succeeded in defining "the people", a process of inclusion and exclusion focused on the creation of identity. Schmitt hated liberalism because he believed that it produced a politics without a rigorously circumscribed "polis" or people; it was bloodless and incapable of generating true intensity of connection.[561] Law was only relevant to the extent that it served this instrumental agenda for a purely majoritarian and ultimately authoritarian anti-democratic politics.[562] And as we have already seen, law was always subservient to the material power that controlled "the state of exception".

The extremes of Schmitt have been softened in our era, but some of his insights still influence contemporary debates, often in an unacknowledged way. Most pointedly, many scholars of a self-described "critical" bent argue that politics remains the dominant force in social life because it is the frame that most explicitly acknowledges the role of power in social relations. It is argued that fields such as law (including international law) and human rights pretend to create forms of equality or level playing fields, but that this is largely false. Scholars and practitioners in these subject areas, especially if they can be described as "liberals", are viewed as mere apologists for the status quo, as justifiers of hegemony, as insensitive to material factors that create and sustain, even reinforce, underlying social and economic inequalities.[563]

For many critical scholars, law fails in creating a level playing field because it is inattentive to the reality of power differentials: "All agents do not participate in social action on an equal level: materially embodied social relations always position agents in socially asymmetrical power relations."[564] On this view, and as an inheritance from Schmitt, law is really nothing more than an instrument in the hands of the powerful. For Schmitt, this was a virtue; to be fair, for critical scholars it is a conclusion rooted in a desire for "realism" and an antidote to the expansive claims of those who promote a determinative role for law in social organisation and the protection of human rights. This concern is shared even by some legal and political theorists of a liberal-centrist bent.[565] I will return to this point shortly.

For many political theorists, especially theorists of democracy, politics is superior to law in a different, structural sense: "Modern constitutions are generally understood as emerging from the people in an act of constituent power."[566] This conception of the national constitution as pre-legal is rooted in a particular understanding of social contract theory, especially the writings of Rousseau,[567] wherein the contract is a one-off agreement concluded before the formation of society that establishes a written constitution as hierarchically superior to all other law.[568] Habermas adopted an interesting hybrid position, suggesting that law in the constitutional state "should illuminate once again the original idea of the self-constitution of a community of free and equal citizens".[569] Yet "the people" is itself constructed under a rule of law. This is what Habermas calls "constitutional patriotism".[570] Legitimate law must enact a political will that is itself shaped by law.[571]

We have already seen that the founders of modern sociology put forward an amended version of the idea that politics pre-dates law. Rather than focusing upon the "will of the people" as the ability to collectively generate the constitution and resulting forms of "self-legislation", Weber stressed the politics of identity construction as the grounding of society and state. The political system is legitimised by its ability to create a shared sense of peoplehood (and nation).[572] For both Durkheim and Weber, this implied that law could only ever be *relatively* autonomous from politics. Law was important because it was one of the means of social integration, but it was a medium serving the politics of integration, not an independent force. Law was legitimated through its "distinct capacity for transmitting powerfully integrative ethical-political substances through society".[573]

Yet from the earliest Enlightenment justifications for democracy, "popular sovereignty" was only ever a theoretical construct, and was not seen as an ideal. Early theorists of popular sovereignty, including Rousseau and Madison, often cited as originators of modern democracy, did not exalt popular self-rule.[574] Hannah Arendt argued this point in her influential comparison of the French and American revolutions, suggesting that the former consumed itself precisely because it idealised the morality of "the people", disconnecting itself from any practical institutions like law. The American revolutionaries, in contrast, drew on traditions, including legal traditions, to account for the role of power in political life.[575] In *The Federalist Papers,* Madison, Hamilton and Jay argued explicitly that any form of direct, popular democracy endangers "both the public good and the rights of other citizens". They stressed that representatives were required, constituting a delegation "of the government ... to a small number of citizens".[576] The government they proposed was for a "republic" not a "democracy" precisely because they believed that unfettered democracy would lead to ignorant populism.[577] Hamilton was indeed prescient. In a powerful discourse from 1792, he warned of a time when a "man unprincipled in private life[,] desperate in his fortune" and "bold in his temper" would rise to power mounted on "the hobby horse of popularity" and "throw things into confusion that he may 'ride the storm and direct the whirlwind'".[578]

What is more, in most cases the "people", understood as a "nation", did not even exist as the justifications for democracy were articulated in the eighteenth century. Since Hegel, theorists have suggested instead that political democracy (and constitutions that formally enacted it) arose not from deliberate collective choice, but from the rise of centralised institutions.[579] I would add that these institutions had a legal basis that seems to have existed prior to the expression of "popular will".[580]

A German-American constitutional scholar, Matias Kumm, poses the central question provocatively: what if "the idea of sovereignty as ultimate authority – a conception of constitutionalism tied to the coercive institutions of the state and a conception of legitimacy and democracy reductively tied to the self-governing practices of 'We the People', is deeply misguided"?[581] Is there a better, more accurate and fruitful description of the relationship between law and politics in contemporary societies?

I believe that there is. The key lies in the argument that legality is legitimated in a relatively autonomous way, and is not dependent upon a political constitution that pre-dates law.[582] Legal systems are held together by "those *intrinsic qualities* that give law its authority and without which there is neither law nor authority".[583] If law is legitimated through its intrinsic qualities, this suggests that a "circular" understanding of legality, in which authority is internal to law, leads to a more robust account of law's role and effects in society than a "linear" understanding, which must locate "law's starting point in something other than law itself", something like popular sovereignty.[584] A circular understanding allows law to serve its crucial function as a check on power, not its mere handmaiden. Law, ethics and political power interact and shape one another, but they are relatively independent forces.[585] To be clear, constitutions gain their force from legitimacy that is built internally by law, but they are not "self-enforcing" and are, of course, shaped by social, cultural and political contexts.[586]

Linear theories of law, on the other hand, trace "authority" and "legitimacy" back to an originating source of law. In Mark Walter's evocative phrase, law is "held up by a string". The traditions of natural law fit this description because the source of law is the deity or reason. All law reaches back to an external moral framework created through divine revelation or right thinking. But linearity is also characteristic of legal positivism. Although for various types of positivists the source of law is described differently, there is always an originating source and – what matters for present purposes – that source is outside law itself. For John Austin, the source of law was the power of the unconstrained sovereign.[587] Hans Kelsen described his "*grundnorm*" simply as a logical postulate, an external source for law simply had to exist because law could not justify itself.[588] Later, Herbert Hart argued that the source of law was simply a "social fact" constituted through official practice, what he called a "rule of recognition".[589]

Despite this intellectual baggage, the very concept of constitutionalism is often described as an ideal of "government established by law and limited by law from exercising arbitrary power".[590] How can government be established "by law" if law itself is established by something other than law? It cannot, which is the basis of the theory of "political constitutionalism", represented today by proponents such as Jeremy Waldron. Waldron argues that it is democratic principles that legitimate a legal order; these principles fall outside law, so the constitution is a political, not a legal, construct.[591] The fundamental question for all constitutions, on this theory, is: what "people" serves as the source of authority, or constituted power?[592]

As David Dyzenhaus argues, "political constitutionalists and legal positivists seem committed to the claim that the legal constitution is ultimately a formal one – one that consists only of formal authorization rules".[593] There are no substantive commitments in the constitution, no matter how limited. "Authority" and "legitimacy" are merely expressions of right process within law, finding their ultimate justification in external political morality, the justification of a people's agreement to be governed.

A similarly linear move is made by realists in international relations who, however unwittingly, support a view of constitutionalism close to that of Carl Schmitt. As we have seen, Schmitt argued that the sovereign has unbounded power to throw off ordinary law in cases of emergency or exception: "Sovereign is he who decides on the exception."[594] Realists share this form of positivist linearity, where authority is rooted outside law, in the ability to escape the application of law through the exercise of material power.

An alternative, "circular", tradition of law and constitutionalism holds that the constitution is a legal construct, not an instrument of material power or even of constitutive political power.[595] This tradition is grounded in the "practical reasoning" or "practical wisdom" of Aristotle (*phronesis*), wherein law is best understood as a discursive exercise, as a form of rhetoric that is purposive, not merely descriptive of fact, and inherently connected to argument.[596] Although I have argued that all practices – including law – are built not only on discourse, but on actions, the rhetorical tradition in law has been powerful and has produced helpful insights. Rhetoric was advanced beyond its classical formulations[597] by the secular humanists of the Enlightenment, thinkers such as Giambattista Vico, who argued that many of life's important conundrums are simply not amenable to the rationalist, dualistic and doubt-focused analysis propounded by Descartes. Instead, life's challenges call for creativity in drawing analogies and in finding similarities amongst seemingly different elements, thereby creating new understandings of reality. This process is the mature exercise of judgement or practical reason, a demonstration of prudence in the light of experience over time.[598]

Starting from a quite different position, Bourdieu also emphasised the role of legal rhetoric, and explained its influence on political life – especially in the modern state. For Bourdieu, the power of lawyers is grounded in the specificity of legal language. Legal words come to form the legitimate representation of reality, occupying a disproportionate space in relation to other "ordinary" social actors. Legal words become the social capital for precedents and solutions, which may involve re-interpreting or re-working (in Bourdieu's word, "transgressing") existing rules. Lawyers, as experts, have the power to legitimate those transgressions through their use of language.[599] What this means is that lawyers are central actors in the modern state, but they are distinct from purely political actors; law is not the same as political power.

I argue that all law, including the constitution itself, is created and refined, shifted and reinforced through continuing practices of contestation, interpretation, application and actions including enforcement. These practices are themselves shaped, and what counts as practical reason or prudence are guided, by "strands of normative value", themselves subject to continuing debate, interpretation and further working out in practices of legality.[600]

This circular understanding of law founds a constitutional order that is distinctively legal, not subservient to politics, but not entirely disconnected either. Fundamental norms of good governance exist within law itself.[601] In the term favoured by legal theorist Lon Fuller, to whose work I shall return shortly, they are the "*internal* morality of law". In one of the most creative discursions of modern legal theory, Fuller derives his principles of internal morality by way of a *reductio ad absurdum.* He traces out the utterly flawed reasoning and practices of "King Rex", thereby showing that even if we have trouble defining legal perfection, we sure can tell what bad law looks like.[602] As well as providing an insightful account of the largely procedural content of the rule of law, this legally focused construction of constitutionalism obviates the need to identify constituent authority outside law since law's authority is provided by internal qualities.[603] That said, I regret Fuller's use of the term "internal morality of law" because I think that it obfuscates and misdirects. It certainly caused much confusion in subsequent debates. I do, however, accept Fuller's underlying argument, as I shall detail later.

Legal sociologist Chris Thornhill upholds the view that law, and the national constitution, are not the product of popular will. Law therefore has an authority separate from political authority. However, he pushes the argument much further:

> [T]he subjective author of democratic law has been moved *from a position outside* the legal system *to a position inside* the legal system. As a result, *the law refers to the law as the ground of law's authority,* and processes of legal construction classically pertaining to political actions now widely occur as elements in a process of *secondary constitution making,* in which already defined legal norms are re-articulated.[604]

Through this process of "secondary constitution making", which Thornhill argues is largely grounded in transnational norms of human rights, what had been political arguments and decisions have now become legalised. In Thornhill's estimation, "Politics Becomes the Law":

> The elemental structure of democracy is no longer shaped by the translation of a political will, condensed around the practices of citizens, into legal form. Now, at a basic level, democracy is more usually shaped by the inner-legal projection of obligatory norms and concepts of legal validity, in which primary norm-setting functions are internalized, and recursively produced within the law. In fact, the structure of democracy is no longer founded in processes of norm formation that are discernably political.[605]

I challenge this claim. It is a dramatic over-reach, and could serve to justify the common criticism that contemporary jurists too often exaggerate the role of lawyers, judges and courts. In asserting legal–social hegemony, lawyers in Western societies, and especially in the United States, aggregate power and actually come to undermine participatory government.[606]

To understand the frustration that many social scientists, politicians and even so-called "ordinary citizens" feel about law and lawyers, it is worth returning to the 1960s and that brilliant, if flawed, book, *Legalism*, by the Harvard political theorist, Judith Shklar, that I have already drawn upon. Her central argument was that legalistic thinking exerted a stranglehold on social organisation, and political and moral discourse. Shklar defined "legalism" as:

> the ethical attitude that holds moral conduct to be a matter of rule following, and moral relationships to consist of duties and rights determined by rules. Like all moral attitudes that are both strongly felt and widely shared it expresses itself not only in personal beliefs but also in philosophical thought, in political ideologies, and in social institutions.[607]

The sheer power of law had led theorists to define rigid boundaries between law and other forms of social organisation and influence, and to isolate law from its societal contexts.[608] Shklar argued that all legal theory was ultimately formalistic and rule-bound. The legalist tried to structure "all possible human relations into the form of claims and counterclaims" because this would allow them to find the applicable rules that were simply "there".[609] As a "social ethos ... following rules gives actions their worth in every case".[610]

Shklar refused to see any distinction whatsoever amongst competing branches of legal theory, arguing that they only conducted a "family quarrel among legalists".[611] She reduced one of the touchstone moments of modern jurisprudence, the "Hart–Fuller debate", to an implicit agreement that "justice is a matter of the equal application of rules" and that, conversely, determinable rules are the "very condition of justice".[612] Shklar thought that all legal theory presupposed that justice and law are co-equal ideas; justice, and therefore law, comes to colonise all fields of endeavour and thought,[613] so we have ever-increasing claims to diverse forms of justice: "political, social, and natural, to name but a few".[614] For legalists, "[t]he man who is determined to honour claims made under a given standard is just, though he may be neither kind, generous, nor amiable".[615] A powerful cultural referent is Shylock in *The Merchant of Venice*, who extols justice with no measure of mercy. In my view, Shklar here pushes her point too far and compromises the power of her argument. I will return to this problem later. For now, it suffices to emphasise Shklar's central insight that lawyers, and especially legal theorists, often overstate law's influence and suppress other forms of socio-political organisation and thought.

In critiquing the dominating claims of the law, and indeed of justice as the primary virtue, Shklar partook of a lively tradition. Reaching back to Aristotle, Thomas Aquinas argued that the common good (*bonum commune*) was rooted in justice and peace. However, in Thomistic thought, "justice" referred "to the preservation of a certain form of equality or a proper relation among persons".[616] Kant, who is typically associated with a liberalism rooted in a core theory of justice, believed that the legitimacy of law was derived from its capacity to guarantee liberty, not justice.[617] Hegel, too, saw law as "the realm of realized freedom".[618]

Habermas stressed the need for law to focus as much on freedom as on "distributive justice"[619] – a concept that he believed emphasised too much what one has rather than what one can do. Still, Habermas was far more sanguine about the role of law in complex contemporary societies than Shklar because he saw law as the only medium in which it is possible to establish morally obligated relationships of mutual respect even among strangers.[620] Habermas nonetheless saw morals as a separate source of obligation working together with law. And he argued that there was no possibility of any rule of law in society in the absence of what he called "radical democracy"; only this form of politics allowed for the existence of law.[621]

After Shklar, other philosophers continued to challenge the hegemony of "justice" as the justification for law and as the primary measure of social good. Perhaps the leading critic is Michael Sandel, who argued in *Liberalism and the Limits of Justice* that:

> The breakdown of certain personal and civic attachments may represent a moral loss that even a full measure of justice cannot redeem. Does it go without saying that a rent in the fabric of implicit understandings and commitments is morally repaired so long as everyone "does what he ought" in the aftermath?[622]

Sandel also emphasised that justice is no more unifying a concept than morals or religion, and so had no greater capacity to build social cohesion.[623] Adopting a different tack, Canadian philosopher James Tully explicitly seeks to build a "public philosophy" that is "oriented to freedom before justice", and that seeks to identify "the possible practices of freedom in which free and equal subjects could speak and exchange reasons more freely over how to criticize, negotiate, and modify their always imperfect practices".[624] Finally, some contemporary critics of human rights argue that there has been an overvaluing of formal rights (as rules) and of justice at the expense of alternative mobilising claims such as freedom, equality and social welfare. They assert that legal remedies have been emphasised, with potentially more effective alternative political strategies overlooked and even undermined.[625]

The circular conception of law's sources of authority, when linked to the pragmatist thought and practice theory that I have described above, reveals an escape route from both the legalism that Shklar decries and its dangerous opposite, a denigration of law as the mere servant of power. To build that case, I will first articulate a specific understanding of what we mean when we invoke the idea of "law". Then I will argue that this understanding provides a framing for the "rule of law" that meets the complex needs of our time.

Notes

552 Lion Feuchtwanger, *The Oppermanns* (London: Persephone Books, 2020), 376 (first published in Germany in 1933).

553 *Arendt Human Condition*, 191

554 Reports can be found on the website of the Office of the UN High Commissioner for Human Rights, available at: www.ohchr.org.

555 For further detail, see United Nations, Working Group on Enforced or Involuntary Disappearances, *Country Visit to Nepal: Report* (2004), UN Doc. A/HRC/19/58/Add.4.

556 See Roger Cotterrell, *Law's Community: Legal Theory in Sociological Perspective* (Oxford University Press, 1997), 8 ("Law is an aspect of society, not an autonomous force acting upon it") (hereinafter *Cotterrell Law's Community*).

557 Tim Wu, "What Really Saved the Republic From Trump?" *New York Times*, 10 December 2020, available at: www.nytimes.com/2020/12/10/opinion/trump-constitution-norms .html?action=click&module=Opinion&pgtype=Homepage.

558 Carl Schmitt, *The Concept of the Political* , trans. George Schwab (University of Chicago Press, 2007), 79 [hereinafter *Schmitt Concept*].

559 *Risse On Justice*, 294 (where Arendt is seen as one of Aristotle's inheritors in this argument).

560 *Schmitt Concept*, 46–8. See also *Risse On Justice*, 357–9; Pauer-Studer, 59.

561 Quoted in Lacroix and Pranchère, 197. See also *Risse On Justice*, 359–61.

562 See *Dyzenhaus Legitimacy*, 646; *Dyzenhaus Hobbes*, 57 (arguing that for Schmitt, "[l]aw is a mere instrument of state power, which the state deploys at its convenience"). Hannah Arendt warned about the dangers of pure instrumentalism in politics as well. *Arendt Human Condition*, 229 ("We are perhaps the first generation which has become fully aware of the murderous consequences inherent in a line of thought that forces one to admit that all means, provided that they are efficient, are permissible and justified to pursue something defined as an end").

563 In the field of international law, the most sophisticated proponent of this view is Martti Koskenniemi, *From Apology to Utopia. The Structure of International Legal Argument* (Cambridge University Press, 2006) [hereinafter *Koskenniemi Apology*]; Martti Koskenniemi, *The Politics of International Law* (London: Hart, 2011), 36 ("The fight for an international Rule of Law is a fight against politics, understood as a matter of furthering subjective desires, passions, prejudices and leading into an international anarchy"). See also David Kennedy, *A World of Struggle: How Power, Law and Expertise Shape Global Political Economy* (Princeton University Press, 2016). In law more generally, see Roberto Mangabeira Unger, *The Critical Legal Studies Movement* (Cambridge, MA: Harvard University Press, 1986); David Kennedy, "The Stakes of Law, or Hale and Foucault!" (1991) 15 *Legal Studies Forum* 327. In human rights, see Stephen Hopgood, *The Endtimes of Human Rights* (Ithaca, NY: Cornell University Press, 2013). Samuel Moyn, "Human Rights and the Crisis of Liberalism", in Stephen Hopgood, Jack

Snyder and Leslie Vinjamuri (eds), *Human Rights Futures* (Cambridge University Press, 2017), 261, adopts the inverse position, arguing that contemporary liberals have actually abandoned the radical insights of classical liberalism in favour of a bureaucratised status quo. For a critique of critical legal studies from a more radical perspective, see Sousa Santos, 20–2 (on "celebratory post-modernism" that does not even aim for emancipation).

564 M. Kurki and Adriana Sinclair, "Hidden in Plain Sight: Constructivist Treatment of Social Context and Its Limitations" (2010) 47 *Int'l Politics* 1, 10.

565 *Kratochwil Status*, 1, 3, 9.

566 Duke, 45.

567 Thornhill, 203–4.

568 David Dyzenhaus, "Constitutionalism in an Old Key: Legality and Constituent Power" (2012) 1 *Global Constitutionalism* 229, 255 [hereinafter *Dyzenhaus Constitutionalism*].

569 *Habermas Discourse*, 393.

570 For a full discussion, see Jan-Werner Müller, *Constitutional Patriotism* (Princeton University Press, 2007).

571 Thornhill, 36–7.

572 Thornhill, 103 (discussing Weber); Eisenstadt, xxx.

573 Thornhill, 110–12.

574 Thornhill, 48.

575 Lang, 227. It is interesting to note that Nazi legal theorists, like their French revolutionary counterparts, saw the "legal revolution" brought about by the new order as grounded purely in the people's will. Of course, the Nazi end-goal was different: to embed an all-powerful state that could resist any social opposition. Pauer-Studer, 51–2.

576 Madison, Hamilton and Jay, *Federalist Papers*,10, quoted in Thornhill.

577 See, e.g., David Runciman, "Biden Wants Unity and Democracy. But in the US These Have Always Been in Conflict", *The Guardian*, 25 January 2021, available at: www.theguardian.com/commentisfree/2021/jan/25/joe-biden-unity-democracy-us-institutions-president-founding-fathers.

578 Alexander Hamilton, "Objections and Answers respecting the Administration of the Government" (1792), available at: https://founders.archives.gov/documents/Hamilton/01-12-02-0184-0002.

579 Thornhill, 62, 63 ("It is widely noted, historically, that reasonably uniform national peoples only came into being a long time after their first construction as the original authors of democratic polities"), 72.

580 *Walters on Dicey*, 227, 347.

581 Mattias Kumm, "The Cosmopolitan Turn in Constitutionalism: An Integrated Conception of Public Law" (2013) 20 *Indiana J. Global Legal Studies* 605, 611, available at: www.repository.law.indiana.edu/ijgls/vol20/iss2/4 [hereinafter *Kumm Cosmopolitan Turn*].

582 See especially *Walters on Dicey*, 135–7, 178, 187, 203, 205, 347. The following paragraphs are adapted from Jutta Brunnée and Stephen Toope, "Interactional Legal Theory, the International Rule of Law and Global Constitutionalism", in Anthony Lang and Antje

Wiener (eds), *Global Constitutionalism* (Cambridge University Press, 2017), 170 [hereinafter *Brunnée and Toope Constitutionalism*].

583 *Dyzenhaus Constitutionalism*, 233 (italics added). See also *Walters on Dicey*, 296, 298.

584 Mark Walters, "The Unwritten Constitution as a Legal Concept", in David Dyzenhaus and Malcolm Thorburn (eds), *Philosophical Foundations of Constitutional Law* (Oxford University Press, 2016), 33, 40 [hereinafter *Walters Unwritten Constitution*].

585 *Dyzenhaus Legitimacy*, 652; *Dyzenhaus Constitutionalism*, 255.

586 Ignatieff, 188.

587 John Austin, *Lectures on Jurisprudence, or The Philosophy of Positive Law*, 4th edn, ed. R. Campbell (London: John Murray, 1879; reprint Bristol: Thoemmes Press, 2002). See also *Walters on Dicey*, 180, 262.

588 Hans Kelsen, *Pure Theory of Law* (Berkeley: University of California Press, 1967; reprint Union, NJ: Lawbook Exchange, 2009).

589 H. L. A. Hart, *The Concept of Law*, Clarendon Law Series, 2nd edn (Oxford University Press, 1994).

590 *Walters Unwritten Constitution*, 37.

591 Jeremy Waldron, *Political Political Theory: Essays on Institutions* (Cambridge, MA: Harvard University Press, 2016), ch. 2.

592 Walters traces this conception in part to the sixteenth-century political theory of Jean Bodin. *Walters on Dicey*, 183–4. Carl Schmitt also argued that the constitution is a political creation external to law. As we have seen, he went further to argue that the *Volk* (people) who gave legitimacy to the constitution had to be homogeneous. *Schmitt Crisis*, 9. He also believed that the guardian of the people's will was the supreme leader (at first the president of the Reich and ultimately the führer). Pauer-Studer, 36, 41, 71 (the latter on an influential successor to Schmitt).

593 David Dyzenhaus, "The Idea of a Constitution: A Plea for *Staatsrechtslehre*", in David Dyzenhaus and Malcolm Thorburn (eds), *Philosophical Foundations of Constitutional Law* (Oxford University Press, 2016), 9, 16.

594 *Schmitt Theology*. That Schmitt suggested that the sovereign was using "law" to overthrow normal law was, I believe, a fundamental misconception. His "law" was actually just power.

595 See *Walters on Dicey*, 367, 370.

596 Aristotle, *The Nicomachean Ethics*, X:ix. For a compelling modern articulation of this understanding of law, see White 166, 199 and James Boyd White, *The Legal Imagination*, 45th anniversary edn (New York: Aspen, 2018).

597 For a thoughtful contemporary reading of the complexity – even multiplicity – of the classical rhetorical tradition, see Laura Viidebaum, *Creating the Ancient Rhetorical Tradition* (Cambridge University Press, 2021).

598 Francis Mootz, "Vico's 'Ingenious Method' and Legal Education" (2008) 83 *Chicago-Kent L. Rev.* 1261, 1282. Later pragmatist thinkers also challenged Descartes' concept of intuitive certainty, arguing that provisional insight always had to be open to displacement through further, often shared, experience. See John Dewey, *The Quest for Certainty* (New York: Capricorn, 1960). Walters argues that even Dicey, who is often

described as a "formalist", was on the same journey towards understanding law – and the rule of law – primarily in rhetorical terms, not as a collection of rules but as a culture, a "legal turn of mind". *Walters on Dicey*, 282, 298, 360, 368.

599 Pierre Bourdieu, *Sur l'État: Cours au Collège de France 1989–92* (Paris: Éditions du Seuil, 2012), especially lecture of 3 October 1991. I thank Ron Levi for drawing this important work to my attention, and for sharing insight into its implications.

600 *Walters Unwritten Constitution*, 34.

601 *Walters Unwritten Constitution*, 47; *Walters on Dicey*, 296, 298.

602 *Fuller Morality*, 33–8.

603 *Dyzenhaus Constitutionalism*, 233. Fuller made the same point in chiding his positivist critics for "falsification of reality" by simply assuming the existence of lawmaking authority. *Fuller Morality*, 148.

604 Thornhill, 275 (italics in original).

605 Thornhill, 277.

606 A clear example of the hegemonic view of law in contemporary society is Ronald Dworkin, *Law's Empire* (Cambridge, MA: Belknap Press of Harvard University Press, 1986), vii [hereinafter *Dworkin Empire*] ("We live in and by the law. It makes us what we are . . .").

607 *Shklar Legalism*, 1.

608 *Shklar Legalism*, 2.

609 *Shklar Legalism*, 10.

610 *Shklar Legalism*, 104.

611 *Shklar Legalism*, 106.

612 *Shklar Legalism*, 109–10. The debate between the legal theorist H. L. A. Hart and Lon Fuller took place largely on the pages of the *Harvard Law Review*, and pitted Oxford's sophisticated positivist, Hart, against Harvard's sociological legal theorist, Fuller. I will return to the Hart–Fuller debate in Chapter 8, in the section on "The Rule of Law".

613 For the most thoughtful and "uncompromising" defence of justice as "the first virtue of social institutions" just "as truth is for systems of thought", see *Rawls Justice*, 3–4. Though it is revealing that even this most sophisticated of thinkers fell back on a stunningly legalistic measure for the assessment of public reason: "how would our argument strike us presented in the form of a supreme court opinion?" John Rawls, *Political Liberalism* (New York: Columbia University Press, 1993), 254 [hereinafter *Rawls Liberalism*].

614 *Shklar Legalism*, 119. Now we might add "economic" and "environmental" justice. See also p. 120 ("Justice, as an operative private virtue, may depend upon the acceptance of freedom and equality as social values, but no purpose is served by speaking of economic, social, or political justice, beyond attaching the sacred name of justice to social ends which, however worthy, do not form a part of justice and may, in fact, come into conflict with it"). The pragmatist philosopher John Dewey argued in parallel that "justice", like other seemingly abstract terms ("democracy" or "freedom"), can be understood only in relation to human experience and contested history. Their

invocation opens debate, and does not settle arguments. See the discussion in Sullivan, 56. See also *Cotterrell Law's Community*, 316–17.

615 *Shklar Legalism*, 116.

616 Duke, 88. See also Robert Cover, "The Supreme Court 1982 Term Forward: Nomos and Narrative" (1983) 97 *Harvard L. Rev.* 4, 11–12 (on Jewish traditions of appropriate purposes in the world, uniting justice, kindness and peace).

617 *Habermas Discourse*, 28. See also *Sandel Limits*, 5, 9.

618 Quoted in Thornhill, 71, fn 74. Amartya Sen argues with great force that notions of freedom and liberty are actually included within a properly expansive understanding of justice. Sen, 59 (aligning with John Rawls on this point), 63 (on liberty being a condition for "public reason"), 301, 317 (on the diverse content in the concepts of liberty and freedom), 304 (on the importance of personal freedom).

619 *Habermas Discourse*, 418. See also *Risse On Justice*, 49 (distinguishing Rawls and Habermas). For a summary of other challenges to justice, especially distributive justice, as *the* core virtue, see *Risse On Justice*, 21–2 (where various thinkers posit that survival, security, agency, efficiency, caring, recognition and participation are all undermined by a focus on justice). Risse describes "distributive justice" as "making sure each person has their proper place in this effort [of humanity] and can enjoy the fruits of collective labor". *Risse On Justice*, 126.

620 *Habermas Discourse*, 459–61.

621 *Habermas Discourse*, xlii–iii (Preface).

622 *Sandel Limits*, 33, see also 179.

623 *Sandel Limits*, 203, 207.

624 Tully, 551–2.

625 See, e.g., Stephen Hopgood, Jack Snyder and Leslie Vinjamuri, "Introduction: Human Rights Past, Present, and Future", in Stephen Hopgood, Jack Snyder and Leslie Vinjamuri (eds), *Human Rights Futures* (Cambridge University Press, 2017), 1, 22; Jack Snyder, "Empowering Rights Through Mass Movements, Religion, and Reform Parties", in Stephen Hopgood, Jack Snyder and Leslie Vinjamuri (eds), *Human Rights Futures* (Cambridge University Press, 2017), 88, 106, 109; Moyn, 274.

CHAPTER EIGHT

Interactional Law and the Rule of Law

> If the people be led by laws, and uniformity sought to be given them by punishments, they will try to avoid the punishment, but have no sense of shame. If they be led by virtue, and uniformity sought to be given them by the rules of propriety, they will have the sense of shame, and moreover will become good.
>
> Confucius, *The Analects*[626]

> You are not obliged to complete the work, but neither are you free to desist from it . . .
>
> Rabbi Tarfon[627]

OVER THE LAST TWENTY YEARS, Jutta Brunnée and I have developed what we call an "interactional" understanding of international law, connecting insights from IR constructivism and practice theory to the legal theory of Lon Fuller.[628] I will shortly lay out the basic approach, but want now to make a strong claim that "interactional law" is an expression of the intellectual traditions I canvassed in Part II of this book. As such, it is not limited to the context of international law, but can inform our understanding of all law. And it helps to point the way to a more hopeful future because it posits an understanding of the rule of law that is appropriately modest but, in part for that reason, fruitful in addressing the anxieties of our era. The rule of law so understood assists us in reconfiguring public authorities of the state, providing ways for them to be more responsive to the fundamental human aspirations towards both autonomy (being able to make choices about one's own life trajectory) and communication (the need for interaction and a sense of community), while also upholding social diversity.[629] This possibility should be reassuring in our anxious times.

In developing our understanding of the rule of law and of the role of legal rules in contemporary societies, Brunnée and I were influenced by Lon Fuller because, amongst twentieth-century legal theorists, he was the most insightful in explaining the essential "horizontality" of all law.[630] Fuller argued that what is often assumed to be a vertical relationship – of authority and subordination – is better understood as a reciprocal relationship in which citizens "accept as law and generally observe" a promulgated body of rules and, in turn, are able to expect that the government and its officials will abide by and apply these rules.[631]

The conceptual apparatus of IR constructivism also provided useful insight into the emergence, maintenance and operation of social norms. Constructivists argued that "norms" are standards of behaviour created through mutual expectation in a social setting, and further that the identity and behaviour of social actors is made up of culture, ideas, institutions, discourse and social norms. Together, these elements shape the perception of "interests". In other words, interests are not strictly speaking "chosen" but are constructed in social interaction and shaped by identity.[632] Those insights connect to the tradition of Aristotelean "practical reason" and to elements of pragmatism I have previously discussed. In turn, practice theory illuminates the dynamic interplay between actors pursuing their ends and legal norms enabling, guiding or constraining them in these pursuits. More specifically, it helps us to understand law as a distinctive set of practices focused on interpretation, justification, contestation and creative action that is rooted in overlapping communities of practice. Practices of law do not create or sustain immutable truths; they provide frames rooted in constitutive rules or anchoring practices that may themselves change over time if they are not constantly reinforced through continuing practice.

Drawing on these influences, the interactional law framework has three interrelated elements. First, building on constructivist insights from international relations, Brunnée and I posit that legal norms can arise only in the context of social norms based on shared understandings (pragmatism's "Background"). The constructivist discussion of shared understandings also reveals both how *social* norms stabilise and how they shift.[633] Secondly, what distinguishes law from other types of social ordering is not simply provenance from a particular hierarchical source – the sovereign power, a legislature, a court – but adherence to a series of internal criteria of legality that were comprehensively, but not definitively, described by Fuller: generality, publicity or promulgation, non-retroactivity, clarity, non-contradiction, not asking the impossible, constancy, and congruence between rules and official action.[634] When linked to these criteria of legality, social norms can become relatively fixed as law. But that fixity is never permanent. Brunnée and I posit, thirdly, that when the shared social understandings in which legal norms are grounded erode, or undergo significant shifts, law too will be under pressure to adjust. Reinforcement, adjustment or demolition of legal norms takes place in and through practices of legality (norm application and interpretation that also satisfies the legality requirements). Continuing practices of legality are crucial to generating a distinctive legal legitimacy and a sense of commitment among those to whom law is addressed.

Fuller's notion of "congruence between rules and official action" encapsulates the idea of reciprocal relationships that I just mentioned and merits a few additional observations. In this conception of reciprocity, lawgivers of the state can only expect that citizens will "accept as law and generally observe" the promulgated body of rules when they meet the criteria of legality.[635] In turn, if they are to be guided by these rules, citizens must be able to expect that the government will also abide by and apply the rules. As well, actions of officials must be congruent with explicit laws, and consonant with the requirements of legality.[636] More than that, law can guide self-directed human interaction only if relatively stable patterns of expectation, or shared understandings, emerge and if law is anchored in them. Through dynamic participatory processes law generates and must continue to maintain its own authority. There is no single external point of origin for law, be it a rule of recognition, a grundnorm or a presumed moral basis created through divine revelation or right thinking.[637] Law is not held up by a string, but is internally validated and must be self-reinforced through continuing practices.

In other words, as I have emphasised, basic norms of good governance are found within law itself.[638] As long as legal rules are grounded in shared expectations and largely meet the criteria of legality, law serves as its own source of authority because it is viewed as legitimate by the people to whom law is directed and through whom law is created.[639] It will have built its own "epistemic practical authority". Law exists, then, on a continuum, being expressed, interpreted, debated, contested, reinforced and sometimes dismantled through the work of communities of practice, their engagement with other such communities in parallel social fields such as politics and sociology, and their influence in the wider world.

Another way of explaining processes that generate and maintain legal authority is that the criteria of legality are crucial in shaping the patterns of a practice of legality. Remember Adler's definition of practices, that they consist of "socially meaningful patterned actions that, performed more or less competently, simultaneously embody, act out, and possibly reify background knowledge and discourse in and on the material world".[640] As we have seen, background knowledge serves to frame particular practices and, in turn, these practices maintain that background knowledge, which participants in the practice come to take for granted.[641] For example, one anchoring practice of law is the idea that both sides to a dispute have a right to be heard before any judgement is given by an official of the state, be it a judge or a civil servant in less consequential matters. Citizens might tolerate instances of arbitrary decision-making for a time, but if too many people experience a failure to be heard the process of decision-making will soon be viewed as unfair and illegitimate. If landlords have the right to launch cases to evict tenants for breach of a lease, but tenants are not afforded a right to explain the circumstances of the purported breach, tenants will soon organise and rebel against the adjudicative process in question.

However, even important anchoring practices – part of background knowledge – are not fixed for eternity. In interaction with other communities of practice, background knowledge is challenged and new knowledge can be created; that is why the background does not produce stasis. Within legal communities of practice, the criteria of legality are the relatively stable, socially constructed background knowledge that partially constitutes the practices of law. They provide the meaningful content of legal interaction and allow for interpretation along similar standards. And we have seen that they function to preclude claims that all *de facto* authority or power is actually "law". What is more, in deeply diverse societies, including international society, these criteria imbue law with a measure of cross-cultural commonality because they are largely procedural and do not demand commitment to a particular version of the good life.[642] The criteria of legality can operate and discipline legal claims even in the face of differences, divisions and cultural particularities.[643]

What Fuller termed "congruence" of purported rules and official action also plays a central role as the third element of interactional law: the practice of legality. It reveals that congruence is more than just "compliance" or conformity of conduct with a given rule. Congruence encompasses a wide range of practices such as legal argumentation, interpretation, contestation, implementation or enforcement measures through which actors demonstrate adherence to the specific norm as well as support for its legality. Therefore, the congruence requirement can be met even when some actors violate or distort existing legal norms, provided that other participants in the legal system work to uphold those norms. Law does not have to be perfectly supported to retain its authority. Consider the case of traffic laws. They are breached quite commonly, but most people follow traffic rules most of the time. They therefore retain their congruence, even though they cannot be constantly enforced, nor can every breach be sanctioned.

It is through a continuing practice of legality that existing norms are buttressed or adjusted through law's distinctive patterns of interaction. Inversely, when a practice of legality degrades (i.e., the criteria of legality are no longer met in practice or failure to uphold the norm becomes endemic), legal norms can be undermined and destroyed.[644] An emphasis on the *practice* of legality highlights that law's application, interpretation and enforcement are all part of a continuum that either supports and subtly adjusts, or undermines, legal norms.[645]

A dramatic example of how these shifts occur is the fate of capital punishment across many different legal systems. Where once the idea of putting people to death for capital crimes was widely accepted, in many societies the shared expectation began to change. Civil society, religious and legal communities of practice started to question the legitimacy of state-sanctioned killing as a punishment for crime. The issue took on international dimensions as some countries, notably Germany, international NGOs and intergovernmental human rights organisations launched campaigns to halt the application of the death penalty. Public opinion in many parts of the world started to shift, and formal legal institutions began to make decisions that undermined the rules concerning capital punishment. Juries sometimes refused to convict in capital cases, or judges found ways not to impose the penalty, deploying mechanisms of interpretation and delay. Appeal processes proliferated, and in many cases even those people sentenced to death escaped its application. In some cases, legislatures formally abolished the death penalty, but in others the penalty simply faded away in practice. It must be said, however, that in other societies social support for state-sanctioned killing remained strong. In those countries, and sometimes even within sub-units of federal states, the death penalty persists as a vital legal norm. The rule of law can accommodate a fairly wide – but not infinite – diversity of values.

To sum up, in Brunnée's and my description of the life-cycle of legal norms, social norms emerge from shared understandings, but must meet the criteria of legality (a specific type of background knowledge) to generate authority as law. It is the criteria of legality that provide standards against which one can measure purported legal norms. The standards are procedural in the main, although they tend to support important claims to autonomy and communication. But they are not linked to specific substantive definitions of democracy or rights or liberal economics, so they can function in highly diverse societies. Even then, legal norms, and the reciprocity upon which interactional law relies, require constant reinforcement through a continuing practice of legality if they are not to fall into disuse or be actively destroyed. If the law deviates from the practices and understandings that prevail within society, it risks being unintelligible to social actors – unclear or unreasonable – and impaired in its legality. When the conflict between a society's shared understandings and its legal rules is too stark, legality can come under significant strain. Actors' ability to rely on the law in their decision-making, and their commitment to the law, is fostered by adherence to the requirements of legality, especially congruence between official action and the law.

With this understanding of law in mind, we can now step back and examine in more detail how a "rule of law" can, amongst its various purposes, help us navigate through our new age of anxiety. The starting point is to remind ourselves of the pragmatist conception of truth:

> We have seen, however, that the pragmatist position ought to be a modest one. One call for modesty is on the inquirer, who must assume that there is a right answer to the question at hand, but not assume that he has the right answer in hand. The right answer, if there is one, is that which would be arrived at were inquiry to be pursued as far as it could fruitfully go.[646]

From this approach we can extrapolate that one cannot create a rule of law by fiat; it has to be built together in communities of practice and through them engage with the wider community, interacting with the insights and contributions of other communities of practice, and ultimately requiring the continuing confidence of the wider populace. Furthermore, even when it is built up and continuously supported, the rule of law alone cannot eliminate all social ills. It must work in conjunction with other socio-political frameworks and institutions, such as representative government, an effective public service and the ability of citizens (often through the media) to criticise the policies and practices of all organisations in society.

A telling example is the appropriate scope of personal privacy in public spaces. More and more of our urban environments are subject to CCTV surveillance. A robust rule of law can ensure that there are safeguards against governmental abuse in such surveillance, but it cannot answer all the important social questions about the deployment of CCTV in the first place. Is it an effective deterrent to crime? Might it have differential impact in relation to certain groups of people? Does the deployment of facial recognition technologies add new ethical issues to the mix? Are CCTV technologies sufficiently robust to be reliable? Might they contain biases in the algorithms? To answer these questions, legal communities of practice would have to interact with communities of sociologists, psychologists and technologists. And the insights from these communities of practice would have to be considered by legislators, the police, the media, NGOs, merchant associations and many others.

The answers that a rule of law provides to social challenges are invariably contingent because shared investigation, interpretation, contestation and reinforcement through concrete action never end. However, a modest rule of law connects legal communities of practice with a broader mix of agents – state practitioners, corporations, scientists, experts and other related communities of practice – all of whom need to learn to cope with uncertainty-causing anxiety that differs according to the field of forces at play in nationalist populism, globalism, and the rise of new technologies and dominating network platforms. In our era, I have argued that these fundamental sources of anxiety can be addressed effectively only through the building up of "epistemic practical authority" across a range of interacting communities of practice. Remember that Adler defined such authority as "the legitimate power to rule on the adoption of practices and their meanings".[647] The rule of law is one of the most powerful forms of epistemic practical authority if it is built in ways that I will shortly describe. That is why it has a central role to play in helping our societies manage and lessen debilitating anxiety, and why it can provide fresh impetus to public authorities in building more inclusive societies that support human autonomy and facilitate human communication.

THE RULE OF LAW

The rule of law is a slippery concept with many definitions offered up over time.[648] At its most general, the concept could mean only that "formalized, predictable, regularized power is substituted for … arbitrary … power".[649] But that definition is not good enough because it treats the study of law and the study of power as one and the same. I have argued that law and power are related to one another in most "intricate ways", that law can be an exercise of power but that it also tames power. Law can be experienced by the people to whom it is directed as a power over oneself or as a balancing of forces that provides a sense of security. As such, it can be conducive to social peace, being a source of comfort.[650] And, crucially, law is itself constrained in the ways that it can legitimately deploy its own power.

The English jurist, A. V. Dicey, who is commonly thought to have coined the term "rule of law", postulated three components: that government must rule through law crafted "in the ordinary legal manner" and not through discretionary action; that citizens and government officials are all equal before the law and subject "to the ordinary law of the realm"; and that the jurisdiction of ordinary courts "in particular cases" – a commitment to inductive reasoning – is the best source of legal protection, rather than reference to "general principles of the constitution" or supposedly universal concepts. The common thread is a commitment to the "ordinary" in constitutional practice and interpretation. For Dicey, constitutional rules were not exceptional, but part of the woof and warp of everyday law.[651] Though often criticised, this conception has been highly influential, with contemporary thinkers relying on the tripartite framework, often implicitly.[652] Indeed, it has been said that in any discussion of the rule of law "[y]ou cannot escape Dicey".[653] Continental scholars of the civil law tradition have placed less emphasis upon the role of court interpretation, and have focused instead on the nature of the state. Is the state itself law-based, or merely power-based? Thus, the French version, *État de droit*, or the German, *Rechtsstaat*.[654]

In a recent contribution, Pavel describes the rule of law as "a moral ideal" that is made operative through both "formal features" similar to the "criteria of legality" posited by Fuller, and "substantive features" focused on equality and autonomy.[655] These were also the key features in Hannah Arendt's understanding of politics: the uniqueness and equality of each person fully revealed only in "sheer human togetherness".[656] Pavel emphasises that:

> The rule of law ideal embodies both a horizontal relationship of equality among the law's subjects, such that no subject has more power or authority over others, and a vertical relationship between officials and subjects, such that officials are constrained to respect the autonomy of subjects.[657]

I have argued that Fuller would go further than this and suggest that the relationship between officials and subjects is itself horizontal in the important sense that official action must be "congruent" with legal norms. Only when this is true will "subjects" accept the legitimacy of law's claims to authority.[658] Nonetheless, Pavel appropriately focuses on the central issue in any debate over the content of the rule of law: the relative importance of "formal" and "substantive" elements in the definition.

This central division of opinion is often framed around the metaphor of a "thin" – largely formal, or perhaps more accurately, procedural – rule of law and a "thick" rule of law, replete with substantive obligations.[659] Distinguished jurists, including Lord Bingham, late of the UK House of Lords, and influential scholars like Oxford's John Finnis argue the necessity for social goods such as freedom and equality, as well as protections of human rights (or natural rights[660]), to be included within the rule of law. The rule of law and concepts of *justice* are, for these thinkers, intimately linked.[661] Remember that Judith Shklar saw this linkage as unfortunate and a manifestation of "legalism". In the words of Lord Bingham:

> A state which savagely represses or persecutes sections of its people cannot on my view be regarded as observing the rule of law, even if the transport of the persecuted minority to the concentration camp or the compulsory exposure of female children on the mountainside is the subject of detailed laws duly enacted and scrupulously observed.[662]

The common justifications for the thick version of the rule of law are that procedural guarantees are not enough to preclude abuse and tyranny, and that core moral values cannot be protected by legal procedure alone.

For the sake of argument, if one were to accept the demand for a substantive rule of law, it remains to decide the content. Some theorists have adopted an expansive view to include all individual, political and social rights rooted in conceptions of the good life, including freedom and equality.[663] The rights to life and physical integrity, freedom of opinion and thought, and the right to private property are often included, as well as what Americans would call "due process" rights, that is, rights to fair and equal treatment within the justice system.[664] McCorquodale adopts a somewhat more circumscribed position (intended to translate the rule of law into the international system) in which he draws on Diceyan elements, albeit re-phrased, such as the need for "legal order", "equal application of the law", and the importance of "settlement of disputes before an independent legal body". But he also includes in his relatively "thick" understanding of the rule of law, the corpus of international human rights protections.[665]

In the passage I cited above, Lord Bingham was explicitly distinguishing his position from that of the influential legal theorist, Joseph Raz, who had argued that a legal system that promoted slavery or discrimination on the basis of sex could still be a rule of law system if the rules were properly enacted and equally applied.[666] Provocatively, Raz once called the rule of law little more than a slogan.[667] Here he was joined by Judith Shklar who described the rule of law as nothing but "ruling class chatter".[668]

In my view, Dicey's conception of the rule of law was closer to Raz's than to Bingham's. Although Dicey did focus on what he called that "special attribute of English institutions", the court of general jurisdiction, Dicey was not thereby importing extensive substantive rights and freedoms into the rule of law itself. He was only suggesting that if a society *wants* to protect rights, courts are the best way of doing so because inductive reasoning is safer than attempts to inculcate high principle through law.[669] Dicey was fundamentally committed to what is called "parliamentary sovereignty", to a legislature that shapes the law. Walters argues convincingly that for Dicey, the sovereignty exercised by Parliament is essentially legal, designed first and foremost to control against the arbitrary exercise of executive authority.[670] However, I do not think that this commitment resulted in a full-scale importation of a bill of rights into the English constitution.[671] Parliament could still override rights; it just had to do so through legislation. The executive could not do so by decree.[672]

Chesterman argues in a similar fashion as concerns the possibility of an effective rule of law in international society. He demands "clarity" and the abandonment of

> ... the additional role that the rule of law sometimes plays as a Trojan horse to import other political goals such as democracy, human rights, and specific economic policies. It is a price worth paying, however, as these substantive goals may properly be seen as distinct from the rule of law – folding them into its robes reduces it to a rhetorical device at best, a disingenuous ideological tool at worst.[673]

Legal theorist Robert Summers argued a parallel point, from the perspective of state legal systems, favouring a purely formal rule of law because of its political neutrality.[674] That said, his "formal" version, focusing on proper procedure, was still wide-ranging, including eighteen requirements.[675] Habermas, too, although he did not use the term "rule of law", argued for a procedural (formal) "paradigm of law" that did not favour "a particular ideal of society, a particular vision of the good life, or even a particular political option".[676]

I do not think that we have to choose between dichotomous positions, the purely formal or the purely substantive conceptions of the rule of law.[677] In a thoughtful reconsideration of Hobbes' understanding of law in society, Dyzenhaus suggests that one can "infer from the fact that law is a human creation that it will include principles of legality that condition the content of positive law in a way that explains why people would consent to be governed by law rather than by some other means".[678] Dyzenhaus explains that even for Hobbes, the ruler "rules through law but also in accordance with the rule of law".[679] A key passage is found in *Behemoth*:

> ... the Power of the mighty has no foundation but in the opinion and the beleefe of the people ... [and] if men know not their duty, what is there that can force them to obey the laws? An army you will say? But what shall force the army?[680]

One can trace this conception of authority back to Aristotle, who argued that there was a fundamental distinction between "kingship" where the passions of the ruler are constrained by "the normative and coercive force of the law" and "tyranny" where no such constraint existed".[681]

Fuller describes the rule of law as existing where "formal institutions are established guaranteeing to the members of the community some participation in the decisions by which their interests are affected".[682] Given his background in the common law tradition, it is not surprising that Fuller focused attention on adjudication, though he argued strenuously that courts are only one aspect of a legal system and that they are often not appropriate to settle what he called "polycentric", meaning multifaceted, disputes.[683] But for a legal system and legal rules to be both legitimate and effective, Fuller believed that in the relevant society there had to exist a widespread desire to pursue some shared human purpose – he gave federalism and a system of exchange (contract) as two examples.[684] These shared purposes serve as premises or starting points for the working out of legal rules in institutions. As Fuller succinctly put it, "communication and persuasion presuppose some shared context of principle",[685] or what Searle would call "Background". It should be obvious then that Fuller's legality requirements, while largely autonomous from substantive values, are not completely divorced from shared understandings – and collective purposes – in society.[686]

Fuller insisted further that notwithstanding their essentially procedural nature, legality requirements would make it harder in practice for substantive injustices to be perpetrated by legal means:

> It has been said that most of the world's injustices are inflicted, not with the fists, but with the elbows. When we use our fists we use them for a definite purpose, and we are answerable to others and to ourselves for that purpose. Our elbows, we may comfortably suppose, trace a random pattern for which we are not responsible, although our neighbor may be painfully aware that he is being systematically pushed from his seat. A strong commitment to the principles of legality compels a ruler to answer to himself, not only for his fists, but for his elbows as well.[687]

John Finnis put forward a similar argument, emphasising that "[a]dherence to the Rule of Law ... is always liable to reduce the efficiency for evil of an evil government, since it systematically restricts the government's freedom of manoeuvre".[688] This is a fundamental point: limitations on action that are largely procedural can have a profound effect on a government's ability to use its elbows to push citizens around. Tyrants (or for that matter, many powerful private interests) do not like procedural limits on their freedom of action because they are effective in restricting power.

Fuller's discussion of the "internal morality of law"[689] – what Brunnée and I call the criteria of legality – provides a compelling framework to imagine a rule of law that is primarily procedural, but that contains enough substantive constraint for law to play its necessary disciplining function on the exercise of power.[690] As we have seen, Fuller argued that if the criteria of legality were largely met, law could control tyrants, both their fists and their elbows, while also ensuring healthy political discourse (communication) within society, and supporting the autonomy of citizens.[691] An obvious example is the requirement that legal rules be made public or, to use the technical term, "promulgated". Only when laws are known will citizens be able to shape their behaviour in accordance with a rule, thereby avoiding liability. In tyrannical regimes, secret laws – often termed "presidential edicts" or "public order directives" – are deployed to trap hapless individuals. What is more, known laws are subject to contestation in the public sphere, through formal political and juridical mechanisms or even in protests on the street.

Fuller never required absolute adherence to the criteria of legality.[692] Like specific legal rules, the rule of law is an imperfect creation. It is not an achieved, or even achievable, ideal but an aspiration.[693] Again, in the words of Lord Bingham:

> The concept of the rule of law is not fixed for all time. Some countries do not subscribe to it fully, and some subscribe to it only in name, if that. Even those who subscribe to it find it difficult to apply all its precepts quite all the time . . . It remains an ideal, but an ideal worth striving for, in the interest of good government and peace, at home and in the world at large.[694]

This is equally true of national and international legal and political orders.[695]

My understanding of the rule of law presupposes that law is not grounded simply in the will of the sovereign or even of Parliament; it is not merely the fiat of state power, nor is it rooted in a hierarchy of rules.[696] *Humans* are not subjected to law; human *conduct* in its broadest form, including the creation of institutions, is subjected to the governance of shared – and communally created – rules.[697] No law, even law in seemingly hierarchical state systems, is merely the imposition of authority or power from above.[698] That is because, when understood as a purposive activity rooted in shared social understandings and goals, law depends for its continuing existence on reciprocity, the "effective interaction and cooperation between citizens and law-making and law-applying officials".[699]

An important implication, and one that is often misrepresented in common parlance, is that law is not something that can be simply "enforced" by raw power. Mechanisms of enforcement are important as part of continuing practices of legality, but only in totalitarian regimes such as North Korea do public authorities depend almost entirely on the threat of physical force to embed rules. In most contexts, law operates because citizens believe it must. They display fidelity to law to advance social purposes and are more inclined to do so when they think that public officials are also bound by legal rules. Even in criminal law settings, where state power can be most severe, most of us do not break the law only because we fear that we will be punished. If we all routinely committed credit card fraud, systems of exchange would break down and our social and economic purposes would be undermined. What is more, we know that public officials are also bound not to commit fraud, and are tasked to create systems of validation and cross-referencing that make such fraud difficult to commit.

For Fuller, reciprocity was necessary to support the fundamental autonomy of human beings. Individuals are not just instruments of the state or the community; their unique purposes must be respected.[700] However, as I have already emphasised, Fuller always balanced human autonomy against an equally fundamental need for human communication, made manifest in what he called "the morality of duty".[701] Citizens are not merely subjects but are interacting agents creating law through specific processes of communication and action, and they have responsibilities one to another in society.

In a tense, though politely academic, exchange with the great English legal philosopher H. L. A. Hart, where both thinkers seemed to be arguing at cross-purposes, Fuller suggested that Hart's legal positivism would have validated Nazi law, making critique impossible. This was perhaps unfair,[702] but it gave Fuller the opportunity to explain why his internal characteristics of law would have allowed a clear judgement that Nazi "law" was not law at all.[703] As we have seen, Fuller argued that certain conditions must be in place to allow human beings to pursue their purposes through law and for law to guide their actions and interactions.[704] If these legality conditions were not largely fulfilled, then the processes of law creation, be it through executive action, legislation, adjudication or negotiation, would be fundamentally flawed and, I would add, lacking in distinctive legal legitimacy. This means that the very idea of a "dual state", with some law established within the constitutional system and a separate form of law that is actually authoritarian edict validated by power, is impossible in the sense that the latter is simply not law.[705] Sean Rehaag summarises Fuller's position clearly:

> Fuller contended that the systemic procedural irregularities in which Nazi dictates were embedded departed so seriously from the principles of legality that at least some Nazi dictates could not reasonably be characterized as legal. These irregularities included extensive use of legislation to retroactively render criminal acts (including mass murder) lawful, secret regulations and legislation, and political interference with the judiciary such that the interpretation and application of laws became subject to executive whims. Given these irregularities, according to Fuller post-Nazi German courts could legitimately refuse to allow individuals to avoid legal repercussions for heinous acts committed under the colour of Nazi "law".[706]

For Fuller, then, the rule of law is created through the generation of "fidelity to law" when strong – though not necessarily perfect – adherence to the criteria of legality within legal communities of practice produces law that is legitimate in the eyes of the persons to whom it is addressed.[707]

In other words, the rule of law is internal to law itself, just as we saw that the legal constitution of a country is itself a legal, and not a purely political, construction.[708] An example of how this "fidelity" works is, perhaps surprisingly, tax law. No one really enjoys paying taxes. We grumble and sweat over our tax forms, or we give up and ask an accountant to fill them in for us. However, when tax law is seen to be public, with the rules relatively clear and understandable, and when those rules are seen to be applied by officials in a non-retroactive and consistent manner, most people will voluntarily pay their taxes. The contrary is equally true, and in many states with a weak set of rule of law principles and practices, the rate of effective tax collection is low.[709] I believe that recognising that the rule of law generates its own "fidelity" when law is perceived as legitimate is a key building block in constructing societies that are stable but also capable of needed change, helping us to address our current anxieties. I will return to this point shortly.

To summarise, then, following Fuller's middle ground between thick conceptions of the rule of law that incorporate contested political commitments, and thin conceptions that deliver little but formal "due process", I emphasise that social learning is possible through processes of law. This learning has the potential to drive limited shared understandings across cultures, building up a distributed background knowledge. Therefore, an admittedly modest rule of law is achievable even in a pluralist society, be it national or international.[710] Fuller always argued that criteria of legality exist on a sliding scale, not as an all-or-nothing package. So, too, the rule of law; when I suggest a "modest" conception is possible, I mean that it will not likely fulfil every possible aspiration, but will provide a framework that is useful in the creation of accountable public authority, protective of people and generative of societal health.[711] A good example is the mechanism of judicial review of executive action. Getting the balance right between empowered political actors who gain legitimacy from elections and the sober second thought of judges who are tasked to ensure that the executive follows the law is always complicated. But it is important that the public actions of governmental officials are open to scrutiny and tested against established law. Otherwise, politically instrumental decisions can threaten the rights, and even the safety, of individuals and groups.

The rule of law involves practices of social actors that are shaped and sometimes even controlled by criteria of legality that allow these actors (members of overlapping communities of practice) to pursue their purposes and organise their interactions. The embedding of these criteria of legality in continuing practice generates a distinctive form of legal legitimacy thereby building a sense of commitment among those to whom law is addressed, helping to explain legal obligation. One might call this a "culture of legality".[712] An example of just such a culture of legality in operation is the system that allows for the circulation of aeroplane traffic around the world. Grounded in the need for communication as well as the desire to allow people to make their own autonomous travel choices, a system of treaties grants overflight rights and landing rights, and supports air safety. The outrage that resulted from the decision of Belarusian President Lukashenko to force down a foreign airline's commercial flight to seize a political opponent demonstrates the widely shared understanding of the need for a rule of law in international aviation.[713]

However, the culture of legality does not require acceptance of a particular construction of the good life or of substantive political and other human rights, so it cannot be dismissed as an exclusionary and value-laden liberal internationalism.[714] Therefore, although many – but certainly not all – of the inspirations I draw upon in this book are derived from "Western" traditions of thought, the intent is to transcend borders and to acknowledge the fundamental *need* for intellectual plurality if we are to build towards truth and create healthy societies that can effectively interact one with another.

The rule of law is not rooted primarily in any specific legal institutions, be it parliaments or courts. The rule of law can therefore exist in international society, where these types of institutions are less developed.[715] This is not to say that institutions are unhelpful in promoting or strengthening practices of legality – institutions, broadly conceived as collections of practices, are important – only that such practices can emerge in diverse ways even in weaker institutional settings. Diplomacy, for example, can be part of a practice of legality even though it is not itself a formal legal institution. International human rights law is often buttressed and advanced through diplomatic actions. So, too, the legal frameworks of arms control.

The reference to various roles of diplomacy emphasises that the aspiration towards a rule of law is not only about constraining power in seemingly hierarchical systems of authority – that is, limiting governmental power within states – although it does perform this function.[716] The rule of law also manages and shapes power within transparently "horizontal" systems like international law.[717] In both settings, it is practices shaped by criteria of legality that limit and channel power, although they may manifest themselves in different ways through the efforts of various social actors.[718] In a national system, the goal is in part to constrain centralised power. In international society the rule of law is more about the equal application of rules, and limiting the self-interested autonomy of states,[719] an autonomy that should not be analogised to the autonomy of individual human beings. I say this because human beings are singular entities that have a capacity to establish their own purposes in life, to create their own "beginnings", to return to Arendt's evocative phrasing (subject, of course, to contextual limitations which can be very real, and can strongly constrain the life choices available to people).[720] States, on the other hand, are artificial constructs that have no real collective intentionality; their purposes are shaped by social and political forces that shift over time, often dramatically. The very existence of a state is determined by the rules of the international order.[721] What is more, the "dignity" of a human being is a strong moral claim; not so the "dignity" of a state.

The version of the rule of law that I defend is one that helps to deliver social stability. Living in a society where rules are relatively predictable and where governmental leaders and civil servants are expected to abide by the same rules as ordinary citizens is reassuring.[722] Just ask the people of Myanmar. They had been moving for over a decade, even if haltingly, towards a country governed by the rule of law when their expectations were completely overturned by yet another military *coup d'état* in 2021. The BBC quoted one anonymous 25-year-old: "Waking up to learn your world has been completely turned upside down overnight was not a new feeling, but a feeling that I thought that we had moved on from, and one that I never thought we'd be forced to feel again."[723] In Myanmar, the overthrow of the rule of law undermines the sense that one can project oneself into the future, and work towards the fulfilment of one's own aspirations. That is tremendously demoralising. Inversely, the relative stability that the rule of law provides can open up vistas of purpose and hope.

At the same time, my understanding of the rule of law does not preclude needed social change because it is rooted in continuing practices that generate authority of a particular kind, what we have seen Adler describe as "epistemic practical authority".[724] Members of communities of legal practice convince others of their discursive and practical competence, revealed in a range of interacting processes including interpretation, negotiation and contestation.[725] In these practices, change can be conceptualised, debated, explained and brought into being. The rule of law, then, may favour stability but its content is not fixed in concrete. Because it is grounded in competent practices that are themselves subject to selection and replication, the rule of law is also open to diverse influences, accommodating cultural difference. It does not impose a fixed set of "ends" that all societies are expected to pursue in exactly the same way; its substantive content is limited, but its procedural content is demanding. That is what helps to establish an appropriate balance between building social stability and shaping change. A modest rule of law also pays attention to the contributions of other forms of social ordering, not claiming to define all debates or to provide the only legitimate answers to social challenges.

This version of the rule of law seems to me to be well attuned to the complex realities of our time, and to the pluralism of our national and international societies, while providing a much-needed discipline in social and political life. There are legitimate constraints to be imposed upon all members of society, including the most powerful. Governments are expected to follow the rules, just as citizens are expected to do. Accusations of misconduct will be dealt with through processes that are public, applicable to all and subject to rules of due process. All of this should be encouraging to citizens who seek to participate in public decision-making while also being "left alone" to get on with their own priorities.

With this understanding of the rule of law in mind, it remains to articulate some of the specific roles that law can play in addressing our prevalent social anxiety, and, finally, to assess what this means for the practice of lawyers and for their education. Because law is rooted in shared normative understandings and is infused with social purpose, it has the capacity not only to resolve disputes and to coordinate action, but also to foster cooperation through the development and reform of social institutions.

Of course, law being only relatively autonomous from politics, the idea of cooperation in law is grounded in a partially cooperative conception of politics as well. That means rejecting the almost purely combative view of politics derived from Hobbes, Weber and Schmitt, in favour of a view that politics is a "struggle between conflicting parties to influence or determine the terms of social co-operation".[726] Please note that I am not suggesting that politics is all "sweetness and light". Politics involves conflicting parties, but its goal should be to contribute to resolving or at least mediating conflict: struggle and cooperation are closely connected and lead to law's role in balancing the two.[727] Habermas argued that his democratic conception of communicative action requires a commitment to cooperation as a product of discourse, rather than mere "strategic interaction", which might be thought of as pure bargaining. Such bargaining could at best lead to the coordination of interests, not real cooperation.[728] Dewey's pragmatist approach to politics was similar. He argued that citizens interact in civil society, and through that interaction – in open discussion – they develop greater diversity of thought. As Adler emphasises: "The public, according to Dewey, must be heard because it carries the practical knowledge and experience of a democracy based on cooperation."[729]

This underlying view of politics as enabling cooperation – Arendt's "power" – while also managing struggle finds concrete expression in an understanding of law that privileges argument, institutionally framed contestation and persuasion, both through law's discursive practice and through the concrete actions of its participants,[730] all taking place within legal communities of practice.[731] As Adler argues, "participants in social practices reflect on, judge and justify, thereby contributing to learning processes within and between communities of practice". Legal communities of practice are but one example of this broader set of processes.[732] However, law is relatively autonomous from other practices, such as political practices, because – like all forms of practice – law's standards of judgement are rooted within the practice itself,[733] creating a particular version of "competent practice" as we have seen.[734]

What are the attributes of competency within legal communities of practice? I imagine that amongst the general public a clear answer would emerge: the ability to argue. The caricatured lawyer is a person who, as a child, always asked "why?" and who later had a wiseacre's answer to all her parents' admonishments. And there are streams of thinking that see law primarily as a particular way to pursue and structure arguments, especially in the common law world, with its focus upon courts.[735] I think that this view is far too narrow, and can be misleading for at least three reasons. First, arguing is by no means unique to law. Politics, as well as all academic endeavours, are also about arguing – though ideally to a common set of shared objectives and aspirations. What is more, the world of law is not just about resolving disputes, though that is important. Law is also about shaping societies and building institutions, framing communities, structuring agreements, and establishing various forms of socio-legal status such as being married, being a commercial partner or being a trustee.

Secondly, limiting our understanding of law to arguments over language tends to focus all attention upon structured, logical deployment of textual analysis. In a fascinating book, the Polish legal theorist Bartosz Brożek argues that we have for too long underestimated the role that intuition and imagination play in the legal mind:

> Mathematicians, physicists, biologists, psychologists, artists, novelists, even the average Joe Bloggs, do not think exclusively in language. They rely on their intuition, explore the fantasy worlds developed by imagination, and do other things to deal with the problems they encounter. Why should lawyers be different?[736]

Brożek goes on to make the crucial point that law is shaped in part by theories that operate at different levels, from quite simple frames that address specific issues (such as *caveat emptor* or buyer beware), to more complex legal theories that cover entire branches of the law (such as liability for wrongs – called tort in the common law or delict in the civil law). Such theories, at whatever level, result from creative thinking as much as from logical linguistic analysis.[737]

Thirdly, we have already seen that all social practices, including law, are about both language and actions in the world.[738] To ignore the concrete material effects of law and to see it only as a communicative or discursive practice would turn law into an ethereal exercise, and discount both the liberating and constraining reality of law for people living in the world. For example, disputes over the scope of human rights law can free someone from prison, subject them to torture, allow the publication of a politically sensitive blog post or prevent access to birth control information. The consequences of legal debate are physical and psychological, not only linguistic and conceptual.

Yet it is true that much of law and legal practice operate *through* language, but in much more specific ways than simply saying that law is about argument. As we have already seen, in any community of practice, what "counts" as a valid argument, and what is seen to be compelling evidence in support of the argument, is shaped by community agreement.[739] That is certainly true of law.

Judith Shklar misconstrued the relative autonomy of law, believing that the process of exercising judgement in law and morals is essentially the same, only on a continuum.[740] I think that this underplays both the socially constructed agreement on what counts as argument and the requirements of legality that help to distinguish law from other forms of reasoning, be they moral, theological or political. Here I can draw upon Habermas for support. Even though he agrees that some basic norms of morality and law "substantively intersect", these "[o]verlapping contents do not blur the boundary between law and morality, which are irreversibly differentiated at the ... level of justification".[741]

Legal communities of practice are constrained not only by self-generated practices of "legitimate" justification, but also by interpretation. Even in traditionally hierarchical systems of law, interpretation is central to legal practice. Within Islamic law, although "inferior" authorities cannot directly change the law, they can interpret it; indeed, all law is subject to interpretation by legal experts, including divine law.[742] Dyzenhaus brings this thought into day-to-day life, arguing that even when playing a children's game – which implies that there are "rules" – the participants are acting as judges or interpreters of the rules that make this activity "the game".[743] Even as simple a game as hide and seek requires the interpretation of some basic rules because rules cannot apply themselves.[744] How fast are you allowed to count to ten? Can you "steal" the hiding place of another participant? Is the first person caught automatically "it" for the next round of the game?

There are commitments implicit in acting as interpreters of the rules. In games more complex than hide and seek, these commitments could include being bound by any text setting out the rule, say in a game of *Monopoly*; offering "reasonable" interpretations of what a rule requires in cases where there is a dispute; taking into account how the rule has previously been interpreted in analogous circumstances; and treating each participant equally in the interpretation.[745] In other words, as I have emphasised repeatedly, rules do not speak for themselves. It is important to note that all participants in the game, members of the community of practice, are held to these commitments, not just those formally denominated "umpires" or "judges". It is this shared responsibility that allows all participants to feel free and equal within the game and ensures that the rules are not read to favour the self-interest of one, or a sub-set, of the participants.[746]

If one moves up a few levels to the constitutions of countries, healthy constitutional systems recognise this shared interpretative responsibility and allow for "transformation through interpretative practice".[747] Even Aristotle, who viewed the textual statements of the prudent legislator as the foundation of law, believed that it was the rational content of the law that was binding, not the "brute fact" that a text has been promulgated.[748] He wrote extensively as well on the role of "equity" in filling gaps in the law.[749] The "living tree" analogy for Canadian constitutional interpretation offered up by Viscount Sankey captures the idea perfectly: text frames legal rules but does not dictate the interpretation or application of those rules in new contexts.[750] Oliver Wendell Holmes argued similarly that the US Constitution is an "organic living" set of institutions that must be reinterpreted and built up over time in the light of changing circumstances.[751]

A defining feature of competence within legal communities of practice is the ability to offer convincing reasons to support legal arguments and judgments. Brożek emphasises that "legal thinking is concerned with persuasion: the lawyer's task is not only to look for solutions to practical problems, those solutions must also be convincing".[752] Such an approach is entirely congenial to pragmatist thinking. As Misak argues:

> [A]ny method for arriving at genuine beliefs (beliefs which aim at truth) must be a method which is driven by reasons and experience ... The shared point is that if you want to have your beliefs governed by reasons, then you will have to expose yourself to different reasons, different perspectives, different arguments. You will have to engage in debate and deliberation.[753]

Perhaps surprisingly, this is a controversial statement in legal theory because it undercuts the oft-argued positivist position that legal authority is independent of content.[754] The issue is thorny. I have argued that while it is true that people do not have to agree continuously to be bound by legal rules, they do nonetheless have to believe that the criteria of legality have been largely met in the creation of the rules. They must also be convinced that a continuing practice of legality supports the rules or their fidelity to law will ultimately be undermined. As we have seen, part of the practice of legality is the congruence of rules and official actions; so too is reasoning and argumentation that respects the requirements of legality. Because law is to a large extent aspirational, never complete or utterly stable, its authority must be continuously reaffirmed.[755] Persuasion is a large part of that story.[756]

Debates in law, as in all social argument, require an exchange of reasons; settled consensus must be open to disruption through future argument.[757] Legal truth, as the pragmatists reveal about all truths, is subject to revision through discovery and reflection in community.[758] Although I do not agree with some of his conclusions, Venzke captures the mood perfectly with his telling phrase that legal actors "*struggle for the law in the law and in interaction with other authorities*, trying to undermine some and support others".[759]

I want to argue further that there are two particular forms of persuasive argument with strong traction in legal communities of practice: reference to precedent and the use of analogy. Most people are familiar with the idea that lawyers like to quote examples from past practice and past decisions. But why? Is it, as Weber and Shklar argued, that law and lawyers are essentially conservative, committed to the "established social order"?[760] Although I have already suggested that the rule of law is indeed an important source of stability in societies, I think it is too easy just to assert conservatism. Precedents matter because they draw on several of Fuller's criteria of legality. There are legal systems, such as Russia's, where precedent is less influential, and in such cases the difference between legal and political decision-making bleeds together in dangerous ways. Having regard to past practice supports the idea that legal rules should be of general application, not being specific to individual status or place or circumstance (though the specifics will be relevant in interpretation). The use of precedent also helps to make the law known because the rules are not picked from thin air, but have grounding in past practices. Clarity of rules is also aided when one can refer back to how a rule has been understood and applied in the past. Most obviously, the constancy requirement is significantly bolstered when precedent guides, *but does not control*, current practice.[761] All in all, some deference – but not slavish following – to past practice supports the continuing legitimacy of law because it aids in predictability and certainty, attributes seen to support a robust rule of law. And it must be added that, in their substance, precedents hold no inherent political orientation; they may be liberal or conservative in spirit, or neither.[762]

A less obvious but, in my view, at least equally important form of persuasive argument in legal communities of practice is the creative use of analogy. Of course, analogy can be related to precedent, drawing on decisions or actions in past circumstances that can be appropriately compared with a new situation.[763] But analogy is a wider concept than precedent and can be deployed by reference to parallel contemporaneous situations or to similar theories, concepts, principles or rules. Speaking of the use of analogical reasoning within sociology, Bourdieu makes the important point that analogy allows the observer to distance oneself from the immediate case, permitting the possibility of generalisation, "which is science [and I would add law] itself".[764]

Analogy has been influential within the tradition of pragmatist philosophy, and borrowed by constructivists in IR theory[765] under the label of "abduction". By abduction, the pragmatist Charles Sanders Peirce was describing reasoning that is an inference to the best explanation.[766] In essence, abduction reflects the everyday problem-solving of human beings, the "ultimate miracle" of human practice.[767] People reason from their experience and borrow insight from analogous situations, moments of reflection and concepts that proved valuable in similar or parallel circumstances.[768] It is no surprise that lawyers should be particularly drawn to abduction because they are so often focused on addressing practical problems that require solutions in the here and now, while also projecting into the future.[769] This helps explain why *qiyas* (analogy) is so important in Islamic legal interpretation. And because lawyers create knowledge together in communities of legal practice, they work out approaches based on shared expectations and shared experience (Background); working from analogies – and reflecting on them, reasoning with them – is second nature.[770]

Abduction is not as neat and tidy as deducing from first principles in an exercise of pure logic. Nor is it as straightforward as deriving a specific lesson from a prior case and simply applying it later. Reasoning from analogy can lead to increased complexity, recognising that issues spill across conceptual borders.[771] For that reason, lawyers do not deploy analogy as their only method of reasoning. They are influenced by both deduction from theory and concept, and induction from data that challenges or supports the abstractions. They streamline, and create heuristics and shortcuts; they deploy intuition and imagination.[772] But I suggest that reasoning from analogy is a particularly powerful, practical way of reasoning to a solution of legal problems. Of course, it must always be conditioned by the criteria of legality. Indeed, it is the criteria of legality that discipline our use of analogies which otherwise might prove faulty because they create false or misleading shortcuts. I will shortly explore a case where faulty analogies proved to be highly dangerous, that is, in the US law governing the interrogation of terrorist suspects in the post 9/11 world.

The focus on solutions emphasises that law, like all human activity – in the tradition of Aristotle – is to a purpose. Law is oriented towards decisions, not just in individual cases but societally as well: decisions on how best to build and sustain institutions of governance; decisions on how to resolve disputes; decisions on the distribution of social goods; decisions on when and how to build a sense of obligation amongst citizens and other social actors; decisions on how to define the status of individuals and bodies corporate. As we have seen, these legal decisions do not take place in a vacuum. They are informed, influenced and sometimes even conditioned by shared social understandings, political realities and material power.[773] In other words, law in its most convincing forms requires critical reflection leading to decision. It is not technocratic but, rather, demands the exercise of practical wisdom in pursuing its purposes.

Because law is oriented towards decision, it is wrong to view it as inevitably a force for stability, although much of the rule of law does seek to provide predictability and the valuing of settled expectations. Law is also creative and can enable change.[774] As I have explained, through the building up and adjustment of shared understandings, *social* norms both stabilise and shift.[775] When supported by criteria of legality, social norms can become relatively fixed as law. But that fixity is never permanent. When the shared social understandings in which legal norms are founded erode, or undergo significant shifts, we have seen that law too will be under pressure to adjust.[776] This can happen as a result of changing material circumstances, as has occurred within environmental law as a result of the increasing scientific knowledge around climate change. It can also result from changing values, as in my example of changing attitudes towards the death penalty. Witness as well the growing recognition of sexual and gender diversity as protected categories in human rights law. New ideas can also spark shifts in social norms that come to modify legal norms, as was the case when commercial partnerships evolved into corporations that could attract outside investors. The legal concept of limited liability was created.

The criteria of legality illustrate that legality – and the rule of law – is in large part about a particular type of stability and a particular approach to enabling, constraining and guiding change.[777] It is important to distinguish two different levels at which the requirements of legality bear on stability and change in law. First, they constitute "Background", collectively held knowledge and experience that is needed for legal practices to occur and for law to exist. While debates may rage about whether or not a given norm is law, or whether or not a given action is in conformity with the law, the parameters for that debate are relatively stable. Participants in processes of legal interpretation, justification and contestation take these parameters for granted as markers of competent legal practice and, by virtue of this routinised recourse to the requirements of legality, also maintain them as background knowledge.

However, this framework is not inherently static, or necessarily supportive of the pre-existing social and political order. First, as I have emphasised, the specific form of legal stability is rooted in interaction and reciprocity; it is therefore an open system, requiring the participation of a range of social actors and drawing upon diverse perspectives. Secondly, the criteria of legality that promote stability also require transparency and accountability, thereby facilitating contestation, and the potential disruption of settled norms. Thirdly, the stabilising tendency of the criteria of legality is moderated by the requirement that the criteria, indeed all law, be grounded in shared social understandings, and by the demand that legal normativity be maintained through a continuing practice of legality.

As we have seen, people act within social structures that shape behaviours, but people also actively reshape those structures.[778] The practice of legality is dynamic, allowing for what Adler calls "creative variation", innovation in practices that builds new background knowledge and in turn recombines and translates practices in novel ways through a process of selective retention.[779] The discipline created through the criteria of legality provides a predictable and reliable framework for promoting substantive change in law, and may also facilitate the shifts in standards that shape behaviour informally, what is sometimes called "soft law".[780] Weber argued that law can be altered by "new lines of conduct which then result either in a change of the meaning of the existing rules of law or in the creation of new rules of law".[781] Put a different way, competent practice in law includes competence in shaping methods of contestation,[782] and also in actively promoting change through the building of new linguistic concepts[783] and institutions, and through the selective modification of practical actions. Competence is not merely about ensuring stability.[784] And I want to re-emphasise that practices of legality demand critical reflection, requiring continuous adjustment, and are not the mere rehearsal of habits.[785]

With its balancing of both stability and change, it is probably fair to say that the rule of law, and specific laws that flow from it and meet its requirements, do not tend to support political revolution.[786] More precisely, to borrow from Hannah Arendt once again, political revolutions – like the French and the Russian – that seek to overturn legal traditions in the name of a morally pure "people" are likely to consume themselves in violence.[787] The rule of law is of its nature contrary to the use of violence to resolve disputes, whereas Mao Tse Tung famously opined that "[p]olitical power grows out of the barrel of a gun".[788] The rule of law is also inevitably resistant to charismatic authority, which we have seen Weber describe as intrinsically revolutionary.[789]

Fuller argued, and I agree, that a specific rule of law rooted in broad (even if inevitably imperfect) compliance with the criteria of legality is likely to preclude most instances where revolutionary change could be justified. Yet Michael Walzer is also right that citizens are not bound to support a state that represses them.[790] For example, the Canadian Supreme Court determined that even within a society shaped by the rule of law, if a clearly defined people can show that it is subject to alien subjugation and exploitation, or otherwise denied any meaningful exercise of its right to self-determination within the state of which it forms a part, it may legitimately claim an "external" right of self-determination, including the right to break up the existing state.[791]

Contrary to John Rawls' view that citizens have no choice in entering or leaving political society,[792] Michael Walzer would seem to suggest that a form of revolution, the choice to "leave" society, or rather to upend it, is open to systematically repressed groups of citizens. So, too, of course, is the option of migration.[793] In the unlikely event of a state regime upholding criteria of legality but engaging in systemic political repression,[794] revolution may be a legitimate option; migration certainly is, although, practically speaking, movement across borders will be limited by the rules of any potential receiving state.[795] Within a rule of law framework that is truly functional, however, evolutionary change is both possible and to be preferred because it is less disruptive, not to say less violent and dangerous, for citizens.

This returns us to a point I made at the outset: the rule of law that I contemplate is modest. It is based in shared social understandings that are transformed into legal obligation when social norms are buttressed by the criteria of legality and then constantly re-enacted in a practice of legality that takes place in legal communities of practice, but is then shared with other overlapping communities of practice in adjacent fields. The rule of law contributes to social and political predictability and relative stability while also providing a framework that allows for, even facilitates, evolutionary change. It is not the answer to all social challenges and it does not seek to displace politics. In the rule-of-law framework I describe, law is only relatively autonomous from other forms of social organisation.[796] But it does play a crucial role in stabilising expectations and in building up a system that supports shared purposes and citizen participation in public decision-making. When the criteria of legality are largely embedded, they generate a shared sense of legitimacy in the system, what Fuller called "fidelity to law". This legitimacy builds public confidence in a system that is seen as broadly fair.

When other social frameworks (the political system, the family, the workplace, social sector institutions) are under stress, as they are now in our age of anxiety, the rule of law as I describe it can be a source of social engagement, security and hope. No, it is not revolutionary; it tends to deliver change over time, not in one fell swoop. But that is a virtue when populist nationalists attack the US Congress and others undermine democratic governance in Poland, India, the Philippines and Brazil to return to only a few of the contemporary examples I discussed early in this book. And when fast-changing surveillance capitalism threatens human autonomy. And when global economic shifts threaten the viability of communities across the world. In these anxious times, sources of stability that also provide a framework for evolutionary but real change are desperately needed. That is what a modest rule of law can help to deliver, and why communities of legal practice, working hand-in-hand with other communities of practice, must work hard to reinforce it.

Notes

626 *The Analects Attributed to Confucius* [Kongfuzi], 551–479 BCE by Lao-Tse [Lao Zi], trans. James Legge (1815–1897), available at: https://china.usc.edu/confucius-analects-2.

627 *Pirkei Avot* 2, available at: www.sefaria.org/Pirkei_Avot.2.16?lang=bi&with=all&lang2=en.

628 See Jutta Brunnée and Stephen Toope, "International Law and Constructivism: Elements of an Interactional Theory of International Law" (2000) 39 *Columbia J. Transn'l L.* 19 [hereinafter *Brunnée and Toope Constructivism*]; *Brunnée and Toope Interactional Account*; Jutta Brunnée and Stephen Toope, "Interactional International Law: An Introduction" (2011) 3 *International Theory* 307–18. For a succinct exposition that highlights practice theory more than earlier versions, see *Brunnée and Toope Stability*. The following paragraphs are adapted from that article.

629 These interacting imperatives, the promotion of autonomy (freedom) and communication, are also explored comprehensively by Sen, 225–320, 415. It has been said that emotions are important in understanding law because emotions contain social information that is crucial to a species (*homo sapiens*) that is "obligatorily gregarious". András Sajó, "The Constitutional Domestication of Emotions", in M. N. S. Sellers (ed.), *Law, Reason and Emotion* (Cambridge University Press, 2017), 55, 59 (quoting F. De Waal).

630 *Fuller Morality*. This concept of how "rule" in law functions is aligned with Hannah Arendt's concept of action because it is not about hierarchy and the mere imposition of constraint. *Arendt Human Condition*, 222.

631 Lon Fuller, "Human Interaction and the Law" (1969) 14 *Am. J. Jurisprudence* 1, reprinted in Kenneth Winston (ed.), *The Principles of Social Order: Selected Essays of Lon L. Fuller*, rev. edn (Oxford: Hart, 2001), 211 [hereinafter *Fuller Human Interaction*]. Hannah Arendt evinced a proximate view of politics, arguing that people in power do

not rule over others, but are empowered by the group to act, an empowerment that may be withdrawn. See Bernstein, 97–8.

632 See *Brunnée and Toope Constructivism*. Social norms were described by the philosopher Philip Pettit as regularities of behaviour to which people generally conform and "disapprove of deviance". Philip Pettit, "Virtus Normativa: Rational Choice Perspectives" (1990) 100 *Ethics* 725, 728. Such norms are internalised by many people in a given society; they become the right thing to do. Greco, 72–3.

633 Antje Wiener, "The Dual Quality of Norms and Governance Beyond the State: Sociological and Normative Approaches to 'Interaction'" (2007) 10 *Critical Rev. Int'l Soc. & Pol. Phil.* 47 [hereinafter *Wiener Dual Quality*]; Wayne Sandholtz, "Dynamics of International Norm Change: Rules against Wartime Plunder" (2008) 14 *EJIR* 101.

634 See *Fuller Morality*. And see Colleen Murphy, "Lon Fuller and the Moral Value of the Rule of Law" (2005) 24 *L. & Phil.* 239, 240–1. Of course, many of these criteria have been discussed for centuries by various legal theorists. For example, Maimonides emphasised that law had to be universal in its prescriptions; Fuller called this "generality". Ralph Lerner, "Moses Maimonides", in Leo Strauss and Joseph Cropsey (eds), *History of Political Philosophy*, 3rd edn (University of Chicago Press, 1987), 228, 233. Strangely, Lechner and Frost also emphasise the "internal" point of view in their conceptualisation of practice (relying only on Herbert Hart's "internal perspective"), but then go on to emphasise the coercive quality of law, rather than its ability to generate its own adherence. Lechner and Frost, 122–3. I think that Fuller's insights could have helped them in distinguishing more clearly between law as "rule acceptance" and law as "obedience to rules".

635 *Fuller Human Interaction*, 235. See also *Dyzenhaus Long Arc*, 16–17, 119, 409 (suggesting that it was Hobbes' focus on the duality of protection by the sovereign and obedience of subjects that pioneered the concept of reciprocity as the basis for a subject's consent to be bound by law). A detailed discussion of the point is found in *Dyzenhaus Long Arc*, ch. 2, especially the idea, at 99 and 101, that for Hobbes the sovereign "is a legally constituted sovereign" and that subjects were to understand the sovereign's rule "as a matter of right rather than unmediated coercive power".

636 *Fuller Morality*.

637 *Brunnée and Toope Constitutionalism*. See also Jan Klabbers, "Constitutionalism and the Making of International Law: Fuller's Procedural Natural Law" (2008) 5 *No Foundations: Journal of Extreme Legal Positivism*, available at: www.helsinki.fi/nofo/Vol4Num1_08.htm, 84, 106.

638 *Walters Unwritten Constitution*, 47.

639 See also *Walters on Dicey*, 204, 281 (arguing that Dicey believed that even parliamentary sovereignty depended upon an ingrained respect for law in the citizenry). I believe that this conception of a modest rule of law rooted in perceived legitimacy is closely tied to Patrick Glenn's argument that legal traditions are about persuasion, not mere power or brute facts. H. Patrick Glenn, "Doin' the Transsystemic: Legal Systems and Legal Traditions" (2005) 50 *McGill L. J.* 863, 881–2, 897.

640 *Adler World Ordering*, 19. See also *Adler and Pouliot Practices*, 3, 6.

641 Searle.

642 *Brunnée and Toope Constitutionalism*. And see Yasuaki Onuma, *International Law in a Transcivilizational World* (Cambridge University Press, 2017), 44, 119; Richard Collins, "Two Idea(l)s of the International Rule of Law" (2019) 8 *Global Constitutionalism* 191, 215 (relying on the work of Michael Oakeshott as transposed into the world of international law by Terry Nardin) [hereinafter *Collins Ideals*].

643 See Anthea Roberts, *Is International Law International?* (Oxford University Press, 2017).

644 See, e.g., *Wiener Contestation*; Machiko Kanetake and André Nollkaemper, "The International Rule of Law in the Cycle of Contestation and Deference", in Machiko Kanetake and André Nollkaemper (eds), *The Rule of Law at the National and International Levels: Contestation and Deference* (Oxford: Hart, 2016), 445.

645 For a concrete illustration of these dynamics at play in international law, see Jutta Brunnée and Stephen Toope, "Norm Robustness and Contestation in International Law: Self-Defence against Non-State Actors" (2019) 4 *J. Global Sec. Studies* 73.

646 *Misak Truth*, 155. See also *Walters on Dicey*, 375.

647 *Adler World Ordering*, 4.

648 Indeed, it has been argued that the rule of law can persist only when there is an indeterminacy as to its core meaning. That is why Christopher May describes it simply as "common sense". I think that this is too imprecise and ill-attuned to value diversity, as we shall see. Christopher May, *The Rule of Law: The Common Sense of Global Politics* (Cheltenham: Edward Elgar, 2014).

649 *Cotterrell Law's Community*, 18 (commenting on the work of Franz Neumann).

650 *Cotterrell Law's Community*, 5–7.

651 A. V. Dicey, *Introduction to the Study of the Law of the Constitution*, 10th edn (London: Macmillan, 1961), 188, 193, 196. The first edition was published as A. V. Dicey, *Lectures Introductory to the Study of the Law of the Constitution* (London: Macmillan, 1885). See also *Walters on Dicey*, 226, 228–9, 255, 366, 374. And as we have seen, the "ordinary" quality of constitutional law also denied the executive authority the ability to declare states of "exception", thereby aggregating power to themselves outside the realm of the quotidian law. *Walters on Dicey*, 276–81, 371–3.

652 See, e.g., Michael Trebilcock and Ronald Daniels, *Rule of Law Reform and Development: Charting the Fragile Path of Progress* (Cheltenham: Edward Elgar, 2009). Chesterman articulates a similar view of the rule of law within nations, focusing on a government of laws (rather than arbitrary power), equality of all before the law, and the application of law to the public authority, exercised through independent courts. Simon Chesterman, "An International Rule of Law" (2008) 56 *Am. J. Comp. L.* 331, 342. Beaulac points out correctly, however, that there is another stream of thought on the rule of law that originated with Chief Justice Marshall in the United States, and which holds that the font of the rule of law is found in a written constitution. See Stéphane Beaulac, "An Inquiry into the International Rule of Law", EUI Working Papers, MWP 2007/14, available at: https://papers.ssrn.com/sol3/papers.cfm?abstract_id=1074562.

653 *Walters on Dicey*, 5 (quoting Frederick H. Lawson).

654 See, e.g., Martin Laughlin, *Foundations of Public Law* (Oxford University Press, 2010), ch. 11. The concepts of "rule of law" and *Rechtsstaat/État de droit* are not interchangeable, as they derive from quite different legal traditions. But since the end of the Second World War, and with the rise of human rights discourse globally, along with "legal reform" promoted in the Global South by international institutions, the conceptualisations associated with "rule of law" have proven more influential. One of the most interesting writers in the *Rechtsstaat* tradition, writing in the shadow of Weimar, was Franz Neumann who argued that the core requirement of the rule of law was that laws had to be "general", meaning abstract rules that are "issued in advance to apply to all cases and all persons". Quoted in *Cotterell Law's Community*, 164–5. For Lon Fuller, "generality" was only one of the elements of the "internal morality of law".

655 Carmen Pavel, "The International Rule of Law" (2020) 23 *Critical Rev. Int'l Soc. & Pol. Phil.* 332, available at: www.tandfonline.com/doi/full/10.1080/13698230.2019.1565714. In listing many of the "criteria of legality" as central to the rule of law, Pavel does not in this section of her article cite Fuller. She does so in her discussion of the substantive elements of the rule of law. See also Terry Nardin, "Theorizing the International Rule of Law" (2008) 34 *Rev. Int'l Studies*, 385 (on the "moral element" of the rule of law).

656 *Arendt Human Condition*, 177–80, 183–4.

657 Pavel, 336.

658 Fuller did not use the term "subjects" of law, preferring the idea of people to whom law is addressed.

659 Brian Tamahana, *On the Rule of Law: History, Politics, Theory* (Cambridge University Press, 2004), 91 et seq. [hereinafter *Tamahana Rule of Law*]; *Walters on Dicey*, 261, 265–6; *Collins Ideals*, 204.

660 John Finnis, *Natural Law and Natural Rights*, Clarendon Law Series, 2nd edn (Oxford University Press, 2011). However, Finnis also argues that the executive should have almost unfettered freedom to decide and act when fundamental constitutional principles are engaged. He is strongly opposed to judicial review, especially by external (i.e., non-national) bodies such as the European Court of Human Rights. See, e.g., John Finnis, "Judicial Power: Past, Present and Future", 2018, available at: http://judicialpowerproject.org.uk/wp-content/uploads/2018/01/Judicial-Power-and-the-Balance-of-Our-Constitution.pdf, 26.

661 See Nardin, 393.

662 Tom Bingham, *The Rule of Law* (London: Penguin, 2010), 67.

663 See, e.g., Ronald Dworkin, *A Matter of Principle* (Cambridge, MA: Harvard University Press, 1985), 11–12; Ronald Dworkin, "The Rule of Law as a Theatre of Debate", in Justine Burley (ed.), *Dworkin and His Critics* (Oxford: Blackwell, 2004), 387–8.

664 Pavel, 337.

665 Robert McCorquodale, "Defining the International Rule of Law: Defying Gravity?" (2016) *ICLQ* 1, 16. A parallel position is adopted by Nardin, who argues for a conception of the rule of law that "both constrains decision-making and protects the moral rights of those who come within its jurisdiction". Nardin, 397.

666 Joseph Raz, *The Authority of Law: Essays on Law and Morality* (Oxford: Clarendon Press, 1979), 221.

667 Joseph Raz, "The Rule of Law and its Virtue" (1977) 93 *LQR*, 195.

668 Judith Shklar, "Political Theory and the Rule of Law", in Allan Hutchinson and Patrick Monahan (eds), *The Rule of Law: Ideal and Ideology* (Toronto: Carswell, 1987), 1.

669 Paul Craig, "Formal and Substantive Conception of the Rule of Law: An Analytical Framework" (1997) *Public L.* 467, 474; *Walters on Dicey*, 279, 362–5. See also Beaulac, 4.

670 *Walters on Dicey*, 372–3.

671 Here I disagree with Walters. *Walters on Dicey*, 230, 235 (though accepting that "the rule of law boiled down to just one procedural rule: governmental power must have parliamentary authorisation").

672 *Walters on Dicey*, 271, 275.

673 Chesterman, 360.

674 Robert Summers, "A Formal Theory of the Rule of Law" (1993) 6 *Ratio Juris* 12.

675 Robert Summers, "The Principles of the Rule of Law" (1999) 74 *Notre Dame L. Rev.* 1691.

676 *Habermas Discourse*, 445. See also *Kumm Cosmopolitan Turn*, 293–301, for a "thin" perspective on constitutionalism and legality (and implicitly the rule of law).

677 Here again I am influenced by the pragmatist Charles Sanders Peirce who argued that in hypotheses, continuities are generally to be preferred over dichotomies. Haack, 88.

678 *Dyzenhaus Constitutionalism*, 255. For a more expansive discussion, see also David Dyzenhaus, "Hobbes on the Authority of Law", in David Dyzenhaus and Thomas Poole (eds), *Hobbes and the Law* (Cambridge University Press, 2012), 186 [hereinafter *Dyzenhaus Hobbes and Law*]. But see *Arendt Totalitarianism*, 139 (arguing a more common view that Hobbes saw the coming together of individuals in society as based entirely on private "interests").

679 *Dyzenhaus Hobbes*, 55; *Dyzenhaus Hobbes and Law*; *Dyzenhaus Long Arc*, 88 et seq., esp. 146–7.

680 Quoted in *Dyzenhaus Long Arc*, 117.

681 Duke, 30, 145. It is important to note, however, that for Aristotle the "rule of law" was not an ideal, but only a way to differentiate amongst essentially defective regimes (all oligarchies and democracies). Regimes with a rule of law were relatively less defective. Duke, 120–1, 147.

682 Lon Fuller, "Adjudication and the Rule of Law" (1960) 54 *Am. Soc. Int'l L. Proc.* 1, 2, 5; Lon Fuller and Kenneth Winston, "The Forms and Limits of Adjudication" (1978) 92 *Harvard L. Rev.* 353, 373 (suggesting that the object of the rule of law is to substitute for violence peaceful ways of settlings disputes). Again, we hear echoes of Arendt's focus on participation as the test of free citizenship. *Arendt Revolution*, 108. This point also connects to Habermas' focus on participation rights in public discourse as essential to democratic citizenship. *Risse On Justice*, 49

683 Fuller and Winston, 395 (with the metaphor of the spider's web representing really complex disputes with shifting centres of gravity; in a spider's web, if one pulls a thread in one direction the entire web shifts and perhaps breaks).

684 Fuller and Winston, 377–8.

685 Fuller and Winston, 372.

686 Indeed, Fuller argued that his "internal morality" requirements were still connected to standards of "external morality". *Fuller Morality, passim.* See also David Luban, "The Rule of Law and Human Dignity: Re-examining Fuller's Canons" (2010) 2 *Hague J. Rule of Law* 29 (on why Fuller's legality principles do entail some "substance"). I therefore do not agree with Reinhold and Zurn who suggest that Fuller's principles of legality are "a minimal version of the concept of the rule of law". Theresa Reinhold and Michael Zurn, "Rules about Rules and the Endogenous Dynamics of International Law: Dissonance Reduction as a Mechanism of Secondary Rule-Making" (2014) 3 *Global Constitutionalism* 236, 243.

687 *Fuller Morality*, 159, see also more generally at 157–70 (discussing various examples, such as the Nazi and apartheid regimes).

688 Finnis, 274. Dicey made a parallel point, suggesting that requiring legislative action to create law (then interpreted in courts) systematically restricted arbitrary executive action. *Walters on Dicey*, 272, 275.

689 As I have already argued, Fuller's use of the phrase "internal morality of the law" was unfortunate. It clouded his reasoning by seeming to suggest a substantive moral content – a shared understanding of the good life – within the law. Yet, in fact, Fuller argued that his was at most a "procedural natural law". *Fuller Morality*, 96.

690 Remember that Dicey too thought that law's essential function was to discipline power (read as "sovereignty") and politics. *Walters on Dicey*, 135–6, 187, 203, 206–7.

691 See David Dyzenhaus, "Fuller's Novelty", in Willem Witteveen and Wibren van der Burg (eds), *Rediscovering Fuller: Essays on Implicit Law and Institutional Design* (Amsterdam University Press, 1999), 97 (noting that, for Fuller, "[t]he moral foundation of law has to be manifest in the institutions of law so that law can fulfil its moral task – the promotion of interaction between individuals subject to the law . . .") [hereinafter *Dyzenhaus Fuller's Novelty*]. Social institutions, including legal institutions, form "webs of significance" through practices that are resilient to individual preferences. See *Cameron Practical Wisdom*, 2–3

692 *Fuller Morality*, 117, 123 (rejecting a bright-line distinction between law and non-law), and esp. at 122 ("[B]oth rules of law and legal systems can and do half exist. This condition results when the purposive effort necessary to bring them into full being has been, as it were, only half successful").

693 Noel Reynolds, "Comment on Robert Summers on The Rule of Law" (1988) 1 *Ratio Juris* 263, 264. "Aspiration is an essential component of political life" argue Finnemore and Jurkovich. Drawing on Fuller, I would add that the same is true within legal frameworks. Martha Finnemore and Michelle Jurkovich, "The Politics of Aspiration" (2020) 64 *Int'l Studies Q.*, 759; Wibren van der Burg, "The Morality of Aspiration: A Neglected Dimension of Law and Morality", in Willem Witteveen and Wibren van der Burg (eds), *Rediscovering Fuller: Essays on Implicit Law and Institutional Design* (Amsterdam University Press, 1999), 169; Cover, 10.

694 Bingham, 174.

695 See McCorquodale, 2; *Tamahana Rule of Law*, 127.

696 *Fuller Morality*, 63 (warning against a confusion between fidelity to law and "deference for established authority"), 107 (distinguishing the rule of law from public order), 115, 148 (emphasising that lawful authority is the "product of law", not its precursor), 168 (explaining why not all governmental action is "legal" in nature), 110 (rejecting the "pyramidal structure of state power" as the essence of law).

697 This distinction is crucial. In the Nazi era, criminal law was transformed from a means to address mischievous human conduct into an instrument of social control focused on the defective personality of the alleged criminal (the "parasite upon the *Volk*"; "the saboteur"; the Jew). Pauer-Studer, 110–11, 113–14.

698 *Fuller Morality*, 221, 233.

699 Gerald Postema, "Implicit Law" (1994) 13 *L. & Phil.* 361, reprinted in Willem Witteveen and Wibren van der Burg (eds), *Rediscovering Fuller: Essays on Implicit Law and Institutional Design* (Amsterdam University Press, 1999), 256, 260. See also *Fuller Morality*, 194–5 ("The quality and terms of the parties' emergent relationship – its 'laws' if you will – constitute an important social reality, but it is a reality brought into being and kept alive by purposive effort and by the way each of the parties interprets the purposes of the other"), 209 (arguing that in a legal system "the existence of a relatively stable reciprocity of expectations between lawgiver and subject is part of the very idea of a functioning legal order").

700 Murphy, 239.

701 *Fuller Morality*, 27–8 (explaining the difference between the "morality of aspiration" and the "morality of duty").

702 Hart did believe that law validly enacted by the Nazis would be "law". See Dyzenhaus' discussion in *Dyzenhaus Long Arc*, 26. However, Hart then argued that people should be able to refuse to obey "immoral" law. *Dyzenhaus Long Arc*, 50, 53. There was absolutely no hint of apology in Hart's reasoning, be it convincing or unconvincing, only a claim that there is a fundamental difference between the validity of law and its morality. H. L. A. Hart, "Positivism and the Separation of Law and Morals" (1957) 71 *Harvard L. Rev.* 593.

703 See Lon Fuller, "Positivism and Fidelity to Law: A Reply to Professor Hart" (1958) 71 *Harvard L. Rev.* 630. For a still-shocking example of how Nazi "law" functioned, see Hansen, 64–5, describing the "obscene public trials" presided over by the fanatic, Roland Freisler ("Freisler, cloaked in red with arms flailing, his face contorted with hatred and rage, screamed at the defendants"). Much of the simulacrum of law created in the Nazi regime was actually nothing more than fiat relying on the führer's raw power, exercised through decree, often secret decree. Pauer-Studer, 5, 45–6, 49, 222.

704 See *Dyzenhaus Fuller's Novelty*.

705 The "dual state" was first described in 1941 by Ernst Fraenkel, *The Dual State: A Contribution to the Theory of Dictatorship*, trans. E. A. Shils et al. (Oxford University Press, 2010). Here I disagree with theorists who argue that during the rise of the Nazis, "law" was used to undermine the "rule of law". See, e.g., Ivan Ermakoff, "Law against the Rule of Law: Assaulting Democracy", *J. L. & Soc.*, 9 October 2020, available at:

https://onlinelibrary.wiley.com/doi/full/10.1111/jols.12253. Following Fuller, I would suggest that the instruments used by authoritarians to destroy democracy and human rights are typically not "law", but the simulacrum, even perversion, of the concept of law. See also the subtle argument of Pauer-Studer, rooted in Fuller but rejecting his terminology of "internal morality of law" that "morality ... [is] a critical parameter for assessing a legal system when it acts as a source for defining the constitutive conditions of the rule of law". Pauer-Studer, 229, and at 152, 214–16, 224–6.

706 Sean Rehaag, "Book Review: The Hart–Fuller Debate in the Twenty-First Century, by Peter Cane (ed.)" (2010) 48 *Osgoode Hall L. J.* 691, 692.

707 See also *Collins Ideals*, 211 (on international law as non-instrumental, as legality expressed in the "autonomy of the legal form itself").

708 See the compelling discussion in Reynolds, 263–4.

709 See, e.g., Marcelo Bergman, *Tax Evasion and the Rule of Law in Latin America: The Political Culture of Cheating and Compliance in Argentina and Chile* (Philadelphia, PA: Penn State University Press, 2009) (arguing that the willingness of citizens to pay taxes is closely related to the social norms that underpin the rule of law; while the threat of enforcement plays a role, its impact is greatest when citizens have other reasons to comply, rooted in a sense that the system is fair and that fellow citizens generally comply; thus, different rule of law traditions explain why tax evasion is relatively common in Argentina whereas compliance rates are relatively high in Chile). See also Dan Kahan, "The Logic of Reciprocity: Trust, Collective Action, and Law" (2003) 102 *Michigan L. Rev.* 71, 82 (commenting on the role of different tax compliance cultures).

710 Habermas makes a similar point about the need for constitutions (with their inbuilt rule of law principles) not to "be conceived as a concrete legal order that imposes a priori a total form of life on society as a whole". *Habermas Discourse*, 263. See also Peer Zumbansen, "The Rule of Law, Legal Pluralism, and Challenges to a Western-centric View: Some Very Preliminary Observations", in Christopher May and Adam Winchester (eds), *Handbook on the Rule of Law* (Cheltenham: Edward Elgar, 2018), 57. See also the magisterial work of Patrick Glenn who "believed in the possibility of a peaceful coexistence in which [legal] traditions engage in perpetual exchange and yet maintain their distinctive identities". *Dedek Action* 3. Glenn's *magnum opus* was *Legal Traditions of the World: Sustainable Diversity in Law*, 5th edn (Oxford University Press, 2014). See also H. Patrick Glenn, *The Cosmopolitan State* (Oxford University Press, 2013).

711 I agree with Cotterrell that the rule of law is an "ideology" in the sense that it is only a part of what we need to build a healthy society. It can only ever be "a partial and limited view of reality". It works alongside other optics and institutions. *Cotterrell Law's Community*, 259.

712 Walters adopts this formulation as well in explaining Dicey's common law constitutionalism. *Walters on Dicey*, 298. I do not share the view that this "culture" is necessarily closely tied to a specific national group, as Dicey seems to have done with his exalting of the English common law tradition. *Walters on Dicey*, 231, 255, 298, 349–50. I suggest that plural traditions can embrace the rule of law form articulated here. Walters seems to offer up some hope of pluralism in practices of the rule of law. This might make a

rule of law more plausible in international society than Dicey would have thought. *Walters on Dicey*, 335–6, 374.

713 See Anton Troianovski and Ivan Nechepurkeno, "Belarus Forces Down Plane to Seize Dissident; Europe Sees 'State Hijacking'", *New York Times*, 23 May 2021, available at: www.nytimes.com/2021/05/23/world/europe/ryanair-belarus.html.

714 See, e.g., Onuma, 119; Jutta Brunnée, "Book Review" (of Onuma) (2018) 59 *Harvard Int'l L. J.* 601.

715 See, e.g., Beaulac, 27–9 (on "an emerging 'international rule of law'"); Chesterman; *Dyzenhaus Hobbes*; McCorquodale; Nardin; Pavel; Bardo Fassbender, "What's in a Name? The International Rule of Law and the United Nations Charter" (2018) 17 *Chinese J. Int'l L.* 761 (on recent, admittedly vague, constructions of the international rule of law within the UN system); and most provocatively perhaps, René Provost, *Rebel Courts: The Administration of Justice by Armed Insurgents* (Oxford University Press, 2021) (on a rule of law practised by armed rebels).

716 Even the critical sociologist Pierre Bourdieu thought that law was relatively autonomous from politics, and was not merely instrumental. See Dezalay and Madsen, 436. Durkheim also argued for the relative autonomy of law, although like Weber, he also saw law as deeply interconnected with politics, as we have seen. Thornhill, 110, 112.

717 Which is why some critics of interdisciplinary research are concerned that connecting international law to international relations theory could neuter law's constraining power. See, e.g., Jan Klabbers, "The Relative Autonomy of International Law or the Forgotten Politics of Interdisciplinarity" (2005) 1 *J. Int'l Rel. & Int'l L.* 35; Martii Koskenniemi, "The Politics of International Law" (1990) 1 *EJIL* 4. Aalberts and Venzke argue strongly why this is not the case. Aalberts and Venzke, esp. at 304 et seq. See also Venzke, 111.

718 On international law as social practices shaped by diverse actors, see *Collins Ideals*, 194–5, 200.

719 Jeremy Waldron, "The Rule of International Law" (2006) 30 *Harvard J. L. & Pub. Pol.* 15, 18 [hereinafter *Waldron Rule of International Law*].

720 Arendt argues, therefore, that there is a crucial difference between human freedom, which is based in action in society, and sovereignty, which presupposes singular power and authority, "contrary to the very condition of plurality". *Arendt Human Condition*, 234.

721 *Waldron Rule of International Law*, 21; *Dyzenhaus Hobbes*, 61.

722 *Cotterrell Law's Community*, 5–7. Stability is also sometimes denominated "order". The risk with that usage is that "order" is too easily conceptualised as an exercise of raw power; the "order" supported by a modest rule of law is entirely different, as this book seeks to explain. See also *Cotterrell Law's Community*, 316–17 (arguing that "order" and "justice" are in balance in any legitimate system of government, but that "order" is primary because it is what allows justice to flourish. Moreover, as we have already seen, "justice" is a more contested concept, evading consensus).

723 NA, "Myanmar Coup: Calls for Suu Kyi Release as Lawmakers Held", BBC News, 2 February 2021, available at: www.bbc.co.uk/news/world-asia-55722226.

724 *Adler World Ordering*, 3.

725 *Adler World Ordering*, 27–8, 236.

726 *Dyzenhaus Legitimacy*, 653.

727 Shklar overlooked this tension, seeing law – or more precisely legalism – as rooted only in "ideologies of agreement". *Shklar Legalism*, 110.

728 *Habermas Discourse*, 272. See also *Risse On Justice*, 47–8 (describing Habermas' focus on cooperation). For a classic description of cooperation in international law, see C. Wilfred Jenks, *The Common Law of Mankind* (New York: Praeger, 1958).

729 *Adler World Ordering*, 293.

730 See Aalberts and Venzke; Risse; *Wiener Contestation* on argumentative practice; Sandholtz on how actions shape norms. Sandholtz, 107. Hannah Arendt also argued for the particular importance of persuasion in the public space as the key to healthy politics because it actually permits the exercise of informed judgement. Bernstein, 100–2.

731 This vision of law aligns well with the late Wittgenstein who argued that rules do not speak for themselves, but are enacted in use. Aalberts and Venzke, 306.

732 *Adler World Ordering*, 29–30.

733 Aalberts and Venzke, 306; Friedrichs and Kratochwil, 712. See also Dennis Patterson, "Law's Pragmatism: Law as Practice and Narrative" (1990) 76 *Virginia L. Rev.* 937, 940.

734 *Adler and Pouliot Practices*, 3.

735 See, e.g., Dworkin; *Walters on Dicey*, 151 ("Dicey obviously thought law is intimately related to judicial decision-making and he would place the common law at the heart of his account of the rule of law"), 332–4.

736 Brożek, 2, 39.

737 Brożek, 99.

738 Sandholtz, 107.

739 Friedrichs and Kratochwil, 712.

740 *Shklar Legalism*, 62.

741 *Habermas Discourse*, 206.

742 Muhammad Hamidullah, *Introduction to Islam* (Paris: Centre culturel islamique, 1969), para. 318(ii).

743 In using the example of a child's game, Dyzenhaus is not adopting a "game theoretic" stance. It is important to distinguish practices from games. Practices may encompass games but practices are concrete and continuing (without a clear beginning, middle and end); they evolve even as they may be partially structured by rules. They are subject to continuing interpretation and contestation. Lechner and Frost, 104–5, 109.

744 *Cameron Practical Wisdom*, 64–5.

745 *Dyzenhaus Hobbes*, 60.

746 *Dyzenhaus Hobbes*, 61.

747 Thomas Franck, "International Institutions: Why Constitutionalize?", in Jeffrey Dunoff and Joel Trachtman (eds), *Ruling the World?: Constitutionalism, International Law, and Global Governance* (Cambridge University Press, 2009), xi.

748 Duke, 164.

749 Duke, 149–65. See also Lacroix and Pranchère, 74–5.

750 *Edwards* v. *Attorney-General of Canada* (1929) 124 UKPC 86. Followed by the Supreme Court of Canada in *Ref. Re BC Motor Vehicles Act* [1985] 2 SCR 486, para. 53 (*per* Lamer CJC). See also the thoughtful discussion in Robert Sharpe, "The Persons Case and the Living Tree Theory of Constitutional Interpretation" (2013) 64 *UNB L. J.* 1.

751 See, e.g., his opinions in *Gompers* v. *United States* (1914) 233 US 604, 610; *Missouri* v. *Holland* (1920) 252 US 416, 433.

752 Brożek, 99. See also the seminal article by H. Patrick Glenn, "Persuasive Authority" (1987) 32 *McGill L. J.* 261 [hereinafter *Glenn Authority*]; *Dyzenhaus Hobbes*, 60–1; Friedrich Kratochwil, *Rules, Norms and Decisions: On the Conditions of Practical and Legal Reasoning in International Relations and Domestic Affairs* (Cambridge University Press, 1989), 18, 240–1; *Cotterrell Law's Community*, 317–18 (on the dichotomy in law between fiat and reason, the latter focusing on persuasion).

753 *Misak Truth*, 106.

754 H. L. A. Hart, *Essays on Bentham* (Oxford University Press, 1983), 254–5. This view flows from Aristotle's argument that citizens did not have to grasp the reasons for law's directive content, even though he believed that law should indeed be practically rational. Duke, 17. However, Aristotle thought that a citizen could be habituated into virtue through following good laws. Duke, 39. Presumably, at that point they might understand the reasons underlying the law, although this is not inevitable.

755 This is not to say that all law is radically indeterminate, only that it is not fixed through text alone, and is subject to reaffirmation and contestation in practice. See Brożek, 113, and following on the need for both top-down reasoning in law based on theories and structures and bottom-up reasoning from day-to-day circumstances. Contra *Koskenniemi Apology*, 67, 591, 596; Reus-Smit, 64 (both arguing that law is inherently indeterminate).

756 See *Glenn Authority*.

757 See *Habermas Discourse*, 30 (on justification as the source of legal legitimacy); *Habermas Transformation*, 33 (on reasons being more important in all "public" debate than the person offering them); Mintzen, 401; Risse, 7. See also Ruggie, 869 (on the distinction between "reasons" and "causes").

758 Cochran, 527, 530, 543.

759 Venzke, 126 (italics added).

760 *Shklar Legalism*, 15 (quoting Tocqueville and suggesting that Weber's "rationality" is what she means by "legalism"), 109. See also *Weber Interpretation*, 183.

761 The pragmatist John Dewey criticised legal reasoning because he thought that reliance on precedent could stultify thought, and preclude the incorporation of subsequent experience in decision-making. See Sullivan, 86–7. Of course, it can, but it need not if sensitively deployed.

762 Within the United States, the many Supreme Court precedents upholding an expansive reading of the Second Amendment of the US Constitution ("the right of the people to keep and bear Arms, shall not be infringed" disconnected from the first clause on the need for a "well-ordered militia") are generally viewed as "conservative",

whereas the consistent reaffirmation of *Brown* v. *Board of Education of Topeka* 347 US 483 (1954) is viewed as "liberal" or even "progressive".

763 See Brożek, 57–8 (noting that the use of analogy to past cases is by no means mechanistic, as cases can be characterised in different ways). See also Brożek, 100–1 (on various types of analogical reasoning).

764 Bourdieu and Wacquant, 233.

765 See, e.g., Wendt, 351–2; Ruggie, 880. Some constructivists in IR have also argued that actors use a "logic of appropriateness", working by way of analogy to apply norms to new situations. See Martha Finnemore and Kathryn Sikkink, "International Norm Dynamics and Political Change" (1998) 52 *IO* 887, relying on the work of March and Olsen, summarised most recently in James March and Johan Olsen, "The Logic of Appropriateness", in Robert Goodin (ed.), *The Oxford Handbook of Political Science* (Oxford University Press, 2011), available at: www.oxfordhandbooks.com/view/10.1093/oxfordhb/9780199604456.001.0001/oxfordhb-9780199604456-e-024?print=pdf. My own view is that pragmatism, read with practice theory, suggests that lawyers are more inclined to a "logic of practicality" that also employs analogy. See *Pouliot Practicality*.

766 I thank Cheryl Misak for clarifying the idea of abduction and providing this succinct phrasing.

767 Friedrichs and Kratochwil, 710.

768 Friedrichs and Kratochwil, 717; Adriana Sinclair, *International Relations Theory and International Law* (Cambridge University Press, 2010), 25–9 (discussing Kratochwil's approach to law and the use of analogy), 49–50 (on analogy). See also *Cameron Practical Wisdom*, 20 (on how practitioners of all types inherit and project into the future at one and the same time).

769 Dezalay and Madsen, 438 ("[J]urists, including academic jurists, do not seek universal knowledge for the sake of universality but also as practical solutions to societal problems").

770 For a powerful articulation and defence of the use of analogy in law, see Cass Sunstein, "On Analogical Reasoning" (1992/3) 106 *Harvard L. Rev.* 741. See also Brożek, 129 (lawyers study and practise, gaining experience that helps them to understand what a "justifiable" claim is within the legal setting). This understanding of law and legal reasoning is completely at variance with Weber's formal-rational (largely deductive) construction of how law functions in society. See Max Rheinstein, "Introduction", to *Weber Law*, xxvi, xlix.

771 See Sunstein; Friedrichs and Kratochwil, 718.

772 Brożek, 2, 5, 6, 8, 100, 153.

773 I agree with Friedrichs and Kratochwil that we need to resist "totalising" explanations for any social phenomena, even explanations like pragmatism read with practice theory, that we may find helpful and congenial. Friedrichs and Kratochwil, 713, fn 56.

774 Adler argues that communities of practice that build and re-build knowledge through evolutionary practices and continuous reflection promote both change and stability, what I term "dynamic stability". *Adler World Ordering*, 39. But see Sousa Santos, who

increasingly over the last twenty years has come to view law as incapable of what he seeks: emancipation of the poor and excluded. Sousa Santos, 525–6.

775 *Wiener Dual Quality*.

776 Even Aristotle, who was always worried about reckless attempts to change the law, believed that legislation (that most formal expression of written law) might have to be reformed "on the basis of subsequent changes in circumstance and improved knowledge". Duke, 112. Duke argues that Aristotle's resistance to legal change was grounded in his belief that fallible human constitutional regimes (usually democracy and oligarchy) could only imperfectly inculcate virtue, so that they required stability to allow for habituation as far as that might be achieved. Duke, 115, 122.

777 For a more complete discussion of stability and change in law, see *Brunnée and Toope Stability*.

778 Wendt; Giddens. See also *Bueger and Gadinger Theory*, 100.

779 *Adler World Ordering*, 30–1, 95. For Adler, this process of retention – with the background knowledge that is incorporated – is in large measure what allows the creation of institutions. *Adler World Ordering*, 252–5.

780 *Brunnée and Toope Stability*. The previous paragraphs are adapted from that article.

781 *Weber Law*, 68; *Weber Interpretation*, 243. Bourdieu articulated the point more generally in arguing that the boundaries between different "fields" and their interaction are constantly "shaped and reshaped both by internal struggles and by external interventions of agents of other related fields: the dynamic of fields is the rule, stability the exception". Bigo, 240.

782 *Wiener Contestation*. It is important to remember Weber's insight that in all "institutional systems" there will always be dissent. Eisenstadt explains the point: "These different orientations to the central symbolic spheres may become foci of conflict and of potential institutional change." Eisenstadt, xliv. Durkheim too saw the possibility of constant change in institutional settings. Armand Cuvillier, "Preface to the French Edition of 1955", in *Durkheim Pragmatism*, xviii. See also Reinhold and Zurn, 253–4 (on three forms of "dissonance" that can lead to legal change).

783 Habermas argued that the language of law can "function as transformer in the society-wide communication circulating between system and lifeworld". *Habermas Discourse*, 81.

784 But see Raymond Duvall and Arjun Chowdhury, "Practices of Theory", in Emanuel Adler and Vincent Pouliot (eds), *International Practices* (New York: Cambridge University Press, 2011), 335, 343 (suggesting that practice theory supports the *status quo* as competency is described by the deployment of existing norms rather than challenges to those norms).

785 As I have emphasised, practice is affected but not dictated by habit. *Contra* Hopf, 540, 545 (arguing that because of the overwhelming power of habits, practice is fixed in the status quo). Aristotle, too, thought that law operated mostly through habit. Duke, 113.

786 See, e.g., *Walters on Dicey*, 224–5. Sousa Santos notes, though, that most historical revolutions took place in the name of law (as a means of correcting corrupt or oppressive regimes), but that the Russian Revolution broke with the tradition, and attacked the edifice of law. Sousa Santos, 524. More recently, the fighters of Islamic

State (ISIS) also pursued a revolutionary dismantling of the edifice of human law, seeking a pure recourse to divine will.

787 *Arendt Revolution, passim*; Lang, 227, 236–7.

788 Quoted in Kamrava, 27.

789 *Weber Theory*, 362. It should be noted that in another work, Weber emphasised that in a sense "reason" is also revolutionary in that it "changes men's attitudes". *Weber Interpretation*, 234.

790 *Walzer Moral Standing*, 222. The great positivist thinker Comte also argued for a "right to insurrection", but only *in extremis*. Auguste Comte, *Discours sur l'ensemble du positivisme* (1848). It seems that Aristotle was ambivalent on the question of any right to overthrow tyranny. Although he argued that no free person should willingly endure tyranny, Duke argues convincingly that Aristotle's position was conditioned by his strong disinclination to support disorder. Duke, 128.

791 *Reference Re Secession of Quebec* [1998] 2 SCR 217.

792 *Rawls Liberalism*, 136.

793 Lechner and Frost, 197 (also challenging Rawls on his view that the state is a "closed society"). Of course, migration may be precluded, and often is, by closed borders and the use of force.

794 Like Fuller, I struggle to identify a political power in the world that upholds a rule of law as defined here, based in the criteria of legality, that can get away with systematic repression. I must be clear that China does not uphold the criteria of legality that Fuller and I identify. It famously promotes a "rule by law", not a rule of law. By that I mean that law is deployed as a force for social control, and sometimes to facilitate commercial and trade relationships, but much of the regulation of social life is opaque. Secret trials are held; arbitrary detention is practised on a massive scale; authority is exercised by Party officials that parallels and sometimes overwhelms the state/public authority. See, e.g., Eric Orts, "The Rule of Law in China" (2001) 34 *Vanderbilt J., Trans'l L.*, 43; Benedict Sheehy, "Fundamentally Conflicting Views of the Rule of Law in China and the West and Implications for Commercial Disputes" (2006) 26 *Northwestern J. Int'l L. & Bus.* 225; NA, "Michael Kovrig: China Begins Espionage Trial Behind Closed Doors", BBC News, 22 March 2021, available at: www.bbc.co.uk/news/world-asia-china-56480219.

795 Kamrava stresses that revolutions, as opposed to chaos and instability, are surprisingly rare in world history, though not, I would add, because of the consistent upholding of the rule of law. Kamrava, 2, 7.

796 In this sense, my argument is parallel to Bourdieu's description of overlapping social "fields" where there are no fixed boundaries. Dezalay and Madsen, 441.

CHAPTER NINE

Lawyers, Practice and Legal Education

I must go away
With my terrors until I have taught them to sing

W. H. Auden, *The Age of Anxiety*[*]

I WANT TO CONCLUDE with some thoughts on what the approach to the rule of law I have traced out means for the contemporary practice of law, and for legal education and scholarship. I will look at the failed practice of some very influential US lawyers in the post 9/11 era to show how the roles and responsibilities of jurists, and more broadly of members of legal communities of practice, intersect with ethical dilemmas associated with the three sources of our contemporary anxiety.

It should be obvious that the emphasis I have placed on the role of communities of practice means that the people who practise law are important to our understanding of the rule of law and of what law can achieve in society. Thoughtful commentators on Weber make a similar point:

> Perhaps the whole legal project is unthinkable without the faith that constitutes lawyers . . . Thinking about the law without thinking realistically about the deal that binds lawyers together is the central error of judgement that Weber warns against.[797]

Habermas, too, argued that law should be viewed from the perspective of "an interpretation community of legal experts".[798] I would expand the point to say that the community is not only one of interpretation, but also of construction, application, contestation and concrete *action*: as I have already detailed, legal practitioners do much more than argue through language.

Members of legal communities of practice discuss, argue and act in the light of shared background knowledge and common purposes. Adler emphasises that all types of practitioner "act in the world with orientations towards ends". Within the framework of the practice, the practitioner is constantly trying to improve on past performance (becoming more "competent") while solving problems in practical ways. Because competence is not measured by efficiency only, practices tend to have ethical content.[799] Like all practitioners, lawyers act and evaluate their actions – reflexively in real time and reflectively later – deploying what Aristotle described as "practical knowledge".[800] Practices therefore change over time, and they come to reshape our background knowledge as well.[801]

Legal communities of practice encompass far more people than would be included in the concept of the legal "profession", and may include students, civil society actors, journalists, professors, civil servants in government, politicians, business people, trade unionists, think tank researchers and writers, diplomats, criminologists and many others. The boundaries of the community are porous. This is a crucial point because, as Weber pointed out long ago, the *profession* of law in the modern era has been shaped fundamentally by the needs of commerce:

> This growing demand for experience and specialized knowledge and the consequent stimulus for increasing rationalization of the law have almost always come from increasing significance of commerce and those participating in it.[802]

I see this as a neutral statement of fact. But the rule of law and law itself, as should be clear from everything I have argued so far, is central to the needs of society broadly construed, not only to the needs of commerce.[803] Examples of non-commercial legal developments that relied on the participation of a wide spectrum of actors, including practising lawyers and law professors but extending far beyond, include the expansion of civil rights for members of the LGBTQ+ community in many countries, the negotiation of climate change treaties, the progressive abolition of the death penalty across the globe, and the reform of national divorce laws over the twentieth century. In these cases, non-governmental organisations, victims' rights groups, lobbyists and activists, civil servants, politicians, diplomats, scientists and many others were variously implicated in legal communities of practice. Even in areas more closely associated with commerce, like changes to trade and investment law, the protection of intellectual property and consumer protection, legal communities of practice have necessarily been highly diverse.

It is also important to distinguish the concepts of "legal community of practice" and "profession of law" for another reason. For a long time, the legal profession has been controlled by localised guilds that restrict entry and more or less effectively monitor the ethics of practice. Those guilds have been constantly criticised for insularity, classism and self-interested behaviours. Bourdieu was fascinated by professions but found them hard to study from a sociological perspective because they tend to co-opt the observer through the use of historically constructed idealisations of their role in society. For Bourdieu, the very goal of a "profession" is to create an homogenised group designed to enhance its own "symbolic power".[804] In "The Force of Law" Bourdieu describes

> … the power of legal doctrine and particularly legal language in turning social reality into legal reality and the way in which the keepers of that power – an increasingly institutionalized legal profession – gradually constructed for themselves a key position in the management of the state.[805]

In Western societies, there can be no doubt that the legal profession accomplished that goal across the nineteenth and twentieth centuries.[806] However, with the rise of populist sentiment globally, professions are, like so many other social institutions, being attacked. I want to separate out the role of professional legal associations (bars) from the groupings of people who constitute legally focused communities of practice. As I have noted, those communities can be more inclusive, including many participants who are not lawyers, and whose practices are far more expansive than the "practice of law" in a professional sense.

I do not want these comments to be interpreted as a slight against practising lawyers, who obviously remain central to communities of legal practice. My point is primarily methodological, defining the scope of what I am examining. In fact, even self-consciously "critical" sociological literature stresses the important role that practitioners (as opposed to theorists) play in advancing knowledge. Practitioners fight in the trenches, so to speak, and then develop insight from that experience. Wacquant argues that for Bourdieu it is fundamentally important to resist construing "the world as a *spectacle*, as a set of significations to be interpreted rather than as concrete problems to be solved practically".[807] Bourdieu was warning that the remote gaze of the critical observer can miss much of the action and disconnect from the real issues of the world.[808]

Of course, this insight aligns with the pragmatist conception of knowledge and truth, that both are created collectively and tested through mutual validation in social practices. We have seen that this consensus theory of knowledge was first articulated by Charles Sanders Peirce, although it built upon Aristotle's insight that we know what values to advance through practical wisdom, which is bound up in prudent action. Of course, not all participants in a community of legal practice are equally competent; some are simply better at persuasion, interpretation, contestation and action of all kinds. Starting with Weber, these sorts of people have been identified as "entrepreneurs" of norms, actions and decisions.[809] As I have noted, pragmatists go on to suggest that all forms of knowledge are best viewed as useful frameworks that are subject to experimentation and necessary reformulation through the creation of new insight, generated in turn through new expressions of competent practice. A similar position was adopted by Habermas: ongoing legal discussion provides only provisional answers heading in the right direction.[810]

But perhaps Habermas is too optimistic here. Practices are not inevitably positive or progressive; even discursive practices in law.[811] As Weber argued, legal practices can produce bureaucratic knowledge that is formalistic and utilitarian – with "professionalised" practitioners focused only on outcomes that appear rational, but that may not be attuned to morals, culture and social norms.[812] If legal knowledge is disconnected from various forms of emotional insight, including intuition and imagination, it can become sterile and misleading.[813] Lawyers can come to privilege "order" above all other social aims.[814] What is worse, legal practices can also reaffirm oppressive behaviours and build new "knowledge" that is corrupt and abusive. The point is that practices matter because they generate social beliefs and actions, not that they are inevitably progressive.

On the other hand, Bourdieu and Foucault are radically sceptical of norms that shape and emerge from communities of practice because both thinkers focus on power relationships that may constrain or pervert the emergence of norms – they want to excavate this problem and reveal the lack of human agency.[815] They see hidden assumptions and power plays everywhere, and especially in the legal profession. Norms that are built and reaffirmed in legal communities of practice are likely to be self-serving; they result in an occupation of the public sphere that simply reflects and reaffirms the importance of law and lawyers.[816] This critique is similar to Shklar's legalism, though this time from a sociological, rather than a political theory perspective.

Although it is certainly possible for law to over-claim and for lawyers to over-reach, I think that the distinction I have drawn between legal communities of practice and the legal profession is important here. Practice communities that include non-lawyers, and that are self-reflective and self-critical, do not in fact claim legal hegemony. I must also frankly admit that I simply reject Foucault and Bourdieu's shared, though differently articulated, fixation with conflicts over power, and the struggle for domination, as the basis or primary driver of all social relationships.[817] Power and its partner, domination, are relevant but so too is the human need for communication and cooperation.

I also want to challenge the implicit critique of theory, and indeed of academia, offered by Bourdieu that I have already mentioned.[818] I do not think that one needs to adopt an either–or position on the need for interpretation and the need for action. A pragmatist focus on practices does not imply that critical reflection is unimportant, quite the contrary. As we have seen, communities of practice engage in all sorts of activities that relate to ideas and debates,[819] as well as action in the world. Theory is embedded in practices.[820] In law, as in all processes of normative articulation, interpretation, contestation and application we need to distance ourselves from the subject matter under consideration.[821] And in such processes of reflexive and reflective learning, being able to draw on the critical analysis of observers of a practice can be really important for participants within the practice.[822] At the same time, observers must do their utmost to understand the practice from within, and not from an abstracted, purely external viewpoint.[823] Observers, including social scientific observers, must try to bury into the practice to understand its relationships, structures and identities. As Hannah Arendt argued so clearly, theory that remains utterly disconnected from practices in the world is likely to be frustratingly irrelevant. It is only through critical reflection and reflexivity that social learning takes place, learning that I have argued is the very basis for both dynamic social stability and requisite evolutionary change.

Critical observers who engage deeply with communities of practice must also be able to translate their insights into comprehensible analysis. More than a decade ago, Friedrichs and Kratochwil pleaded with international relations scholars to "maintain the communicability of our research questions and findings not only to fellow specialists but also to a wider academic audience and, ultimately society at large". They emphasised that "the findings of empirical research and the gist of theoretical debates should be reported in a vocabulary close enough to everyday language to allow for cross-community dialogue".[824] The same must be said for legal analysts and theorists. Law exists in the world; it has profound implications for real people. If the ability to reflect critically is contained to a few hundred academics who write and talk to each other on given issues, practices will be impoverished and fidelity to law in the wider community will decay.[825]

I want to take the argument a step further to suggest that communities of legal practice are *ethically bound* to derive insights and critically reflect upon the data of the world in which we find ourselves. If they fail to do so, they become disconnected from the consequences of legal arguments and decisions. Failing to appreciate consequences can have devastating effects, as we will see shortly in the case of challenges to the rules prohibiting torture. Legal communities of practice are also ethically bound to communicate back into that world in ways that inexpert people can understand. Otherwise, they decouple law from the people who must uphold it. Remember that for Fuller and me, citizens are reciprocally bound to follow rules when the promulgator of the rules is also bound to them. This is a fundamental element of the rule of law. Failing to communicate effectively about the law and its requirements undermines the very possibility of reciprocity. Let me explain this point more fully by reflecting upon what a legal education should help graduates think through and undertake. I will then explore what happens when that process fails in its core purposes.

Every so often a coterie of law professors erupts in a declaration of "crisis" in legal education. Over the last century at least, legal education has seen dramatic shifts and regular cries of concern. I will focus primarily on debates within US legal culture for three reasons. First, they are extremely well-documented and helpfully framed by two insightful reports produced in the early part of the twentieth and twenty-first centuries. Secondly, the cultural power of American law, in an era of globalisation, has meant that disputes over the proper shape of legal education in the United States have transnational influence. Finally, I want to examine in some detail what I take to be deformations of US legal culture, including legal education, in a very specific setting of public law practice, that of US government lawyers in the Office of Legal Counsel of the US Department of Justice in the post-9/11 era. I do so because the stakes were high and the insights to be drawn are important, and not only for US law and lawyers.

In 1914, the Carnegie Foundation – presumably sensing a problem – commissioned the distinguished Austrian civil law expert, Professor Josef Redlich, to visit American university law schools and assess their quality.[826] In a thoughtful and balanced report, Professor Redlich concluded that although the American focus on court cases was perfectly suited to teaching common law legal method, and even represented the "nature" of the common law,[827] it undervalued systematisation and failed to help students to grasp the mission of law in society.[828] I suspect that a similar critique could have been applied to English and Commonwealth (or, rather, Empire) legal education at the time. Redlich went on to suggest that American law professors still needed to create a "scientific system of the common law" enabling students to see the big picture, and this the "case method" demonstrably failed to deliver.[829]

Redlich's Germanic notion of legal science treated law as fundamentally normative, based on understandings of what "ought to be" rather than what "is".[830] That version of a "science" of law stands in stark contrast to another self-proclaimed scientific view of a slightly earlier day, promoted by Christopher Columbus Langdell at Harvard.[831] Langdell famously argued that "[i]f law be not a science … it is a species of handicraft, and may best be learned by serving an apprenticeship …"[832] Like Redlich, Langdell wanted systematisation, but thought that it could be derived from a very specific form of empirical observation borrowed from his understanding of the natural sciences. By parsing court cases and comparing them over time, one could draw out "certain principles or doctrines":

> To have such a mastery of these as to be able to apply them with constant facility and certainty to the ever-tangled skein of human affairs, is what constitutes a true lawyer; and hence to acquire that mastery should be the business of every earnest student of law.[833]

Soon after becoming dean at Harvard, Langdell went so far as to decree that the study of legal theory should no longer be a required part of the curriculum.[834] Inductive reasoning from cases, a form of scientific positivism, was all that mattered to derive legal rules.

Langdell's "science" of legal education was attacked head-on by the American legal realists, scholars who thought that cases were more about politics and who decided them than they were about any scientific principles that could be gleaned from their study. In a harsh essay, Karl Llewellyn castigated the Langdell model because "it blinds, it stumbles, it conveyor-belts, it wastes, it mutilates, and it empties".[835] Llewellyn argued that legal education had to take account of what lawyers do, but also had to consider the development of professional character, not merely the articulation of doctrine. Fifty years later, a distinguished legal historian and theorist felt the need to take on the realist heritage in American law teaching. In a short article from 1985, matching in tone the screed of Llewellyn, Harold Berman argued:

> We have been overwhelmed by the belief that law is politics and politics in a rather narrow sense: not in the sense that Aristotle meant when he said law is politics, but more in the sense of Max Weber and V. I. Lenin meant when they said law is politics …
>
> Of course law is politics. But law is also morality. And law is also history. Law is not only something that is *made* by those who are in power; law is also something that is *given*. The legislators and judges are not only its masters. They are also its creatures.[836]

As between Langdell's science and Llewellyn's realism, Berman responds: "a plague on both your houses".

By the 1990s, the sense that US law schools were in crisis had grown, possibly as a result of the political *ennui* lingering after the Watergate debacle, the financial excesses of the 1980s (after all, this was the era of *The Bonfire of the Vanities*),[837] and the swiftly rising cost of an American legal education. Various *cris de coeur* were published,[838] but for the legal academy at least, the most influential was Yale Dean Anthony Kronman's *The Lost Lawyer.*[839] Calling for the resurrection of a discarded ideal, that of the "lawyer-statesman", Kronman described professionals who exercise practical wisdom infused with the virtue of "civic-mindedness".[840] Legal education needed to avoid both cynicism (one hears echoes of Berman's "law is more than the politics of power") and technocracy (law is not Langdell's doctrinal science; nor is it merely a branch of economics). Yet, intriguingly, Kronman's prescription for legal education was to re-build the late nineteenth-century commitment to Socratic dialogue that Langdell pioneered.[841] For Kronman, however, the point of this dialogue would not be to derive principles from nature (in case law), but to foment the "moral imagination".[842]

At the end of the twentieth century, then, we returned to the beginning, with Redlich's description of the case law method as inherent in the nature of common law, but Kronman appeared to be no closer to answering Redlich's question of how to rise above the details of cases to create a more expansive – social – understanding of law. Indeed, in a forceful critique of North American legal education issued in 2007, the Carnegie Foundation for the Advancement of Teaching, the same foundation that commissioned the Redlich report in 1914, stressed that an over-reliance on the case law method led to "a striking conformity in outlook and habits of thought among legal graduates".[843] While acknowledging, as Redlich had almost a century before, that in its ideal form the case law method provides strong training in logic and is a "potent form of learning by doing",[844] the 2007 Carnegie authors reject the idea that the case law method of teaching is inherent in the common law method, at least as that method is experienced in the practice of law.[845]

The Carnegie authors go further, suggesting that the case law method is both an oversimplification of and an abstraction from "life", and that it undervalues the social effects of law, which in turn tends to mask fundamental ethical issues.[846] A similar perspective had been adopted in a

Canadian report on legal education and scholarship in 1983, where it was argued that Canadian law schools were too focused on "black letter" legal doctrine, and were not open or even attuned to insights from cognate disciplines. The law schools therefore tended to produce graduates who lacked creativity, did not understand the implications of legal constructs and decisions in society, and were simply not humane enough.[847]

Contemporary legal education is often described as helping students to "think like a lawyer"[848] as if that were a monolithic construct. The challenges to the case law method that I have reviewed point to a tough question: what is "thinking like a lawyer" and is it enough for students today? For Kronman, the method, in the idealised form he describes, would excite the moral imagination.[849] For one of the authors of the 2007 Carnegie Report, on the other hand, the case law method and related analytical approaches have served to "domesticate doubt". And we have seen that the second Carnegie Report suggests that the case law method, for all its strengths analytically, can serve to distance law students from the pertinent complexities of life.[850] Perhaps domesticating doubt is part of the problem.[851] To reduce doubt – and with it the reality of uncertainty in life – artificially (by reducing the scope of legal thinking to rules-based "analytical" approaches alone) is to instrumentalise law,[852] to see it only as an exercise in solving disputes rather than society-building, and to reduce the scale of "law's cosmos", to adopt Canadian Supreme Court Justice Nicholas Kasirer's terminology.

Law can be much more than a projection of "oughts" – an imperial project. It can be a way of thinking, a way of knowing and even a way of being – a cosmological project.[853] As I have suggested and tried to model throughout this book, the cosmological project requires openness to the complexities – more, the uncertainties – of life. It demands frames of reference that help us to handle that complexity, be they called "anchoring practices" or "Background". These frames can be grasped only if we connect law to cognate disciplines (philosophy, sociology, anthropology, economics, increasingly computer science, etc.). We then draw on precedent and deploy sophisticated analogy and comparison. All this in the exercise of practical wisdom.[854] The potential to invoke practical wisdom is more likely, Aristotle teaches us, if we work concretely to build political and legal norms and institutions that have the capacity to habituate virtue.[855] Doing so allows participants in legal communities of practice to be reflexive and reflective – self-critical as we work and able also to rise above immediate data. Empathy is also required, that is, the ability to enter into the data and, more importantly, into the shoes of citizens experiencing the rule of law and particular legal rules.[856] It seems to me that these virtues lie at the heart of what it is to be a wise "counsel" to others. Such inculcated virtues also prompt people to be honest and open about their purposes; what Background shapes their desire to contribute to the world of law?[857]

Borrowing Vico's concept, students of the law need to develop a refined capacity to "see new arguments based on probabilities in situations of uncertainty" and not merely quantifiable risk.[858] This approach does not imply that law exists only, or even primarily, in a world of ideas.[859] The rich concept of "practice" I have traced out provides a way of thinking about lived experience as integral to law's ability to reflect upon itself, without turning law into a mere technical exercise. We are not, therefore, presented with the dichotomy that seems to have been assumed in much of the late twentieth-century writing on legal education: law must be corrected and expanded through external critique (the various "law and ..." movements),[860] or it must be acknowledged as purely instrumental by connecting law only to what clients need and want (law as commerce, or law as nothing but politics).[861] Instead, by seeing law as a form of practical wisdom rooted in life experience, the richness of human knowledge can be included within law, but that knowledge is tested in particular ways through communities of legal practice, with their internal evaluations of competent practice. The result is, as Wendel puts it: "the moral and social dimensions of legal reasoning are embedded *within* legal reasoning ... [because] formal knowledge is not prior to practice ..."[862] This conception, of course, is close to Fuller's, and to what Brunnée and I call "criteria of legality". It also reminds us of Dyzenhaus' argument that constitutions are internally legitimated within law, and are not reliant on purely external legitimation from "the will of the people".

In thinking through what all this means for communities of legal practice, teaching law and the ethics of law, it is worth considering a high-profile example where, in my view, legal ethics – and even the competent performance of legal practice – were utterly abandoned in the face of widespread social anxiety, indeed fear. In an important legal decision flowing from the attacks of 11 September 2001, President Bush issued an Executive Order in February of the following year denying Taliban and Al Qaeda prisoners the protections of the Geneva Conventions. The Bush Administration determined that "terrorists and other enemy fighters who did not wear uniforms or carry their arms openly" would not be treated as prisoners of war.[863] As a direct consequence, the Administration asked its legal counsel to provide new guidance on what "techniques" could be employed to get accused Al Qaeda operatives in custody to talk.

At the beginning of August 2002, the head of the Office of Legal Counsel (OLC) in the Department of Justice, Jay Bybee, sent a memo to the Counsel to the CIA, arguing that ten specific techniques, escalating in force up to waterboarding, did not constitute torture.[864] On the same day, a second memo from the OLC, also signed by Bybee, but written primarily by John Yoo, was sent to the White House Counsel, Alberto Gonzales.[865] In transforming the UN Convention Against Torture[866] into US law, Congress had already defined torture narrowly, limiting torture that might give rise to criminal prosecution within the United States to acts "specifically intended" to cause "severe physical ... pain" or "prolonged mental harm".[867] Yoo sought to limit the concept of torture even further, interpreting the US statute so that only pain "associated with a sufficiently serious physical condition or injury such as death, organ failure, or serious impairment of bodily functions" would constitute physical torture.[868] Waterboarding would fall outside this definition; so too burning people with cigarettes, giving them electric shocks or depriving them of sleep for days on end.

The legal analysis that Professor Yoo employed to reach this conclusion has been widely criticised.[869] Starting from the debatable proposition that the statutory requirement that acts causing "severe ... pain" or "prolonged mental harm" is inherently ambiguous, Yoo (and Bybee) looked for analogous definitions of "severe pain" in other US statutes. They chose as the principal analogy a definition of "emergency condition" entitling someone to obtain health-care benefits.[870] In a powerful critique, Wendel asks the right question: "Is it a legitimate legal argument to infer from the emergency health-care benefits statute to a definition of severe pain in the torture statute?" I believe not: "[t]he lawyers' argument feels like someone went fishing around on a computer database looking to match up the search terms, without using their judgment to decide whether the match was on point."[871] This description may be too generous, for with lawyers as well-trained as Yoo, it is hard to believe that he did not exercise independent judgement.

Early the next year, in March 2003, John Yoo sent another memo, this time to the Counsel to the Department of Defense, detailing the international and domestic law applicable to the treatment of detainees. He argued that "national defense" and executive power are paramount considerations, trumping all legal constraints.[872] The thrust of the legal advice being offered to US interrogators was that aggressive techniques were necessary in the "War on Terror", and that "torture" could be read so narrowly as to allow techniques that might otherwise be contrary to international and US law. In other words, by fiat of redefinition in the name of national security, no "torture" was being committed.

In considering what a complete understanding of "practice" looks like, and by connecting that understanding to an approach to legal education rooted in practical wisdom, have we learned anything that might help to explain the actions of those government lawyers? More importantly, can we draw out lessons that might discourage future lawyers from adopting similar positions in eras dominated by anxiety, eras like our own?[873] We can certainly say that the practices adopted by these lawyers, if they had become generalised and not subject to strong resistance, would likely have produced a sense of illegitimacy in the law against torture. If the entire practice verges on incompetency, in the sense that the reasoning and resulting actions do not meet the standards of the relevant legal community of practice, the practice is fundamentally undermined. For that reason it is important to stress that the arguments offered up by the OLC lawyers were strongly rebuffed by various US and international legal communities of practice that encompassed international lawyers, human rights lawyers, NGOs, church groups, political actors, journalists and diplomats. The human right to be protected from torture was ultimately reaffirmed, even strengthened.[874]

When asked by a reporter on network television "Why is waterboarding legal, in your opinion?", former President Bush answered simply "Because the lawyer said it was legal".[875]

That deference – or perhaps abdication of leadership – reveals why lawyers bear a heavy responsibility for the advice they give, the arguments they make, the institutions and systems they design, and the negotiation and dispute settlement they undertake. Lawyers' roles are myriad, and the consequences of legal argument, interpretation, decisions and actions can be enormous. It is common to say that, unlike doctors, legal work is not "life and death". That is not necessarily true. After the early legal opinions were issued authorising aggressive interrogations of terrorist subjects, a CIA detainee in a secret prison in Kabul died of hypothermia after he was stripped and chained outside for many hours.[876] We may never know how many other people died in secret prisons dotted around the world at the behest (and sometimes under the direct control) of US security forces. Or consider the powerful film *Eye in the Sky*, that focused on the decisions of lethal drone operators and the legal advisers who struggled to determine when a strike was lawful. The stakes are even higher when one imagines the role that lawyers typically play in the design of public systems of governance, which affect the lives of hundreds of millions of people. Remember that a brilliant lawyer, Carl Schmitt, offered up legal conceptions that buttressed the Nazi regime. Today, lawyers in various repressive countries help to justify widespread abuses of human rights.

It should come as no surprise that many observers have called upon legal education to focus as much on the education of "citizens" as "professionals",[877] echoing Kronman's desire to create "lawyer-statesmen".[878] Yet one could argue that this call is not precise enough. One would hope that any educated person in our society is exposed to the demands and aspirations of Arendt's free citizenship. Although there is much evidence that the liberal arts ideal of "educating citizens" is collapsing under the weight of specialisation, careerism and high cost,[879] the ideal should presumably remain available to a range of students wider than those who choose to study law, and even if they cannot attend elite universities.

Rather than talking of "citizenship" in general, as important as that is, the more fruitful question is whether or not there are particular aptitudes and virtues associated with being a lawyer, part of a community of legal practice.[880] I have already answered in the affirmative, at least as aptitudes are concerned, in suggesting that the form of reasoning known as "practical wisdom" is what lawyers need to learn and enhance in their education and throughout their day-to-day work. In describing "interactional law", I showed how the very idea of legal obligation, which is often simply assumed, is rooted in shared social understandings which solidify into law when connected to criteria of legality. But this law must be maintained and supported constantly by legal communities of practice if it is not to fade into disuse. The practical wisdom of lawyers, and others who participate in communities of legal practice, constantly navigating through the complex channels of social life, upholds and furthers legal obligation and the rule of law.

In difficult cases or circumstances, there may be no obvious answer to the fundamental questions of "what to do" or "how to decide". Lawyers have to ask themselves even deeper questions: what is the right thing to do, for the right reasons, and in the best possible way in these practical circumstances?[881] The specific aptitudes of reasoning from precedent and by analogy, exercising empathetic judgement, drawing creative inspiration through thoughtful and open-spirited connections to other forms of thought, and sophistication in the design of complex institutions are all relevant, all required in the competent practices of law. But how is this connected to the personal and professional responsibility of lawyers?

A starting proposition for legal education is that:

> ... professor and student are not merely role-players in an abstract game to which their commitment is merely contingent, but are human beings endowed with the capacity and charged with the responsibility for improving the social institutions through which people can pursue their life projects.[882]

Four important ideas are found in this short quotation: first, is that at a high level, not associated with a specific formulation of the good life, law is purposive, not static or simply "received". It exists to protect individual autonomy but also to facilitate the gathering together of people in a society, allowing them to articulate and pursue common purposes through communication. Secondly, law is not abstracted from that society, but rooted in its shared understandings and attendant social norms. Thirdly, law is not a game in the trivial sense, for law actually allows the common purposes of people in society to be furthered. Fourthly, students and law teachers must truly commit to explore law together, for legal education is not instrumental (a "training" school) but is partly constitutive of law itself; professors and students are already part of communities of legal practice. This means that legal education is a critical part of engendering the rule of law and building specific legal norms. Because all knowledge, including legal knowledge, is built through human interaction, legal studies must progressively escape from completely insular, jurisdictionally focused rule-learning into forms of education that promote greater openness to diverse sources of insight and creativity, building towards empathy. We need to discover "the encounter" in legal education.[883]

Even as a law student, then, and certainly as a law professor, one's task is fundamentally connected to the existence and health of law itself. If one believes in the possibility, or even more in the necessity, of a rule of law in society, then one's responsibility is manifest:

> If . . . respect for the law is a way of respecting the inherent dignity and equality of one's fellow citizens, even in circumstances of deep disagreement about what morality requires, then there is something intrinsically good about the rule of law. The ethics in lawyering can therefore be understood not in terms of underlying moral goods to be pursued through legal means, but in terms of the non-instrumental value of legality as a virtue of societies characterized by tolerance and respect for all citizens.[884]

It is in the very reasoning, interpreting, arguing and acting of communities of legal practice that the ethical obligations of law, the personal and professional responsibilities, are assumed and worked out.[885] In Ignatieff's terms, the development of "character" as a lawyer-citizen is more important than an encyclopaedic knowledge of "the rules".[886]

It is now possible to offer tentative explanations as to why some distinguished lawyers in the US Department of Justice's Office of Legal Counsel offered up arguments for the legality of waterboarding and other forms of aggressive interrogation techniques that seem so laboured, so unconvincing. One can start from the proposition that the

Al Qaeda suspects were outside established frameworks of law or that, as non-citizens, their existence was "bare" to borrow Agamben's term.[887] They were not found within the territory of the United States and were not "prisoners of war". Therefore, the society that gives context (shared understandings) to law became harder to identify. In a world that still accords so much value to the state, despite the many challenges to its hegemony, it is still easier to see fluidity and uncertainty in a society denominated "international". The Background is harder to discern. So, the lawyer may assume a degree of interpretative freedom greater than when he or she operates within the bounds of a domestic system of law. Hence, the not altogether disingenuous arguments put forward that international law does not contain a precise definition of torture.[888] But even when trying to define torture using US law, the OLC lawyers managed to play fast and loose with interpretative methods. One could defend their approach by suggesting that they were doing what good lawyers do as part of reasoning through practice: exercising creativity in the use of analogy. How can one say that they went too far?

As I have already hinted, the answer is found in the concept of practical wisdom, and in Vico's notion that in situations of uncertainty lawyers must be helped to develop "the prudence to choose appropriately when the matter is not subject to calculation . . ."[889] As I have stressed, sophisticated practice requires not just creativity and flexibility, but pragmatism – connection to the impact of law in the world. In practice, lawyers must temper ideas with life experience; they create knowledge through the sharing of experience, not just "clever" thoughts. The OLC lawyers found "a way" to argue that the definition of physical pain and suffering could be narrowed. Their argument was superficially creative (looking to a statute on the provision of health care to define pain and suffering as a result of torture) and even clever. But it was neither prudent nor pragmatic because it was not tested against life experience. How else can one explain the anodyne descriptions of what happened to the suspects subjected to aggressive interrogation techniques offered by Professor Yoo and others?[890] The disconnect between what they say they imagined and what actually happened is extreme, because they had no relevant experience to call upon, and it seems no empathetic judgement, or "moral imagination",[891] to adopt Kronman's terminology.

How could that be? How could really smart people who had gone to some of the best law schools in the United States lack pragmatic insight and moral imagination? If one reviews the criticisms of North American legal education lodged quite consistently over the last hundred years, we can tease out a convincing and expansive explanation: the dominance of instrumentalism. In diverse ways, law students have been inculcated with the belief that law is nothing more than a "tool". For followers of Carl Schmitt, or for legal realists and their successors amongst critical theorists, law is what those in power (public and private power) want to see happen. For legal positivists, law is what the hierarchical, pedigreed institutions of society (usually the state) say it is. For the myriad purveyors of "law and . . ." studies, especially law and economics, law is what is used to pursue externally determined ends. As one critical commentator put it, winning is what lawyers are paid to do; that is the test of their effectiveness, nothing more.[892] These instrumental approaches, with their many variations, have dominated law schools, especially in the United States, with ebbs and flows of influence, for the last century. Hannah Arendt warned long ago of "the murderous consequences inherent in a line of thought that forces one to admit that all means, provided that they are efficient, are permissible and justified to pursue something defined as an end".[893]

If law is nothing more than an instrument to pursue goals outside itself, if it has no intrinsic value, the freedom to manipulate is almost complete. As long as one can make "an argument", it is an acceptable argument, denying any evaluation of competent practice. And if the law is but an instrument, the important question is only: "what do I need to have happen in law so that my goals will be met?" One sees this attitude expressly in the argument put forth by Yoo that the president as commander-in-chief could override even the modest limitations on torture contained in US statute law because the limitations prevented the president "from gaining the intelligence he believes necessary to prevent attacks upon the United States".[894] Almost twenty years later, Professor Yoo is still making the underlying argument about the need for presidential power to overcome legal constraint.[895]

Law professors and law students are not disconnected from the practices of law even if they never work directly for a client or step into a courtroom. Teaching and learning together is a key element in the communities of legal practice that constitute law, and they in turn build or destroy our understanding of the rule of law in our society. To the extent that teachers and students conceive of law as infinitely malleable, as merely a tool to achieve exogenous ends, or as a purely intellectual game divorced from consequences for real people, they are helping to destroy the rule of law, exposing our fellow human beings to risks that may be hard to calculate in advance, but are often horrifying in retrospect. Without a widely shared understanding that the rule of law matters in a society, and that all people are both empowered and constrained by law, people can be subjected to torture. People can die. Societies can disintegrate. That is the root of legal ethical responsibilities, both professionally and personally.[896] On the other hand, if a robust commitment to a sophisticated albeit modest version of the rule of law is built up in legal education, it can help to buttress practices of legality that allow for healthy social stability while providing frames for evolutionary change. That rule of law can help to address and manage our current anxieties.

Notes

797 David Kettler and Volker Meja, "Legal Formalism and Disillusioned Realism in Max Weber" (1996) 18 *Polity* 307, 329 (though the authors believe this "faith" is based in formalism; I think it is bound up in the criteria of legality).

798 *Habermas Discourse*, 224.

799 Lechner and Frost, 138.

800 *Adler World Ordering*, 131 (referring to the work of Schazki).

801 *Adler World Ordering*, 218.

802 *Weber Interpretation*, 254. For a contemporary take on this phenomenon, now linked to the political economy of globalisation, see Harry Arthurs, "Law and Learning in an Era of Globalization" (2009) 10 *German L. J.* 629.

803 Though for the stability of contracts and the predictability that business people need, the rule of law and concrete laws are crucial. For example, the role of independent adjudication in commercial disputes is often said to be a *sine qua non* for foreign investment. See, e.g., Joseph Staats and Glen Biglaiser, "The Effects of Judicial Strength and Rule of Law on Portfolio Investment in the Developing World" (2011) 92 *Soc. Sci. Q.* 609.

804 Dezalay and Madsen, 437.

805 Cited in Dezalay and Madsen, 437–8.

806 See, e.g., the work of the great American legal historian, James Willard Hurst, "Lawyers in American Society 1750–1966" (1967) 50 *Marquette L. Rev.* 594, 598 ("It is too narrow

a view to define the instruments of government as the executive, legislative, and judicial branches. Realism requires that we recognize that lawyers in their collective impact, as the bar, constitute in effect a fourth arm of government"). For a wider view on the role of lawyers in constructing Western liberalism, see Kermit Hall, Terence Halliday and Lucien Karpik (eds), *Lawyers and the Rise of Western Political Liberalism: Europe and North America from the Eighteenth to the Twentieth Centuries* (Oxford University Press, 1998).

807 Bourdieu and Wacquant, 39 (in this section of the book, Wacquant is discussing Bourdieu's thought; later, a discussion between the two is transcribed).

808 Lechner and Frost, 12, 49, 73, go further, arguing that even "observers" like social scientists must adopt an internal perspective or misconstrue the realities of a practice.

809 Eisenstadt, xl. See also Finnemore and Sikkink, *passim* (on norm entrepreneurs in international relations); *Kratochwil Status*, 21, 101 et seq.

810 *Habermas Discourse*, 226–7.

811 See Haack, 94–5.

812 *Weber Theory*, 333–40. See also *Weber Law*, 96–7, 321; White, 190.

813 Brożek, 34–8, 40–5. Of course, emotions too can be misleading. Brożek, 35.

814 *Weber Law*, 300; *Weber Interpretation*, 63.

815 See, e.g., Bigo, 226. I think, however, that both Foucault and Bourdieu focus too much on only one conception of power, that is, power as force. If the idea of "power" is expanded to include, for example, the power of duty or obligation, or performative power and legitimacy, power takes on a more collaborative hue. It may even be necessary to fulfil the human need for communication and cooperation. Remember that Arendt saw power as definitionally collective. *Arendt On Violence*, 40–4.

816 Dezalay and Madsen, 438.

817 Dezalay and Madsen, 439, 441 (Bourdieu on power); Lechner and Frost, 67 (Bourdieu on domination, but arguing that he is more subtle in exploring a range of domains in social interaction); Michel Foucault, *Discipline and Punish: The Birth of the Prison*, trans. Alan Sheridan (London: Penguin, 1991), *passim* (Foucault on varieties of power, discipline and an extended notion of "government" over others in society). On the difference between Foucault's disciplinary power and juridical (state) power, see Sousa Santos, 6–7.

818 Bourdieu strongly criticises any rigid distinction between theory and methodology in the social sciences. He suggests that theoretical choices are inevitably bound up in any choice of methodology. Bourdieu and Wacquant, 161 ("The function of the concepts I employ is first and foremost to designate, in a kind of shorthand, within the research procedure, a theoretical stance, a principle of methodological choice, negative as well as positive"), 233. On this point, I fully agree. But he is also negative about any form of "theoreticist theory", and here I think his case is overstated. Bourdieu and Wacquant, 31–2.

819 Anne Peters, "The Rise and Decline of the International Rule of Law and the Job of Scholars", Max Planck Institute, MPIL Research Paper Series No. 2017-16, 2 (manuscript on file with author) (on the role of scholars – theorists – to produce ideas that "have the power to shape attitudes and actions").

820 Lechner and Frost, 208 ("[W]hat we do within the framework of a common institution (a 'practice') is constituted by what we understand ourselves to be doing ('theory')"). On this point, Bourdieu would almost certainly agree. We need not adopt the dichotomy of theory and praxis put forth by Aristotle. Lechner and Frost, 100.

821 See Jochen von Bernstorff, "International Legal Scholarship as a Cooling Medium in International Law and Politics" (2014) 25 *EJIL* 977. On reflexivity, see *Bueger and Gadinger Practice*, 457–8 (on Bourdieu's "reflexive sociology" versus the pragmatist conception of reflexivity). See also Bourdieu and Wacquant, *passim* (on reflexive sociology); Friedrichs and Kratochwil, 711 (on reflexive pragmatism).

822 Tamahana, 524 (though I disagree with Tamahana that legal thinking is practice and social science is external observation; each must contain elements of understanding from inside and external critique). On the way these issues play out for international lawyers, who inevitably have a "dual identity", see *Reus-Smit Liberal Theory*, 585–7.

823 Lechner and Frost, 41–9.

824 Friedrichs and Kratochwil, 726. See also Lechner and Frost, 24, on the need for "concrete" language in social scientific and philosophical discourse.

825 Of course, the ability to create frames for critical public deliberation lies at the heart of Habermas' communicative action as well. *Habermas Discourse*, *passim.*

826 Josef Redlich, *The Common Law and the Case Method in American University Law Schools: A Report to the Carnegie Foundation for the Advancement of Teaching, Bulletin No. 8* (1914), thoroughly reviewed in James Maxeiner, "Educating Lawyers Now and Then: Two Carnegie Critiques of the Common Law and the Case Method" (2007) 35 *Int'l J. Legal Info.* 1. The following paragraphs are adapted from Stephen Toope, "Thinking, Doing, Being: Why 'Practising' Law Matters to the Prevention of Torture", in Helge Dedek and Shauna Van Praagh (eds), *Stateless Law: Evolving Boundaries of a Discipline* (Farnham: Routledge, 2015), 159.

827 Redlich described the case method as "an entirely original creation of the American mind in the realm of law". Maxeiner, 10, 15, 17. This conclusion certainly underplayed the English common law tradition!

828 Maxeiner, 1

829 Redlich, quoted in Maxeiner, 35.

830 Redlich, quoted in Maxeiner, 34.

831 Redlich explicitly rejects Langdell's approach. Redlich, quoted in Maxeiner, 34.

832 Christopher Columbus Langdell, "Address", 5 November 1866, reprinted in (1887) 3 *LQR* 123, 124.

833 Christopher Columbus Langdell, *A Selection of Cases on the Law of Contracts* (Boston, MA: Little, Brown, 1871), vi.

834 David Barnhizer, "The Purposes and Methods of American Legal Education" (2011) 36 *J. Legal Profession* 1, 7.

835 Karl Llewellyn, "On What is Wrong with So-called Legal Education" (1935) 35 *Columbia L. Rev.* 651, 653. See also Jerome Frank, "Why not a Clinical Lawyer-School?" (1933) 81 *U. Penn. L. Rev.* 907.

836 Harold Berman, "The Crisis of Legal Education in America" (1985) 26 *BC L. Rev.* 347, 348. As should be obvious, I do not agree that law "is" any of those things in essence. Rather, law is related to, and only relatively autonomous from, them all.

837 Tom Wolfe, *The Bonfire of the Vanities* (New York: Picador, 2008).

838 See, e.g., Mary Ann Glendon, *A Nation Under Lawyers: How the Crisis in the Legal Profession is Transforming American Society* (Cambridge, MA: Harvard University Press, 1994); Sol Linowitz and Martin Mayer, *The Betrayed Profession: Lawyering at the End of the Twentieth Century* (Baltimore, MD: Johns Hopkins University Press, 1996).

839 Anthony Kronman, *The Lost Lawyer: Failing Ideals of the Legal Profession* (Cambridge, MA: Belknap Press of Harvard University Press, 1993). And see the analysis of Kronman's argument in Mootz, 1265–8.

840 Kronman, 109 (hearkening back to Aristotle).

841 Kronman, 110.

842 Kronman, 113.

843 William Sullivan et al., *Educating Lawyers: Preparation for the Profession of Law* (Stanford, CA: Carnegie Foundation for the Advancement of Teaching, 2007), 186 [hereinafter *Sullivan Educating Lawyers*].

844 *Sullivan Educating Lawyers*, 74.

845 *Sullivan Educating Lawyers*, 81. And it should be noted that the teaching of law has been pursued differently in England than in the United States. There is not, in any event, a single comprehensive "common law method".

846 *Sullivan Educating Lawyers*, 187. See also the detailed discussion of the 2007 Carnegie Report in Maxeiner, *passim*; Toni Fine, "Reflections on U.S. Curricular Reform" (2009) 10 *German L. J.* 717.

847 Social Sciences and Humanities Research Council of Canada, *Law and Learning/Le droit et le savoir: Report of the Consultative Group on Research and Education in Law* (Ottawa: SSHRC, 1983). The report is generally referred to as the "Arthurs Report" after Prof. Harry Arthurs who chaired the Consultative Group. It is fair to say that the report was received with consternation by much of the legal academic community and was largely ignored by the community of practising lawyers. However, it slowly gained influence as can be seen from the many commentaries produced on its twentieth anniversary canvassed in Robert Gordon, "The Law School, the Profession, and Arthurs' Humane Professionalism" (2006) 44 *Osgoode Hall L. J.* 157.

848 See, e.g., Maxeiner, 15 (quoting the Redlich report).

849 See Kronman, 88.

850 See Judith Welch Wegner, "Reframing Legal Education's 'Wicked Problems'" (2009) 61 *Rutgers L. Rev.* 867, 893–4.

851 One of the authors of the Carnegie Report reveals that for most of the law professors and law students surveyed, internalisation of a process of "questioning" was seen as central to legal reasoning. Wegner, 895–6.

852 Or, in James Boyd White's terms, to see law as nothing but a policy instrument, aligning it with economics. White, 200.

853 Nicholas Kasirer, "Bijuralism in Law's Empire and in Law's Cosmos" (2002) 52 *J. Legal Ed.*, 29, esp. 30–1, 36.

854 See Kasirer. This approach to legal thinking is more specific than the "thinking critically" answer that seems so often to be offered as a description of legal reasoning – as if other disciplines had no critical capacity. See Wegner, 900. It is important to emphasise as well that for very practical reasons, lawyers need to revel in uncertainty: most issues that come before them are not "packaged" in any way. Situations have a way of changing, and a "case" may turn out to be about something entirely other than is first imagined. See James Freund, *Lawyering: A Realistic Approach to Legal Practice* (New York: Law Journal Seminars-Press, 1979), 15–16, quoted in Roderick Macdonald and Jason MacLean, "No Toilets in Park" (2005) 50 *McGill L. J.* 721.

855 See, e.g., *Cameron Phronesis*, 6–7; Zena Hitz, "Aristotle on Law and Moral Education" (2012) 42 *Oxford Stud. Ancient Phil.* 263 (discussing in particular the *Nicomachean Ethics* and *Politics*).

856 Hence Brożek's emphasis on both reason and emotion in the legal mind. Brożek, *passim*. See also Jason Beckett, "Rebel Without a Cause? Martii Koskenniemi and the Critical Legal Project" (2006) *German L. J.* 1045, 1071–2 (on objectivity and empathy in the work of a leading international lawyer). Ignatieff makes the same argument more generally about seeing arguments over human rights as a means to expand the "circle of moral concern". Ignatieff, 214.

857 For a parallel argument in IR, see Freidrichs and Kratochwil, 715–16 (claiming complete objectivity is an "obscurantist move").

858 See Mootz, 1295.

859 See Barnhizer, 14 ("No practicing lawyer or judge with whom I have ever interacted sits around in an office and 'ideates'. The point is that idea and action are inseparably connected and intertwined with each reinforcing and informing the other as part of a singular system").

860 See, e.g., Janet Mosher, "Legal Education: Nemesis or Ally of Social Movements?" (1997) 35 *Osgoode Hall L. J.* 613.

861 Consider the experience of this law student interviewed for the 2007 Carnegie Report: "You realize your thinking has changed, your values and the depth of your understanding. It leaves you with less creativity. [Thinking like a lawyer] reduces my role and focuses my attention on being an advocate for someone else." Wegner, 915.

862 W. Bradley Wendel, "Should Law Schools Teach Professional Duties, Professional Virtues, or Something Else? A Critique of the Carnegie Report on Educating Lawyers", 1, 37–8, available at: http://ssrn.com/abstract=1963838 [hereinafter *Wendel Professional Duties*].

863 Much of the detail in this section is derived from *Brunnée and Toope Interactional Account*, ch. 5. For a description of the internal Administration process that resulted in this decision by the president, see Philippe Sands, *Torture Team* (New York: Palgrave Macmillan, 2008), 30–6.

864 Assistant Attorney General Jay S. Bybee, US Department of Justice, Office of Legal Counsel, "Memorandum for John Rizzo, Acting General Counsel of the Central

Intelligence Agency Re: Interrogation of al Qaeda Operative", 1 August 2002, 18, available at: http://luxmedia.vo.llnwd.net/o10/clients/aclu/olc_08012002_bybee.pdf [hereinafter *Bybee Memo*]; see also Scott Shane, David Johnston and James Risen, "Secret U.S. Endorsement of Severe Interrogations", *New York Times*, 4 October 2007.

865 Assistant Attorney General Jay S. Bybee, US Department of Justice, Office of Legal Counsel, "Memorandum for Alberto R. Gonzales, Counsel to the President Re: Standards of Conduct for Interrogation under 18 U.S.C. §2340-2340A", 1 August 2002, available at: www.washingtonpost.com/wpsrv/politics/documents/cheney/torture_memo_aug2002.pdf [hereinafter *First Yoo Memo*]. On the real authorship of the memo, see Jack Goldsmith, *Terror Presidency: Law and Judgment Inside the Bush Administration* (New York: W. W. Norton, 2007), 142.

866 United Nations Convention Against Torture and Other Cruel, Inhuman or Degrading Treatment or Punishment, 26 June 1984, 1465 UNTS 85, Part I, (Reg. No. 24811) (entered into force 26 June 1987), Art. 1 (1).

867 18 USC §2340 (1) (1994).

868 *First Yoo Memo*, 46.

869 See, e.g., W. Bradley Wendel, "The Torture Memos and the Demands of Legality" (2009) 12 *Legal Ethics* 107; Goldsmith; David Luban, "The Torture Lawyers of Washington", in David Luban (ed.), *Legal Ethics and Human Dignity* (Cambridge University Press, 2007), 162.

870 42 USC SS 1395w-22(d)(3)(B). See also Goldsmith, 145.

871 *Wendel Professional Duties*, 34.

872 Deputy Assistant Attorney General John C. Yoo, US Department of Justice, Office of Legal Counsel, "Memorandum for William J. Haynes II, General Counsel of the Department of Defence Re: Military Interrogation of Alien Unlawful Combatants Held Outside the United States", 14 March 2003, 80–1, available at: http://media.washingtonpost.com/wp-srv/nation/pdfs/OLCMemo60–81.pdf.

873 See Stephen Toope, "Human Rights and the Use of Force after September 11th, 2001", in Terry Nardin and Daniel Sherman (eds), *Terror, Culture, Politics: Rethinking 9/11* (Bloomington: Indiana University Press, 2006), 236; Stephen Toope, "Fallout from '9-11': Will a Security Culture Undermine Human Rights?" (2002) 65 *Sask L. Rev.* 281.

874 See Sands, *passim.*

875 See Frank James, "Bush Says Waterboarding was Legal, But Was it Moral?", 9 November 2010, available at: www.npr.org/blogs/itsallpolitics/2010/11/09/131184413/president-bush-would-jesus-ok-waterboarding.

876 Dana Priest, "CIA Holds Terror Suspects in Secret Prisons", *Washington Post*, 2 November 2005, available at: www.washingtonpost.com/wp-dyn/content/article/2005/11/01/AR2005110101644.html.

877 See Kasirer, 33. Kasirer goes on to specify that law graduates should be "cosmopolitan citizens" (Kasirer, 39, citing Daniel Downes and Richard Janda, "Virtual Citizenship" (2008) 13 *Can. J. L. & Soc.* 27).

878 Kronman.

879 See Mark Yates, "The Carnegie Effect: Elevating Practical Training over Liberal Education in Curricular Reform" (2011) 17 *J. Legal Writing Institute* 233, 242–4.

880 See Mootz, 1262; *Kratochwil Status*, 24–5. In making similar arguments, Mootz and Kratochwil both talk of "skills". I prefer the term "aptitudes" because I think it is wider in ambit, encompassing qualities of reason that do not properly fit in the idea of a "skill".

881 *Cameron Practical Wisdom*, 38–9.

882 Macdonald and MacLean, 768.

883 Nicolas Kasirer, "Legal Education as Métissage" (2003) 78 *Tulane L. Rev.* 481, 482.

884 *Wendel Professional Duties*, 17–18.

885 The process is complicated, and often messy. It is rarely heroic, *pace* Ronald Dworkin in *Dworkin Empire*.

886 Ignatieff, 29–30 ("Rules, someone once said, are for people with no character. Woe betide a republic ruled by rules, in other words by people with no character").

887 It is not irrelevant to stress that the removal of the protections of citizenship ("denationalisation") was the first step in the Nazi assault on the Jews and other "foreign" or "degenerate" social elements. See the moving discussion of these issues in Philippe Sands, *East West Street* (London: Weidenfeld & Nicolson, 2016), esp. at 166. See also *Arendt Totalitarianism*, 297.

888 *Brunnée and Toope Interactional Account*, 256–9.

889 Mootz, 1282.

890 John Yoo, *War by Other Means* (New York: Atlantic Monthly Press, 2006), 171–2 ("would limiting a captured terrorist to six hours' sleep, isolating him, interrogating him for several hours, or requiring him to exercise constitute" suffering amounting to torture?). The actual practices used on some "high value" detainees at Guantánamo Bay and elsewhere were in fact much more "aggressive": isolation went on for months; deprivation of sleep was repeated for days on end; during interrogations threats of rape, slaps, the use of pornography and subjection to extremely loud music for hours at a time were common. Interspersed amongst the questions was repeated waterboarding. See Jessica Wolfendale, "The Myth of 'Torture Lite'" (2009) 23 *Ethics & Int'l Affs* 47, 50, 52–4 ("[D]espite the frequency with which the term is used, the distinction between torture and torture lite [e.g., loud music, sleep deprivation] is not one that is recognised in any of the international conventions dealing with torture, but it is embraced by democratic regimes as a partial mitigation of the use of 'torture' broadly").

891 Kronman, 113. Other professional "experts" also failed in their moral imagination in the post-9/11 era. See the defence of the two psychologists who designed the "enhanced interrogation techniques" deployed by some US security services. Sacha Pfeiffer, "Psychologists Who Helped Develop CIA Torture Program to Testify in Sept. 11 Case", *NPR*, 20 January 2020, available at: www.npr.org/2020/01/20/797870699/pre-trial-hearings-set-to-begin-in-case-against-sept-11-terrorists. Hannah Arendt described a similar failure of empathy and imagination in her famous report on the Eichmann trial. Hannah Arendt, *Eichmann in Jerusalem: A Report on the Banality of Evil*, 2nd edn (New York: Penguin, 1965), 287–8 ("He *merely*, to put the matter colloquially, *never realized what he was doing*").

892 Sinclair, 57–8.

893 *Arendt Human Condition*, 229.

894 See Goldsmith, 144 (Goldsmith argues that it was an over-reaching as to the prerogative powers of the president that was one of the greatest weaknesses in the legal analysis of the *First Yoo Memo*).

895 John Yoo, *Defender in Chief: Donald Trump's Fight for Presidential Power* (New York: All Points Books, 2020).

896 Misconceived theories divorced from robust assessment of potential consequences can kill. See Sabina Alkire, "Development: 'A Misconceived Theory Can Kill'", in Christopher Morris (ed.), *Amartya Sen* (Cambridge University Press, 2009), 191.

Conclusion: That a Beginning be Made

OUR CONTEMPORARY SOCIAL and political dynamics can be understood, in part, as a recalibration after the undue optimism of the early 1990s. We witness a divisive counterpoint to what proved to be naive assumptions about common purposes, common values and shared norms. History did not end with the fall of the Berlin Wall.[897] Liberal multilateralism did not triumph. The upswing of globalism in the early 1990s marked a high point of both international cooperation and domestic optimism, at least within Western societies. However, the common ground on which to build has proven to be more restricted and far more fragile than it once seemed. We find ourselves in a new age of anxiety, confronting widespread populist nationalism, persistent fears of the effects of globalism, and deep worry over the economic and psychological consequences of disruptive new technologies and dominating network platforms. The twin, and interrelated, spectres of environmental catastrophe and pandemic illness hang over us. Increasing geopolitical conflict means that even the possibility of nuclear war now seems far less remote than it did five years ago.

Yet, precisely because we live in an age of anxiety, marked by radical uncertainty, we could be liberated to build again upon foundations of thought and models of past action that are our shared heritage. When well-settled heuristics fail us we are forced back to historically informed improvisation, drawing on human creativity and imagination.[898] Turbulent times can be moments of intellectual and societal openness, which may allow for a reaffirmation of a reformed, revitalised rule of law, within countries and internationally.[899] This reaffirmation is one of the means by which we can begin to reshape paralysing anxiety into hope.

My first task was to clarify the differences between two important concepts: risk and uncertainty. "Risk" is best conceived as "known unknowns", possible eventualities that can be calibrated and gauged using the quantifying tools of economic analysis. Uncertainty is fundamentally different. It is the "unknown unknowns", things so unclear as to consequences that they are not amenable to prediction. You cannot calculate real uncertainty. In a world of massive unpredictability, the best we can hope for is that we will strive, collectively and individually, to exercise mature judgement – practical wisdom – demonstrating prudence gleaned from experience.

We will need that sense of prudence and mature judgement to confront contemporary populist nationalism. Arising principally from a widespread – and often quite rational – sense of unfairness and social decay, populism draws on the desire to re-found society in a more economically and politically inclusive way. But it gains ground by allying with nationalist claims of homogeneous peoplehood, meaning that social solidarity becomes strictly circumscribed, with "outsiders" defined and marginalised. Cultural diversity is typically seen by populists as a challenge to the "traditional" myths and ethics of closed societies. The "global" is remote and dangerous because it could undermine both economic self-sufficiency and local community values. Globalism or cosmopolitanism is caricatured as inevitably elitist. In our era, longstanding cosmopolitan values of pluralism have been overwhelmed by forces of neoliberal globalisation that have driven economic dominance rather than inclusion. Populist forces are almost always strengthened when connected to a charismatic leader who articulates the underlying grievance and promises a way out, however unrealistic. The charismatic leader must then deliver results quickly or they will bleed support. Instability is innate and growing.

Our era's anxiety is reinforced by rapidly emerging and increasingly powerful new technologies that threaten jobs and call into question our shared understandings of human autonomy, creativity and privacy. Automated decision-making is growing. Machines already perform many functions that profoundly affect our public and private lives. Artificial intelligence brings much promise for discovery and new ways of understanding, but it is also beginning to create "art" and challenge our essential humanity. The corporations that build and manage networks derive unparalleled power and wealth from their access to personal data. Algorithmic correlations can drive social, political and economic decisions even when divorced from true causal connections. Surveillance by both corporations and states increases apace.

In the face of radical uncertainty, one might be tempted to withdraw. Plutocrats build safe havens in New Zealand or on tiny islands to do just that. I have tried to provide a better answer, accessible to a much wider group of people. The way to control and reduce our anxiety is to reconstruct our resilience individually and socially by drawing upon a rich and plural intellectual heritage that can both reassure and inspire. To paraphrase Alan Bennett's encouraging words from *The History Boys*: we can read the works of people we have never met, people who are long dead, and they can reach out their hands and take ours.

I started with Aristotle's insight that human beings gain practical wisdom not only by following rules, but in the mutual creation and building up of practices. In their interactions, people learn by reflecting upon those practices and reasoning over time. They 'work out' for themselves what they should do. People are not merely passive receivers of habit, tradition and rules. They are active agents in their own social world.

Building on Aristotle, the philosophical pragmatists showed us that our actions as people are oriented to purposes and that we desire to contribute meaningfully to society. Societies are complex adaptive systems, evolving over time. Ours is not a world of static "being", but of dynamic "becoming". Our communities and social structures do not dictate human outcomes, though they do, of course, influence and shape them. We are empowered and can act, drawing on our reason, our experience and our creativity.

Pragmatism's focus on becoming entails the further conclusion that knowledge must be actively sought out rather than simply received; indeed, it is built and re-built for practical purposes through our efforts. What is more, knowledge is constructed mutually through our social interactions; it results from consensus. That is why "facts" in society are as much about understanding as explaining or justifying.

If social reality is not given to us, but built through our shared practices, it follows that we identify "truths" that are recognised as useful frames to guide our understanding and action. Truth can change over time and should be subject to continuous testing through the accumulation of new knowledge in ever-more inclusive dialogue. However, and this is crucially important, just because truth may change does not mean that objectively valid truth is impossible, only that the test of truth is that it will survive the challenge of evidence and reason, given our existing knowledge and ability to inquire. Hannah Arendt warned almost half a century ago that:

> [T]he result of a consistent and total substitution of lies for factual truth is not that the lies will now be accepted as truth, and truth defamed as lies, but that the sense by which we take our bearings of the real world – and the category of truth vs. falsehood is among the mental means to this end – is being destroyed.[900]

The pragmatist concept of truth does not necessitate radical doubt; nor does it support the idea of "alternative facts" to quote a Trumpian trope. Rather, it encourages the acceptance of frames of reference that allow us to function day-to-day in socio-political contexts. Those frames of reference are, however, subject to continued questioning and can be displaced by new knowledge derived from rational inquiry. Intuitively we know this to be true because we see it happening constantly in scientific discovery. Received wisdom is overturned. The sun does not rotate around the earth. Illness is not caused by "vapours".

The pragmatist heritage supports pluralism and diversity within and across societies because it rejects the idea of a human essence or nature outside of culture. Because knowledge is created in human interaction, it emerges within specific cultural contexts. Of course, these contexts are not always supportive of human flourishing; they may be imbued with unfairness and many forms of repression. However, interaction also occurs across cultures and societies so that knowledge, including legal knowledge, can be built across borders. Greater pluralism of thought and experience encourages more perceptive identification of the most important issues and increases the likelihood of achieving more effective solutions to problems. Diversity produces deeper knowledge and challenges partial, repressive cultural "truths".

People do not engage in interaction, either within countries or across societies, from a void. We are all inclined to behave in ways that follow patterns because we are influenced by our abilities, dispositions and capacities, what pragmatist philosophers call "Background". But that Background is not simply a "given" in any society. It is itself built up through human interactions in practice. It can also be modified through reflection and self-criticism, so is at least partially dynamic. Background predilections are a pattern, but not a straitjacket, and are not replicated unvaryingly simply out of habit.

To put the matter differently, despite the influence of Background, humans retain agency in their own lives and in the ordering of their societies. We do this through social learning that takes place in the shared working out of our social practices, both in reflexive thinking as we act in real time and in later reflection. And practices are potentially innovative, change-making and liberating. They are not, however, *necessarily* socially or culturally positive. Practices can reproduce oppression, corruption and other social ills. A perspective on human and social action derived from pragmatism, with its emphasis upon learning through practices, is not naive or idealistic.

Practices are built within society by "communities of practice" that share an interest or even a passion for something, like law, politics, rap music, football or the further development of artificial intelligence. In their interactions, communities of practice learn how to perform the practice better, following constitutive rules (or what are sometimes called "anchoring practices"), meaning rules that allow for the existence of the practice as well as shaping ideas and actions within it. These communities are themselves collective agents in society and they create new knowledge and structure it in particular ways, by allowing for the further selection and replication of ideas and practices. Replication is not automatic; it is selective because our practical wisdom helps guide us as we confront changed material circumstances and novel discoveries or insights.

Communities of practice are sites not only of stability, as they generate shared knowledge and common actions, but also of change and development through their continuing internal interaction, and through engagement with other communities of practice. That engagement may produce friction, but cooperation is possible, indeed necessary, in human society. Friction, or contestation, can actually further cooperation in some cases by working through tensions. Diverse perspectives, even differing measures of truth, can produce richer insight and more practical action with a wider sweep of application. This process is buttressed by the interaction of different communities of practice with differing anchoring practices.

In any community of practice, rules evolve that allow participants to assess what is or is not competent practice. Competence is not merely the performance of single actions in a correct manner, as in knowing the possible moves in a game of chess; it is the more complex ability to understand, interpret and generally act in accordance with the Background – and the constitutive rules – that shape the practice. If incompetence builds within the practice, its legitimacy and effectiveness will be undermined.

The intellectual traditions that I have canvassed reveal a unique type of "authority" in our social world, one not discussed in the famous catalogue proposed by Max Weber. This new form of authority Emanuel Adler calls "epistemic practical authority". It is built up through social discourse and action. It articulates rights and obligations in part through its performative power, understood as the ability of participants in communities of practice to convince others of their linguistic and practical competence, demonstrated through various processes, including interpretation, negotiation, contestation and action.

The emphasis throughout this book on the role of critical reflection within communities of practice should not be read as implying that tradition and habit are unimportant as motivators of human thought and action, nor that emotions are irrelevant. However, humans are uniquely endowed with the ability to reason in conversation with habit and emotion, and through that to learn and to refine our purposes. In our day-to-day practices we question ourselves and each other, we argue and articulate reasons, we interpret and assess, and we decide how to act, individually and collectively. The intellectual heritage of pragmatism and practice theory, rooted in Aristotle and in the so-called process philosophers, reveals clearly that we are not, as individuals or societies, "destined" for anything. We are not trapped in our own history. Our world is a world of dynamic becoming, with flux and change endemic, filled with possibility. I hope that you can join me in finding that idea deeply encouraging in this anxious time.

What is law's role in our world of becoming? It should be clear from my discussion that law should not be viewed as heroic, as *the* answer to all of life's uncertainty and challenge. Yet law does have a useful, even profound, contribution to make in conjunction with other frameworks of analysis and creative discovery. The rule of law is not itself the definition of a well-ordered human society. It is, however, one of the core anchoring practices of a healthy society, made up of ideas, discourses and concrete actions that can help to create and sustain human liberty and all forms of equality, both within and beyond national borders. The rule of law is a particular, and potentially powerful, form of "epistemic practical authority". That is why it can contribute to giving anxious people hope.

To fulfil that role, I have suggested that we must articulate an accurate and fruitful description of the relationship between law and politics in contemporary societies. Law is legitimated internally, and is not dependent upon a political constitution that pre-dates law. Legal systems are upheld by intrinsic qualities, criteria of legality, that provide law with its own sources of legitimated authority. It generates its own fidelity within the communities to which law is addressed. This understanding allows law to serve its crucial function as a check on power, not its mere handmaiden. Law, ethics, morality and political power interact and shape one another, of course, but they are relatively independent forces. Each is also affected and constrained by the material circumstances of societies.

All law is created and refined, shifted and reinforced, through continuing practices of contestation, interpretation, application and actions, including enforcement. This implies that law is not "legalism" as caricatured by myriad critics. Law is not inevitably formalistic and rule-bound. Rules shape law, as they shape all social practices, but, as we have seen, they are patterns and not straitjackets. Even the constitutive (constitutional) rules of law can be reshaped by communities of legal practice. However, there are limits to how that reshaping can take place. These are the limits to what Jutta Brunnée and I call "interactional law".

I began the description of interactional law with the foundational work of Lon Fuller. He argued that while legal relationships within the state are often assumed to be vertical, implying the authority of the sovereign and subordination of the citizen, they are better understood as reciprocal relationships. Citizens accept a body of rules as law, and are generally willing to observe them, because the government will, in turn, abide by and apply the same rules.

Building on this core insight, the interactional law framework has three interrelated elements. First, legal norms arise in the context of social norms based on shared understandings, or Background, that shape the social learning of legal communities of practice. Social norms stabilise and they shift, constantly affecting the underpinnings of legal norms. Secondly, law is distinguishable from other types of social ordering not because of its provenance from a particular hierarchical source of law (the sovereign power, a legislature, a court), but by its adherence to criteria of legality succinctly described by Fuller. These include generality, publicity or promulgation, non-retroactivity, clarity, non-contradiction, not asking the impossible, constancy, and congruence between rules and official action. When buttressed by these criteria of legality, social norms can become relatively fixed as law. The criteria of legality provide the meaningful content of legal interaction and they allow for interpretation according to internally generated standards of competent practice. In deeply diverse societies, these criteria imbue law with a measure of cross-cultural commonality without demanding a commitment to a single, shared conception of the good life.[901]

As long as legal rules remain grounded in shared expectations (social norms) and largely meet the criteria of legality, law can serve as its own source of authority. Its legitimacy is recognised by the people to whom law is directed and through whose practices law is created. Law is not called into existence, then, with an on–off switch. It lives on a continuum, being expressed, interpreted, debated, contested, reinforced and sometimes dismantled through the continuous work of communities of practice, their engagement with other such communities in parallel fields such as politics and sociology, and their influence in the wider world.[902]

What Fuller termed "congruence" of purported rules and official action plays a central role as the third element of interactional law: the continuing practice of legality. Reinforcement, adjustment or demolition of legal norms takes place in and through practices of legality that are required to build a continuing, distinctive legal legitimacy and a sense of commitment among those to whom law is addressed. Congruence is more than just "compliance" (conformity of conduct with a given rule) because it encompasses a wide range of practices, including legal argumentation, interpretation, contestation, implementation or enforcement measures through which actors demonstrate adherence to the norm as well as support for its legality. That is why the congruence requirement can be met even when some actors violate or distort existing legal norms, as was the case with the Office of the Legal Adviser's torture memos, provided that other participants in the legal system work effectively to uphold those norms.

With this understanding of how legal obligation works in society, the role of the rule of law in helping us to navigate through our new age of anxiety becomes clearer. If we accept the pragmatist understanding of truth, that it can best be described as the position that would be arrived at were inquiry to be pursued as far as it could fruitfully go, then it becomes obvious that the rule of law cannot be, by itself, *the* answer to all social ills. Nor is it something that can simply be imposed on people as an exercise of either political or legal fiat. The rule of law can only be built successfully together in communities of practice that then reach into the wider community. At all times, legal communities of practice interact internally and with other communities of practice (political, sociological, diplomatic, etc.) that supply their own insights and undertake their own actions. Only with this approach will the rule of law gain support and with it, the continuing confidence of the wider population.

Because the rule of law depends upon the continuing acceptance of its legitimacy, legal communities of practice are constrained in their discourse and actions by self-generated practices of legitimate justification, amounting to competent practice. Convincing reasons must be offered to support legal arguments, judgements and actions.

Two particular forms of argument are particularly persuasive within legal communities of practice: reference to precedent and the use of analogy. Both are examples of competent practice because they are grounded in the criteria of legality, and not because lawyers are essentially conservative, a claim made by some critics. But precedent and analogy can produce complexity in justification. Participants in legal communities of practice must therefore deploy a range of reasoning and arguing methods, including deduction from theory and concept, and induction from specific cases or circumstances. Lawyers thereby streamline, using heuristics and shortcuts. They draw on their intuition and imagination to identify creative solutions to problems, moving beyond simple justification. That said, creativity is limited by the criteria of legality and anchoring practices. A competent lawyer cannot legitimately "argue anything".

A pragmatic focus on solutions emphasises that law, like all human activity, works to a purpose. Law orients itself towards decisions, not just in individual cases, but societally as well. Yet legal decisions never emerge from a vacuum. Law's purposes are informed and shaped by shared social understandings, political realities and material power. That is why law is only relatively autonomous from other social phenomena.

When other social institutions, such as the political system, the family, the workplace and the social sector, are under severe stress, as they all are now in our new age of anxiety, the modest rule of law that I describe can be a source of security. Indeed, one of the most important contributions of the rule of law is in furthering social and political predictability and relative stability, while also providing a framework that facilitates evolutionary change. However, as should be abundantly clear, a sense of security, and even optimism, can arise from an effective rule of law only if the various component parts of legal communities of practice work together to maintain competency and legitimacy.

The implications for legal education of my understanding of the rule of law, and of legal rules, are profound. It is quite common for law professors to declare "crises" in the study of law, especially in North America. I resist that terminology but do worry that many generations of law students have been led astray. A series of thoughtful studies and deep reflections by leading academic educators suggests that too much emphasis has been placed on logic, and pseudo-scientific reasoning in the law, and not enough on what is termed "abduction". Abduction is reasoning across categories, often by way of analogy. It requires the identification of similarities amongst seemingly different elements, thereby creating fresh understandings of social reality. It is grounded in practical reason, which demands empathy, not only thinking in logical categories of induction or deduction, as important as they are.

The rich concept of "practice" I have detailed reveals that life experience is central to law's ability to reflect critically upon itself. Participants in legal communities of practice have to draw on the practicalities of life to temper ideas and institutions as they promote solutions to complex problems. In practice, lawyers create knowledge through the sharing of experience, not just clever ideas. Scaling back variables simply to make a solution more elegant is contrary to the spirit of pragmatism which accepts the inevitable messiness of social existence. The competent practice of law must address the dual realities of complexity and uncertainty, always striving to identify and address potential unintended consequences.

In the troubling example I offered of smart lawyers from some of the top law schools of the United States who managed to argue their way into supporting torture and providing legal cover for its application, we see a failure of competent practice. The lawyers in the Office of Legal Counsel found "a way" to argue that the definition of physical pain and suffering could be narrowed. Their argument was superficially creative, even clever. But it was neither prudent nor pragmatic because it was not tested against life experience. The failure was in part due to a lack of empathy and moral imagination. But it was also more technical: making arguments and justifying actions that would not stand up against the criteria of legality.

Their approach was grounded in a faulty assumption about what law is: they conceived of law as nothing more than a tool or instrument for other purposes, with no purposes or requirements of its own. Unfortunately, these lawyers could draw on a long tradition that brings together strange bedfellows, from followers of Carl Schmitt who believe that everything is politics and nothing is law, to legal realists and critical theorists who see law as merely an expression of power, to positivists for whom law is only what a sovereign authority says it is, to law and economics proponents who judge law only on its ability to deliver on completely independent, external ends. The common, deeply damaging, denominator is legal instrumentalism.

If law has no intrinsic value, the freedom to manipulate is almost complete. I do not care if my arguments, interpretations, decisions or actions are incompetent within the strictures of a community of practice, or that they fail to uphold the internal criteria of legality, as long as these failures do not undermine my external goal. To the extent that participants in law view it as infinitely malleable, or as an intellectual game where the consequences for real people are of little import or interest, they are undermining the rule of law and exposing our fellow human beings to even deeper uncertainty with potentially devastating results.

In his brilliant analysis of the origins of the First World War, Cambridge historian Christopher Clark described a generation of political leaders as "sleepwalkers".[903] To be fair, those leaders, like those of the present day, were living through a period of profound uncertainty. As one reviewer of *The Sleepwalkers* emphasised: "Statesmen at various levels and in at least five countries were testing a system whose workings were beyond their comprehension. No single logic, no master narrative led to a determinable end. There were structural limits to policy-making."[904]

But the joy of Clark's account is that he largely eschews structural analysis, rejecting any sense of inevitability in the march to war. His is primarily an account of flawed human beings making a series of bad choices that blocked more sensible options. As Thomas Laqueur writes:

> Clark's story is "saturated with agency". Many actors (the crowned heads of Europe, military men, diplomats, politicians and others), each with their own objectives, acting as rationally and irrationally as humans are wont to act, made decisions that foreclosed on others and collectively led the world into an unimaginable and un-imaged war. Collectively, they produced the greatest "black swan event" in world history.[905]

Our generation is anxious in part, I think, because we fear that just such unintended consequences may flow from an inability to work our way through the deep uncertainty of our era.

I hope that this book has revealed that we do have the intellectual resources to conceive of and implement prudent action in the face of uncertainty. It requires of us that we call upon the wells of practical wisdom that have been built up with time and experience, that we adopt pragmatic stances to the creation of knowledge and the identification of truth about our societies and relationships, and that we work together in communities of practice to identify and advance shared purposes. We then have to test out those purposes in continuing social interaction, reflecting deeply on consequences and on how we may need to adjust our aspirations and re-work our practices and institutions.

One of the wellsprings of practical wisdom is our inheritance of legal thought, which spans across cultures and traditions. Part of that inheritance is an approach to the rule of law that is inherently modest, not triumphalist. I have suggested that in deeply plural contemporary societies, both national and international, we are best advised to offer a middle ground between the thick (substantive) and thin (procedural) conceptions of the rule of law. We cannot assume, much less insist on, a commonly shared conception of the good life, or the "correct" purposes of human existence. Nor can we draw on expansive understandings of various forms of "justice", be they legal, environmental, political or social, to define the rule of law. In plural societies, all forms of justice remain contested.

Alternatively, by adopting Fuller's criteria of legality, we can imagine and build up a rule of law that is primarily procedural, but that contains enough constraint for law to play its necessary disciplining function on those who exercise power on our behalf. At the same time, the rule of law I describe also supports Arendt's understanding of power: "the human ability not just to act but to act in concert".[906] It does so by focusing on two fundamental human needs, autonomy and communication. It creates effective frameworks for cooperation, both in the facilitation of public discourse and in the design of healthy institutions. The rule of law is created when strong adherence to the criteria of legality, and a continuing practice of legality, generate fidelity to law in the population because law is generally seen to be legitimate. But like specific legal rules, the rule of law is always imperfect; it remains an aspiration that must constantly be reinforced.

Indeed, and as I acknowledged at the beginning of this book, the rule of law envisaged here is under severe pressure, buffeted by the three forces of uncertainty and anxiety that I have discussed at some length. I have tried to set out the intellectual resources at our disposal for active resistance to further undermining of the rule of law. Resistance is primarily the job of active citizens in political groupings within states and at the level of international society. It is also, of course, the job of communities of practice and of institutions in the widest sense: structured coalitions of people around shared purposes, be it in civil society (for example, in NGOs), in the public sphere (governmental or intergovernmental) and even, sometimes, in the private sphere (such as anti-corruption groups organised by the corporate sector). The crucial point is constantly to reassert that law is not only relatively distinct from power, it must have the capacity to challenge and discipline power if it is to serve one of its most important social purposes.

And we who live in Western countries also have a crucial role in challenging actions within our own societies that undermine the rule of law. When a British tabloid called judges of the UK High Court "enemies of the people" after a particular decision related to the Brexit quagmire, it is to the shame of elected politicians that they did not stand up and cry foul.[907] Meanwhile, in Israel the Chief Justice of the Supreme Court felt compelled to push back against vicious political attacks:

> Recently, voices are growing among us seeking to present the principle of the rule of law as "the rule of the legal scholars" and as a stumbling block that stands in the way of what is called by those people "governance". There is no greater error than this.[908]

Eternal vigilance is not only the price of liberty; it is the prerequisite to a stable rule of law. As we have seen over the last few years, we are not fully protected from assaults on the rule of law by our formal institutions even in well-established democracies.

I end with the inspiring example of Hannah Arendt, a young German Jew who wrote her doctoral dissertation at Heidelberg on *Love and Saint Augustine*, struggling to carve out her own future, distinct from that of her dominating Nazi-supporting supervisor and lover, the philosopher Martin Heidegger.[909] Drawing on her PhD work decades later, living as an exile in the United States, Arendt reminded us of Augustine's pithy statement: "that a beginning be made man was created". Arendt went on to argue that it is this very beginning that "is the supreme capacity of man; politically it is identical with man's freedom".[910] Like Arendt, we must recognise the plurality of our world and of most national societies, and yet struggle to help citizens identify and build shared purposes through a mutual recognition of our equality within and across nations.[911] That requires active participation in society, upholding Arendt's "free citizenship" not as submission to authority, but through reciprocal recognition by leaders and citizens of our mutual deference to a reformed and revitalised, albeit modest, rule of law. Arendt reminds us as well that because of the inherent uncertainty of human and social relations, our actions can have unpredictable consequences. To live together we have to work to forgive one another for the mistakes made, and consequences unintended.[912] If we can manage that, defeating our era's easy recourse to constant blame and anger, together we can work our way through pervasive, debilitating anxiety. Let us begin.

Notes

897 *Pace* Francis Fukuyama, *The End of History and the Last Man* (New York: Penguin, 2012).

898 *Katzenstein and Seybert Uncertainty*, 38 (quoting Patrick Jackson), 39–40, 47.

899 Lorna McGregor, "The Thickening of the International Rule of Law in 'Turbulent' Times", available at: www.ejiltalk.org/the-thickening-of-the-international-rule-of-law-in-turbulent-times.

900 *Arendt Between Past*, 257. See also Adler and Drieschova.

901 This open-spirited approach is completely consistent with legal pragmatist thinking which does not require "authoritative announcements concerning . . . [a] vision of the good life". Rather, the legal pragmatist is "trying to empower intelligent decision making within the present community by rendering the legal past explicit while laying out possible futures". Sullivan, 117.

902 See *Dyzenhaus Long Arc*, 32.

903 Christopher Clark, *The Sleepwalkers: How Europe Went to War in 1914* (London: Penguin, 2013).

904 Thomas Laqueur, "Some Damn Foolish Thing" (2013) 35 *London Rev. Books*, available at: www.lrb.co.uk/the-paper/v35/n23/thomas-laqueur/some-damn-foolish-thing (reviewing Christopher Clark's *The Sleepwalkers*).

905 Laqueur.

906 *Arendt On Violence*, 44.

907 James Slack, "Enemies of the People: Fury Over 'Out Of Touch' Judges Who Have 'Declared War on Democracy' by Defying 17.4m Brexit Voters and Who Could Trigger Constitutional Crisis", *Daily Mail*, 3 November 2016, available at: www.dailymail.co.uk/news/article-3903436/Enemies-people-Fury-touch-judges-defied-17-4m-Brexit-voters-trigger-constitutional-crisis.html.

908 Raoul Wootliff, "Supreme Court Chief Slams Attack on Justice System; AG: 'No one's Above the Law'" *Times of Israel*, 5 December 2019, available at: www.timesofisrael.com/supreme-court-chief-slams-attack-on-justice-system-ag-no-ones-above-the-law.

909 See *Scott on Arendt*, 298

910 *Arendt Totalitarianism*, 478–9. And see *Arendt Human Condition*, 177. Arendt left Germany illegally in the early 1930s after being detained by the Nazi authorities. She had agreed to help some Zionist friends by researching anti-Semitic propaganda. She did not admit that work under questioning, and her release was something of a miracle. See Bernstein, 3–4.

911 Arendt saw the "explicitness of equality" in the secular "commandment of neighbourly love". She thought that this commandment legitimated the simultaneous love of one's own people and of all people. *Scott on Arendt*, 304, 308. Sousa Santos, 546, 595, argues too for a contemporary form of "subaltern cosmopolitanism" that allows for expressions of solidarity across national borders for those denied basic human dignity; this is opposed to neoliberal economic globalisation.

912 *Arendt Human Condition*, 237–41.

Bibliography

BOOKS

Adamson, Peter (ed.). *Interpreting Avicenna: Critical Essays* (Cambridge University Press, 2013).

Adler, Emanuel. *World Ordering: A Social Theory of Cognitive Evolution* (Cambridge University Press, 2019). [*Adler World Ordering.*]

Adler, Emanuel and Vincent Pouliot (eds). *International Practices* (New York: Cambridge University Press, 2011).

Agamben, Giorgio. *Homo Sacer: Sovereign Power and Bare Life*, trans. Daniel Heller-Roazen (Stanford University Press, 1998).

State of Exception (University of Chicago Press, 2005).

Ahmed, Akbar. *Discovering Islam: Making Sense of Islamic History* (New York: Routledge, 1998).

Anderson, Benedict. *Imagined Communities: Reflections on the Origin and Spread of Nationalism* (London: Verso, 1983).

Arendt, Hannah. *The Origins of Totalitarianism* (New York: Meridian, [1951] 1958). [*Arendt Totalitarianism.*]

Between Past and Future: Eight Exercises in Political Thought (New York: Penguin, 1961). [*Arendt Between Past.*]

Eichmann in Jerusalem: A Report on the Banality of Evil, 2nd edn (New York: Penguin, 1965).

On Violence (New York: Houghton Mifflin Harcourt, 1970). [*Arendt On Violence.*]

On Revolution (London: Penguin, [1963] 1990). [*Arendt Revolution.*]

The Jewish Writings, ed. Jerome Kohn and Ron Feldman (New York: Schocken, 2007).

The Human Condition, 2nd edn (University of Chicago Press, 2018). [*Arendt Human Condition.*]

Arestis, Philip and Malcolm Sawyer (eds). *Neo-Liberal Economic Policy: Critical Essays* (Cheltenham: Edward Elgar, 2004).

Aristotle. *[The Nicomachean] Ethics*, trans. J. A. K. Thomson (Harmondsworth: Penguin, 1976). [*The Nicomachean Ethics.*]

Attenborough, David. *A Life on Our Planet: My Witness Statement and a Vision for the Future* (London: Penguin, 2020).

Auden, W. H. *The Age of Anxiety: A Baroque Eclogue* (Princeton University Press, 2011).

Austin, John. *Lectures on Jurisprudence, or The Philosophy of Positive Law*, 4th edn, ed. R. Campbell (London: John Murray, 1879; reprint Bristol: Thoemmes Press, 2002).

Averroes. *Averroes' Tahafut Al-Tahafut*, trans. Simon Van Den Bergh, vols 1 and 2 (n.p.: Gibb Memorial Trust, 2008).

Bail, Chris. *Breaking the Social Media Prism: How to Make Our Platforms Less Polarizing* (Princeton University Press, 2021).

Bennett, Alan. *The History Boys* (London: Faber & Faber, 2004).

Bergman, Marcelo. *Tax Evasion and the Rule of Law in Latin America: The Political Culture of Cheating and Compliance in Argentina and Chile* (Philadelphia, PA: Penn State University Press, 2009).

Berlin, Isaiah. *To Define Populism* (London: Isaiah Berlin Virtual Library, 1967), available at: http://berlin.wolf.ox.ac.uk/lists/bibliography/bib111bLSE.pdf.

Bernstein, Richard. *Why Read Hannah Arendt Now?* (Cambridge: Polity, 2018).

Bhaskar, Roy. *The Possibility of Naturalism* (New York: Humanities Press, 1979).

Bingham, Tom. *The Rule of Law* (London: Penguin, 2010).

Bourdieu, Pierre. *Outline of a Theory of Practice* (Cambridge University Press, 1977).

Sur l'État: Cours au Collège de France 1989–92 (Paris: Éditions du Seuil, 2012).

Bourdieu, Pierre and Loïc Wacquant. *An Invitation to Reflexive Sociology* (University of Chicago Press, 1992).

Brożek, Bartosz. *The Legal Mind: A New Introduction to Legal Epistemology* (Cambridge University Press, 2020).

Brunnée, Jutta and Stephen Toope. *Legitimacy and Legality: An Interactional Account of International Law* (Cambridge University Press, 2010). [*Brunnée and Toope Interactional Account.*]

Bueger, Christian and Frank Gadinger. *International Practice Theory*, 2nd edn (Cham: Palgrave Macmillan, 2018). [*Bueger and Gadinger Theory.*]

Burleigh, Michael. *Populism Before and After the Pandemic* (London: Hurst, 2021).

Burley, Justine (ed.). *Dworkin and His Critics* (Oxford: Blackwell, 2004).

Cameron, Maxwell. *Political Institutions and Practical Wisdom: Between Rules and Practice* (New York: Oxford University Press, 2018). [*Cameron Practical Wisdom.*]

Capps, Patrick and Henrik Olsen (eds). *Legal Authority beyond the State* (Cambridge University Press, 2018).

Castells, Manuel. *The Rise of the Network Society: The Information Age, vol. 1: Economy, Society and Culture* (Oxford: Blackwell, 1996).

The Internet Galaxy: Reflections on the Internet, Business, and Society (Oxford University Press, 2002).

Cave, Stephen, Kanta Dihal and Sarah Dillon (eds). *AI Narratives: A History of Imaginative Thinking about Intelligent Machines* (Oxford University Press, 2020).

Clark, Christopher. *The Sleepwalkers: How Europe Went to War in 1914* (London: Penguin, 2013).

Cohen, Elizabeth. *The Political Value of Time: Citizenship, Duration, and Democratic Justice* (Cambridge University Press, 2018).

Cole, Alyson. *The Cult of True Victimhood: From the War on Welfare to the War on Terror* (Stanford University Press, 2006).

Comte, Auguste. Discours sur l'ensemble du positivisme (1848).

Cotterrell, Roger. *Law's Community: Legal Theory in Sociological Perspective* (Oxford University Press, 1997). [*Cotterrell Law's Community.*]

Deaton, Angus. *The Great Escape: Health, Wealth, and the Origins of Inequality* (Princeton University Press, 2013).

Dedek, Helge (ed.). *A Cosmopolitan Jurisprudence: Essays in Memory of H. Patrick Glenn* (Cambridge University Press, 2022). [*Dedek Jurisprudence.*]

Dedek, Helge and Shauna Van Praagh (eds). *Stateless Law: Evolving Boundaries of a Discipline* (Farnham: Ashgate, 2015; London: Routledge, 2016).

Deibert, Ronald. *Reset: Reclaiming the Internet for Civil Society* (Toronto: House of Anansi Press, 2020).

Dewey, John. *How We Think* (Boston, MA: D. C. Heath, 1910). [*Dewey Think.*]

Human Nature and Conduct (New York: Henry Holt, 1922). [*Dewey Human Nature.*]

The Quest for Certainty (New York: Capricorn, 1960).

"Logical Conditions of a Scientific Treatment of Morality", in *The Middle Works, 1899–1924*, ed. Jo Ann Boydston (Carbondale: Southern Illinois University Press, 1985), 38.

"Experience and Nature", in *The Later Works, 1925–53*, ed. Jo Ann Boydston (Carbondale: Southern Illinois University Press, 1996). [*Dewey Experience.*]

Dicey, A. V. *Introduction to the Study of the Law of the Constitution*, 10th edn (London: Macmillan, 1961).

Dick, Philip. *Second Variety*, reprint (Floyd, VA: Positronic Publishing, 2015).

Dieleman, Susan, David Rondel and Christian Voparil (eds). *Pragmatism and Justice* (New York: Oxford University Press, 2017).

Dostoyevsky, Fyodor. *Crime and Punishment,* trans. Richard Pevear and Larissa Volokhonsky (New York: Vintage, 1993).

Drieschova, Alena, Christian Bueger and Ted Hopf (eds). *Conceptualising International Practices: Directions for the Practice Turn in International Relations* (Cambridge University Press, 2021).

Du Bois, William. *Souls of Black Folk* (New York: Dover, 1994).

Duke, G. *Aristotle and Law: The Politics of Nomos* (Cambridge University Press, 2020).

Dunoff, Jeffrey and Joel Trachtman (eds). *Ruling the World?: Constitutionalism, International Law, and Global Governance* (Cambridge University Press, 2009).

Durkheim, Emile. *Sociology and Philosophy* (London: Cohen & West, 1953). [*Durkheim Sociology.*]

Durkheim, Emile. *The Division of Labor in Society* (New York: Free Press, 1964).

Durkheim, Emile. *Pragmatism and Sociology* (Cambridge University Press, 1983). [*Durkheim Pragmatism.*]

Dworkin, Ronald. *A Matter of Principle* (Cambridge, MA: Harvard University Press, 1985).

Dworkin, Ronald. *Law's Empire* (Cambridge, MA: Belknap Press of Harvard University Press, 1986). [*Dworkin Empire.*]

Dyzenhaus, David. *The Long Arc of Legality: Hobbes, Kelsen, Hart* (Cambridge University Press, 2022). [*Dyzenhaus Long Arc.*]

Dyzenhaus, David and Thomas Poole (eds). *Hobbes and the Law* (Cambridge University Press, 2012).

Dyzenhaus, David and Malcolm Thorburn (eds). *Philosophical Foundations of Constitutional Law* (Oxford University Press, 2016).

Ebers, Martin and Susana Navas (eds). *Algorithms and Law* (Cambridge University Press, 2020).

Ericsson, Anders and Robert Pool. *Peak: Secrets from the New Science of Expertise* (Boston, MA: Houghton Mifflin Harcourt, 2016).

Ermakoff, Ivan. *Ruling Oneself Out: A Theory of Collective Abdications* (Durham, NC: Duke University Press, 2008).

Feuchtwanger, Lion. *The Oppermanns* (London: Persephone Books, 2020; first published in Germany in 1933).

Fichte, Johann Gottlieb. *Addresses to the German Nation,* ed. Gregory Moore (Cambridge University Press, 2008).

Finnis, John. *Natural Law and Natural Rights,* Clarendon Law Series, 2nd edn (Oxford University Press, 2011).

Foucault, Michel. *Discipline and Punish: The Birth of the Prison*, trans. Alan Sheridan (London: Penguin, 1991).

Fraenkel, Ernst. *The Dual State: A Contribution to the Theory of Dictatorship*, trans. E. A. Shils et al. (Oxford University Press, 2010).

Freund, James. *Lawyering: A Realistic Approach to Legal Practice* (New York: Law Journal Seminars-Press, 1979), 15–16.

Fukuyama, Francis. *The End of History and the Last Man* (New York: Penguin, 2012).

Fuller, Lon. *The Morality of Law*, rev. edn (New Haven, CT: Yale University Press, 1969).

Gelder, Sarah van (ed.). *This Changes Everything: Occupy Wall Street and the 99% Movement* (San Francisco, CA: Berrett-Koehler, 2011).

Gellner, Ernest. *Nations and Nationalism* (Oxford: Blackwell, 1983).

Giddens, Anthony. *Central Problems in Social Theory: Action, Structure and Contradiction in Social Analysis* (London: Macmillan, 1979).

Goodhart, David. *The Road to Somewhere: The Populist Revolt and the Future of Politics* (London: Penguin, 2017).

Goodin, Robert (ed.). *The Oxford Handbook of Political Science* (Oxford University Press, 2011), available at: .www.oxfordhandbooks.com/view/10 .1093/oxfordhb/9780199604456.001.0001/oxfordhb-9780199604456-e-024? print=pdf

Glendon, Mary Ann. *A Nation Under Lawyers: How the Crisis in the Legal Profession is Transforming American Society* (Cambridge, MA: Harvard University Press, 1994).

Glenn, H. Patrick. *The Cosmopolitan State* (Oxford University Press, 2013).

Legal Traditions of the World: Sustainable Diversity in Law, 5th edn (Oxford University Press, 2014).

Goldsmith, Jack. *Terror Presidency: Law and Judgment Inside the Bush Administration* (New York: W. W. Norton, 2007).

Greco, John. *The Transmission of Knowledge* (Cambridge University Press, 2021).

Habermas, Jürgen. *The Structural Transformation of the Public Sphere*, trans. T. Berger (Boston, MA: Polity, 1989). [*Habermas Transformation.*]

Legitimation Crisis, trans. Thomas McCarthy (Cambridge: Polity, 1992).

Between Facts and Norms: Contributions to a Discourse Theory of Law and Democracy, trans. W. Rehg (Cambridge, MA: MIT Press, 1996). [*Habermas Discourse.*]

Hall, Kermit, Terence Halliday and Lucien Karpik (eds). *Lawyers and the Rise of Western Political Liberalism: Europe and North America from the Eighteenth to the Twentieth Centuries* (Oxford University Press, 1998).

Hamidullah, Muhammad. *Introduction to Islam* (Paris: Centre culturel islamique, 1969).

The Emergence of Islam (Islamabad: Islamic Research Institute, 1993).

Hamilton, Alexander. "Objections and Answers respecting the Administration of the Government" (1792), available at: https://founders.archives.gov/documents/Hamilton/01-12-02-0184-0002.

Hansen, Randall. *Disobeying Hitler: German Resistance after Operation Valkyrie* (Toronto: Doubleday Canada, 2014).

Hart, H. L. A. *Essays on Bentham* (Oxford University Press, 1983).

The Concept of Law, Clarendon Law Series, 2nd edn (Oxford University Press, 1994).

Heaney, Seamus. *The Redress of Poetry: Oxford Lectures* (London: Faber & Faber, 1995).

Hegel, Georg. *The Phenomenology of Spirit*, ed. and trans. Terry Pinkard and Michael Baur (Cambridge University Press, 2018).

Hildebrandt, Mireille and Ekatarina De Vries (eds). *Privacy, Due Process and the Computational Turn: Philosophers of Law Meet Philosophers of Technology* (Abingdon: Routledge, 2012).

Hiruta, K. (ed.). *Arendt on Freedom, Liberation, and Revolution* (London: Palgrave Macmillan, 2019).

Hobsbawm, Eric. *Nations and Nationalism since 1780* (Cambridge University Press, 1990).

Holmes, Oliver Wendell. *The Common Law* (London: Macmillan, 1882).

Hopgood, Stephen. *The Endtimes of Human Rights* (Ithaca, NY: Cornell University Press, 2013).

Hopgood, Stephen, Jack Snyder and Leslie Vinjamuri (eds). *Human Rights Futures* (Cambridge University Press, 2017).

Huntington, Samuel. *The Clash of Civilizations and the Remaking of the World Order* (London: Simon & Schuster, 1997).

Husserl, Edmund. *The Crisis of the European Sciences and Transcendental Phenomenology* (Chicago, IL: Northwestern University Press, 1970).

Hutchinson, Allan and Patrick Monahan. *The Rule of Law: Ideal and Ideology* (Toronto: Carswell, 1987).

Ignatieff, Michael. *The Ordinary Virtues: Moral Order in a Divided World* (Cambridge, MA: Harvard University Press, 2017).

International Commission of Jurists. *Turkey: the Judicial System in Peril* (2016).

Ishiguro, Kazuo. *Klara and the Sun* (London: Faber & Faber, 2021).

Jacobs, K., S. Moser and J. Buizer (eds). The US National Climate Assessment (2015), available at: https://link.springer.com/chapter/10.1007/978-3-319-41802-5_9.

Janssens, Liisa (ed.). *The Art of Ethics in the Information Society* (Amsterdam: University of Amsterdam Press, 2016), available at: https://mediarep.org/handle/doc/14317.

Jenks, C. Wilfred. *The Common Law of Mankind* (New York: Praeger, 1958).

Kamrava, Mehran. *A Concise History of Revolution* (Cambridge University Press, 2020).

Kanetake, Machiko and André Nollkaemper (eds). *The Rule of Law at the National and International Levels: Contestation and Deference* (Oxford: Hart, 2016).

Katzenstein, Peter and Lucia Seybert (eds). *Protean Power: Exploring the Uncertain and Unexplained in World Politics* (Cambridge University Press, 2018).

Kelsen, Hans. *Pure Theory of Law* (Berkeley: University of California Press, 1967; reprint Union, NJ: Lawbook Exchange, 2009).

Kennedy, David. *A World of Struggle: How Power, Law and Expertise Shape Global Political Economy* (Princeton University Press, 2016).

Kindi, Vasso and Theodor Arabatzis (eds). *Kuhn's The Structure of Scientific Revolutions Revisited* (New York: Routledge, 2012).

Koh, Harold. *The Trump Administration and International Law* (Oxford University Press, 2019).

Koskenniemi, Martti. *From Apology to Utopia: The Structure of International Legal Argument* (Cambridge University Press, 2006). [*Koskenniemi Apology.*]

The Gentle Civilizer of Nations: The Rise and Fall of International Law 1870–1960 (Cambridge University Press, 2009). [*Koskenniemi Civilizer.*]

The Politics of International Law (London: Hart, 2011).

Kraemer, Joel (ed.). *Perspectives on Maimonides: Philosophical and Historical Studies* (Oxford: Littman Library of Jewish Civilization, Oxford University Press, 1991).

Kratochwil, Friedrich. *Rules, Norms and Decisions: On the Conditions of Practical and Legal Reasoning in International Relations and Domestic Affairs* (Cambridge University Press, 1989).

The Status of Law in World Society: Meditations on the Rule and Role of Law (Cambridge University Press, 2014). [*Kratochwil Status.*]

Krieger, Heike, Georg Nolte and Andreas Zimmermann (eds). *The International Rule of Law: Rise or Decline?* (Oxford University Press, 2019).

Kronman, Anthony. *The Lost Lawyer: Failing Ideals of the Legal Profession* (Cambridge, MA: Belknap Press of Harvard University Press, 1993).

Krygier, Martin, Adam Czarnota and Wojciech Sadurski (eds). *Anti-Constitutional Populism* (Cambridge University Press, 2022).

Kuhn, Thomas. *The Structure of Scientific Revolutions: 50th Anniversary Edition* (University of Chicago Press, 2012).

Lacroix, Justine and Jean-Yves Pranchère. *Human Rights on Trial: A Genealogy of the Critique of Human Rights* (Cambridge University Press, 2018).

Lang, Anthony and Antje Wiener (eds). *Global Constitutionalism* (Cambridge University Press, 2017).

Langdell, Christopher Columbus. *A Selection of Cases on the Law of Contracts* (Boston, MA: Little, Brown, 1871).

Larson, Erik. *The Splendid and the Vile* (New York: Random House, 2020).

Latour, Bruno. *Science in Action: How to Follow Scientists and Engineers Through Society* (Cambridge, MA: Harvard University Press, 1987).

Laughlin, Martin. *Foundations of Public Law* (Oxford University Press, 2010).

Lave, Jean and Etienne Wenger. *Situated Learning: Legitimate Peripheral Participation* (New York: Cambridge University Press, 1991).

Lawson, Philip. *The East India Company: A History* (London: Routledge, 1993).

Lechner, Silviya and Mervyn Frost. *Practice Theory and International Relations*, 1st pbk edn (Cambridge University Press, 2020).

Lincoln, Bruce. *Authority: Construction and Corrosion* (University of Chicago Press, 1991).

Linowitz, Sol and Martin Mayer. *The Betrayed Profession: Lawyering at the End of the Twentieth Century* (Baltimore, MD: Johns Hopkins University Press, 1996).

Luban, David (ed.). *Legal Ethics and Human Dignity* (Cambridge University Press, 2007).

Madison, James, Alexander Hamilton and John Jay. *Federalist Papers* (London: Penguin, 1987).

May, Christopher. *The Rule of Law: The Common Sense of Global Politics* (Cheltenham: Edward Elgar, 2014).

May, Christopher and Adam Winchester (eds). *Handbook on the Rule of Law* (Cheltenham: Edward Elgar, 2018).

Misak, Cheryl. *Truth, Politics, Morality: Pragmatism and Deliberation* (London: Routledge, 2000). [*Misak Truth.*]

Frank Ramsey: A Sheer Excess of Powers (Oxford University Press, 2020). [*Misak Ramsey.*]

Mishra, Pankaj. *Age of Anger: A History of the Present* (New York: Farrar, Straus & Giroux, 2017).

Moffitt, Benjamin. *The Global Rise of Populism: Performance, Political Style, and Representation* (Stanford University Press, 2016).

Morris, Christopher (ed.). *Amartya Sen* (Cambridge University Press, 2009).

Morson, Gary and Morton Shapiro. *Cents and Sensibility: What Economics Can Learn from the Humanities* (Princeton University Press, 2018).
Mudde, Cas and Cristóbal Rovina Kaltwasser. *Populism: A Very Short Introduction* (Oxford University Press, 2017).
Müller, Jan-Werner. *Constitutional Patriotism* (Princeton University Press, 2007).
Nardin, Terry and Daniel Sherman (eds). *Terror, Culture, Politics: Rethinking 9/11* (Bloomington: Indiana University Press, 2006).
Neuman, Gerald (ed.). *Human Rights in a Time of Populism: Challenges and Responses* (Cambridge University, 2020).
Nollkaemper, André et al. (eds). *International Law as Profession* (Cambridge University Press, 2017).
Norris, Pippa and Ronald Inglehart. *Cultural Backlash: Trump, Brexit, and Authoritarian Populism* (Cambridge University Press, 2019).
Nussbaum, Martha. *Poetic Justice: The Literary Imagination and Public Life* (Boston, MA: Beacon Press, 1995).
The Fragility of Goodness: Luck and Ethics in Greek Tragedy and Philosophy (Cambridge University Press, 2001), vol. II.
Obama, Barack. *A Promised Land* (London: Viking, 2020).
Onuma, Yasuaki. *International Law in a Transcivilizational World* (Cambridge University Press, 2017).
Pais, Abraham. *Subtle is the Lord: The Science and the Life of Albert Einstein* (Oxford University Press, reissued 2005).
Pauer-Studer, Herlinde. *Justifying Injustice: Legal Theory in Nazi Germany* (Cambridge University Press, 2021).
Peierls, Rudolph. *Surprises in Theoretical Physics* (Princeton University Press, 1979).
Peirce, Charles Sanders. *Collected Papers of Charles Sanders Peirce*, vols 1–8, ed. Charles Hartshorne, Paul Weiss and Arthur Burks (Cambridge, MA: Belknap Press, 1901), vol. 8.
Piketty, Thomas. *Capital in the Twenty-First Century*, trans. Arthur Goldhammer (Cambridge, MA: Harvard University Press, 2014).
Popper, Karl. *A World of Propensities* (Bristol: Thoemmes, 1990).
Porter, Theodore. *Trust in Numbers: The Pursuit of Objectivity in Science and Public Life*, new edn (Princeton University Press, 2020).
Posner, Richard. *Law, Pragmatism and Democracy* (Cambridge, MA: Harvard University Press, 2003).
Przeworski, Adam. *Crises of Democracy* (Cambridge University Press, 2019).
Provost, René. *Rebel Courts: The Administration of Justice by Armed Insurgents* (Oxford University Press, 2021).
Rawls, John. *A Theory of Justice* (Cambridge, MA: Harvard University Press, 1971). [*Rawls Justice.*]

Political Liberalism (New York: Columbia University Press, 1993). [*Rawls Liberalism.*]

Raz, Joseph. *The Authority of Law: Essays on Law and Morality* (Oxford: Clarendon Press, 1979).

Redlich, Josef. The Common Law and the Case Method in American University Law Schools: A Report to the Carnegie Foundation for the Advancement of Teaching, Bulletin No. 8 (1914).

Risse, Mathias. *On Justice: Philosophy, History, Foundations* (Cambridge University Press, 2020). [*Risse On Justice.*]

Roberts, Anthea. *Is International Law International?* (Oxford University Press, 2017).

Roethke, Theodore. *The Collected Poems of Theodore Roethke* (New York: Doubleday, 1961).

Rorty, Richard. *Consequences of Pragmatism* (Minneapolis: University of Minnesota Press, 1982). [*Rorty Consequences.*]

Truth and Progress: Philosophical Papers (Cambridge University Press, 1998).

Philosophy and Social Hope (New York: Penguin, 1999).

Ross, Alex. *Wagnerism* (London: 4th Estate, 2020).

Runciman, David. *How Democracy Ends* (London: Profile, 2018).

Sandel, Michael. *Liberalism and the Limits of Justice*, 2nd edn (Cambridge University Press, 1998). [*Sandel Limits.*]

The Tyranny of Meritocracy: What's Become of the Common Good? (New York: Penguin, 2021). [*Sandel Meritocracy.*]

Sands, Philippe. *Torture Team* (New York: Palgrave Macmillan, 2008).

East West Street (London: Weidenfeld & Nicolson, 2016).

Schatzki, Theodore et al. (eds). *The Practice Turn in Contemporary Theory* (London: Routledge, 2001).

Schmitt, Carl. *The Crisis of Parliamentary Democracy*, trans. Ellen Kennedy (Cambridge, MA: MIT Press, 1985). [*Schmitt Crisis.*]

Political Theology: Four Chapters on the Concept of Sovereignty, trans. George Schwab (Cambridge, MA: MIT Press, 1986). [*Schmitt Theology.*]

The Concept of the Political, trans. George Schwab (University of Chicago Press, 2007). [*Schmitt Concept.*]

Constitutional Theory, trans. Jeffrey Seitzer (Durham, NC: Duke University Press, 2008).

Schwartzberg, Melissa and Philip Kitcher (eds). *Truth and Evidence* (New York: New York University Press, 2021).

Scott, James. *Seeing Like a State: How Certain Schemes to Improve the Human Condition have Failed* (New Haven, CT: Yale University Press, 1998).

Searle, John. *Speech Acts: An Essay in the Philosophy of Language* (Cambridge University Press, 1969).

The Construction of Social Reality (New York: Free Press, 1995). [*Searle Construction.*]

Sellers, M. N. S. *Law, Reason, and Emotion* (Cambridge University Press, 2017).

Sen, Amartya. *The Idea of Justice* (Cambridge, MA: Belknap Press, 2009).

Shklar, Judith. *Legalism* (Cambridge, MA: Harvard University Press, 1964).

American Citizenship: The Quest for Inclusion (Cambridge, MA: Harvard University Press, 1991). [*Shklar Legalism*]

Shute, Stephen and Susan Hurley (eds). *On Human Rights: The Oxford Amnesty Lectures 1993* (New York: Basic Books, 1993).

Sinclair, Adriana. *International Relations Theory and International Law* (Cambridge University Press, 2010).

Skinner, Quentin. *The Foundations of Modern Political Thought, Vol. 2: The Age of Reformation* (Cambridge University Press, 1978).

Slobodian, Quinn. *Globalists: The End of Empire and the Birth of Neoliberalism* (Cambridge, MA: Harvard University Press, 2018).

Smith, Adam. *The Theory of Moral Sentiments* (New York: Penguin, 2009).

Social Sciences and Humanities Research Council of Canada. *Law and Learning/ Le droit et le savoir: Report of the Consultative Group on Research and Education in Law* (Ottawa: SSHRC, 1983).

Soper, J. Christopher and Joel Fetzer. *Religion and Nationalism in Global Perspective* (Cambridge University Press, 2018).

Sousa Santos, Boaventura de. *Toward a New Legal Common Sense: Law, Globalization, and Emancipation*, 3rd edn (Cambridge University Press, 2020).

Stern, Nicholas. *Why are We Waiting?: The Logic, Urgency, and Promise of Tackling Climate Change* (Cambridge, MA: MIT Press, 2015).

Stiglitz, Joseph. *The Price of Inequality* (London: Penguin, 2013).

Stopford, John, Susan Strange and John Henley. *Rival States, Rival Firms: Competition for World Market Shares* (Cambridge University Press, 1991).

Strevens, Michael. *The Knowledge Machine: How Irrationality Created Modern Science* (New York: Liveright, 2020).

Sullivan, Michael. *Legal Pragmatism: Community, Rights and Democracy* (Bloomington: Indiana University Press, 2007).

Sullivan, William et al. *Educating Lawyers: Preparation for the Profession of Law* (Stanford, CA: Carnegie Foundation for the Advancement of Teaching, 2007). [*Sullivan Educating Lawyers.*]

Tamahana, Brian. *On the Rule of Law: History, Politics, Theory* (Cambridge University Press, 2004). [*Tamahana Rule of Law.*]

Taylor, Charles. *Human Agency and Language* (Cambridge University Press, 1985).

Thornhill, Chris. *The Sociology of Law and the Global Transformation of Democracy* (Cambridge University Press, 2018).

Trebilcock, Michael and Ronald Daniels. *Rule of Law Reform and Development: Charting the Fragile Path of Progress* (Cheltenham: Edward Elgar, 2009).

Unger, Roberto Mangabeira. *The Critical Legal Studies Movement* (Cambridge, MA: Harvard University Press, 1986).

Vaidhyanathan, Siva. *Antisocial Media: How Facebook Disconnects Us and Undermines Democracy* (Oxford University Press, 2018).

Vessey, Mark, Karla Pollmann and Allan Fitzgerald (eds). *History, Apocalypse, and the Secular Imagination* (Bowling Green, OH: Philosophy Documentation Center, 1999).

Viidebaum, Laura. *Creating the Ancient Rhetorical Tradition* (Cambridge University Press, 2021).

Waldron, Jeremy. *Political Political Theory: Essays on Institutions* (Cambridge, MA: Harvard University Press, 2016).

Wallace-Wells, David. *The Uninhabitable Earth: A Story of the Future* (London: Penguin, 2019).

Walters, Mark. *A. V. Dicey and the Common Law Constitutional Tradition: A Legal Turn of Mind* (Cambridge University Press, 2020). [*Walters on Dicey.*]

Walzer, Michael. *Spheres of Justice: A Defense of Pluralism and Equality* (New York: Basic Books, 1983). [*Walzer Spheres of Justice.*]

Weber, Max. *The Theory of Social and Economic Organization* (New York: Free Press, 1964). [*Weber Theory.*]

Max Weber on Law in Economy and Society (Cambridge, MA: Harvard University Press, 1966). [*Weber Law.*]

Max Weber on Charisma and Institution Building: Selected Papers (University of Chicago Press, 1968). [*Weber Charisma.*]

The Interpretation of Social Reality (London: Joseph, 1970). [*Weber Interpretation.*]

The Vocation Lectures, ed. David Owen and Tracy Strong (Indianapolis, IN: Hackett, 2004).

Wenger, Etienne, Richard McDermott and William Snyder. *Cultivating Communities of Practice: A Guide to Managing Knowledge* (Cambridge, MA: Harvard Business School Press, 2002).

Wenger-Trayner, Etienne et al. *Learning in Landscapes of Practice: Boundaries, Identity, and Knowledgeability in Practice-Based Learning* (New York: Routledge, 2015).

Wenger-Trayner, Etienne and Beverly Wenger-Trayner. "Introduction to Communities of Practice: A Brief Overview of the Concept and Its Uses", BETreat Workshops (2015), available at: https://wenger-trayner.com/introduction-to-communities-of-practice.

Werbach, Kevin (ed.). *After the Digital Tornado: Networks, Algorithms, Humanity* (Cambridge University Press, 2020).

Westerman, Pauline et al. (eds). *Legal Validity and Soft Law* (New York: Springer, 2018), available at: https://link.springer.com/chapter/10.1007/978-3-319-77522-7_5.

White, James Boyd. *The Legal Imagination*, 45th anniversary edn (New York: Aspen, 2018).

Whitehead, Alfred North. *Process and Reality*, ed. David Griffin and Donald Sherburne, corrected edn (New York: Free Press, 1978).

Wiener, Antje. *The Invisible Constitution of Politics: Contested Norms and International Encounters* (Cambridge University Press, 2008).

Contestation and Constitution of Norms in Global International Relations (Cambridge University Press, 2018). [*Wiener Contestation.*]

Winston, Kenneth (ed.). *The Principles of Social Order: Selected Essays of Lon L. Fuller*, rev. edn (Oxford: Hart, 2001).

Witteveen, Willem and Wibren van der Burg (eds). *Rediscovering Fuller: Essays on Implicit Law and Institutional Design* (University of Amsterdam Press, 1999).

Wittgenstein, Ludwig. *Philosophical Investigations*, ed. Peter Hacker and Joachim Schulte, 4th edn (Chichester: Wiley-Blackwell, 2009).

Tractatus Logico-Philosophicus, trans. C. K. Ogden (Gothenburg: Chiron Academic Press, 2016).

Wolfe, Tom. *The Bonfire of the Vanities* (New York: Picador, 2008).

Yoo, John. *War by Other Means* (New York: Atlantic Monthly Press, 2006).

Defender in Chief: Donald Trump's Fight for Presidential Power (New York: All Points Books, 2020).

Young, Iris Marion. *Justice and the Politics of Difference* (Princeton University Press, 2011).

ARTICLES IN JOURNALS AND EDITED COLLECTIONS

Aalberts, Tanja and Ingo Venzke. "Moving Beyond Interdisciplinary Turf Wars: Towards an Understanding of International Law as Practice", in André Nollkaemper et al. (eds), *International Law as Profession* (Cambridge University Press, 2017), 287.

Adler, Emanuel. "Control power as a Special Case of Protean Power: Thoughts on Peter Katzenstein and Lucia Seybert's Protean Power: Exploring the Uncertain and Unexpected in World Politics" (2020) 12 *Int'l Theory* 422.

Adler, Emanuel and Alena Drieschova. "The Epistemological Challenge of Truth-Subversion to the Liberal International Order" (2021) *IO*, available at: www.cambridge.org/core/journals/international-organization/article/

epistemological-challenge-of-truth-subversion-to-the-liberal-international-order/D2B6C964CBAAD892DB7ED5A62DBB2932.

Adler, Emanuel and Vincent Pouliot. "International Practices: Introduction and Framework", in Emanuel Adler and Vincent Pouliot (eds), *International Practices* (New York: Cambridge University Press, 2011), 16. [*Adler and Pouliot Practices.*]

Alarie, Benjamin, Anthony Niblett and Albert Yoon. "How Artificial Intelligence Will Affect the Practice of Law" (2018) 68 *UTLJ* 106.

Alkire, Sabina. "Development: 'A Misconceived Theory Can Kill'", in Christopher Morris (ed.), *Amartya Sen* (Cambridge University Press, 2009), 191.

Allcock, John. "Editorial Introduction to the English Translation", in Emile Durkheim, *Pragmatism and Sociology* (Cambridge University Press, 1983), xxxiv.

Anghie, Anthony. "The Evolution of International Law: Colonial and post-Colonial Realities" (2006) 27 *Third World Q.* 739.

Arthurs, Harry. "Law and Learning in an Era of Globalization" (2009) 10 *German L. J.* 629.

Baer, Susanne. "The Rule of – and Not by Any – Law. On Constitutionalism" (2018) 71 *Current Legal Problems* 335.

Baker, J. H. "The Law Merchant and the Common Law Before 1700" (1979) 38 *Cambridge L. J.* 295.

Barnhizer, David. "The Purposes and Methods of American Legal Education" (2011) 36 *J. Legal Profession* 1.

Bayamlıoğlu, Emre and Ronald Leenes. "The 'Rule of Law' Implications of Data-driven Decision-making: a Techno-regulatory Perspective" (2018) 10 *Law, Innovation and Technology* 295.

Beaulac, Stéphane. "An Inquiry into the International Rule of Law", EUI Working Papers, MWP 2007/14, available at: https://papers.ssrn.com/sol3/papers.cfm?abstract_id=1074562.

Beckett, Jason. "Rebel Without a Cause? Martii Koskenniemi and the Critical Legal Project" (2006) *German L. J.* 1045.

Berman, Emily. "A Government of Laws and Not of Machines" (2018) 98 *SSRN J.* 1279, available at: www.ssrn.com/abstract=3098995.

Berman, Harold. "The Crisis of Legal Education in America" (1985) 26 *BC L. Rev.* 347.

Berman, Lawrence. "The Ethical Values of Maimonides within the Context of Islamicate Civilization", in Joel Kraemer (ed.), *Perspectives on Maimonides: Philosophical and Historical Studies* (Oxford: Littman Library of Jewish Civilization, Oxford University Press, 1991), 13. [*Berman Maimonides.*]

Bernstein, Steven and Marion Laurence. "Practices and Norms: Relationships, Disjunctures and Change", in Alena Drieschova, Christian Bueger and Ted Hopf (eds), *Conceptualising International Practices: Directions for the Practice Turn in International Relations* (Cambridge University Press, 2021), 77.

Bernstorff, Jochen von. "International Legal Scholarship as a Cooling Medium in International Law and Politics" (2014) 25 *EJIL* 977.

Besson, Samantha. "Whose Constitution(s)? International Law, Constitutionalism, and Democracy", in Jeffrey Dunoff and Joel Trachtman (eds), *Ruling the World?: Constitutionalism, International Law, and Global Governance* (Cambridge University Press, 2009), 381.

Bigo, Didier. "Pierre Bourdieu and International Relations: Power of Practices, Practices of Power" (2011) 5 *Int'l Pol. Sociology* 225.

Black, Deborah. "Certitude, Justification, and the Principles of Knowledge in Avicenna's Epistemology", in Peter Adamson (ed.), *Interpreting Avicenna: Critical Essays* (Cambridge University Press, 2013), 120.

Blokker, Paul. "Populism as a Constitutional Project" (2019) 17 *Int'l J. Constitutional L.* 535.

Bogojevic, Sanja. "Erosion of the Rule of Law: How Populism Threatens Environmental Protection" (2019) 31 *J. Environmental L.* 389.

Brown, Chris. "The 'Practice Turn', Phronesis and Classical Realism: Towards a Phronetic International Political Theory" (2012) 40 *Millennium: J. Int'l Studies* 439.

Brown, Thomas. "Populism and Nationalism: Implications for the International Order", 12 January 2017, 7, available at: https://lordslibrary.parliament.uk/research-briefings/lln-2017-0002.

Brunnée, Jutta. "Book Review" (2018) 59 *Harvard Int'l L. J.* 601.

"Challenging International Law: What's New?" *Opinio Juris Blog*, 13 November 2018, available at: http://opiniojuris.org/2018/11/13/challenging-international-law-whats-new.

"Multilateralism in Crisis" (2018) 112 *Proceedings ASIL* 335.

Brunnée, Jutta and Stephen Toope. "International Law and Constructivism: Elements of an Interactional Theory of International Law" (2000) 39 *Columbia J. Transn'l L.* 19. [*Brunnée and Toope Constructivism.*]

"Interactional International Law: An Introduction" (2011) 3 *International Theory* 307.

"Interactional Legal Theory, the International Rule of Law and Global Constitutionalism", in Anthony Lang and Antje Wiener (eds), *Global Constitutionalism* (Cambridge University Press, 2017), 170. [*Brunnée and Toope Constitutionalism.*]

"International Law and the Practice of Legality: Stability and Change" (2018) 49 *Victoria U. Wellington L. Rev.* Special Symposium Issue 429. [*Brunnée and Toope Stability.*]

"Norm Robustness and Contestation in International Law: Self-Defence against Non-State Actors" (2019) 4 *J. Global Sec. Studies* 73.

Bueger, Christian and Frank Gadinger. "The Play of International Practice" (2015) 59 *Int'l Studies Q.* 449. [*Bueger and Gadinger Practice.*]

Bussani, Mauro. "How to Do Comparative Law: Some Lessons to Be Learned", in Helge Dedek (ed.), *A Cosmopolitan Jurisprudence: Essays in Memory of H. Patrick Glenn* (Cambridge University Press, 2022), 29.

Cameron, Maxwell. "Democratic Virtue Ethics: Phronesis in Politics and Political Science", unpublished manuscript on file with author. [*Cameron Phronesis.*]

Casey, Anthony and Anthony Niblett. "Self-Driving Laws Focus Feature: Artificial Intelligence, Big Data, and the Future of Law" (2016) 66 *U. Toronto L. J.* 429.

Cath, Corinne. "Governing Artificial Intelligence: Ethical, Legal and Technical Opportunities and Challenges" (2018) 376 *Phil. Trans. R. Soc. A* 20180080, available at: https://royalsocietypublishing.org/doi/full/10.1098/rsta.2018.0080.

Chesterman, Simon. "An International Rule of Law" (2008) 56 *Am. J. Comp. L.* 331.

Cladis, Mark. "Durkheim's Individual in Society: A Sacred Marriage?" (1992) 53 *J. History of Ideas* 71.

Cochran, Molly. "Deweyan Pragmatism and Post-Positivist Social Science in IR" (2002) *Millennium: J. Int'l Stud.* 525.

Cohen, Julie. "Networks, Standards, and Network-and-Standard-Based Governance", in Kevin Werbach (ed.), *After the Digital Tornado: Networks, Algorithms, Humanity* (Cambridge University Press, 2020), 58.

Cole, Daniel. "'An Unqualified Human Good': EP Thompson and the Rule of Law" (2001) 28 *J. L. and Society* 177.

Collins, Richard. "Two Idea(l)s of the International Rule of Law" (2019) 8 *Global Constitutionalism* 191.

Coombe, Rosemary. "The Recognition of Indigenous People's Knowledge in International Law" (2001) 14 *St Thomas L. Rev.* 275.

Cotterrell, Roger. "The Durkheimian Tradition in the Sociology of Law" (1991) 25 *L. & Soc. Rev.* 923.

Cover, Robert. "The Supreme Court 1982 Term Forward: Nomos and Narrative" (1983) 97 *Harvard L. Rev.* 4.

Craig, Paul. "Formal and Substantive Conception of the Rule of Law: An Analytical Framework" (1997) *Public L.* 467.

Cuvillier, Armand. "Preface to the French Edition of 1955", in Emile Durkheim, *Pragmatism and Sociology* (Cambridge University Press, 1983), xviii.

Czarnota, Adam. "*Sources of Constitutional Populism: Democracy, Identity and Economic Exclusion*", in Martin Krygier, Adam Czarnota and Wojciech Sadurski, *Anti-Constitutional Populism* (Cambridge University Press, 2022), 495.

Dedek, Helge. "Where the 'Real Action' Is: From Comparative Law to Cosmopolitan Jurisprudence", in Helge Dedek (ed.), *A Cosmopolitan Jurisprudence: Essays in Memory of H. Patrick Glenn* (Cambridge University Press, 2022), 3.

Denvir, Catrina et al. "The Devil in the Detail: Mitigating the Constitutional and Rule of Law Risks Associated with the use of Artificial Intelligence in the Legal Domain" (2018) 47, available at: https://papers.ssrn.com/abstract=3426337.

Dewey, John. "Logical Method and the Law" (1924) 10 *Cornell L. Rev.* 17.

Dezalay, Yves and Mikael Madsen. "The Force of Law and Lawyers: Pierre Bourdieu and the Reflexive Sociology of Law" (2012) 8 *Annual Rev. L. & Soc. Sci.* 433.

Downes, Daniel and Richard Janda. "Virtual Citizenship" (2008) 13 *Can. J. L. & Soc.* 27.

Dunoff, Jeffrey and Joel Trachtman. "A Functional Approach to International Constitutionalization", in Jeffrey Dunoff and Joel Trachtman (eds), *Ruling the World? Constitutionalism, International Law, and Global Governance* (Cambridge University Press, 2009), 3.

Duvall, Raymond and Arjun Chowdhury. "Practices of Theory", in Emanuel Adler and Vincent Pouliot (eds), *International Practices* (New York: Cambridge University Press, 2011), 335.

Dworkin, Ronald. "The Rule of Law as a Theatre of Debate", in Justine Burley (ed.), *Dworkin and His Critics* (Oxford: Blackwell, 2004), 387.

Dyzenhaus, David. "Herman Heller and the Legitimacy of Legality" (1996) 16 *Oxford J. Legal Studies* 641. [*Dyzenhaus Legitimacy.*]

"Fuller's Novelty", in Willem Witteveen and Wibren van der Burg (eds), *Rediscovering Fuller: Essays on Implicit Law and Institutional Design* (University of Amsterdam Press, 1999), 97. [*Dyzenhaus Fuller's Novelty.*]

"Constitutionalism in an Old Key: Legality and Constituent Power" (2012) 1 *Global Constitutionalism* 229. [*Dyzenhaus Constitutionalism.*]

"Hobbes on the Authority of Law", in David Dyzenhaus and Thomas Poole (eds), *Hobbes and the Law* (Cambridge University Press, 2012), 186. [*Dyzenhaus Hobbes and Law.*]

"Hobbes on the International Rule of Law" (2014) 28 *Ethics & Int'l Affairs* 53. [*Dyzenhaus Hobbes.*]

"The Idea of a Constitution: A Plea for *Staatsrechtslehre*", in David Dyzenhaus and Malcolm Thorburn (eds), *Philosophical Foundations of Constitutional Law* (Oxford University Press, 2016), 9.

"Lawyer for the Strongman", *Aeon,* 12 June 2020, available at: https://aeon.co/essays/carl-schmitts-legal-theory-legitimises-the-rule-of-the-strongman. [*Dyzenhaus Lawyer.*]

Ebers, Martin. "Regulating AI and Robotics: Ethical and Legal Challenges", in Martin Ebers and Susana Navas (eds), *Algorithms and Law* (Cambridge University Press, 2020), 37.

Eisenstadt, S. N. "Introduction", *Max Weber on Charisma and Institution Building: Selected Papers* (University of Chicago Press, 1968), ix.

Eldridge, J. T. "Introductory Essay", in Max Weber, *The Interpretation of Social Reality* (London: Joseph, 1970), 12.

Ermakoff, Ivan. "Law against the Rule of Law: Assaulting Democracy", *J. L. & Soc.*, 9 October 2020, available at: https://onlinelibrary.wiley.com/doi/full/10.1111/jols.12253.

Fassbender, Bardo. "What's in a Name? The International Rule of Law and the United Nations Charter" (2018) 17 *Chinese J. Int'l L.* 761.

Fine, Toni. "Reflections on U.S. Curricular Reform" (2009) 10 *German L. J.* 717.

Finnemore, Martha and Michelle Jurkovich. "The Politics of Aspiration" (2020) 64 *Int'l Studies Q.* 759.

Finnemore, Martha and Kathryn Sikkink. "International Norm Dynamics and Political Change" (1998) 52 *IO* 887.

Finnis, John. "Judicial Power: Past, Present and Future", 2018, available at: http://judicialpowerproject.org.uk/wp-content/uploads/2018/01/Judicial-Power-and-the-Balance-of-Our-Constitution.pdf.

Fitzmaurice, Malgosia. "The Dilemma of Traditional Knowledge: Indigenous Peoples and Traditional Knowledge" (2008) 10 *Int'l Community L. Rev.* 255.

Franck, Thomas. "International Institutions: Why Constitutionalize?", in Jeffrey Dunoff and Joel Trachtman (eds), *Ruling the World? Constitutionalism, International Law, and Global Governance* (Cambridge University Press, 2009), xi.

Frank, Jerome. "Why not a Clinical Lawyer-School?" (1933) 81 *U. Penn. L. Rev.* 907.

Frega, Roberto. "Pragmatism and Democracy in a Global World" (2017) 43 *Rev. Int'l Studies* 720.

Friedrichs, Jörg and Friedrich Kratochwil. "On Acting and Knowing: How Pragmatism Can Advance International Relations Research and Methodology" (2009) 63 *IO* 701.

Frischmann, Brett and Evan Selinger. "Why a Commitment to Pluralism Should Limit How Humanity Is Re-Engineered", in Kevin Werbach (ed.), *After the Digital Tornado: Networks, Algorithms, Humanity* (Cambridge University Press, 2020), 155.

Fuller, Lon. "Positivism and Fidelity to Law: A Reply to Professor Hart" (1958) 71 *Harvard L. Rev.* 630.

"Adjudication and the Rule of Law" (1960) 54 *Am. Soc. Int'l L. Proc.* 1.

"Human Interaction and the Law" (1969) 14 *Am. J. Jurisprudence* 1, reprinted in Kenneth Winston (ed.), *The Principles of Social Order: Selected Essays of Lon L. Fuller*, rev. edn (Oxford: Hart, 2001), 211. [*Fuller Human Interaction.*]

Fuller, Lon and Kenneth Winston. "The Forms and Limits of Adjudication" (1978) 92 *Harvard L. Rev.* 353.

Galston, William. "The Populist Challenge to Liberal Democracy" (2018) 29 *J. of Democracy* 5.

Glenn, H. Patrick. "Persuasive Authority" (1987) 32 *McGill L. J.* 261. [*Glenn Authority.*]

"Doin' the Transsystemic: Legal Systems and Legal Traditions" (2005) 50 *McGill L. J.* 863.

"The Cosmopolitan State" (2013) 61 *Kansas L. Rev.* 735.

Gordon, Robert. "The Law School, the Profession, and Arthurs' Humane Professionalism" (2006) 44 *Osgoode Hall L. J.* 157.

Graham, Daniel. "Heraclitus", *The Stanford Encyclopedia of Philosophy*, available at: https://plato.stanford.edu/archives/fall2019/entries/heraclitus.

Grimmelmann, James. "Regulation by Software" (2005) 114 *Yale L. J.* 1719.

Gutas, Dimitri. "Avicenna's Philosophical Project", in Peter Adamson (ed.), *Interpreting Avicenna: Critical Essays* (Cambridge University Press, 2013), 28.

Haack, Susan. "On Legal Pragmatism: Where Does 'The Path of the Law' Lead Us?" (2005) 50 *Am. J. Jurisprudence* 71.

Haas, Peter and Ernst Haas. "Pragmatic Constructivism and the Study of International Institutions" (2002) 31 *Millennium: J. Int'l Studies* 573.

Habermas, Jürgen. "Why Europe Needs a Constitution" (2001) 11 *New Left Rev.* 5.

Harkens, Adam. "The Ghost in the Legal Machine: Algorithmic Governmentality, Economy, and the Practice of Law" (2018) 16 *J. Info. Comms & Ethics in Soc.* 16.

Hart, H. L. A. "Positivism and the Separation of Law and Morals" (1957) 71 *Harvard L. Rev.* 593.

Hekma, Gert. "Queers and Muslims: The Dutch Case", *Global Citizenship: Human Rights, Urban Diversity, and Environmental Challenges* (2011) 27, available at: https://core.ac.uk/download/pdf/46721093.pdf.

Hellmann, Gunther. "Pragmatism and International Relations" (2009) 11 *Int'l Studies Rev.* 638.

Hildebrandt, Mireille. "The New Imbroglio: Living with Machine Algorithms", in Liisa Janssens (ed.), *The Art of Ethics in the Information Society* (University of Amsterdam Press, 2016), available at: https://mediarep.org/handle/doc/14317.

"Algorithmic Regulation and the Rule of Law" (2018) *Phil. Trans. R. Soc. A* 376: 20170355, 1, available at: http://dx.doi.org/10.1098/rsta.2017.0355. [*Hildebrandt Algorithmic Regulation.*]

"Law as Computation in the Era of Artificial Legal Intelligence: Speaking Law to the Power of Statistics" (2018) 68 *UTLJ* 12.

Hitz, Zena. "Aristotle on Law and Moral Education" (2012) 42 *Oxford Stud. Ancient Phil.* 263.

Hopf, Ted. "The Logic of Habit in International Relations" (2010) 16 *EJIR* 539.

Hopgood, Stephen, Jack Snyder and Leslie Vinjamuri. "Conclusion: Human Rights Futures", in Stephen Hopgood, Jack Snyder and Leslie Vinjamuri (eds), *Human Rights Futures* (Cambridge University Press, 2017), 311.

"Introduction: Human Rights Past, Present, and Future", in Stephen Hopgood, Jack Snyder and Leslie Vinjamuri (eds), *Human Rights Futures* (Cambridge University Press, 2017), 1.

Hosanagar, Kartik and Alex Miller. "Who Do We Blame for the Filter Bubble? On the Roles of Math, Data, and People in Algorithmic Social Systems", in Kevin Werbach (ed.), *After the Digital Tornado: Networks, Algorithms, Humanity* (Cambridge University Press, 2020), 103.

Howse, Robert. "Epilogue: In Defense of Disruptive Democracy – a Critique of Anti-Populism" (2019) 17 *Int'l J. Constitutional L.* 641.

Humphreys, Stephen. "Legalizing Lawlessness: On Giorgio Agamben's State of Exception" (2006) 17 *EJIL* 677, available at: www.ejil.org/pdfs/17/3/208.pdf.

Huq, Aziz. "Artificial Intelligence and the Rule of Law", 12 March 2021, available at: https://papers.ssrn.com/sol3/papers.cfm?abstract_id=3794777.

Hurst, James Willard. "Lawyers in American Society 1750–1966" (1967) 50 *Marquette L. Rev.* 594.

Ibrahim, Ahmed Fekry. "The Sunni Legal Tradition: An Overview of Pluralism, Formalism, and Reform", in Helge Dedek (ed.), *A Cosmopolitan Jurisprudence: Essays in Memory of H. Patrick Glenn* (Cambridge University Press, 2022), 180.

Jäger, Anton. "The Myth of 'Populism'" (2018) *Jacobin Magazine*, available at: https://jacobinmag.com/2018/01/populism-douglas-hofstadter-donald-trump-democracy?fbclid=IwAR0h2rssdH9KobXBFxK4S19-y2UMJ6Hf2NgPofsFP0tpj177Z5ERgaerUNU.

Johnson, Douglas. "In Defence of Democratic Populism", in Gerald Neuman (ed.), *Human Rights in a Time of Populism: Challenges and Responses* (Cambridge University Press, 2020).

Kahan, Dan. "The Logic of Reciprocity: Trust, Collective Action, and Law" (2003) 102 *Michigan L. Rev.* 71.

Kanetake, Machiko and André Nollkaemper. "The International Rule of Law in the Cycle of Contestation and Deference", in Machiko Kanetake and André Nollkaemper (eds), *The Rule of Law at the National and International Levels: Contestation and Deference* (Oxford: Hart, 2016), 445.

Kasirer, Nicholas. "Bijuralism in Law's Empire and in Law's Cosmos" (2002) 52 *J. Legal Ed.* 2.

"Legal Education as Métissage" (2003) 78 *Tulane L. Rev.* 481.

Katzenstein, Peter and Lucia Seybert. "Power Complexities and Political Theory", in Peter Katzenstein and Lucia Seybert (eds), *Protean Power: Exploring the Uncertain and Unexplained in World Politics* (Cambridge University Press, 2018), 267. [*Katzenstein and Seybert Power.*]

"Uncertainty, Risk, Power and the Limits of International Relations Theory", in Peter Katzenstein and Lucia Seybert (eds), *Protean Power: Exploring the Uncertain and Unexplained in World Politics* (Cambridge University Press, 2018), 27. [*Katzenstein and Seybert Uncertainty.*]

Kennedy, David. "The Stakes of Law, or Hale and Foucault!" (1991) 15 *Legal Studies Forum* 327.

Kettler, David and Volker Meja. "Legal Formalism and Disillusioned Realism in Max Weber" (1996) 18 *Polity* 307.

Klabbers, Jan. "The Relative Autonomy of International Law or the Forgotten Politics of Interdisciplinarity" (2005) 1 *J. Int'l Rel. & Int'l L.* 35.

"Constitutionalism and the Making of International Law: Fuller's Procedural Natural Law" (2008) 5 *No Foundations: Journal of Extreme Legal Positivism*, available at: www.helsinki.fi/nofo/Vol4Num1_08.htm 84.

Koskenniemi, Martii. "The Politics of International Law" (1990) 1 *EJIL* 4.

Kraut, Richard. "Aristotle's Ethics", *The Stanford Encyclopedia of Philosophy*, Edward Zalta (ed.), available at: https://plato.stanford.edu/archives/sum2018/entries/aristotle-ethics.

Kroll, Joshua et al. "Accountable Algorithms" (2017) 165 *U. Penn. L. Rev.* 633. [*Kroll Algorithms.*]

"The Fallacy of Inscrutability" (2018) 376 *Phil. Trans. R. Soc. A* 20180084, available at: https://royalsocietypublishing.org/doi/10.1098/rsta.2018.0084.

Krygier, Martin. "The Challenge of Institutionalisation: Post-Communist 'Transitions', Populism, and the Rule of Law" (2019) 15 *Euro. Constitutional L. Rev.* 544.

"Introduction: Anti-Constitutional Populism", in Martin Krygier, Adam Czarnota and Wojciech Sadurski, *Anti-Constitutional Populism* (Cambridge University Press, 2022), 1.

"Too Much Information", in Helge Dedek (ed.), *A Cosmopolitan Jurisprudence: Essays in Memory of H. Patrick Glenn* (Cambridge University Press, 2022), 117.

Kumm, Mattias. "The Legitimacy of International Law: A Constitutionalist Framework of Analysis" (2004) 15 *EJIL* 907. [*Kumm Legitimacy.*]

"The Cosmopolitan Turn in Constitutionalism: An Integrated Conception of Public Law" (2013) 20 *Indiana J. Global Legal Studies* 605, available at: www.repository.law.indiana.edu/ijgls/vol20/iss2/4. [*Kumm Cosmopolitan Turn.*]

Kurki, M. and Adriana Sinclair. "Hidden in Plain Sight: Constructivist Treatment of Social Context and Its Limitations" (2010) 47 *Int'l Politics* 1.

Kyle, Jordan and Yascha Mounk. "The Populist Harm to Democracy: An Empirical Assessment", Tony Blair Institute for Global Change (2018), available at: https://institute.global/insight/renewing-centre/populist-harm-democracy.

Lamont, Michelle. "From 'Having' to 'Being': Self-worth and the Current Crisis of American Society" (2019) 70 *Brit. J. Sociology* 660, 7–8, available at: www.researchgate.net/publication/333749456_From_%27having%27_to_%27being%27_self-worth_and_the_current_crisis_of_American_society.

Lang, Anthony. "Constitutions are the Answer!: Hannah Arendt and the Egyptian Revolution", in K. Hiruta (ed.), *Arendt on Freedom, Liberation, and Revolution* (London: Palgrave Macmillan, 2019), 225.

Langdell, Christopher Columbus. "Address", 5 November 1866, reprinted in (1887) 3 *LQR* 123.

Laqueur, Thomas. "Some Damn Foolish Thing" (2013) 35 *London Rev. Books*, available at: www.lrb.co.uk/the-paper/v35/n23/thomas-laqueur/some-damn-foolish-thing (reviewing Christopher Clark's *The Sleepwalkers*).

Lerner, Ralph. "Moses Maimonides", in Leo Strauss and Joseph Cropsey (eds), *History of Political Philosophy*, 3rd edn (University of Chicago Press, 1987), 228.

Llewellyn, Karl. "On What is Wrong with So-called Legal Education" (1935) 35 *Columbia L. Rev.* 651.

Logan, David. "Known Knowns, Known Unknowns, Unknown Unknowns and the Propagation of Scientific Enquiry" (2009) 60 *J. Experimental Botany* 712.

Luban, David. "The Torture Lawyers of Washington", in David Luban (ed.), *Legal Ethics and Human Dignity* (Cambridge University Press, 2007), 162.

"The Rule of Law and Human Dignity: Re-examining Fuller's Canons" (2010) 2 *Hague J. Rule of Law* 29.

Macdonald, Roderick and Jason MacLean. "No Toilets in Park" (2005) 50 *McGill L. J.* 721.

MacIntosh, Duncan. "Autonomous Weapons and the Nature of Law and Morality: How Rule-of-Law-Values Require Automation of the Rule of Law" (2016) 30 *Temple Int'l and Comp. L. J.* 99.

Maldonado, Julie et al. "Engagement with Indigenous Peoples and Honouring Traditional Knowledge Systems", in K. Jacobs, S. Moser and J. Buizer (eds), *The US National Climate Assessment* (2015), available at: https://link.springer.com/chapter/10.1007/978-3-319-41802-5_9.

March, James and Johan Olsen. "The Logic of Appropriateness", in Robert Goodin (ed.), *The Oxford Handbook of Political Science* (Oxford University Press, 2011), available at: www.oxfordhandbooks.com/view/10.1093/oxfordhb/9780199604456.001.0001/oxfordhb-9780199604456-e-024?print=pdf.

Marsden, Christopher. "The Regulated End of Internet Law, and the Return to Computer and Information Law?", in Kevin Werbach (ed.), *After the Digital Tornado: Networks, Algorithms, Humanity* (Cambridge University Press, 2020), 35.

Martini, Mario. "Regulating Algorithms: How to Demystify the Alchemy of Code?", in Martin Ebers and Susana Navas (eds), *Algorithms and Law* (Cambridge University Press, 2020), 100.

Maxeiner, James. "Educating Lawyers Now and Then: Two Carnegie Critiques of the Common Law and the Case Method" (2007) 35 *Int'l J. Legal Info.* 1.

Mayer-Schönberger, Viktor. "Regulating the Feedback Effect", in Kevin Werbach (ed.), *After the Digital Tornado: Networks, Algorithms, Humanity* (Cambridge University Press, 2020), 122.

McCorquodale, Robert. "Defining the International Rule of Law: Defying Gravity?" (2016) *ICLQ* 1.

McGregor, Lorna. "The Thickening of the International Rule of Law in 'Turbulent' Times", available at: www.ejiltalk.org/the-thickening-of-the-international-rule-of-law-in-turbulent-times.

Mindus, Patricia. "The Wrath of Reason and the Grace of Sentiment: Vindicating Emotion in Law", in M. N. S. Sellers (ed.), *Law, Reason, and Emotion* (Cambridge University Press, 2017), 202.

Mintzen, Jennifer. "Reading Habermas in Anarchy: Multilateral Diplomacy and Global Public Spheres" (2005) 99 *Am. Pol. Sci. Rev.* 401.

Mirza, Mahan. "Buruni's Thought and Legacy" (2011) 5 *Religion Compass* 609.

Misak, Cheryl. "A Pragmatist Account of Legitimacy and Authority: Holmes, Ramsey and the Moral Force of Law", in Susan Dieleman, David Rondel and Christopher Voparil (eds), *Pragmatism and Justice* (Oxford University Press, 2017), 295 [*Misak Legitimacy*.]

"Nothing Scoundrelous About Truth", in Melissa Schwartzberg and Philip Kitcher (eds), *Truth and Evidence* (New York: New York University Press, 2021), 176. [*Misak Scoundrelous*.]

"Kitcher on Moral Progress", in Philip Kitcher (ed.), *Homo Quaerens: Progress, Truth, and Values* (forthcoming, manuscript on file with the author). [*Misak Moral Progress.*]

Mootz, Francis. "Vico's 'Ingenious Method' and Legal Education" (2008) 83 *Chicago-Kent L. Rev.* 1261.

Mosher, Janet. "Legal Education: Nemesis or Ally of Social Movements?" (1997) 35 *Osgoode Hall L. J.* 613.

Moss, Jonathan, Emily Robinson and Jake Watts. "Brexit and the Everyday Politics of Emotion: Methodological Lessons from History" (2020) 68 *Pol. Studies* 837, available at: https://journals.sagepub.com/doi/pdf/10.1177/00323217 20911915.

Moyn, Samuel. "Human Rights and the Crisis of Liberalism", in Stephen Hopgood, Jack Snyder and Leslie Vinjamuri (eds), *Human Rights Futures* (Cambridge University Press, 2017), 261.

Müller, Dennis, Maurice Chiodo and James Franklin. "A Hippocratic Oath for Mathematicians? Mapping the Landscape of Ethics in Mathematics", December 2021, Arxiv platform, Cornell University, available at: https:// arxiv.org/pdf/2112.07025.pdf (preprint version).

Murphy, Colleen. "Lon Fuller and the Moral Value of the Rule of Law" (2005) 24 *L. & Phil.* 239.

Nardin, Terry. "Theorizing the International Rule of Law" (2008) 34 *Rev. Int'l Studies* 385.

Navas, Susana. "Creativity of Algorithms and Copyright Law", in Kevin Werbach (ed.), *After the Digital Tornado: Networks, Algorithms, Humanity* (Cambridge University Press, 2020), 221. [*Navas Creativity.*]

"Robot Machines and Civil Liability", in Martin Ebers and Susana Navas (eds), *Algorithms and Law* (Cambridge University Press, 2020), 157.

Naylor, David. "On the Prospects for a (Deep) Learning Health Care System" (2018) 320 *JAMA* 11, available at: www.researchgate.net/publica tion/327407622_On_the_Prospects_for_a_Deep_Learning_Health_Care_ System.

Nelken, David. "Learning from Patrick Glenn: Tradition, Change, and Innovation", in Helge Dedek (ed.), *A Cosmopolitan Jurisprudence: Essays in Memory of H. Patrick Glenn* (Cambridge University Press, 2022), 161.

Nuseibeh, Sari. "Al'Aql al-Qudsi: Avicenna's Subjective Theory of Knowledge" (1989) 69 *Studia Islamica* 39.

Orts, Eric. "The Rule of Law in China" (2001) 34 *Vanderbilt J. Transn'l L.* 43.

Parsons, Talcott. "Introduction", to Max Weber, *The Theory of Social and Economic Organization* (New York: Free Press, 1964), 16.

Patterson, Dennis. "Law's Pragmatism: Law as Practice and Narrative" (1990) 76 *Virginia L. Rev.* 937.

Pavel, Carmen. "The International Rule of Law" (2020) 23 *Critical Rev. Int'l Soc. & Pol. Phil.* 332, available at: www.tandfonline.com/doi/full/10.1080/13698230.2019.1565714.

Peristiany, J. "Introduction", in Emile Durkheim, *Sociology and Philosophy* (London: Cohen & West, 1953), xxvix. [*Durkheim Sociology.*]

Peters, Anne. "The Rise and Decline of the International Rule of Law and the Job of Scholars", Max Planck Institute, MPIL Research Paper Series No. 2017-16 (manuscript on file with author).

Pettit, Philip. "Virtus Normativa: Rational Choice Perspectives" (1990) 100 *Ethics* 725.

Posner, Eric. "Liberal Internationalism and the Populist Backlash Symposium: The Forefront of International Law" (2017) 49 *Arizona State L. J.* 795.

Postema, Gerald. "Implicit Law" (1994) 13 *L. & Phil.* 361, reprinted in Willem Witteveen and Wibren van der Burg (eds), *Rediscovering Fuller: Essays on Implicit Law and Institutional Design* (Amsterdam University Press, 1999), 256.

Pouliot, Vincent. "The Logic of Practicality: A Theory of Practice of Security Communities" (2008) 62 *IO* 257. [*Pouliot Practicality.*]

Price, Huw. "Truth as Convenient Friction" (2003) 100 *J. Phil.* 167.

Raz, Joseph. "The Rule of Law and its Virtue" (1977) 93 *LQR* 195.

Rehaag, Sean. "Book Review: The Hart–Fuller Debate in the Twenty-First Century, by Peter Cane (ed.)" (2010) 48 *Osgoode Hall L. J.* 691.

Reinhold, Theresa and Michael Zurn. "Rules about Rules and the Endogenous Dynamics of International Law: Dissonance Reduction as a Mechanism of Secondary Rule-Making" (2014) 3 *Global Constitutionalism* 236.

Reus-Smit, Christian. "The Strange Death of Liberal International Theory" (2001) 12 *EJIL* 573. [*Reus-Smit Liberal Theory.*]

"Protean Power and Revolutions in Rights", in Peter Katzenstein and Lucia Seybert (eds), *Protean Power: Exploring the Uncertain and Unexplained in World Politics* (Cambridge University Press, 2018), 59.

Reynolds, Noel. "Comment on Robert Summers on the Rule of Law" (1988) 1 *Ratio Juris* 263.

Rheinstein, Max. "Introduction" to Max Weber, *Max Weber on Law in Economy and Society* (Cambridge, MA: Harvard University Press, 1966), xxvi.

Risse, Thomas. "Let's Argue!: Communicative Action in World Politics" (2000) 54 *IO* 1.

Rodrik, Dani. "Is Populism Necessarily Bad Economics?" *AEA Papers and Proceedings* 108 (2018) 196–9, available at: https://doi.org/10.1257/pandp.20181122.

Rorty, Richard. "Human Rights, Rationality, and Sentimentality", in Stephen Shute and Susan Hurley (eds), *On Human Rights: The Oxford Amnesty Lectures 1993* (1993), 111. [*Rorty Human Rights.*]

"Justice as a Larger Loyalty", in Susan Dieleman, David Rondel and Christian Voparil (eds), *Pragmatism and Justice* (New York: Oxford University Press, 2017), 21.

Rouvroy, Antoinette. "The End(s) of Critique: Data-behaviourism vs. Due-process", in Mireille Hildebrandt and Ekatarina De Vries (eds), *Privacy, Due Process and the Computational Turn: Philosophers of Law Meet Philosophers of Technology* (Abingdon: Routledge, 2012), 143.

Ruggie, John. "What Makes the World Hang Together? Neo-utilitarianism and the Social Constructivist Challenge" (1998) 52 *IO* 855.

Sadurski, Wojciech. "Institutional Populism, Courts, and the European Union", in Martin Krygier, Adam Czarnota and Wojciech Sadurski (eds), *Anti-Constitutional Populism* (Cambridge University Press, 2022), 506.

Sajó, András. "The Constitutional Domestication of Emotions", in M. N. S. Sellers (ed.), *Law, Reason and Emotion* (Cambridge University Press, 2017), 55.

Sampson, Thomas. "Brexit: The Economics of International Disintegration" (2017) 31 *J. Econ. Perspectives* 163, available at: www.aeaweb.org/articles?id=10.1257/jep.31.4.163.

Sandholtz, Wayne. "Dynamics of International Norm Change: Rules against Wartime Plunder" (2008) 14 *EJIR* 101.

Sandro, Paolo. "Unlocking Legal Validity: Some Remarks on the Artificial Ontology of Law", in Pauline Westerman et al. (eds), *Legal Validity and Soft Law* (New York: Springer, 2018), available at: https://link.springer.com/chapter/10.1007/978-3-319-77522-7_5.

Seybert, Lucia and Peter Katzenstein. "Protean Power and Control Power: Conceptual Analysis", in Peter Katzenstein and Lucia Seybert (eds), *Protean Power: Exploring the Uncertain and Unexplained in World Politics* (Cambridge University Press, 2018), 3.

Sharpe, Robert. "The Persons Case and the Living Tree Theory of Constitutional Interpretation" (2013) 64 *UNB L. J.* 1.

Sheehy, Benedict. "Fundamentally Conflicting Views of the Rule of Law in China and the West and Implications for Commercial Disputes" (2006) 26 *Northwestern J. Int'l L. & Bus.* 225.

Shklar, Judith. "Political Theory and the Rule of Law", in Allan Hutchinson and Patrick Monahan (eds), *The Rule of Law: Ideal and Ideology* (Toronto: Carswell, 1987), 1.

Smith, Blake. "Why Jürgen Habermas Disappeared" (2021) *Foreign Policy*, available at: https://foreignpolicy.com/2021/02/07/why-jurgen-habermas-disappeared.

Snyder, Jack. "Empowering Rights Through Mass Movements, Religion, and Reform Parties", in Stephen Hopgood, Jack Snyder and Leslie Vinjamuri (eds), *Human Rights Futures* (Cambridge University Press, 2017), 88.

Somers, Kim and François Vaillancourt. "Some Economic Dimensions of the Sovereignty Debate in Quebec: Debt, GDP, and Migration" (2014) 30 *Oxford Rev. Econ. Pol.* 237.

Staats, Joseph and Glen Biglaiser. "The Effects of Judicial Strength and Rule of Law on Portfolio Investment in the Developing World" (2011) 92 *Soc. Sci. Q.* 609.

Steinrötter, Björn. "The (Envisaged) Legal Framework for Commercialisation of Digital Data within the EU", in Martin Ebers and Susana Navas (eds), *Algorithms and Law* (Cambridge University Press, 2020), 269.

Summers, Robert. "A Formal Theory of the Rule of Law" (1993) 6 *Ratio Juris* 12.

"The Principles of the Rule of Law" (1999) 74 *Notre Dame L. Rev.* 1691.

Sunstein, Cass. "On Analogical Reasoning" (1992/3) 106 *Harvard L. Rev.* 741.

Swidler, Ann. "What Anchors Cultural Practices", in Theodore Schatzki et al. (eds), *The Practice Turn in Contemporary Theory* (London: Routledge, 2001), 74.

Tamahana, Brian. "An Analytical Map of Social Scientific Approaches to the Concept of Law" (1995) 15 *Oxford J. Legal Stud.* 501.

Thomas, Martin. "After Mers-el-Kébir: The Armed Neutrality of the Vichy French Navy, 1940–43" (1997) 112 *Eng. Hist. Rev.* 643.

Toope, Stephen. "Fallout from '9-11': Will a Security Culture Undermine Human Rights?" (2002) 65 *Sask L. Rev.* 281.

"Human Rights and the Use of Force after September 11th, 2001", in Terry Nardin and Daniel Sherman (eds), *Terror, Culture, Politics: Rethinking 9/11* (Bloomington: Indiana University Press, 2006).

"Thinking, Doing, Being: Why 'Practising' Law Matters to the Prevention of Torture", in Helge Dedek and Shauna Van Praagh (eds), *Stateless Law: Evolving Boundaries of a Discipline* (Farnham: Ashgate, 2015; London: Routledge, 2016), 159.

Trackman, Leon. "The Evolution of the Law Merchant: Our Commercial Heritage" (1980) *J. Maritime L. & Comm.* 1.

Tully, James. "Political Philosophy as a Critical Activity" (2002) 30 *Political Theory* 533.

van der Burg, Wibren. "The Morality of Aspiration: A Neglected Dimension of Law and Morality", in Willem Witteveen and Wibren van der Burg (eds), *Rediscovering Fuller: Essays on Implicit Law and Institutional Design* (Amsterdam University Press, 1999), 169

Vecchiarelli Scott, Joanna. "Hannah Arendt's Secular Augustinianism", in Mark Vessey, Karla Pollmann and Allan Fitzgerald (eds), *History, Apocalypse, and the*

Secular Imagination (Bowling Green, OH: Philosophy Documentation Center, 1999), 293. [*Scott on Arendt.*]

Venzke, Ingo. "Semantic Authority, Legal Change and the Dynamics of International Law", in Patrick Capps and Henrik Olsen (eds), *Legal Authority beyond the State* (Cambridge University Press, 2018), 102.

Vinjamuri, Leslie. "Human Rights Backlash", in Stephen Hopgood, Jack Snyder and Leslie Vinjamuri (eds), *Human Rights Futures* (Cambridge University Press, 2017), 114.

Voeten, Erik. "Populism and Backlashes against International Courts" (2019) *Perspectives on Politics* 1.

Waldron, Jeremy. "What is Cosmopolitan?" (2000) 8 *J. Political Phil.* 227.

"The Rule of International Law" (2006) 30 *Harvard J. L. & Pub. Pol.* 15. [*Waldron Rule of International Law.*]

"Rule-of-Law Rights and Populist Impatience", in Gerald Neuman (ed.), *Human Rights in a Time of Populism: Challenges and Responses* (Cambridge University Press, 2020), 43.

Walker, Neil. "Cosmopolitan Attachments", in Helge Dedek (ed.), *A Cosmopolitan Jurisprudence: Essays in Memory of H. Patrick Glenn* (Cambridge University Press, 2022), 280.

Walters, Mark. "The Unwritten Constitution as a Legal Concept", in David Dyzenhaus and Malcolm Thorburn (eds), *Philosophical Foundations of Constitutional Law* (Oxford University Press, 2016), 33. [*Walters Unwritten Constitution.*]

Walzer, Michael. "The Moral Standing of States: A Response to Four Critics" (1980) 9 *Philosophy & Pub. Affs* 209. [*Walzer Moral Standing.*]

Warren, Jean-Philippe. "Secularism in Quebec", *The Canadian Encyclopedia*, 26 November 2020, available at: www.thecanadianencyclopedia.ca/en/article/secularism-in-quebec.

Wegner, Judith Welch. "Reframing Legal Education's 'Wicked Problems'" (2009) 61 *Rutgers L. Rev.* 867.

Wendel, W. Bradley. "Should Law Schools Teach Professional Duties, Professional Virtues, or Something Else? A Critique of the Carnegie Report on Educating Lawyers", available at: http://ssrn.com/abstract=1963838. [*Wendel Professional Duties.*]

"The Torture Memos and the Demands of Legality" (2009) 12 *Legal Ethics* 107.

Wendt, Alexander. "The Agent–Structure Problem in International Relations Theory" (1987) 41 *IO* 335.

Werbach, Kevin, "Digital Tornado: The Internet and Telecommunications Policy (1997) Selected Excerpts", in Kevin Werbach (ed.), *After the Digital Tornado: Networks, Algorithms, Humanity* (Cambridge University Press, 2020), 13, 23–4.

"Introduction", in Kevin Werbach (ed.), *After the Digital Tornado: Networks, Algorithms, Humanity* (Cambridge University Press, 2020), 1.

White, James Boyd. "Economics and Law: Two Cultures in Tension" (1987) 54 *Tennessee L. Rev. J.* 161.

Wiener, Antje. "Contested Compliance: Intervention on the Normative Structure of World Politics" (2004) 10 *EJIR* 190.

"The Dual Quality of Norms and Governance Beyond the State: Sociological and Normative Approaches to 'Interaction'" (2007) 10 *Critical Rev. Int'l Soc. & Pol. Phil.* 47. [*Wiener Dual Quality.*]

Wiener, Antje and Uwe Putter. "The Quality of Norms is What Actors Make of It: Critical Constructivist Research on Norms" (2009) *J. Int'l L. & Int'l Relations* 2.

Wolfendale, Jessica. "The Myth of 'Torture Lite'" (2009) 23 *Ethics & Int'l Affs* 47.

Wouters, Jan. "International Law, Informal Law-Making", in Heike Krieger, Georg Nolte and Andreas Zimmermann (eds), *The International Rule of Law: Rise or Decline?* (Oxford University Press, 2019), 242.

Wu, Tim. "Will Artificial Intelligence Eat the Law? The Rise of Hybrid Social-Ordering Systems" (2019) 119 *Col. L. Rev.* 2001.

Yates, Mark. "The Carnegie Effect: Elevating Practical Training over Liberal Education in Curricular Reform" (2011) 17 *J. Legal Writing Institute* 233.

Zalnieriute, Monika, Lyria Bennett Moses and George Williams. "The Rule of Law and Automation of Government Decision-Making" (2019) 82 *MLR* 425.

Zeitlin, Irving. "The Political and Social Theory of Max Weber" (1991) 60 *U. of TQ* 404.

Zuboff, Shoshana. "*Caveat Usor*: Surveillance Capitalism as Epistemic Inequality", in Kevin Werbach (ed.), *After the Digital Tornado: Networks, Algorithms, Humanity* (Cambridge University Press, 2020), 174.

Zumbansen, Peer. "The Rule of Law, Legal Pluralism, and Challenges to a Western-centric View: Some Very Preliminary Observations", in Christopher May and Adam Winchester (eds), *Handbook on the Rule of Law* (Cheltenham: Edward Elgar, 2018), 57.

Index